LEARNING PARTNERSHIPS

LEARNING PARTNERSHIPS

Theory and Models of Practice to Educate for Self-Authorship

Marcia B. Baxter Magolda
Patricia M. King

Sty/us

STERLING, VIRGINIA

Published in 2004 by

Stylus Publishing, LLC
22883 Quicksilver Drive
Sterling, Virginia 20166

**Library of Congress
Cataloging-in-Publication Data**
    Learning partnerships : theory and models
      of practice to educate for self-authorship /
      edited by Marcia B. Baxter Magolda and
      Patricia M. King.—1st ed.
      p. cm.
    Includes bibliographical references and index.
    ISBN 1-57922-084-3 (alk. paper)—
    ISBN 1-57922-085-1 (Paperback : alk. paper)
    1. College teaching. 2. Education, Higher—
    Aims and objectives. 3. Constructivism
    (Education) 4. Teacher-student
    relationships. 5. Self-culture. I. Baxter
    Magolda, Marcia B., 1951– II. King,
    Patricia M., 1950–

LB2331 .L393 2004
378.1'2—dc22
2003024659

To my spouse, Peter, and my mother, Marjorie,
for our lifelong learning partnerships
Marcia Baxter Magolda

To my friend and colleague, Karen Strohm Kitchener,
for our 30-year learning partnership
Patricia M. King

CONTENTS

LIST OF ILLUSTRATIONS
AND TABLES

Marcia B. Baxter Magolda, Distinguished Professor, Department of Educational Leadership, Miami University (Ohio)

Jennifer A. Buckley, Project Associate, National Survey of Student Engagement, Center for Postsecondary Research, Policy, and Planning, Indiana University

Katie Egart, Coordinator, Urban Leadership Internship Program, Miami University (Ohio)

Carolyn Haynes, Professor, School of Interdisciplinary Studies and Director, University Honors Program, Miami University (Ohio)

Melissa P. Healy, Assessment Co-Coordinator, Urban Leadership Internship Program, Miami University (Ohio)

Anne M. Hornak, ROSES Coordinator and Academic Adviser, College of Engineering, Michigan State University

Patricia M. King, Professor and Director, Center for the Study of Higher and Postsecondary Education, University of Michigan

Kathleen Knight Abowitz, Associate Professor, Department of Educational Leadership, Miami University (Ohio)

Peter M. Magolda, Associate Professor, Department of Educational Leadership, Miami University (Ohio)

Rebecca Mills, Vice President for Student Life, University of Nevada, Las Vegas

Anna M. Ortiz, Associate Professor, Department of Educational Psychology, Administration, and Counseling, California State University, Long Beach

Terry D. Piper, Vice President, Student Affairs, University of California, Northridge

Judy L. Rogers, Associate Professor, Department of Educational Leadership, Miami University (Ohio)

Karen L. Strong, Associate Vice President for Student and Campus Life, University of Nevada, Las Vegas

Terry M. Wildman, Professor of Educational Psychology, and Director, Center for Excellence in Undergraduate Teaching, Virginia Polytechnic Institute and State University

Kevin Yonkers-Talz, Codirector, Casa de la Solidaridad, Santa Clara University

ACKNOWLEDGMENTS

Learning partnerships are the central focus of this book, so it is fitting to acknowledge that many learning partnerships stand at its foundation. The learning partnership between the two of us began more than 20 years ago at Ohio State University, where our mutual interest in assessing intellectual development brought us together. Although our research agendas in the intervening years reflect distinct emphases in exploring college students' intellectual development, they converge around our core conceptions of the developmental journey and the conditions necessary to promote development. We have both been involved in long-term longitudinal studies of intellectual development and learning from which we have experienced the complexity and social construction of knowledge. In interviews with our study participants, we have witnessed firsthand that learners' identities are central to their cognitive maturity. We have heard repeatedly that mutual knowledge construction—the sharing of authority and expertise among knowledgeable peers—leads to complex cognitive capacity as well as to an integrated sense of identity and mature relationships. Our mutual construction of knowledge around these complex issues with our research participants is what leads us to value self-authorship as the central goal of higher education. We are grateful to all those longitudinal participants, as well as those who participated in myriad other studies, for sharing their ways of making meaning with us and for helping us develop a vision for 21st-century higher education.

Our commitment to that vision led to the learning partnerships with the educators who contributed chapters to this book. These authors took advantage of or created opportunities to mutually construct knowledge: By exploring the concept of self-authorship in diverse contexts and conceptualizing practice to promote it, they contributed to the innovative practices that are the main body of this volume. The educators whose work is featured here all recognize the complexity of the developmental journey as well as the intricacies of promoting development in today's higher-education institutions. They have taken significant risks to envision and enact new possibilities to promote learning. We appreciate the complexity of the work in which they are engaged, respect their courage to shift to new paradigms, and value the insights we have gained from their attempts to put theoretical concepts into practice. Their educational practice has been shaped by our theoretical constructions, which have in turn been shaped by their educational practice. We also appreciate their willingness to describe and reflect on their practice in these chapters and to engage with us in the iterative process of crafting and revising these descriptions, cheerfully responding to our requests for clarification, examples, or nuanced language. Our understanding and appreciation for the process of promoting development—as well as the complexities of capturing these experiences in words—has deepened as a result of our partnerships with these authors.

We are both graduate faculty members who are actively engaged in the preparation of future professionals for higher education and student affairs roles. These roles afford us frequent opportunities to engage in mutual construction of knowledge and in discussions about individuals' developmental journeys with students in class each week and with faculty, student affairs staff, and other professional colleagues around topics of mutual interest we wish to better understand and address.

Our theoretical constructions have been influenced by scholars whose groundbreaking work brought the developmental journey to the forefront of educational practices, particularly the late William G. Perry Jr. and James Rest, Clyde A. Parker, Karen Strohm Kitchener, Mary F. Belenky, Blythe McVicker Clinchy, Nancy R. Goldberger, Jill M. Tarule, Robert Kegan, and Kurt W. Fischer. Innovative scholars who envisioned collaborative relationships between learners and educators, particularly Gloria Ladson-Billings, Henry Giroux, and Ira Shor, shaped our construction of that relationship as a mutual partnership. We are indebted to our faculty colleagues at our home institutions (Miami University and the University of Michigan) and across the country who challenged our thinking, supported our efforts to sustain our research agendas, and served as learning partners for us. Student affairs educators on these and other campuses have also been learning partners, mutually constructing with us how to influence and organize the cocurriculum to promote self-authorship. We are grateful to both teaching faculty and professional colleagues for keeping us grounded in the realities of everyday campus life. Graduate students at our home institutions have patiently read our work as it has evolved, engaged in intense conversations with us to help us clarify theoretical constructs, conducted their own research to expand our work in new directions with new populations, experimented with our ideas in their professional practice, and persuaded other professionals to consider our work in crafting educational practice. We cherish the challenges, insights, and long-standing support we have enjoyed from our learning partnerships with current and former students. We also appreciate the tangible weekly support we have enjoyed from our office colleagues, including Jan Clegg and Peggy Bower (Miami University), and Melinda Richardson (University of Michigan).

Significant learning partnerships promote growth while simultaneously making us feel at home with ourselves and those around us. Because the scholarly work of knowledge construction centrally involves our identities and relationships, our partnerships with people beyond our academic roles are crucial. Both of us wish to acknowledge the important roles members of our families have played in our own meaning making and in our ability to sustain our energy in projects like this. Both of our mothers, Marjorie A. Baxter and B. Marjorie Brown, have been lifelong learning partners for us, offering wisdom, emotional support, and practical assistance and showing by example the power of their own courage, remarkable vitality, and ways of caring. Other family members have provided partnerships that are central to our feeling at home. Marcia's spouse, Peter Magolda, is both an intellectual and an emotional partner, generously offering his mind and heart, strengthening her and their partnership. Ardath Sunderland, Marcia's sister and a 35-year veteran teacher, is a model of sustained commitment to learning. Pat's children, David, Brian, and Ellen, not only provide good examples for developmental concepts discussed in class and public speeches, but are also daily reminders of the complexity and mystery of human development and of the joys and heartbreaks of the journey toward self-authorship. To all our immediate and extended family members and close friends who enrich our sense of being at home through our partnerships with you, we express our love and gratitude.

October 2003
Marcia B. Baxter Magolda
Oxford, Ohio

Patricia M. King
Ann Arbor, Michigan

PREFACE

> You are so the master of your own destiny at college. It's such a time of stretching and growing all the way around. You test the ground and see how it feels in a lot of different areas. And you are trying to fly off cliffs, and you crash a few times, and you soar a few times. *Gwen* (Baxter Magolda, 1992, p. 362)

Gwen captures the essence of learning—taking risks to try something new, crashing on the initial attempts, and soaring after one develops expertise. Her comments also emphasize a crucial aspect of college learning—that college students must learn to be the masters of their own destinies.

College is a time of transformation. It is the time when adolescent dependence on authorities must be gradually replaced with adult responsibility as a citizen. Educators focus their energy on helping students make this transformation. Faculty encourage students to learn the foundations of their disciplines yet encourage them to think critically about existing ideas to contribute to future progress. Student affairs educators specify the boundaries of acceptable behavior yet encourage students to construct their own values that will lead to productive community participation. Parents gradually relinquish authority, hoping their daughters and sons will take it up wisely. Much guidance is available throughout the college environment regarding how to make adult decisions, yet students are encouraged to make the decisions themselves. The balance of providing guidance and enabling responsibility is a delicate one. Educators try to make *learning to fly* as safe as possible, yet a certain amount of crashing is to be expected. Balancing the degree of risk during college with the necessity of expertise for adult life is a constant learning curve in which educators sometimes crash and sometimes soar.

The complexity of contemporary life necessitates that higher education prepare students to be lifelong learners and responsible citizens. This book offers a grounded theory and practical examples of how these goals can be achieved at the course, program, and institutional levels. It describes the developmental maturity—self-authorship—that undergirds lifelong learning and responsible citizenship. The Learning Partnerships Model, a result of a 17-year longitudinal study of young adult development (Baxter Magolda, 2001), is a means of blending guidance and enabling responsibility to promote self-authorship. Implementation of these partnerships in multiple college contexts demonstrates how developmental maturity and context-specific learning goals can be achieved simultaneously.

The Learning Partnerships Model: Blending Connection and Autonomy to Enable Self-Authorship

During college and certainly by the time young adults graduate from college, society expects them to assume positions of responsibility in public and private life. As employees, parents, and partners, they are expected to manage complexity and engage multiple perspectives. They are expected to gather and judge relevant evidence from others to make decisions without being consumed by pleasing everyone. They are expected to act in ways that benefit themselves and others equitably and contribute to the common good. The Learning Partnerships Model introduces learners to these expectations by portraying learning as a complex process in which learners bring their own perspectives to bear on deciding what to believe and simultaneously share responsibility with others to construct knowledge. Because this vision of learning is a challenge to authority-dependent learners, the Learning Partnerships Model helps learners meet the challenge by validating their ability to learn, situating learning in learners' experience, and defining learning as a collaborative exchange of perspectives.

Meeting responsible citizenship expectations requires the emergence of a distinctive mode of meaning making that Sharon Parks (2000) describes as "becoming critically aware of one's own composing of reality" (p. 6). Adolescence is a time of learning the realities others have composed; college is a time of learning that others have in fact composed what constitutes reality. Adult life requires joining in the composition, composing one's own reality in the context of one's relationships with others and the surrounding community. Robert Kegan (1994) calls composing one's own reality *self-authorship*. He describes self-authorship as internally coordinating beliefs, values, and interpersonal loyalties rather than depending on external values, beliefs, and interpersonal loyalties.

Mark, a participant in a longitudinal study of young adult learning and development, described the concept of self-authorship this way:

> Making yourself into something, not what other people say or not just kind of floating along in life, but you're in some sense a piece of clay. You've been

formed into different things, but that doesn't mean you can't go back on the potter's wheel and instead of somebody else's hands building and molding you, you use your own, and in a fundamental sense change your values and beliefs. (Baxter Magolda, 2001, p. 119)

Mark recognized that as a child and adolescent he had assumed various shapes influenced by external guidance. He described the transformation of taking himself, the core piece of clay, back to the potter's wheel to remold with his own hands. Reshaping the clay represents the coordination of beliefs, values, and interpersonal loyalties that stems from composing one's own reality.

The Learning Partnerships Model enables this shift from authority dependence to self-authorship by challenging learners to see the composing of reality in complex terms and supporting them in coordinating their beliefs, values, and interpersonal loyalties. The model demonstrates how to achieve the balance between guidance and empowerment in ways that help diverse learners develop self-authorship. Learning partnerships challenge authority dependence via *three core assumptions* about learning: knowledge is complex and socially constructed, one's identity plays a central role in crafting knowledge claims, and knowledge is mutually constructed via the sharing of expertise and authority. Portraying knowledge as the complex result of experts negotiating what to believe gives learners access to the process of learning and deciding what to believe. Assuming that one's identity plays a central role in this process opens the door for learners to see their role in knowledge construction—to recognize the need to use their own hands to mold their beliefs. Assuming that knowledge is mutually constructed emphasizes the shared responsibility to engage multiple perspectives to decide what to believe. All three assumptions emphasize autonomy through personal responsibility for learning and molding beliefs. They simultaneously emphasize connection through the necessity to connect to one's own and others' perspectives.

Learning partnerships support self-authorship via *three principles:* validating learners' capacity as knowledge constructors, situating learning in learners' experience, and defining learning as mutually constructing meaning. Validating learners' capacity to learn and construct knowledge is necessary for them to realize that they can go back to the potter's wheel. Situating learning in their experience instead of the experience of authority gives them a context from which to bring their identity to learning. Defining learning as a mutual process of exchanging perspectives to arrive at knowledge claims supports their participation in the social construction of knowledge. The three principles model autonomy through encouraging learners to bring their experience and construct their own perspectives. The principles model connection through encouraging learners to connect to their own and others' experience and ideas.

The blend of challenge and support in the Learning Partnerships Model provides guidance and empowerment simultaneously, modeling the blend of connection and autonomy inherent in the nature of self-authorship. Coordination of beliefs, values, and interpersonal loyalties requires a complex integration of autonomy and connection. Mark illustrates autonomy in using his own hands to remold his identity and internal belief system. In coordinating his interpersonal loyalties, he recognizes the value of his connection to others and how this connection can be incorporated into authoring his life. Mark found "a truer identity that leads to understanding and informs important life decisions" (Baxter Magolda, 2001, p. 67). This truer identity led him to this perspective on moving to another state for his wife's education:

> If I wanted to exert some kind of control, or draw a line in the sand, I could—I have that kind of authority. But why would I do that? In terms of the process, Michele has ideas about where she wants to go. . . . I'd have to take the bar exam again, which is not something I look forward to, but I kind of accept Michele now as a kind of engine in part for my life. This move isn't just about her; more horizons for me just by going along with her to a new environment. You get more energy and enthusiasm from moving from one place to another. It is longer than a rush, an infusion—become focused, learn new things, grow. Her moving is an engine for me to develop as well. (Baxter Magolda, 2001, p. 67)

The way Mark molds himself takes his wife's interests into account. He composes his reality by perceiving her move as good for her and as an opportunity for his growth. He chooses to use his authority in ways that balance autonomy and connection. Learning partnerships help learners achieve autonomy in the context of connection to others to arrive at the balance Mark demonstrates.

Dawn, another participant in the longitudinal study, also spoke to this intricate balance. Having been diagnosed with multiple sclerosis in her early 30s, Dawn reflected on her life:

> For quite a long time I've been introspective, pursuing that knowledge of self, sense of self, spiritual centeredness—this has evolved over time, but the MS diagnosis accelerated it even more. I think it is fulfilling something that I've always wanted; never thought I'd get it quite this way. You follow the Tao of life, Zen moment, go with the flow, take on whatever comes your way—I always wanted that and I'm finally getting it. There are days when I

don't have it, but for the most part I do. I'm trying to make something better out of myself and make the world a better place with me in it. I feel more deeply connected to my spiritual center than I ever have before in my life.

My illness, well not an illness, a condition—it will not control my life. I have way too much to do and accomplish to let it get in my way. It challenges me. And I'm okay to give it that much leeway. I've maintained since the beginning that this is definitely a gift. It can be viewed as unfortunate, but at the same time it has gotten me into this way of thinking, exploring my world, that is different. I go deeper within myself. When you face that you can't do something, the door opens to something you can do. Enjoy yourself and immerse yourself in that. I do control it; it will not control me.

Like Mark, Dawn pursued a truer identity, a deeper sense of self, to guide how she understood her diagnosis. Her sense of autonomy is clear in her choice to frame her condition as a gift and her determination to control it. At the same time, it challenged her to go with the flow of life. Her sense of connection to herself and the larger world emerged as she explained striving for that balance:

Finding the balance between [going with the flow] and me saying I have control over myself, not letting this condition get the best of me. Knowing how to make things happen and let things happen. When you find the balance between those things, life is spectacular. That is kind of a trust thing—trusting that you know yourself enough to dance that line. Know when to make something happen and when to let it happen. Trusting yourself that you know that space. I don't quite know myself enough to trust that yet. I'm working on it. I'm getting close. That deepest self-knowledge to know you can stay there at that middle point and have that balance. That is a constant process for me. To be able to say this is my life and it's on my terms; I love that.

Although Dawn is molding herself, she is doing it in the context of what arises in her life. She is connected to her inner self and connected to the world. Outside influences shape her, yet she coordinates them with her internal belief system and values to shape herself. She knows how to make things happen (her autonomy) and when to let things happen (her connection to the world around her). As she conveys, it is an intricate dance to stay on that line, in that space. Having the balance she speaks of reflects coordinating her beliefs, values, and interpersonal loyalties in the context of the external world around her. Dawn conveys both the intricacy and the work involved in achieving this balance. Learning partnerships actively engage learners in this work, guiding them toward the empowerment Dawn exhibits as she faces life's challenges.

Self-authorship is the capacity to internally define a coherent belief system and identity that coordinates engagement in mutual relations with the larger world. This internal foundation yields the capacity to actively listen to multiple perspectives, critically interpret those perspectives in light of relevant evidence and the internal foundation, and make judgments accordingly. Grounding in the internal foundation counteracts the need for approval, yielding openness to new possibilities and diverse others. It enables what Judith Jordan (1997) calls mutuality in which each person is able to "represent her or his own experience in a relationship, to act in a way which is congruent with an 'inner truth' and with the context, and to respond to and encourage authenticity in the other person" (p. 31). Thus, self-authorship, in its intricate blend of autonomy and connection, enables meaningful, interdependent relationships with diverse others grounded in an understanding and appreciation for human differences and the cultural practices and values these differences reflect. Learning partnerships engage learners in these interdependent relationships.

Self-Authorship as the Central Goal of Higher Education

Most expectations of college graduates could be captured by the overarching goal of effective citizenship. *Greater Expectations: A New Vision for Learning as a Nation Goes to College* advocates intentional learners who "consciously choose to act in ethical and responsible ways. Able to place themselves in the context of a diverse world, these learners draw on difference and commonality to produce a deeper experience of community" (Association of American Colleges and Universities, 2002, p. 22). Consciously choosing to act in ethical and responsible ways requires composing one's own reality in the context of the realities of others. Cognitive complexity is necessary to understand context, interpret multiple frames of reference and evidence, and justify choices. An internal sense of self is needed to act on the internal belief system. The capacity for mutuality is necessary for ethical action for the common good. Thus, effective citizenship requires self-authorship because it requires complexity in defining one's belief system, a coherent identity, and mutual relations.

These three dimensions of self-authorship are also common learning outcomes desired by many higher-education institutions. Most mission statements emphasize critical thinking or the ability to interpret, coordinate, and evaluate diverse evidence to make judgments. This is both the process and the outcome of defining an internal belief system. Most college mission statements advocate developing an internal value system to guide action.

Similarly, they emphasize understanding multiple cultures, appreciating difference, and working collaboratively with others. An internal foundation is crucial to this capacity for intercultural maturity (Kegan, 1994; King & Baxter Magolda, 2003).

Substantial evidence suggests that self-authorship is uncommon during college. Traditional age students rely heavily on external authorities and sources for their beliefs and values (Baxter Magolda, 1992; Kegan, 1994; King & Kitchener, 1994). Some model autonomy as they attempt to master the expectations of authorities; others model connection as they attempt to meet authorities' expectations (Baxter Magolda, 1992). Yet these do not constitute authentic autonomy and connection because no internal foundation of beliefs and values exists. They are, instead, socialized styles or patterns of operating that are influenced by external affirmation. Those who graduate from college without the internal foundation follow external formulas for adult life (Baxter Magolda, 2001). As young adults recognize the need to compose their own realities and begin to do so either near the end of college or after graduation, they realize the need for both authentic autonomy and connection. Developing their internal belief and value systems, those "truer identities" Mark and Dawn spoke of, enables them to author their own lives in the context of mutual relations with their communities.

This book advocates self-authorship as a central goal of higher education for the 21st-century and the Learning Partnerships Model as a means of achieving that goal. Promoting self-authorship during college requires finding the delicate balance between guiding learners and enabling them to be responsible. Too much guidance affirms reliance on external formulas. Yet enabling responsibility must be balanced with guidance until learners develop the internal mechanisms to act responsibly. As Sharon Parks (2000) notes, "How a young adult is met and invited to test and invest this new consciousness with its emerging new capacities will make a great difference in the adulthood that lies ahead" (p. 6). Just as learners are learning to dance in the space between authority dependence and self-authorship, educators must learn to dance in the space between guidance and empowerment. Maintaining these delicate balances is achievable through learning partnerships.

Applications and Outcomes of the Learning Partnerships Model

The Learning Partnerships Model emerged from Marcia Baxter Magolda's 17-year longitudinal study of young adults' learning and development. Based on nearly 1,000 narratives from participants' undergraduate, graduate, employment, and personal life experiences, the Learning Partnerships Model offers an empirically grounded yet flexible approach to promote self-authorship and learning. The Learning Partnerships Model's use in college classrooms, experiential learning, community development, curricular reform, and organizational development illustrates its value and flexibility in promoting self-authorship and learning in numerous contexts.

Learning Partnerships: Theory and Models of Practice to Educate for Self-Authorship is a story of the outcomes of this model in diverse contexts, including multiple student populations, multiple educational contexts, and both curricular and cocurricular arenas. In-depth narratives about learning partnerships in these multiple contexts illustrate various forms the key elements of the Learning Partnerships Model take with learners at diverse junctures of the journey toward self-authorship. Part 1 of the book explores the centrality of self-authorship in meeting contemporary higher-education learning goals. Narratives from the longitudinal study demonstrate the nature of self-authorship and its role in the learning goals of cognitive maturity, an integrated identity, mature relationships, and effective citizenship. Narratives from longitudinal participants and participants in a course observation study (Baxter Magolda, 1999) describe the nature and nuances of the Learning Partnerships Model in promoting these learning goals.

Part 2 contains exemplars of the Learning Partnerships Model in action in higher-education contexts. Carolyn Haynes describes use of the model in the conceptualization and implementation of an undergraduate writing curriculum in Miami University's School of Interdisciplinary Studies in Chapter 3. Self-authorship outcomes are evident in scoring of senior projects and assignments. Anne Hornak and Anna Ortiz illustrate using the model in conjunction with Ortiz and Rhoads's (2000) Multicultural Education Framework in a community college business course in Chapter 4. An ethnographic study of the course outcomes reveals progress toward self-authorship. In Chapter 5, Katie Egart and Melissa Healy demonstrate the model's use in conceptualizing and implementing the Urban Leadership Internship Program based at Miami University. The 10-week internship in major urban areas in the Midwest results in self-authorship evident in reflective journals, assignments, and interviews. Kevin Yonkers-Talz describes use of the Learning Partnerships Model in Casa de la Solidaridad, a semester-length exchange program sponsored by Santa Clara University and the University of Central America, in Chapter 6. American students from Jesuit colleges spend a semester living and working among the poor in El Salvador; ongoing reflection built in to their experience and interviews before, during, and after the program convey the self-authorship gains they experience. In Chapter 7 Terry Piper and Jennifer Buckley share self-authorship outcomes from a 10-year implementation of the model in the community standards process in residential life at the University of Nevada, Las Vegas. A quality-of-life assessment and a qualitative study show that self-authorship results from residents engaging in creating their living standards. Chapter 8 shifts to graduate education as Judy Rogers, Peter Magolda, Marcia Baxter Magolda, and Kathleen Knight Abowitz describe the Learning Partnerships Model as the foundation of a master's of science program in college student personnel. Use of the model to create core values, pedagogy, and the curriculum yielded self-authorship gains evident in assessments with current students, graduating students, and graduates of the program. The variations of implementation of the Learning Partnerships Model in these exemplars, the diversity of contexts in which they occurred, and the multiple populations of students involved support the model's utility to promote self-authorship in academic and student affairs arenas.

The Learning Partnerships Model transforms educational practice and necessitates transformations in faculty development and student affairs organization. Part 3 addresses transformations undertaken at two institutions where implementation of the Learning Partnerships Model played a central role in transforming faculty and student affairs educators' work to promote student learning. Faculty development efforts at Virginia Polytechnic Institute and State University reveal the transformations that stem from structuring teaching, learning communities, and advising in a partnership model. The organization of the University of Nevada, Las Vegas, Student Affairs Division models organizational structures that support learning partnerships among staff and with students.

The book concludes with a synthesis of implications of the Learning Partnerships Model for holistic educational practice. A two-part framework provides a structure for educators to analyze and design educational practice using the Learning Partnerships Model. The assessment phase of this structure guides readers in defining learning goals in particular educational contexts; identifying what ways of making meaning of beliefs, self, and relationships are required to meet those learning goals; and assessing their particular learners' current ways of making meaning. The design phase of this structure guides readers in designing their particular practice to craft the best balance of guidance and empowerment for particular learners in the context.

The authors invite you to explore the space between guidance and empowerment through the narratives that follow. The book models a learning partnership. We offer complex, diverse examples of the Learning Partnerships Model and invite you to consider them in the contexts of your educational philosophy and practice. We share our struggles with engaging in learning partnerships and transformations we have experienced to illustrate the central role of self in the social construction of knowledge. We write in first person to emphasize the central role of self. Learners' narratives of their struggles and transformations emphasize the same point and demonstrate the mutual construction of learning partnerships. We offer the model and design process for its implementation as guidance to empower you to craft your own learning partnerships. Our hope is that this book, with its rich description of learning partnerships and tangible evidence of their effectiveness in meeting contemporary learning goals, will inspire readers to return to the potter's wheel to remold assumptions about teaching and learning to enable self-authorship during the college experience.

Marcia B. Baxter Magolda

References

Association of American Colleges and Universities. (2002). *Greater expectations: A new vision of learning as a nation goes to college.* Washington DC: Author.

Baxter Magolda, M. B. (1992). *Knowing and reasoning in college: Gender-related patterns in students' intellectual development.* San Francisco: Jossey-Bass.

Baxter Magolda, M. B. (1999). *Creating contexts for learning and self-authorship: Constructive-developmental pedagogy.* Nashville: Vanderbilt University Press.

Baxter Magolda, M. B. (2001). *Making their own way: Narratives for transforming higher education to promote self-development.* Sterling, VA: Stylus.

Jordan, J. V. (1997). A relational perspective for understanding women's development. In J. V. Jordan (Ed.), *Women's growth in diversity: More writings from the Stone Center* (pp. 9–24). New York: Guilford.

Kegan, R. (1994). *In over our heads: The mental demands of modern life.* Cambridge, MA: Harvard University Press.

King, P. M., & Baxter Magolda, M. B. (2003). Toward a developmental model of intercultural maturity: An holistic approach to collegiate education. In C. Rust (Ed.), *Improving student learning: Improving student learning theory and practice—10 years on. Proceedings of the 2002 10th International Symposium* (pp. 269–284). Oxford: Oxford Brookes University.

King, P. M., & Kitchener, K. S. (1994). *Developing reflective judgment: Understanding and promoting intellectual growth and critical thinking in adolescents and adults.* San Francisco: Jossey-Bass.

Ortiz, A. M., & Rhoads, R. A. (2000). Deconstructing whiteness as part of a multicultural educational framework: From theory to practice. *Journal of College Student Development, 41*(1), 81–93.

Parks, S. D. (2000). *Big questions, worthy dreams: Mentoring young adults in their search for meaning, purpose, and faith.* San Francisco: Jossey-Bass.

SELF-AUTHORSHIP AS THE COMMON GOAL OF 21ST-CENTURY EDUCATION

Marcia B. Baxter Magolda

[Learning is] like a starfish. You start in the center and suddenly you are going out in every different direction to try to really step back and take a look at the whole picture. When I was first learning [oncology], I sold a growth factor that is used in a variety of cancers with a variety of different [chemotherapies] so it's the best thing to be selling when you are learning oncology because you really do have to get a great big overview. Now with my specialty, I know a lot about leukemia, specifically acute leukemia, and some other hematological issues. So I understand blood and how when things aren't working in your marrow what happens. It's just being responsible that when you read something and it mentions something and you don't know what it is about, you have to do more research. So that you know you get the full gist of it. And it's always changing. It's been a great journey and it's been very fulfilling work. (Gwen, in Baxter Magolda, 2003, p. 231)

Gwen described the kind of learning college educators espouse—taking responsibility to explore what one does not understand, working to see the "big picture," realizing that knowledge evolves, and viewing learning as a life-long process. Gwen's perspective on learning stemmed from her commitment to helping medical personnel treat cancer patients as effectively as possible—work she finds personally fulfilling. A participant in a 17-year longitudinal study of young adult learning and development (Baxter Magolda, 1992, 2001), Gwen expressed this perspective at age 32, 10 years after her college graduation.

Gwen's ability to identify personally fulfilling work hinged on a shift that she, like most of her peers in the longitudinal project, experienced during her 20s. It was a shift from accepting knowledge from authorities to constructing knowledge herself, made possible by a shift from defining herself through others' perceptions to defining herself based on internally constructed values (Baxter Magolda, 2001). Similarly, Sharon Parks (2000) asserted that between the ages of 17 and 30, a distinctive mode of making meaning emerges that "includes: (1) becoming critically aware of one's own composing of reality, (2) self-consciously participating in an ongoing dialogue toward truth, and (3) cultivating a capacity to respond—to act—in ways that are satisfying and just" (p. 6). Gwen became critically aware of her role in composing reality, was dedicated to participating in finding new cancer treatments, and wanted to act in ways that were satisfying to her and just to the patients she served. This distinctive mode of making meaning—which developmental scholars call self-authorship (Baxter Magolda, 2001; Kegan, 1994)—captures the complexity inherent in typical college learning outcomes, such as critical thinking, mature decision making, appreciation of multiple perspectives and difference, and interdependent relationships with others.[1] It also captures the complexity inherent in contemporary adult life; these same learning outcomes are essential for young adults to be productive in their professions and their personal lives and as citizens in a diverse society. This chapter synthesizes the key expectations of 21st-century higher education and analyzes the developmental demands these expectations place on college students. The developmental transformations required to meet these learning expectations illustrate that educational reform must address learning as transformation rather than focusing exclusively on skill acquisition to effectively prepare graduates for adult life.

Key Components of 21st-Century Higher Education

A common educational goal in American higher education is to improve student learning for the purpose of preparing young adults for the professional, civic, and personal challenges of adult life. Numerous reports address educational needs at the dawn of the 21st-century, most emphasizing the complexity of life in contemporary society as a key dynamic. Writing about the need for commitment in a complex world, Parks Daloz, Keen, Keen, and Daloz Parks (1996) outlined this purpose of a college education:

> At their best, colleges provide space and stimulus for a process of transformation through which students move from modes of understanding that are relatively dependent upon conventional assumptions to more critical, systemic thinking that can take many perspectives into account, make discernments among them, and envision new possibilities. The deep purpose of higher education is to steward this transformation so that students and faculty

---

[1]Adapted from Baxter Magolda (2003).

together continually move from naïveté through skepticism to commitment rather than becoming trapped in mere relativism and cynicism. This movement toward a mature capacity to hold firm convictions in a world which is both legitimately tentative and irreducibly interdependent is vitally important to the formation of citizens in a complex and changing world. (p. 223)

This transformation is the shift from primarily accepting knowledge from authorities to constructing knowledge oneself, as Gwen experienced. These authors emphasize that the complexity of the world simultaneously requires systemic thinking, the ability to judge knowledge claims offered by authorities, constructing convictions, and openness to new possibilities. As such, becoming aware of one's own role in composing reality carries implications beyond intellectual growth.

A Holistic Approach

Addressing the complexities of this kind of transformation, Willimon and Naylor (1995) wrote that a college education should

provide a conceptual framework and a process to facilitate the search for meaning that attempts to integrate the spiritual, intellectual, emotional, and physiological dimensions of life, . . . encourag[ing] students . . . to formulate a *personal strategy* to address the most important quest human beings face—the need for their lives to have enduring meaning. (p. 130)

Their holistic approach to integrating the multiple dimensions of life is echoed in educational reform reports from professional associations. *Powerful Partnerships* (1998), a joint report of the American Association of Higher Education, American College Personnel Association, and National Association of Student Personnel Administrators, includes among learning expectations for students making connections among ideas, experience, contexts, and self and others; actively searching for meaning and taking responsibility for learning; developing an integrated sense of identity that extends to the larger world; and engaging with others in risk taking, critiquing ideas, and sharing diverse experiences.

Reports from both student affairs and academic organizations advocate this holistic approach to 21st-century education. *The Student Learning Imperative,* a report calling for explicitly focusing student affairs work on learning, advanced these hallmarks of a college-educated person:

(a) complex cognitive skills such as reflection and critical thinking; (b) an ability to apply knowledge to practical problems encountered in one's vocation, family, or other areas of life; (c) an understanding and appreciation of human differences; (d) practical competence skills (e.g., decision making, conflict resolution); and (e) a coherent integrated sense of identity, self-esteem, confidence, integrity, aesthetic sensibilities, and civic responsibility. (American College Personnel Association, 1994, p. 1)

These hallmarks link cognitive complexity, identity development, mature relationships, and applying maturity in all these dimensions in everyday life.

Similarly, the Association of American Colleges and Universities advocated a holistic approach in addressing the role colleges play in effective citizenship in a diverse democracy. This can be seen in several excerpts from its report *American Pluralism and the College Curriculum: Higher Education in a Diverse Democracy* (1995), which asserts that "students must learn, in every part of their educational experience, to live creatively with the multiplicity, ambiguity, and irreducible differences that are the defining conditions of the contemporary world" (p. xxii). Yet the authors recognized that learning to live with difference required understanding one's own history and identity:

> Because one's own particular inheritances and experiences form an interpretive framework both for the construction of identity and for all further learning, all students should be encouraged to study these inheritances and to become conversant with and conscious of the images, symbols, stories, and vocabularies that comprise their own experience of cultural connections and particularities. (p. 21)

These authors also recognized that understanding oneself would be insufficient. They advocated understanding others' histories and identities as well, writing,

> Because our graduates will be part of a society that depends on engagement across difference, they need studies and experiences that enable them to become fluent in one another's vocabularies and histories and to discover value in other ways of conceiving the world. (p. 21)

Finally, they noted,

> Because issues of cultural diversity and racial inequity go directly to the core of human identity and self-knowledge, students should encounter these topics affectively as well as intellectually, learning to draw on experience and human empathy as well as rationality and analysis. (p. 22)

They concluded that these premises warranted a commitment to fostering "grounded selves, capable of connection as well as autonomy" (p. 23).

Recognizing the connections among cognitive, identity, and relationship dimensions of these expectations for appreciating diversity (King & Baxter Magolda, 1996), Patricia King and I offered a holistic conceptualization of intercultural maturity (King & Baxter Magolda, 2003). Intercultural maturity includes the ability to use multiple cultural frames to construct knowledge, engaging in meaningful relationships with diverse others that are grounded in appreciation of difference, and the capacity to openly engage challenges to one's beliefs. Similarly, Lisa Landreman (2003) offered a holistic conceptualization of intercultural consciousness. She argued that "achieving consciousness implies an understanding of self and identity (intrapersonal) in a historical and socio-cultural-political context (interpersonal), achieved through reflection (cognitive) and action" (p. 66).

The interweaving of cognitive, identity, and relationship dimensions of learning are evident in one of the most recent reports on contemporary higher education. *Greater Expectations: A New Vision for Learning as a Nation Goes to College* (Association of American Colleges and Universities, 2002), also frames learning in the context of the complexity of adult life. The authors advocate intentional learning:

> In a turbulent and complex world, every college student will need to be purposeful and self-directed in multiple ways. Purpose implies clear goals, an understanding of process, and appropriate action. Further, purpose implies intention in one's actions. Becoming such an intentional learner means developing self-awareness about the reason for study, the learning process itself, and how education is used. Intentional learners are integrative thinkers who can see connections in seemingly disparate information and draw on a wide range of knowledge to make decisions. They adapt the skills learned in one situation to problems encountered in another: in a classroom, the workplace, their communities, or their personal lives. As a result, intentional learners succeed even when instability is the only constant.
>
> For intentional learners, intellectual study connects to personal life, formal education to work, and knowledge to social responsibility. Through understanding the power and implications of education, learners who are intentional consciously choose to act in ethical and responsible ways. Able to place themselves in the context of a diverse world, these learners draw on difference and commonality to produce a deeper experience of community. (pp. 21–22)

This vision of intentional learning illustrates the complexity of undergraduate learning required to address the complexity of contemporary campus and adult life. It portrays the intentional learner as empowered through intellectual and practical skills, such as mental agility, intellectual power, flexibility, and creative problem solving; the latter stem from integrating multiple sources of knowledge and transforming that knowledge into judgment and action. The intentional learner is also informed by knowledge and ways of knowing, necessitating "a deep understanding of the world's variety, as well as a knowledge of Western culture" (p. 24). The intentional learner is responsible for personal actions and civic values, requiring understanding and respect for one's own and others' identities and cultures, active participation in learning and society, and ethical action for the benefit of individuals and society. This comprehensive vision of 21st-century higher education conveys the magnitude of higher education's expectations of college students.

Contemporary College Learning Outcomes

Collectively, these reports suggest that contemporary college learning outcomes should include the following:

- *Cognitive maturity,* characterized by intellectual power, reflective judgment, mature decision making, and problem solving in the context of multiplicity

- An *integrated identity,* characterized by understanding one's own particular history, confidence, the capacity for autonomy and connection, and integrity

- *Mature relationships,* characterized by respect for both one's own and others' particular identities and cultures and by productive collaboration to integrate multiple perspectives

Maturity in these three areas combines to enable effective citizenship—coherent, ethical action for the good of both the individual and the larger community. Effective citizenship requires the ability to evaluate possible actions, interpret contexts and consequences, and make wise choices—all characteristics of cognitive maturity. For these choices to be coherent and ethical requires an internal belief system and an internal identity that together guide action. Ethical action for the good of the individual and larger community requires the capacity for mutuality and interdependence characteristic of mature relationships: it requires understanding of and commitment to one's own interests in interaction with understanding and commitment to the interests of others. To act ethically as a citizen requires intercultural maturity, or the ability to use multiple cultural frames, engage in relationships with diverse others grounded in appreciation of difference, and consideration of social identities in a global and national context (King & Baxter Magolda, 2003). Although young adults

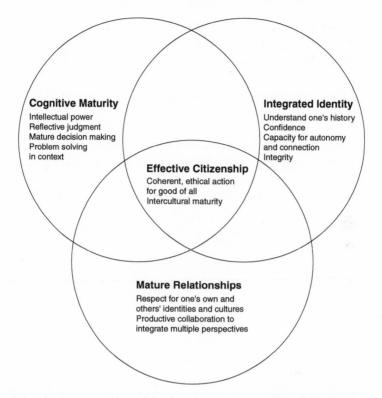

Cognitive Maturity
Intellectual power
Reflective judgment
Mature decision making
Problem solving
in context

Integrated Identity
Understand one's history
Confidence
Capacity for autonomy
and connection
Integrity

Effective Citizenship
Coherent, ethical action
for good of all
Intercultural maturity

Mature Relationships
Respect for one's own and
others' identities and cultures
Productive collaboration to
integrate multiple perspectives

Figure 1.1 An integrated model of contemporary college learning outcomes.

can be influenced to act as effective citizens by others whose opinions they value, genuine achievement of this learning outcome as a free choice requires integration of cognitive maturity, integrated identity, and mature relationships. Figure 1.1 portrays the relationships among these learning outcomes.[2]

Although considerable agreement exists about the desirability of these learning outcomes—and in fact has for many years—educational practice has yet to be substantively reformed to facilitate these outcomes. The slow pace of change in higher education, faculty training in their discipline rather than in pedagogy, and the historical bifurcation of academic and student affairs all contribute to lack of reform. Reform has also been hindered by the lack of attention to the developmental foundations on which complex learning outcomes stand and the lack of attention to the way these foundations interrelate to support these outcomes. The substantive learning outcomes called for in

[2]For a more specific portrayal of how cognitive, identity, and relationship dynamics interrelate in intercultural maturity, see King and Baxter Magolda (2003).

the myriad national reports discussed earlier in this chapter require self-authorship, or the internal capacity to define one's beliefs, identity, and relations with others (Baxter Magolda, 2001).

Developmental Foundations of Contemporary College Learning Outcomes

Figure 1.2 highlights the developmental foundations of cognitive maturity, integrated identity, mature relationships, and effective citizenship. Mature capacity in three dimensions of development—epistemological, intrapersonal, and interpersonal—intertwine to form self-authorship to support these learning outcomes.

How people use assumptions about the nature, limits, and certainty of knowledge to make knowledge claims is the *epistemological* dimension of

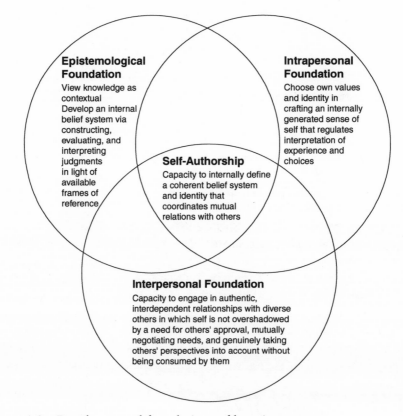

Figure 1.2 Developmental foundations of learning outcomes.

development.[3] Cognitive maturity requires viewing knowledge as contextual, or as constructed using relevant evidence in a particular context. A contextual view of knowledge recognizes that multiple perspectives exist, depending on how people structure knowledge claims. It further requires the capacity to participate in constructing, evaluating, and interpreting judgments in light of available evidence and frames of reference. Contextual knowers construct knowledge claims internally, critically analyzing external perspectives rather than adopting them uncritically. Increasing maturity in knowledge construction yields an internal belief system that guides thinking and behavior yet is open to reconstruction given relevant evidence. Cognitive outcomes such as intellectual power, reflective judgment, mature decision making, and problem solving depend on these epistemological capacities. This dimension is central to achieving cognitive maturity and is a necessary ingredient for achieving the other learning outcomes.

How people view themselves and construct their identities is the *intrapersonal* dimension of development.[4] An integrated identity requires the ability to reflect on, explore, and choose enduring values. It requires coordinating various characteristics to form a coherent identity that gains stability over time yet is open to growth. To be coherent and enduring, this integrated identity must be internally constructed rather than adopted to seek external approval. An integrated identity serves as a foundation for interpreting experience and conducting oneself in the world. Understanding one's particular history, confidence, the capacity for autonomy and connection, and integrity all depend on these intrapersonal capacities. These intrapersonal developmental capacities are central to achieving an integrated identity as well as necessary for attaining the other learning outcomes. For example, constructing an internal belief system and using it in decision making (i.e., cognitive maturity) requires an internal identity that is not overly dependent on the views of others. Similarly, choosing one's values and identity characteristics (i.e., integrated identity) requires contextual knowing in which one takes responsibility for constructing knowledge.

How people view themselves in relation to others and how they construct relationships is the *interpersonal* dimension of development. Mature relationships are characterized by respect for both one's own and others' particular identities and cultures as well as by productive collaboration to negotiate and

---

[3]For extensive theories of college students' epistemological development see Perry (1970), Belenky et al. (1986), King and Kitchener (1994), and Baxter Magolda (1992).

[4]For extensive theories of college students' identity development, see Chickering and Reisser (1993), Josselson (1987, 1996), and Kegan (1994). These theories also address interpersonal development.

integrate multiple perspectives and needs. The developmental capacity for interdependence stands at the base of this learning outcome. Interdependence requires openness to other perspectives without being consumed by them. An integrated identity makes this interdependence possible by prioritizing self-approval as a criteria with which to judge others' perspectives. This is not a return to egocentricity but rather a turning away from self-sacrifice to please others (evident in Kurt's narrative later in this chapter). Kegan (1994) describes this as having relationships rather than being had by them. From this vantage point, it is no longer threatening to see differences (e.g., cultural, political, and geographical) or to acknowledge that people hold multiple perspectives; this capacity enables the individual to become interculturally mature (Kegan, 1994; King & Baxter Magolda, 2003). Mutuality (Jordan, 1997) is possible because of the capacity to explore others' perspectives as well as one's own. These interpersonal capacities are central to mature relationships as well as to the other learning outcomes. For example, both constructing an internal belief system (i.e., cognitive maturity) and achieving an integrated identity require avoiding being consumed by others' perspectives. Similarly, authentic engagement in interdependent relationships requires an integrated identity. It also requires the acceptance of multiple perspectives and the internal belief system possible with cognitive maturity.

Maturity on all three developmental dimensions yields self-authorship. Among my longitudinal participants, self-authorship took the form of acknowledging the uncertainty of knowledge and crafting their own internal belief systems. Simultaneously, it involved intense self-reflection to explore and select their internal values and identity. They negotiated or renegotiated relationships that balanced their internal beliefs and identity with those of others in a mutual fashion. Kegan (1994) described this self-authorship as fourth order, a way of making meaning in which values, beliefs, convictions, generalizations, ideals, abstractions, interpersonal loyalty, and intrapersonal states of mind emerge from being co-constructed with others external to the self. The fourth order of meaning making

> takes all of these as objects or elements of its system, rather than the system itself; it does not identify with them but views them as parts of a new whole. This new whole is an ideology, an internal identity, a *self-authorship* that can coordinate, integrate, act upon, or invent values, beliefs, convictions, generalizations, ideals, abstractions, interpersonal loyalties, and intrapersonal states. It is no longer *authored by* them, it *authors them* and thereby achieves a personal authority. (p. 185)

Kegan noted that half to two thirds of the adult population in his studies did not reach the fourth order. My participants' transformation to self-authorship evolved over their 20s and early 30s, enabling them to become effective citizens in their public and private lives. Thus, achieving the 21st-century learning outcomes of cognitive maturity, integrated identity, and mature relationships that together enable effective citizenship requires engaging young adults in the transformation from authority dependence to self-authorship.

The longitudinal participants' narratives reveal the phases of the journey toward self-authorship, providing a foundation from which educators can join young adults on the journey. A brief overview of that journey is provided next; readers who desire the more detailed version can find it in *Making Their Own Way* (Baxter Magolda, 2001). My particular construction of this journey from the longitudinal data was, of course, informed by key theories of college students' epistemological (e.g., Belenky, Clinchy, Goldberger, & Tarule, 1986; King & Kitchener, 1994; Perry, 1970), intrapersonal, and interpersonal (e.g., Chickering & Reisser, 1993; Josselson, 1987; Kegan, 1994) development. The role these theories played in my constructions is addressed in *Knowing and Reasoning in College* (Baxter Magolda, 1992).

Journeys Toward Self-Authorship

The three stories that follow illustrate self-authorship and its development from three vantage points. Al's story places the epistemological dimension in the forefront as he recounts his development as a decision maker. Thus, the learning outcomes of cognitive maturity and effective citizenship in his role as a physician are evident. Dawn's story brings the intrapersonal dimension to the foreground as she focuses on the development of her identity. The learning outcome of an integrated identity is most clear in her story. Kurt's story highlights the interpersonal dimension as he traces the evolution of his role in relationships, illustrating the mature relationships learning outcome. Although all three stories reflect the collective learning outcomes and developmental dimensions, bringing various components to the forefront helps demonstrate their unique dynamics. The stories begin with the participants' portrayal of self-authorship to illuminate this concept. The journey toward self-authorship is then traced from their prior experience. Table 1.1 provides an overview of the journey toward self-authorship.

Cognitive Maturity: Al's Story

Al, a family doctor at the age of 33, described his medical decision-making process in a way that reveals the central nature of self-authorship:

> Medical decision-making is a logical, clear process—you have a set of facts, you put them together and come to a conclusion that makes sense. With my

Table 1.1 Developmental Journey Toward Learning Outcomes

Dimension	External formulas	Crossroads	Self-authorship
Epistemological	View knowledge as certain or partially certain, yielding reliance on authority as source of knowledge; lack of internal basis for evaluating knowledge claims results in externally defined beliefs	Evolving awareness and acceptance of uncertainty and multiple perspectives; shift from accepting authority's knowledge claims to personal processes for adopting knowledge claims; recognize need to take responsibility for choosing beliefs	View knowledge as contextual; develop an internal belief system via constructing, evaluating, and interpreting judgments in light of available evidence and frames of reference
Intrapersonal	Lack of awareness of own values and social identity, lack of coordination of components of identity, and need for others' approval combine to yield an externally defined identity that is susceptible to changing external pressures	Evolving awareness of own values and sense of identity distinct from external others' perceptions; tension between emerging internal values and external pressures prompts self-exploration; recognize need to take responsibility for crafting own identity	Choose own values and identity in crafting an internally generated sense of self that regulates interpretation of experience and choices

Interpersonal	Dependent relations with similar others are source of identity and needed affirmation; frame participation in relationships as doing what will gain others' approval	Evolving awareness of limitations of dependent relationships; recognize need to bring own identity into constructing independent relationships; struggle to reconstruct or extract self from dependent relationships	Capacity to engage in authentic, interdependent relationships with diverse others in which self is not overshadowed by need for others' approval; mutually negotiating relational needs; genuinely taking others' perspectives into account without being consumed by them

level of confidence with my own ability and skills and knowledge, I don't have any trouble making those decisions. Here are a set of facts, here is what I think; I'm competent and comfortable in that decision. You've made good decisions in the past; once you've made a few, you realize you know what you are doing. . . . If I'm in a situation where I have control of the variables it is a piece of cake for me. It is hard when I know what needs to be done, but there is no way for me to make it happen. I just have to sit back and hope—that is where praying and hope and God come into it for me—leave that in hands of God—I can't fix this. I leave that to God to fix for me.

Initially, it sounded as though Al viewed medical decisions as factual. However, extended conversations clarified that he used his knowledge base to interpret factual data and determine when uncertainty was acceptable. Asked if he ever encountered not controlling the variables in medical decisions, he responded,

Yes, 95% of the time things go like you expect. You need to recognize that in the other 5% this isn't what I expected, so I get help. As long as I know I'm doing as much as I can, and I'm getting help when it is over my head, I'm comfortable with unpredictability of a situation. The range of situations is so broad, you have to recognize when you don't know what is going on or someone is sicker than they should be. That has become fairly easy for me to make those distinctions. Can I afford to figure this out myself or get help now? I can deal with that when I know I'm not jeopardizing someone's health—you can't have an ego about that. That gets simple for me. Are they sick or not? Do I know what it is or not? If I can recognize those four things, I'm in good shape. If they are sick and I don't know, get someone else involved. That is pretty much it. Those four situations. I should write that down! I've had some people in my office in the last couple of weeks that have something strange going on. I don't know what it is, but they are getting better. I can't label it, but that is not a problem. None of them needed to be in the hospital and they are gradually improving, so I saw them every 3 to 5 days, repeated blood work to make sure things are improving. I always have an out—send someone to the university medical center.

These comments suggest that Al sees medical decisions as complex and ambiguous. He uses relevant evidence to interpret patients' health conditions. Usually his judgments, which stand on his acquired knowledge and previous experience, play out as he anticipates they will. When they do not, he analyzes multiple perspectives, evaluates new evidence to try to make sound judgments, and recognizes that he may not be able to figure out what is going on. Al's medical knowledge and confidence in that knowledge help him cope with uncertainty to a degree. When Al does not know what to make of the patient's situation, he enlists the help of specialists with more knowledge and experience than he possesses. He recognizes that in some cases even the specialists cannot cure patients, a sign that he is aware of the inevitable uncertainty of knowledge. Al also acts in the best interests of his patients. His belief that "you can't have an ego" about getting help conveys effective citizenship as a physician. His patients' health supercedes his interest in solving problems himself, leading to ethical action. Al's cognitive maturity grounds his ability to make contextual medical decisions, yet it is augmented by his integrated identity and mature relationships. His internal identity supports his confidence as a physician who does not have to portray an all-knowing image to his patients or colleagues. His minimal ego needs enable him to engage in authentic relations with others and bring in other experts as necessary. His work is guided by his internal belief system, his internal identity, and his commitment to do what is best for his patients. His self-authorship grounds effective medical practice.

Al's self-authorship as a person and a physician evolved over his mid- to late 20s. On graduating from college, Al still relied on *external formulas* to guide his decisions. Having multiple job offers as a college senior, Al chose a position as a computer consultant because he thought it had the most potential. Reflecting on this position in his first year on the job, he said,

> I made the right decision as far as where I can go with it. If I do well, my monetary rewards are going to be much higher much quicker. As far as my status it will go up much quicker and much higher. And also the variety of learning experiences are going to be much more so in this job. I think I'll be a little more marketable coming out of this. I think as far as a good beginning ground you can't do any better than where I'm at. If you stay with it, the rewards are very good, too. But if you don't, you've made so many contacts and you've had the kind of background and training that you can pretty much go anywhere or get into just about any grad school.

Al's criteria for a good starting position included financial reward, experience, and marketability. These criteria focus on being perceived positively by others. In considering his first full-time position, Al did not entertain internal criteria, such as his values and identity. It did not take long (his second year working) for these internal dynamics to emerge in his work:

> In school, I think I always did what I thought was right. On my job, even if I think it's right, I can't do it all the time. You have all those other factors that come in now, some ethical, some just financial, some you have to just do the things the way they're done. Whereas, I think in school I always did what I thought was right. And that always got me pretty far. I guess you come out [of college] a little bit of an idealist and you always want to do it the best way or the way you think. But then you have more pieces to the puzzle, so

you have to consider those, whereas before you didn't. So obviously that adds to the complexity of the picture. I'm learning there are times when I need to suppress what comes right to the top of my head. The old stop, think about it a little more, take a step back before you jump into it. Even though I don't like it, it has helped me find that control a little bit more. I've always been pretty closed minded about things, kind of always had my vision of what is right and what's wrong and what should be done and what I like to do and what I don't like to do. And I'm trying to be a little more open-minded. I've been reading a lot of books, just trying to get different perspectives. I realize that there are a lot of other ways to look at things and a lot of other ways to do things. And my way's not always the best way. I need to open myself to some of the other ways and kind of mesh them all together maybe and come up with a new, better way. I wasn't happy because I was always frustrated. The way I wanted to do things wasn't the way things were happening. I have had to learn to just roll with whatever we came up with or whatever was decided. And that's something I've struggled with. But I'm working on it. I'm still struggling with it, but I think it's making me a better person for it. It's been a lot of work. It's hard to change yourself that way.

Al's story of the struggle between doing things his way and doing things the company's way reveals both his reliance on external authority and his recognition that he needs to be open to multiple perspectives. Because doing things his way in college served him well, he did not encounter these conflicts in college. Finding out that he could not always do things his way in his job led him to try to change himself. He suppressed his initial reactions when they conflicted with the company preference. He read books to obtain new perspectives in his quest to be more open-minded. He tried to accept decisions and work with them instead of debating their merits. He tried to resolve his frustration over things not being done his way by accepting external authority.

Although Al achieved some success in managing his frustrations by exploring multiple perspectives, his effort to be more open to multiple perspectives and his reflection on himself at work led him to the *crossroads* of the journey toward self-authorship. His growing sense of his values led him to change careers. Describing the situation, he said,

After you've worked a year or so, you start to realize you're going to be working the rest of your life. I mean, you realize you're going to have to get a job, but you really don't feel what it's all about until you get out there and do it. After a year, I learned a lot with the company I worked for. And I didn't dislike it. I just figured I'm going to work until I'm 65 anyway, I ought to do what I've always thought I wanted to do. And if I'm ever going to do it, I need to get started. Even that freshman year in college, I thought maybe

I would want to be a doctor. But what was holding me back was (a) I wasn't sure I wanted to spend that much time getting there, and (b) I have never been a real science fan. Now I'm looking at the end of the road rather than what it takes to get there. I think the bottom line is, "Are you going to be happy in what you're doing?" The biggest thing is what am I really doing? In my job, I never really felt like it was the kind of help I wanted to give to people. How I can do a job faster to me is not as important as helping a kid get through cancer. So that's what I looked at in making the decision. I'm somewhat involved in the church. And at times I almost felt like I was cheating people. My billing rate was $120 an hour. And here I am, a year out of school and the company can charge $120 an hour for me to sit in a meeting. I was just like, "Great day! I'm definitely not doing work worth that much." And I just feel like I want to spend my life helping people more than just making companies more efficient, which is a good thing, but it's just not the kind of good I want to do. (Baxter Magolda, 2001, pp. 101–102)

Al's evolving awareness of his own values and sense of identity distinct from others' perceptions led him back to a career he had considered earlier. Tension between his emerging internal values and external pressures prompted this self-exploration and his sense that his current work did not involve the kind of good he wanted to do. Recognizing the need to take responsibility for crafting his own adult identity led him out of the crossroads into self-authorship.

Developing self-authorship takes time and energy. Al took additional undergraduate courses in science to prepare for medical school, took the MCAT, and worked in computer consulting while waiting to enroll in medical school. Over the next few years, he steadily worked toward developing his own internal belief system, values, and identity. Part of this process involved increasingly accepting uncertainty. Al described how he faced this:

I don't second-guess decisions; that has changed. I used to have stomach trouble! I've gotten better at this over the last 3 to 5 years. I came to the realization that it isn't worth it. The role of religion and Christ in my life is part of this. Worrying isn't going to change anything. There is a poem by—I can't remember— but the last line is something like 10% is what happens, 90% is how we respond. That is the attitude I try to take. Looking too far back and too far ahead is pointless. This attitude, and religion, alters goals and what is really important. I major on the majors and minor on the minors. If you keep what is really important in perspective, the daily grind doesn't get to you that much. Keeping things that matter in focus yields a sense of peace and calm; you don't need to get worked up. That alone isn't it; it is both ideas—a combination of knowing Christ is there and a way of thinking that you have to take on. Maybe I just don't need to understand everything. That is one of the struggles I have. I'm still working on that. It is tough because I like to know why; I'm a fixer, solution kind of guy—I like to know the variables so I can deal with them. If there are no variables, it is tough to deal. (Baxter Magolda, 2001, pp. 144–145)

As Al explored balancing uncertainty and responsibility for his life, he also struggled to balance uncertainty and judgment several years later as a medical resident:

> I'm not that comfortable making judgments; there is always uncertainty. You have to get used to it, you have to do what you know to do and use your best judgment. Right now I don't have confidence in my knowledge base; I'm not to that point yet. I don't know enough. I wouldn't be comfortable with the final decision. Even as a resident, you can be the final decision-maker; others say it is good to get that experience. It forces you to learn more; when you are in that situation you are going to work through it before you make a plan. Now I can take my best shot, and my doc is watching my back. Being in that situation will force me to learn more. I need to start doing that more now. (Baxter Magolda, 2001, p. 150)

As a medical resident, Al knew he needed to use his best judgment and continue to take responsibility for his decisions. He was not yet comfortable with his knowledge base but was clearly aware that using what he did know to make a medical plan was the way to gain this confidence. Handling uncertainty meant constructing, evaluating, and interpreting judgments in light of available evidence and frames of reference in order to make a medical plan.

The learning outcome of cognitive maturity is a key thread of Al's story. His first job after college challenged his notion that he always knew the right way to do things. His quest to become more open-minded led him to a career change that took his values into account, marking the beginning of an internal belief system. His encounter with medical knowledge and uncertainty in medical school honed his ability to accept uncertainty yet construct reasonable medical judgments within complex contexts. His ability to be an effective citizen as a physician and person hinges on his achievement of cognitive maturity. It also hinges on his achievement of an internal identity and interdependent relations with others.

An Integrated Identity: Dawn's Story

Dawn is a creative person who divides her professional energy between theater and cooking. At age 33, Dawn clearly articulated self-authoring her identity:

> There is so much processing going on, what I do on a daily basis, trying to fit all the pieces of the puzzle together. I think I'm definitely at a point where I

am really defining a lot about my life. Not that it is discovering new things—I'm sure I am—but bringing everything that I've ever thought and believed into a much clearer focus for myself. I'm in very deep thought about evaluating what is important, what is not so important, what gives me comfort, emotionally, mentally, discovering these things. Specifying these things that accomplish these things for me. I'm starting to realize that the more specific you are, the much more simple things become. It's definitely true in my theater work. I push my actors when I'm directing, or when I am acting, to being specific about how you communicate, physically, vocally. To put that in a bigger scale, knowing exactly how you are going to handle things. Am I going to get angry about this? Be very positive about this? If you are very specific in your frame of mind in how you approach and handle things, that makes it much simpler. The whole thought process of just taking stock of where you are in your life. It's like putting your life through a sieve, getting the big awkward chunks out of your life, getting the nice finely sifted residue—it is kind of sorting it all out. What is the essence of you and what isn't? What is important to the essence of you and what isn't? Do I get upset because somebody didn't cook a tenderloin right? Maybe in the moment, but in the bigger picture it doesn't mean anything. Life goes on. Defining that picture. Deciding what is important. It is all interconnected; I find myself thinking about things now answering this question that I was talking about a while back. It's a process of thought and understanding, some decision making that goes into it. You have to decide what it is that you want and don't want. Little by little, things take a much more specific shape. Who is to say, tomorrow I might wake up and have something that occurs in my day that sets me on a completely different road, so there I am again sifting and rebuilding with all this new information that I have. I don't suppose it happens that rapidly. I think I'll be on this path for a while until it is time to go in another direction.

Dawn's comments reveal that she is interpreting experiences she encounters along the way, deciding what to keep and omit to form her sense of herself. As she sifts the awkward chunks out of her life, she finds handling everyday life simpler. Getting to what she calls "the essence of you" is the key to her life taking a specific shape, to defining a path to follow until new experience reshapes it, processing each new experience in the context of the essence of who she is. Asked how she decided on the essence of herself, she responded,

I knew that was coming. This is kind of a funny analogy, but it is kind of like trying on clothes. You know if something doesn't fit you and it doesn't feel right. Given everything you know from birth to now, your experience, you instinctively choose what feels right and what doesn't. When you are exposed to new information, you try it on, if it doesn't feel right, you get rid of it, if it fits you keep it. I suppose there is a much deeper philosophical way to explain it than that—but that's the easiest way I can define it. You take in information and see how it feels given your accumulation of life experiences to that point. If it feels right you keep it; if it doesn't, you let it go. As far as thinking how that relates to like deeper issues, um, I think a lot of it also has to relate to the self, how you view yourself. If you respect yourself, if you have confidence in your ability, that changes your whole perspective. If you respect yourself, it is pretty much a given that you will respect others. Treating others with compassion and understanding can only happen when you've achieved a certain level of that yourself. Just thinking about the energy of the world and how we treat each other and how—that is a big defining thing for me right now. Stepping into that realm of not judging people, treating them with compassion, acting in my life without judging and with compassion. That is a step that I'm trying to take for myself right now; relates to the karma idea—you get back exactly what you give. If you are always putting forth things that are positive in the world, you get things that are positive right back at you. That is how the world works; it may not come back immediately. It is a simpler, more peaceful way of living. That right there eliminates a lot of daily stresses and makes the day much more pleasant. It contributes to you as an individual being a better person and getting more out of life.

Dawn's trying-on-clothes metaphor conveys that knowing and accepting one's body is central to deciding whether clothes fit. Similarly, Dawn's integrated identity, so grounded internally that she labels it instinctive, guides her determination of what fits the essence of herself. It also leads to respecting herself and confidence in her ability, factors she views as central to respecting others. Her commentary on treating others with compassion and understanding reveals the intricate relationship of autonomy and connection. Because Dawn established an internal identity that enables her to respect herself—a component of autonomy—she is able to engage in authentic relationships with others—a component of connection. Dawn's commentary clarifies that the concept of self-authorship is not self-centered but rather a mutual, reciprocal dynamic of relations with others. These reflections explicitly place respecting the self at the core of one's meaning making and interactions with others.

The perspective Dawn shared at 33 was more than 10 years in the making. As a college student, Dawn followed the *external formulas* offered by authorities. She started college in pre-med, changed to English, and then in her junior year changed her major again. Her story about the junior year change reveals the external focus of these decisions:

I'm finally off academic probation. I think it's finally getting into the subject area that I want to study. I've changed my mind as everybody does, about five hundred times, but finally [found] something that I really enjoy and it doesn't bother me to have to do a lot of work for it. I'm now a history and theater major. There's a lot involved with it, but it's also something that I can just do forever and never get enough of.

Asked how she decided on this change, Dawn explained,

> Actually it's been kind of a several months thing. It took awhile, especially with the theater. I had to think about what I'm going to do in the future. But I felt strongly enough about it that that's what I wanted to do. And there are several things I can do with it after I graduate. So that was just kind of the way I decided to do it. [The most important thing] was the fact that I really enjoyed it. That's what made me, "Why don't I just make this my career?" But then I had to stop and think, "Well, there could be something holding me back as far as what can I do with it?" So I had to figure out—I thought it over a lot, and figured, "What the heck. If it's what I want to do, why be unhappy doing something else?" It seems so much easier for me to get the grades doing something that I like to do.

Dawn described her choice as hinging on being able to get the necessary grades, liking what she was doing, and being able to do something with it on graduation. This vague explanation suggests that these were external criteria for success. Despite her emphasis on doing something she liked, Dawn's decision seemed to rest on a superficial examination of her values.

Dawn's interest in theater increased as time passed. After her graduation, she was far less concerned about what she might do with it, evident in the following story:

> Right now I'm doing theater at a professional theater, which is something I never expected to be doing right out of college. I was thinking about just going home and working through the summer and seeing what happens. I feel very lucky. But it also makes me feel extremely confident that if, right out of school, I can be getting these opportunities that I am getting, it charges me to just go full speed ahead into the next thing and to continue to search out more opportunities where I can go next. I'm still kind of a tumbleweed that wherever I land, that's where I'll be. But I try to keep that flexibility just so that—because I just know so many things can come up. I try to keep myself flexible to make the choice wherever I want to go. Coming and having this internship right now and having the success that I feel that I've had with it and the experiences that I've gained, and then to be offered another one for next year—it's kind of overwhelming. But I just feel so determined to do what I want to do. And I think that's what adds to my confidence, my excitement. I kind of sat down and had a conversation with

myself not too long ago and just kind of tried to assess what was happening in my life and where things were going. And I just felt so exuberant about everything. We often think being in the theater, "What if I don't make it?" Right now I don't think that's a possibility. And I don't mean that to sound in any way conceited or anything. I feel that confident. If things aren't going to fall into place for me, which I'm sure they're not, but I feel like I have the confidence and the stamina and the smarts to make something happen for me. You should probably go back and dig out a tape from when I was a sophomore and it would be such a drastic change from now. I don't feel like I can expend that energy in what if, what if. And if by some odd stroke of luck I don't [make it] . . . I have the wealth in the experience to move me in another direction to whatever comes next. I mean, this is all just a wonderful, wonderful life experience to be having. Fortunately, it's in what I want to be doing. It's like for the first time in my life, I know I'm in the career vein that I have always wanted to be in and should be in. I think there's a lot of floundering that goes on while you're in school, "What's my major? What am I going to do with my life?" And I think I've found where I need to be and want to be.

Dawn expected to go home and work to make money and accepted that she might not immediately get theater opportunities. She did get a theater internship, which boosted her confidence. Her comments reveal an increasing recognition that she plays a role in her career path. The confidence she gained through this internship made her "determined" to do what she wants to do and helped her conclude that she had the smarts to make it happen. She was still aware that external factors might alter her plans, but she was emerging from the *crossroads* with a strong internal sense of self.

Dawn continued her theater work simultaneously with learning to cook. She found both to be creative outlets, yet the theater work had the most influence on her growth toward self-authorship. By her late 20s, she described having achieved the internal sense of self that characterizes self-authorship:

The more you discover about yourself, the more you can become secure with it. And that obviously leads to greater self-confidence because you become comfortable with who you really are. My confidence level is so much better than it ever has been. I'm more willing to express my ideas and take chances expressing my ideas. "Who cares what people think?" sort of thing. When you're not as self-confident, you're afraid that people are going to laugh at what you think or you're afraid that they're going to think you're stupid— it's all those petty, little things that inhibit us. Whereas when you're confident, you are more willing to say, "This is my opinion; this is why I hold this opinion. You may agree with it or not, but this is what—with my mind I have formulated this opinion and that's how I think and feel." I'm not as afraid to be willing to say that because of what I am this is how I feel. I try not to step on people's toes with my opinions, be offensive about it, but if someone asks me for my opinion or advice or how I think and feel about something, I will definitely tell them. And I think self-awareness too, because you realize that it doesn't really matter if other people agree with you or not. You can think and formulate ideas for yourself and ultimately that's what's important. You have a mind and you can use it. That's probably the most important thing, regardless of the content of what your thoughts and opinions are. I suppose it's very idealistic to think that everybody can see that. It's the fact that you can form an opinion that's more important than the opinion itself. But I don't think that happens. So it's kind of a self-confidence and self-awareness thing. (Baxter Magolda, 2001, pp. 152–153)

Becoming comfortable with herself helped Dawn express her ideas. It formed the basis for the confidence to construct her beliefs and share them with others without fear of ridicule. Her internal sense of self allowed her to overcome her concerns about others' approval so that she could be herself.

Solidifying her internal sense of self prompted Dawn to share another significant dimension of her journey with me in our 10th annual interview:

One of the biggest things—it hasn't come up in any of our conversations before—was accepting the fact that my sexual orientation is out of the mainstream. It was a big thing for me. It started for me when I was in school. You finally get to a point where you can feel comfortable enough that you don't care what people think about you. The turning point was in the last couple of years. It brought out interesting things in me. It has taken me probably five years to feel solid. Now, I don't care if you know if I'm gay and what you think. It doesn't matter and this is who I am. Dealing with that with family; I told my parents three years ago. That's been an interesting process. (Baxter Magolda, 2001, p. 182)

Dawn's comment on taking 5 years to feel solid about this suggests the arduous process of achieving an internal sense of self. We talked about why her sexual orientation had not entered our previous conversations. Dawn said,

It wasn't that I couldn't talk about it; becomes a personal thing. Now I am at that point that I am comfortable—it doesn't bother me. A big thing in the last couple years in my life. That has contributed a great deal to how I see things and how I think. Getting to where I am now, the confidence thing; you know you have the inner strength to stand apart from the mainstream. I don't have to be a duck in a row, following what everyone else is doing.

Whether it has to do with being gay or not. The best way I can explain it is learning to walk. You get stronger and finally run. It is a release, where you are willing to let go of clutter that people throw at you. (Baxter Magolda, 2001, p. 183)

Dawn was settled in her internal foundation and had the strength to balance her own needs with others' expectations. For her, this was the central dynamic of achieving self-authorship.

Mature Relationships: Kurt's Story

At age 33, Kurt described entering into a significant relationship from a self-authored perspective:

> I always look to do things from the inside out. I don't look for opportunities to provide me with the internal state of mind; I first concentrate on that internal state of mind. Lynn Grabhorn wrote a book called *Excuse Me, Your Life Is Waiting*. It talks about being clear with what you want, and then when it happens, experiences come in to support that because you attract those things to you. I'm clear on what I want and what I want to feel, then these experiences develop and come my way. I attribute the plant manager position to this. I didn't go asking for this. It just kind of falls in there. To me it is like the important piece is to begin with the end in mind. What do I want to accomplish with the situation I'm in? It is even larger in how do I want to live my life, how my marriage will turn out, all those things. It is not conscious. Something presents itself to me and this is the next logical step.
>
> Dating my fiancée falls into this process. The situation kept coming back for me. For 3 or 4 years we were friends. She asked me to go skiing, I asked her to a movie one time, she said sorry. Working with her it was difficult— me as a manager wanted to be conscious of harassment; we are told over and over again, it is okay to ask once, but not more. The timing wasn't right. Then I thought, it is here, it is here for a reason, available to you. See what might come from it.

Kurt articulated that once he knows what he wants, he identifies opportunities and situations that help him reach his goals. While he focused on being a good manager and avoiding harassment, he postponed dating his friend and coworker. At a later point as his internal state of mind focused on wanting a relationship, he decided to see what might materialize. Asked how he knew that he wanted to marry this woman, he offered,

> One thing that is very apparent to me—I spent the entire decade of my 20s getting in touch with who I was and what is important to me. From the time

we started dating, there weren't any questions, it got to a point of—it was weird. We went into the relationship with a totally different set of goals and objectives [than in earlier relationships]. To the extent that we could, more than any other relationship I've had, we entered into it as complete people. We weren't lacking for anything, weren't needing affirmation, or needing each other to give us something to complete us. From a perspective of infatuation, I have never had that with her—have had it with other women, but it's the pendulum thing again. Always been in middle with her; wonderful thing of us sharing our lives with each other, we both have a similar set of beliefs, allowing me to be that whole person that I already am. Not having to put on an act. I haven't felt the whole infatuation thing, just an even keel kind of thing. That has allowed me to feel great about making the commitment. The support from her—the beautiful thing about that—I don't need to change a single thing and still be loved as much or more than I was this morning. Hopefully that is the environment I create for her as well. Accepted, respected and loved by me. That's how it has come to be and how I've been able to commit to that and feel great about it. (Baxter Magolda, 2003, p. 234)

Kurt's key point was that he and his fiancée entered this relationship with different objectives than he was used to carrying into relationships—the notion that each of them entered as a complete person. They entered this relationship with respect for both of their particular identities and collaborated productively to integrate multiple perspectives. Knowing who he was and what was important to him (an integrated identity) created an internal state of mind that led him to pursue this relationship. It was also the foundation for his entering it genuinely, without pretenses or needs for affirmation. Thus, like Dawn, Kurt articulated that self-authorship yielded authentic mutuality. Mutual respect, loving each other as they are, and not needing affirmation combine to enable Kurt and his fiancée to enjoy interdependence.

Kurt mentioned spending most of his 20s getting in touch with himself. Like Al, Dawn, and their peers in the longitudinal study, Kurt followed external formulas when he graduated from college. Talking about an internship he accepted after college, Kurt shared,

One of the priorities was to be happy with what I was doing. I define happiness as having a real high degree of self-worth, like I'm really into things and I'm really making a difference in what I'm doing. I had a summer position with this law firm but it was glorified busy work. It was just coming to work and get the job done and then go home. There were a couple of ways I established my self-worth, by really attracting these people that I worked with. Not necessarily just having it be a job, but become friends with them. And then taking on projects, stuff that my supervisor had wanted to do for the last two or three years that she never had time to do. So I really think that I'll get a lot of self-worth out of that position. I've been wanting to be an attorney. That's been something that's driven me ever since sixth grade. I was steered away from that for a while. People were saying, "Kurt, there are too many attorneys. Go be something else. Be a businessman." And I'm like, "Okay." So I did that, and then I took a couple of years in the business school, and I'm like, "No, I don't want to do this. I want to be an attorney." The fact that I still think I want to be an attorney motivated me to go after this position, because they're going to be paying for my law school. I was like, "Kurt, as long as the opportunity presents itself, you can't let those kinds of things pass you by and not take advantage of them." Another priority I had for this position was, I guess it was just because it's the right thing for me to do right now. In two or three years I'll be able to wrap up being a legal assistant, and if I want to become an attorney, then I'll know I want to become an attorney. And then I'll just have the next logical step.

Kurt's initial comments on self-worth hint at an integrated identity. As he continued, however, it became clear that he based his self worth on becoming friends with his colleagues and pleasing his supervisor by doing projects she did not have time to complete. Those around him influenced his career choices. The position of legal assistant served as a formula for knowing his career goals and achieving them.

Dissatisfaction with his role as a legal assistant led Kurt to reflect further on his career goals and himself. He, too, found himself at a *crossroads:*

I'm the kind of person who is motivated by being wanted, I think. I've gone to a couple of workshops and, either fortunately or unfortunately, I'm the kind of person who gets my self-worth on whether or not other people accept me for what I do or other people appreciate what I'm doing. . . . I'm coming from a position where I get my worth and my value from other people, which is, I think, wrong for me to do. But that's where I am right now. I feel like whether or not I choose to be happy is dependent upon me and only me. If I say, "You made me mad," or the converse, "You made me happy," then I'm giving all of the power that I have to you. The power of choice is mine; I have a choice of how I want to perceive each and every situation in my life. . . . Obviously I'm not to that point yet because I choose to make myself happy and make myself sad on what other people are thinking. But I think I'd like to someday get to a point where I can say, "Okay, that's your perception. I am not dependent on you for my happiness or my sadness." And I think that would be a very strong, very spiritual place to be. (Baxter Magolda, 2001, pp. 98–99)

Kurt's reflections yielded greater awareness of his dependence on others. His desire to take control of his meaning making and to retain the power to determine his feelings led him to work toward moving his internal voice to the foreground in relationships. It was not easy to get through this crossroads, as his comments over the next few years reveal:

> It has been like my own personal spiritual path—exploring, trying to understand why I am here, what I have to contribute to life on earth. I am motivated by personal satisfaction and what would make me happy, I kind of abandoned [external reassurance]—[I have] more of a self-acceptance rather than external—like job or friends. I'm letting go of external influence to a large extent. I've done personality assessments, and one of the tenets of self [for me] is gaining acceptance through pleasing other people, sometimes sacrificing my own needs. I'm letting go of that to become more in tune with who I am and what makes me happy. I would not have imagined working for a hardware store three years after college. I came to an acceptance of what *is* in life, rather than changing externals. It's a great job, and I have fun doing it. Self-acceptance, being able to say, "Yes, this is my choice, and I'm happy with it." By doing what I want I have abandoned [self-sacrifice], but fall back into it sometimes. Learning is a process, slow and steady. It is still hard to stand up for my needs and too easy to meet others'. Like, "Can you work late?" when I have been planning on going home early. (Baxter Magolda, 2001, pp. 126–127)

Two years later, Kurt felt this even more deeply and drew the distinction between talking about it and living it:

> My philosophy, what I'm looking for out of life, is the same: The ability to influence the world around me in a positive way. What has changed is that it has further unfolded in my life—two years ago I was talking about it; now I'm living it. That's a totally huge difference. I probably thought I was living it then; that is a big change. What is inside impacts what is outside, but it comes from inside. The inside is not influenced by others. You have to learn that it does come from inside. For a while you think others can make decisions; you learn in the end that it comes down to you. There is a poem, something like "Man in the Glass." It talks about going through life, but the only person you answer to is the man in the glass—the mirror, looking at yourself. I can't remember the exact lines, but one is that the most important person is the person in the glass. My parents have instilled that a lot. They never gave answers, just said, "You get out on your own and we'll support you." My experience with the law firm set me on the road to where I am now. I thought it would bring me happiness, tried to live society's plan for me; no way! Then it was like, "Okay, I don't think there is any self-actualization in what society has planned, what other people planned." In order to self-actualize yourself, you have to look inside yourself. (Baxter Magolda, 2001, p. 127)

Kurt accepted where he was in life at the moment, not worrying about what other people thought regarding his working in a hardware store 3 years out of college and working on developing the internal voice that would guide him in the future. Despite occasional struggles with others' expectations, his internal self-definition remained in the forefront of his identity. This shaped his relationships with others, as is evident in his description of a romantic relationship that was not working out:

> This relationship is deteriorating. I wanted to hold onto it. What to do? Then it didn't feel right—maybe it isn't the relationship I should be holding onto. One thing I recognize in myself is that I have a tendency to overcommit myself to things. I go around committing to everyone who needs something, then see what is left for Kurt. Sometimes there is something left, sometimes not. I have to start cutting out some before I can give to Kurt. For me, balance is not a conscious thing—it just happens when I am following what feels right and what doesn't. If I go out to try to get balance, you can bet I won't get it. The act of consciously trying to do it eliminates the possibility of achieving it. I don't know why that is. For me, if I want balance, I have to be balanced. If I want peace, I have to be [at] peace. If I go out and look for it, it is elusive—it's outside. I have stopped looking for it outside myself. (Baxter Magolda, 2001, p. 173)

This long road to stop looking for happiness outside himself led Kurt to the complete person he was able to take into his relationship with his wife in his early 30s. The reason he was not looking for something to complete himself in this new relationship is that he was already complete. He had come to peace with the notion that he had to look inside himself to create whom he wanted to be. His authentic, interdependent relationship with his spouse was possible because he had achieved an integrated sense of self.

Self-Authorship as the Central Goal of Higher Education

These three narratives reveal that college students encounter complex decisions about their academic majors and careers, the nature of their identities, and the nature of their relationships with others. Making these decisions from the vantage point of external formulas is risky. Doing what others expected or what they perceived others expected led my longitudinal study participants to conflicts between their own needs, desires, and interests and those of others. Relying on external authority allowed them to succeed in college but was insufficient for life after graduation. The lack of necessity to reflect on their values, beliefs, and identities during college reinforced reliance on external authority.

The narratives also illustrate the interconnectedness of epistemological, intrapersonal, and interpersonal dimensions of development. Defining one's internal belief system is interwoven with crafting an integrated sense of self. The integrated sense of self is central to the capacity to implement and refine the internal belief system. Entering mature relationships with others is possible from the vantage point of the integrated sense of self. Appreciating multiple perspectives in relationships hinges on the cognitive maturity that emerges from the internal belief system. Thus, self-authorship, or the internal capacity to define one's beliefs, identity, and relations with others, stands at the core of the contemporary college learning outcomes identified in national reform reports. Subsequently, a holistic approach to education for the 21st century must focus on self-authorship as its central goal.

Transforming Educational Practice to Promote Self-Authorship

Adopting self-authorship as the central goal of higher education has substantial implications for educational practice. Given the complexity and difficulty of the journey toward self-authorship and the need for it during college, weaning students away from authority dependence must begin at the outset of college. Faculty who believe that students must acquire a particular knowledge base before being engaged in knowledge construction will need to address both goals simultaneously rather than waiting, for example, until the junior year to start teaching students how to develop internal belief systems. Student affairs educators who believe that students must be taught how to act and relate to others must accomplish these goals simultaneously with affording students autonomy to craft their own identities and relations with others. Placing self-authorship as the central goal of higher education necessitates providing a new form of guidance. This new form of guidance—detailed in this book as the Learning Partnerships Model—engages students immediately in the complexity of college and young adult life and provides the balance of autonomy and support necessary for students to move toward internal beliefs, identities, and constructions of relationships. A new partnership will be necessary between educators and learners to achieve this delicate balance. Partnerships to promote self-authorship require sharing authority, mutually constructing meaning, and facing complexity squarely. Educators will need to transform their role as authorities, their assumptions about learners' capabilities, and their assumptions about educational practice.

This new form of guidance is certainly not a new concept. Numerous scholars advocate using similar concepts. John Dewey's (1916) conceptualization of education as the reorganization and reconstruction of experience and

Jean Piaget's (1970) conceptualization of intellectual development as the reorganization and reconstruction of meaning stand at the foundation of many of these perspectives. Both took experience as the starting point for learning and development, advocating that people came to understand the world by virtue of organizing their experiences. Encountering experiences inconsistent with one's current organization (called dissonance) prompted a need for resolving the discrepancy. Piaget (1970) advanced the idea that this resolution took place either through incorporating the new experience into the original organization or, if that failed, through reorganizing one's assumptions to accommodate the new experience. The latter process represented growth to a more complex way of making meaning. Proponents of constructivist teaching, collaborative learning, the use of narrative in teaching, and incorporating care in education all emphasize student experience, sharing authority, the importance of relationships between educator and student, and students coming to their own conclusions. Proponents of liberatory, empowering, and critical education endorse focusing on students' experience, sharing authority, and mutual construction of new possibilities. Proponents of constructive-developmental pedagogy emphasize that in addition to knowing *what* learners experience, educators must know *how* learners interpret their experience. The latter refers to the way we make meaning or the organizing principles we use to interpret our experiences. Constructive-developmentalists argue for connecting teaching to students' ways of making meaning in order to create the conditions to promote growth to more complex meaning making.

William Perry (1970), the pioneer of understanding adults' ways of making meaning, emphasized the importance of listening to students and respecting their current perspectives. Using his work, Laurent Daloz (1986) suggested mentoring adult students by providing a structure for learning based on listening to their ways of making meaning, sharing ourselves in the learning relationship, and recognizing the difficult nature of changing one's way of viewing the world. Daloz painted the developmental picture as a journey through which adults needed companionship and guidance to move successfully. Kegan (1994) proposed a bridge metaphor to provide this company. Regarding students as on one side of a bridge and the educational goal on the other, he argued that educators must create conditions that simultaneously respect and welcome students' ways of making meaning on their side of the bridge yet facilitate their journey toward the other end. Similarly, Belenky et al. (1986) offered a midwife metaphor for what they called "connected teaching." They described a connected teacher as one who shares the process of knowing and serves as midwife to "assist the students in giving birth to their own ideas, in making their own tacit knowledge explicit and elaborating it" (p. 217).

Other scholars have offered more specific portrayals of promoting growth in college environments. King and Kitchener (2002) translated their 20 years of research on the Reflective Judgment Model as well as other literature to form seven suggestions for promoting reflective thinking. They emphasized respecting students' epistemological assumptions; engaging students in exploring ill-structured problems; providing opportunities to study lines of reasoning, analyze others' views, and defend their own views; teaching students how to gather, evaluate, and interpret data; giving frequent feedback and encouraging practice of reasoning skills in multiple settings; and helping students reflect on their assumptions about knowledge. Michael Ignelzi (2000) translated Kegan's work to the college classroom, offering a conceptualization similar to King and Kitchener's. He recommends appreciating students' current understanding of their experience, giving students good directions for the journey toward self-authorship and accompanying them on the trip, encouraging students to collaborate with peers in the journey, and providing opportunities for celebrating growth to new places yet reminiscing about leaving old ones.

Valuing students' experience also contributes to creating inclusive and culturally relevant pedagogy. Gloria Ladson-Billings (1994) described teachers who practice culturally relevant methods like this:

> They demonstrate a connectedness with all of their students and encourage that same connectedness between the students. They encourage a community of learners; they encourage their students to learn collaboratively. Finally, such teachers are identified by their notions of knowledge: They believe that knowledge is continuously re-created, recycled, and shared by teachers and students alike. They view the content of the curriculum critically and are passionate about it. Rather than expecting students to demonstrate prior knowledge and skills they help students develop that knowledge by building bridges and scaffolding for learning. (p. 25)

Thus, enhancing the cultural relevance of educational practice is a part of this new form of guidance.

The assumptions and principles of the Learning Partnerships Model, organized from the longitudinal participants' narratives, reinforce the tenets advanced by constructivist-developmental scholars. These conceptualizations revolve around valuing students' current experience and how they understand it, engaging them in new experiences, and building mutual partnerships among learners and between learners and educators. Assuming that knowledge is complex and socially constructed respects learners' ways of understanding knowledge. Assuming self as central to knowledge construction values and respects student experience. Sharing authority and expertise creates bridges and scaffolding for learners based on their current meaning making. Validating learners as knowers and situating learning in their experience support them in using these structures to move toward self-authorship. The Learning Partnerships Model's three assumptions and three principles welcome learners' histories, identities, and cultures into learning and help educators understand and appreciate them. The model's blend of connection and autonomy resonate with notions of mutuality inherent in descriptions of the development of women (e.g., Belenky et al., 1986; Gilligan, 1982; Surrey, 1991), African Americans (e.g., Daniel Tatum, 1997; Day Shaw, 2001; Fries-Britt, 2000), Asian Americans (e.g., Atkinson, Morten, & Sue, 1998), and Latinos (e.g., Torres, 2003).

The Learning Partnerships Model for Promoting Self-Authorship in College

The holistic nature of the journey toward self-authorship requires a holistic approach to higher education. The traditional separation of cognition and affect that manifests in students experiencing college as two separate worlds—the curricular and the cocurricular—works against achieving self-authorship. The narratives in this chapter demonstrate that achieving cognitive maturity requires achieving an integrated identity that is not obsessed with others' approval. The implications of these observations are dramatic: academic goals cannot be met without attention to intrapersonal and interpersonal development. Similarly, an integrated identity requires exploring multiple values, reflection, and judgment about what to believe and the ability to construct a value system. Thus, intrapersonal complexity cannot be achieved without the corresponding cognitive maturity. By the same token, mature relationships require the ability to deal with multiple perspectives that comes with cognitive maturity and the ability to hold one's own value system that comes with intrapersonal complexity. In order to promote development in all three dimensions simultaneously, academic and student affairs educators must take a collaborative approach to 21st-century education. Partnerships with students are one dynamic of this collaboration, as the student is the central player in coordinating making meaning of his or her collective college experience. Partnerships between academic and student affairs educators are another dynamic of this collaboration to model a holistic approach for students and present students with consistent expectations for developing internal beliefs and values.

This book explores a Learning Partnerships Model that is designed to intentionally promote self-authorship. Academic and student affairs educators, in partnership with students, have implemented the model; it also shapes potential collaboration among academic and student affairs.

Despite the enormity of the challenge to promote self-authorship during college, evidence suggests that it is not only possible but also manageable. A framework for promoting self-authorship—the Learning Partnerships Model—emerged from my longitudinal participants' stories of employment, graduate school, and personal life experiences in their 20s (Baxter Magolda, 2001). Their stories revealed the nature of partnerships that engaged them in reflecting on and crafting their internal belief systems, identities, and relations with others. I share their narratives in chapter 2 to illuminate the nature of the Learning Partnerships Model.

References

American Association of Higher Education, American College Personnel Association, & National Association of Student Personnel Administrators. (1998). *Powerful partnerships: A shared responsibility for learning.* Washington, DC: Author.

American College Personnel Association. (1994). *The student learning imperative.* Washington, DC: Author.

Association of American Colleges and Universities. (1995). *American pluralism and the college curriculum: Higher education in a diverse democracy.* Washington, DC: Author.

Association of American Colleges and Universities. (2002). *Greater expectations: A new vision of learning as a nation goes to college.* Washington DC: Author.

Atkinson, D. R., Morten, G., & Sue, D. W. (1998). *Counseling American minorities.* Boston: McGraw-Hill.

Baxter Magolda, M. B. (1992). *Knowing and reasoning in college: Gender-related patterns in students' intellectual development.* San Francisco: Jossey-Bass.

Baxter Magolda, M. B. (2001). *Making their own way: Narratives for transforming higher education to promote self-development.* Sterling, VA: Stylus.

Baxter Magolda, M. B. (2003). Identity and learning: Student Affairs' role in transforming higher education. *Journal of College Student Development, 44*(2), 231–247.

Belenky, M., Clinchy, B. M., Goldberger, N., & Tarule, J. (1986). *Women's ways of knowing: The development of self, voice, and mind.* New York: Basic Books.

Chickering, A. W., & Reisser, L. (1993). *Education and identity* (2nd ed.). San Francisco: Jossey-Bass.

Daloz, L. A. (1986). *Effective teaching and mentoring: Realizing the transformational power of adult learning experiences.* San Francisco: Jossey-Bass.

Daniel Tatum, B. (1997). Racial identity development and relational theory: The case of Black women in White communities. In J. V. Jordan (Ed.), *Women's growth in diversity: More writings from the Stone Center* (pp. 91–106). New York: Guilford.

Day Shaw, J. (2001). *An application of Baxter Magolda's Epistemological Reflection Model to Black and Latino students.* Unpublished doctoral dissertation, Florida State University, Tallahassee.

Dewey, J. (1916). *Democracy and education.* New York: Free Press.

Fries-Britt, S. (2000). Identity development of high-ability Black collegians. In M. B. Baxter Magolda (Ed.), *Teaching to promote intellectual and personal maturity: Incorporating students' worldviews and identities into the learning process. New Directions for Teaching and Learning* (pp. 55–65). San Francisco: Jossey-Bass.

Gilligan, C. (1982). *In a different voice.* Cambridge, MA: Harvard University Press.

Ignelzi, M. (2000). Meaning-making in the learning and teaching process. In M. B. Baxter Magolda (Ed.), *Teaching to promote intellectual and personal maturity: Incorporating students' worldviews and identities into the learning process. New Directions for Teaching and Learning* (pp. 5–14). San Francisco: Jossey-Bass.

Jordan, J. V. (1997). A relational perspective for understanding women's development. In J. V. Jordan (Ed.), *Women's growth in diversity: More writings from the Stone Center* (pp. 9–24). New York: Guilford.

Josselson, R. (1987). *Finding herself: Pathways to identity development in women.* San Francisco: Jossey-Bass.

Kegan, R. (1994). *In over our heads: The mental demands of modern life.* Cambridge, MA: Harvard University Press.

King, P. M., & Baxter Magolda, M. B. (2003). *Toward a developmental model of intercultural maturity: A holistic approach to collegiate education.* In C. Rust (Ed.), *Improving student learning: Theory and practice—10 years on* (pp. 269–284). Oxford: Oxonian Rewley Press.

King, P. M., & Baxter Magolda, M. B. (1996). A developmental perspective on learning. *Journal of College Student Development, 37*(2), 163–173.

King, P. M., & Kitchener, K. S. (1994). *Developing reflective judgment: Understanding and promoting intellectual growth and critical thinking in adolescents and adults.* San Francisco: Jossey-Bass.

King, P. M., & Kitchener, K. S. (2002). The Reflective Judgment Model: Twenty years of research on epistemic cognition. In B. K. Hofer & P. R. Pintrich (Eds.), *Personal epistemology: The psychology of beliefs about knowledge and knowing* (pp. 37–61). Mahwah: NJ: Erlbaum.

Ladson-Billings, G. (1994). *The dreamkeepers: Successful teachers of African American children.* San Francisco: Jossey-Bass.

Landreman, L. (2003). *Improving the preparation of a global citizenry through the reconceptualization of intercultural competence as a higher education outcome.* Unpublished manuscript, University of Michigan, Ann Arbor.

Parks Daloz, L., Keen, C. H., Keen, J. P., & Daloz Parks, S. (1996). *Common fire: Lives of commitment in a complex world.* Boston: Beacon.

Parks, S. D. (2000). *Big questions, worthy dreams: Mentoring young adults in their search for meaning, purpose, and faith.* San Francisco: Jossey-Bass.

Perry, W. G. (1970). *Forms of intellectual and ethical development in the college years: A scheme.* Troy, MO: Holt, Rinehart and Winston.

Piaget, J. (1970). *Structuralism.* New York: Basic Books.

Surrey, J. L. (1991). The "Self-in-relation": A theory of women's development. In
    J. V. Jordan, A. G. Kaplan, J. B. Miller, I. P. Stiver, & J. L. Surrey (Eds.), *Women's
    growth in connection: Writings from the Stone Center* (pp. 51–66). New York:
    Guilford.
Torres, V. (2003). Factors influencing ethnic identity development of Latino college
    students in the first two years of college. *Journal of College Student
    Development, 44*(4), 532–547.
Willimon, W. H., & Naylor, T. H. (1995). *The abandoned generation: Rethinking
    higher education.* Grand Rapids, MI: Eerdmans.

2

LEARNING PARTNERSHIPS MODEL

A FRAMEWORK FOR PROMOTING SELF-AUTHORSHIP

Marcia B. Baxter Magolda

He takes the approach that he wants you to do it on your own. He will help you plot through your ideas and he will help you sort out what you are thinking and help direct you and he still encourages you to work independently. He just makes his office setting very comfortable. He'll ask "What are you confused about?" and he will ask your opinion on the matter rather than telling you what you should do. He will ask you exactly what is happening and what you need help with and try to direct you from there rather than presenting himself in a way that is kind of intimidating. . . . I think the way I see it is that he wants you to feel that you are at the same level as him, not in as far as the same knowledge, he wants the atmosphere to be such that you feel comfortable asking him or talking to him in any way. (Erica, in Baxter Magolda, 1999, pp. 133–134)

Erica's comments reflect the learning partnership she experienced with Professor Snowden, the instructor of her zoology course. The course introduced scientific complexity by virtue of Professor Snowden's statement on the syllabus that he wanted students to understand the tentative nature of scientific facts, and he wanted them to learn to think like scientists. Erica's description of Professor Snowden's approach to helping students meet these goals conveys the integration of challenge and support and the blend of connection and autonomy that characterize learning partnerships. Professor Snowden challenged Erica to work through her ideas to construct her own perspective yet supported her by helping her sort through her thinking. By respecting Erica as a capable learner, Professor Snowden offered connection and support that made her comfortable exploring her thinking with him. Refraining from telling her what to do in favor of help-ing her figure it out through accessing her thinking conveyed to Erica that Professor Snowden wanted her to think autonomously. This chapter describes the Learning Partnerships Model conceptualized from the charac-teristics Erica and other learners portrayed as central to their journeys toward self-authorship.

Origins of the Learning Partnerships Model

The Learning Partnerships Model emerged from a 17-year longitudinal study of young adults' learning and development (Baxter Magolda, 1992, 2001). Grounded in the constructivist-developmental tradition of Perry's (1970) and Belenky, Clinchy, Goldberger, and Tarule's (1986) work, the college phase of the study traced epistemological development during college. Using an inductive approach consistent with this tradition (Piaget, 1950) yielded dialogue during the college interviews about classroom and campus condi-tions that promoted or hindered developmental growth. Extensive data emerged from the 432 interviews conducted during the first 5 years of the study. Of 101 students interviewed in their first year of college, 95 returned for the sophomore-year interview, 86 for the junior-year interview, 80 for the senior-year interview, and 70 for the fifth-year interview. The partici-pants were all students at Miami University, a public liberal arts institution with an enrollment of 16,000. Two students who transferred to other insti-tutions their junior year remained in the study. The group was balanced by gender during the first year (51 women and 50 men) and remained reason-ably so throughout the study. Only three participants were members of underrepresented populations.

Because I intended the longitudinal study to explore possibilities for devel-opment, the stories and my interpretations of them offer one possible portrayal of development during college and the conditions that promote it. I provide in-depth narratives elsewhere (Baxter Magolda, 1992, 2001) to help readers judge the degree to which this portrayal is applicable to other con-texts. Miami attracts primarily traditional age students who have high entrance test scores and high school grades, are highly involved, and are highly motivated to succeed. The campus culture reinforces academic success and campus involvement. The participants were enrolled in all six divisions of the University (Applied Sciences, Arts and Science, Business Administration, Education and Allied Professions, Interdisciplinary Studies, and Fine Arts), involved in various campus activities (e.g., organizations related to academic majors, service organizations, Greek life, and leadership positions), and employed in diverse settings (e.g., computer labs, recreation centers, residence life, dining halls, and local businesses). Nine studied abroad while in college.

Continuing the constructivist approach to the study in the postcollege phase broadened the contexts in which to explore conditions to promote self-authorship. Study participants moved to diverse geographic locations, enrolled in various graduate and professional schools, accepted employment in multiple fields, and engaged in the diverse complexities of young adult life. Interviews reflected the participants' intrapersonal and interpersonal growth as well as their epistemological growth (see chapter 1 for a description of these dimensions) due in part to their shift from college to multiple contexts and due in part to my realization that their development could be best understood by integrating the multiple dimensions of development. Thirty-five participants have remained in the study for 17 years, yielding approximately 450 interviews from the 6th to the 17th year. These postcollege interviews, taking place in the participants' 20s and early 30s, reveal a more comprehensive understanding of the Learning Partnerships Model than was evident in the college years and show that it is applicable beyond the college years.

Participants' graduate or professional educational opportunities were another major source of data to identify the conditions that promoted self-authorship. Of the 35 longitudinal participants who currently remain in the study, 24 pursued some form of graduate or professional education. Seven others who are no longer in the study but participated in the early years after college also pursued graduate or professional study. The participants collectively attended a wide range of institutions, from small, private colleges to major research universities for their graduate/professional studies. Twelve participants completed their degrees part time while working full time. The majority worked for 1 to 3 years prior to pursuing graduate degrees, whereas those going into law, medicine, and the seminary generally began immediately after college graduation. The pursuit of advanced education was equally prevalent among women (16) and men (15). Eight participants pursued master's degrees in business in either business administration (6), economics (1), or international affairs (1). Six pursued master's degrees in education: 4 in teaching, 1 in supervision, and 1 in educational technology. Five studied social sciences, resulting in 2 master's degrees in psychology, 2 in social work, and 1 PhD in organizational behavior. Eight participants studied in professional schools: 2 in medicine, 3 in law, 2 in seminary, and 1 in culinary arts. Four participants pursued continuing education in teacher licensure, computer technology, mathematics education, and art history.

Postcollege employment provided another major source of experiences that promoted self-authorship. Participants entered the workforce in numerous occupations in diverse settings. Some followed the same career path from college graduation to their 30s, whereas others frequently changed paths. Although some stayed with the same institution or company for this span of time, most moved to new institutions or companies at least once or twice over these years. The two most prevalent work settings for the 35 participants remaining in the study were business and education. Fifteen participants, 8 women and 7 men, work in the business arena. One is an accountant. The majority work in sales and services, including insurance, computers, pharmaceutical or medical equipment, advertising, marketing, real estate, and chemical sales. A few work in retail sales, primarily in clothing and furniture. One participant owns a retail business. Ten participants are educators—9 in K–12 settings and 1 in higher education. Two of these participants are men, both of whom work in K–12 where 1 is a principal. The federal government employed 1 participant (a male) as an economist. Five (3 men and 2 women) work in human services in counseling, social work, services for the blind, and the Christian ministry. The group includes 2 practicing attorneys (1 female and 1 male), 1 physician (a male), and 2 restaurant professionals.

Finally, community and personal life contexts offered insights into the conditions that promote self-authorship. Many participants pursued leadership positions and volunteer work in their communities. These experiences often involved using their business or human relations skills to help others whose lives differed significantly from those of the participants. Interaction with diverse others contributed to the conditions for self-authorship to emerge. Participants' personal lives entailed intense relationship development, such as finding life partners, having children, and coping with parental or their own divorces. Thirty-three of the participants married after college; three of those divorced and two remarried. Twenty-five had children during their twenties or early thirties. In addition, six participants encountered major health problems. Responding to and managing these life experiences yielded important insights into the conditions that promote self-authorship.

An observational study provided one more source for exploring conditions that promote self-authorship (Baxter Magolda, 1999). In the interest of directly observing the optimal learning conditions described by longitudinal participants, I observed three semester-length college courses. I chose a large education course for first- and second-year students to observe how self-authorship might be prompted in younger students and two upper-division courses (i.e., zoology and mathematics) to observe how it might be promoted for more advanced students. Attending the course sessions, interviewing the instructors, and interviewing students in the courses confirmed the insights the longitudinal participants shared and yielded more tangible possibilities for translating their insights to educational practice.

All four contexts—college education, graduate or professional education, employment, and community and personal life—not only revealed the conditions that promote self-authorship but also demonstrated how crucial achieving self-authorship in one's early to mid-20s is for success in adult life. Minimal self-authorship was often the source of struggle in all these contexts. The stories in this chapter illustrate how educators can help learners successfully resolve these struggles to internally define their belief systems, identities, and relations with others in adult life.

The Learning Partnerships Model

I identified conditions that promote self-authorship from analyzing these multiple contexts and their influence on participants' journeys toward self-authorship (Baxter Magolda, 2001). Despite diversity across contexts, environments that promoted self-authorship consistently operated on *three key assumptions* and *three key principles*. The assumptions modeled the expectation for self-authorship in each developmental dimension, challenging learners to move toward self-authorship. The principles offered the support necessary to do so. The combination of these assumptions and principles forms the Learning Partnerships Model shown in Figure 2.1.

Learners were exposed to epistemological, intrapersonal, and interpersonal complexity via the three assumptions. First, these environments conveyed *knowledge as complex and socially constructed.* Whether engaged in a course assignment, job responsibility, or volunteer role, participants encountered challenges through multiple interpretations, ambiguity, and the need

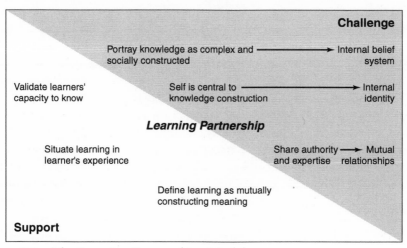

Figure 2.1   The Learning Partnerships Model.

to negotiate what to believe with others. This complexity modeled the epistemological growth—the capacity to wisely choose from among multiple alternatives—needed for self-authorship. Framing knowledge as complex and socially constructed gave rise to the second assumption—that *self is central to knowledge construction.* Encouragement to define themselves and bring this to their way of learning, work, and relationships emphasized the intrapersonal growth, the internal sense of self, needed for self-authorship. The third assumption evident in these environments was that *authority and expertise were shared in the mutual construction of knowledge among peers.* The invitation and necessity to participate as equal partners in this mutual construction modeled the interpersonal growth, or the ability to function interdependently with others, needed for self-authorship. These three assumptions were tightly linked in environments that were most effective in promoting self-authorship.

These three assumptions were usually not explicitly stated, however. They were, instead, enacted through the approach educators, employers, or other adults used when interacting with the longitudinal participants. These assumptions complemented *three principles for educational practice* initially identified from the college phase of the study (Baxter Magolda, 1992). These principles were derived from college experiences that longitudinal participants reported as aiding intellectual development and were further supported by the observation study in which the principles' use in college courses promoted students' intellectual development (Baxter Magolda, 1999). Participants' stories in their 20s provide further evidence that these three principles help educators join learners at their current developmental place in the journey and support movement toward self-authorship. These were powerful supports because they modeled and encouraged a blend of connection and autonomy. Thus, the three assumptions challenge learners to journey toward self-authorship, while the three principles bridge the gap between their current developmental place and authoring their own beliefs, identities, and relationships.

The first principle, *validating learners' capacity to know,* was evident in employers' soliciting employees' perspectives and trusting their judgments as well as in educators' interest in learners' experiences and respect for their beliefs. This validation invited participants into the knowledge construction process, conveyed that their ideas were welcome, and offered respect that boosted their confidence in themselves. Soliciting their perspectives reinforced the importance of connection with others' perspectives yet blended it with the autonomy implied in constructing one's own ideas. The second principle, *situating learning in learners' experience,* was evident in educational and employment settings that used participants' existing knowledge and experience as the basis for continued learning and decision making. Participants perceived the use of their current knowledge and experience as a sign of respect (emphasizing connection); it simultaneously gave them a foundation for enhancing their learning or work (the potential for autonomy). The third principle, *mutually constructing meaning,* involved educators or employers connecting their knowledge to that of the participants to arrive at more complex understandings and decisions. This welcomed participants as equal partners in knowledge construction, helped them clarify their own perspectives (emphasizing autonomy), and helped them learn how to negotiate with others (emphasizing connection). The blend of connection and autonomy inherent in mutually constructing meaning supported learners in moving toward the mutuality characteristic of self-authorship (described in chapter 1).

These three principles promoted self-authorship by modeling it and providing participants the kind of support they needed to shift from external to internal self-definition. Because participants were at varying places along the journey, the company they needed varied accordingly. Situating learning in learners' experience and mutual construction of meaning helped educators and employers connect to and stay in tune with participants' development. Mutual construction helped educators and employers understand participants' journeys. This connection aided but did not overshadow learners taking initiative, learning by doing, and experiencing consequences of their choices to grow toward self-authorship.[1]

The data from which the Learning Partnerships Model were constructed suggest that it is most effective when the assumptions and principles are used intentionally to create learning partnerships. As will be evident in the exemplars that follow, however, the assumptions and principles sometimes occurred naturally. For example, situating learning in learners' experience can be done intentionally, or it can occur by virtue of being directly immersed in what one is learning, as was the case in many employment settings. Similarly the complexity and social construction of knowledge was evident in some contexts regardless of whether educators or employers explicitly emphasized it. Thus, using the Learning Partnerships Model intentionally is a matter of capitalizing on the assumptions and principles naturally occurring in a context and building in the others to achieve the combination of challenge and support that the collective set of assumptions and principles provide.

---

[1]Adapted from the preface of Baxter Magolda (2001).

Exemplars: The Learning Partnerships Model in Action

Participants' narratives reveal the nuances of the Learning Partnerships Model in educational, employment, and community life settings. The variations of the model within and across these contexts illustrate that the model's basic assumptions and principles can be used flexibly and creatively rather than prescriptively. Exemplars from the longitudinal participants' graduate education illustrate the nature of learning partnerships in multiple academic disciplines. Undergraduate exemplars reveal that traditional age students are capable of and appreciate participating in learning partnerships. Employment exemplars demonstrate the Learning Partnerships Model in diverse employment contexts and model types of learning partnerships that could be adopted by college educators in both academic and campus employment contexts. Community life exemplars show various forms the Learning Partnerships Model can take in everyday interactions with others and model learning partnerships college educators could translate to college community life, service learning, cultural immersion programs, and study abroad.

Graduate Education Exemplars

After working in business for a year after college, Andrew pursued his MBA. His story recounts numerous aspects of his graduate program that model learning partnerships and how this experience affected him. The three core assumptions are evident in this story about one of his courses:

> In graduate school there was a lot more taking a position and defending it. There were a lot of things where there wasn't exactly a right answer. But you could come up with better answers and explain why you got to them. I had a management class where we were in essence running a business. We ran a simulated airline. There was no one right answer because we had nine groups and nine airlines in the class and all of them chose different philosophies in how they wanted to run their business. And three completely different airlines finished up at the top. In fact, the way our airline did it was different, the teacher said, than any other class had ever done. We just took a completely different approach, yet it was still successful. He even said in the grading of our report that he completely disagreed with it, but it was well argued and reasoned out, and he still gave us an A. I guess I kind of respected that aspect of—you know, "We agree to disagree." I like not always thinking there was one right answer because when you go out and try to deal with a lot of things, there isn't always one right answer. I think too much as an undergraduate we're taught to believe in black and white and there is no gray. And I think there's a lot more gray than there is black and white. (Baxter Magolda, 2001, p. 197)

Rewarding multiple philosophies and approaches to running a successful business conveyed knowledge as complex and socially constructed. Students were encouraged to bring themselves into knowledge construction because the members of the group had to develop and support their approach. Taking and defending a position in the face of no right answer modeled the complexity of knowledge construction. The instructor's respect for Andrew's team, despite his disagreement with their approach, reflected sharing expertise and authority among knowledgeable peers. The instructor validated Andrew and his classmates as knowers by giving them responsibility to seek better answers and support them as well as affirming them for providing reasonable arguments for their stance. Running the simulated airline situated learning in their experience. Doing so as a team reinforced the definition of learning as mutually constructing meaning. Because Andrew had already discovered that gray prevailed over black and white in the business world, he appreciated the opportunity to explore it further in his studies. His economics course provided a similar opportunity:

> We had to pick a topic and kind of take a position—we had to use economic tools, supply and demand charts, and explain why we thought is was correct or incorrect. Which was something I had *never* done in economics. Someone had to explain why supply side economics would reduce the federal deficit or would not. You had to argue it. And we weren't told what topic to choose— it was our own decision. . . . Defending your point and getting your point across is important. You are presented with a lot—you have to defend your position and why you chose something . . . people asking questions "why?" You have to reason why you did something. Every time I do something I think through it a little more. Asking that why question a lot more. (Baxter Magolda, 2001, pp. 197–198)

Again, the complexity and social construction of knowledge was evident in using economic tools to defend multiple positions. Andrew had to bring himself to the task to choose his topic, choose his position, determine how to support it, and ask himself why he believed a particular perspective. This sharing of expertise and authority helped Andrew establish the habit of reasoning in defining his beliefs. He had to make his beliefs his own and defend them with his peers. He was supported in doing so by being validated as a learner and having learning situated in his own experiences.

Sharing expertise and authority among diverse peers added another dimension to Andrew's graduate experience and modeled another component of the Learning Partnerships Model:

> For graduate school, something that added a lot was dealing with the different cultures and the people from different countries and backgrounds. Graduate

school was very heterogeneous, very mixed, very unlike my undergraduate. And I think it was much better just because of that. You had people who came from different backgrounds with different opinions. And I think when you're put in a class where too many are exactly the same, a lot of things are not brought out just because you don't have anybody that's being a devil's advocate. I think a little bit of antagonism is good for learning because it forces you to think why you believe what you believe and all that. It's not just a bunch of robots taking stuff in. (Baxter Magolda, 2001, p. 200)

This mutual construction of knowledge, even if it seemed somewhat antagonistic, forced Andrew to clarify why he held his beliefs. It also caused him to question perspectives he had accepted earlier without exploration:

I mean, just a lot of things we're taught in business are from an American perspective and American approach. Well, that's not necessarily the best and most correct way. In fact, at least in the manufacturing environment, we're getting our rear ends kicked. The Japanese have a much better approach that seems to be working. They challenged a lot of what we took as standard. They even argued with some of the financial theories, which supposedly aren't one of the things that you debate. But it was really good. We had people from communist countries that just had a very different perspective. And a lot of what they said made sense from the type of situations they were dealing with. (Baxter Magolda, 2001, p. 200)

Andrew's openness to questioning the "standard" approach reflected growth on all three dimensions of development. As he gained experience in constructing and defending his own beliefs, he gained epistemological complexity. Learning to value diverse perspectives, whether from classmates taking a different approach to business or from classmates from different cultural contexts, helped Andrew achieve interpersonal complexity, or the ability to meaningfully consider and appreciate others' perspectives. Being consistently asked to decide for himself and learning to connect to others and to his own internal belief system also led to intrapersonal complexity. Although it is certainly possible that Andrew's year of work experience contributed to this growth, he linked specific aspects of his graduate program to his growth toward self-authorship.

Alice pursued a master's in counseling immediately following her college graduation. Although her program differed greatly from Andrew's, it offered another exemplar of the Learning Partnerships Model. She described it like this:

We did a lot of videotaping and audio taping that were reviewed with the professor and kind of critiqued with different counseling styles. And I thought that was real helpful. I guess just memorizing the concepts and writing them down is one thing, but then practicing them is a whole different ball game. And it helped me to find out which styles felt more natural for me, and it has kind of helped me evolve into what theoretical background that I adhere most strongly to. By doing it some of them really feel better, seem to fit better than others. And the actual doing them on tape really helped in that process, I think. (Baxter Magolda, 2001, p. 208)

Being new at counseling, Alice found learning situated in her own experience very helpful. Practicing counseling styles helped her meet the challenge her professors presented to construct her own theoretical framework. She explained this further:

Well, you read all these hundreds of different counseling theories and it's just real overwhelming and confusing. They tell you that they want you to work with it and develop your own—not that you have to pick one theory and say, "I'm this," and never do anything else. But they kind of want you to have in the back of your mind that you should be trying to evolve and select one that you feel is going to work best for you. You know, just try them on and see which ones fit your own personal philosophy and things like that. And by actually doing them and seeing them on tape, that helped me to do that process. (Baxter Magolda, 2001, pp. 208–209)

The challenge to develop her own theoretical foundation, one that is consistent with her own personal philosophy, was a more difficult task than Alice had been accustomed to as an undergraduate. Professors in her counseling program portrayed knowledge as complex and socially constructed. Further, it was clear that she was responsible for constructing her counseling knowledge in a way that fit her as a person. She learned more about the challenge of self as central to knowledge construction, as she reported here:

The hands-on experience through my practicum and internship has made me realize nobody else is in this room with me when I'm doing this counseling session. And so, for me to be clear on these issues, I need to figure them out for myself. Not to say that I'm ever going to figure them out, but to know where I stand on them and to think them through. And I think that's kind of encouraged that process. It's you and your client sitting there. I feel like if I'm not sure where I stand or I'm not clear on what the issues are and what the arguments are both ways and process that myself, then I don't see how I can be of any help at all to this client. So I think that's really encouraged me to do that. (Baxter Magolda, 2001, p. 209)

Learning situated in her experience brought home the realization that it was just she and her client in the counseling relationship. She realized the necessity to work out her own stance, tentative as it must be because of the multitude of counseling theories and clients' diverse therapeutic needs. The process of practicing and mutually constructing knowledge with her instructors and supervisors supported her in meeting this challenge. Validation as a learner led her to see herself as capable of constructing her own counseling style. She shared her sense of the outcome:

> I think that I'm more independent. I'm more of a self-thinker, if that makes sense. I'm questioning things more, and I'm not taking—just because I take notes and then that's the way it is and that's all that's been written and that's law. I'm finding that I'm really questioning things and issues. Like with the dual diagnosis. I'm really sorting stuff out for myself instead of just taking notes about everybody else's opinion. In that way I think I'm a lot different. (Baxter Magolda, 2001, p. 210)

As a self-thinker, Alice established her own beliefs internally in the context of others' opinions and available knowledge, blending autonomy and connection. She had gained the intrapersonal confidence through establishing her own internal identity as a counselor to sort perspectives out for herself. Although she did not speak directly to interpersonal complexity, her growth on the epistemological and intrapersonal dimensions suggests that she could maintain her own identity and beliefs in mutual relations with others.

Undergraduate Education Exemplars

A few longitudinal participants described conditions that promoted self-authorship during their undergraduate experience. More substantive examples, however, are available from the course observation study with its combination of observational and interview data (Baxter Magolda, 1999). The zoology course Erica spoke of at the outset of this chapter modeled learning partnerships because of Professor Snowden's emphasis on integrating multiple disciplinary perspectives, recognizing that facts are tentative and subject to revision, and engaging students in thinking like scientists. This emphasis on the complexity and social construction of knowledge was apparent to Rich, a student in the course:

> The whole focus of most of my classes in college have been just regurgitating the facts, with the exception of a few like Winter Biology where the base facts were given to you on the ground level and where the actual learning was coming in above and beyond that. The learning was coming in where he would ask, "What do you think about this?" and you couldn't just look on your notes, you couldn't just remember what he said. It is not just blatant

memorization; learning comes into it when you are utilizing the ideas towards something new that hasn't been done. That kind of set-up seems to stimulate me more than just being like a computer and storing this information to really do nothing with. This class gave more interest into the applications, what is going on right now, ideas of it, theories on what they don't know. The other classes it was "here is what we know and you have to know it too." There wasn't any fairly mutual exchange between the instructor and the class, no formulations of ideas beyond. (Baxter Magolda, 1999, p. 122)

Rich had lost interest in storing facts like a computer and regurgitating them on command. He preferred to use the facts as a foundation for exploring and constructing new knowledge. He elaborated on the mutual exchange between the instructor and the class that was absent in his other classes:

[The lecture] has got to have structure because everybody is not on the same level. And it's got to have a mediator that can guide the group idea in the right direction and that lets certain instances of false knowledge kind of seep into the fact and encourage the idea to come out—but if it is wrong, fine, subtlety set it aside so it doesn't get into the collective. It takes some serious skills dealing with people, their collective knowledge. It is the best way to utilize other students' knowledge at least for me. There is a fine line—if I say something that is fundamentally wrong, you have to isolate that response as an instructor and figure out why that student came to that conclusion instead of being like, "No that is the wrong answer." Chris [Professor Snowden] would find out why that came about and steer it over to the rest of the idea; "Okay that is not quite right, but how did you get there? Is this how you got there?" That is what I mean by subtly bringing it back or saying that I would not be wrong if I came out and said something. (Baxter Magolda, 1999, p. 126)

These comments are Rich's interpretation of the class interactions that took place. Professor Snowden routinely engaged students in thinking with him about data and possible interpretations. As Rich reported, Professor Snowden respectfully pursued the source of students' contributions and mutually constructed meaning with them in ways that helped them correct faulty assumptions. Professor Snowden modeled epistemological complexity by noting that scientific knowledge construction is fraught with assumptions that must be pursued to determine the most reasonable interpretation. Inviting students into this process of analysis situated learning in their experience, validated them as capable of constructing knowledge, and taught them how to mutually construct meaning with others. Professor Snowden also modeled the core assumption that one brings oneself to the process of deciding what to believe.

In addition to modeling the core assumptions and principles through lecture and classroom interaction, Professor Snowden did so through the assignments. Students read primary literature on a topic of their choice and presented their findings to the class to simulate scientific conference presentations. They were also asked to write a grant proposal to seek funding for the research questions they had generated. Jill shared her thoughts regarding the overall nature of the course and these assignments:

> There are some things that are left in the air but I think that is in a good sense. There are things that we don't quite understand yet, that would lend to grant proposals that would lend to further research. I think that is the key in science; you have to have questions to move further in science. It is the whole idea that science is futuristic, you are coming up with new ideas, you want to invent new things, you need to utilize other research to come up with your own. I think he sparks questions and I think that is what science is about—questioning things, pulling things together from different sources (that is what research is), everything that has been done in science, you take something that someone else has learned and you say I have an idea, this work proves this side of my project. I just did a report on cancer and cancer of the kidney. First someone develops an idea that it is in the cortex and then someone realizes that it is in the tubules that run through the cortex, and even portions outside of the cortex, and then someone takes the ideas of these portions and say I discovered it looks like these type of cells, so that limits it to just the tubules that run in the tubules. I think you have to learn from what other people have done and apply it and ask questions and that is how you move forward and make discoveries. I think by asking questions constantly you come up with ideas for research and new discoveries. (Baxter Magolda, 1999, p. 120)

Jill, too, recognized the complexity and social construction of knowledge in the constant use of questions to lead to new discoveries. She accepted that some things are always uncertain in scientific work. She also recognized how various discoveries are coordinated to lead to future questions, an example of sharing expertise and authority among members of the scientific community in knowledge construction. The assumption of self as central was evident to her as well, as revealed in these comments:

> His point was he wanted us to learn how to be scientists. I just realized that by making us write this grant proposal, we have to put what we have learned—our topic, our seminar—into a question and be a scientist about it and make a revelation. I have been sitting here talking about how science is moving forward and asking questions and that is exactly what we are doing by writing the grant proposal. That is why it is so scary, that is what science

is about and if you can't do it and you can't write a proposal than maybe you shouldn't be in science. But I think the key to really being a scientist is to not just follow what other people are saying about their discoveries but to go out on your own. I think he is doing that. (Baxter Magolda, 1999, p. 130)

Although Jill was not totally confident going out on her own with discoveries, she recognized the challenge of acknowledging her own central role in constructing scientific knowledge. She felt validated by Professor Snowden's trusting that students could generate their own questions and write grant proposals. Having these experiences situated learning in her own experience and engaged her in mutually constructing knowledge with others.

In an end-of-semester interview, Professor Snowden shared his sense of the grant proposal assignment:

> The purpose of the proposal was accomplished in the sense that they [students] have a better idea now what it means to do primary research and how it is reported. Some of the things one has to think about if you are going to continue work—what it would take to write a proposal, how hard it is to define a question. Maybe a lot of what they got out of this isn't going to show up as a high quality proposal on a piece of paper and that's okay. Because in some ways they weren't ever in a position to do this and of course they found it extremely difficult, because it is extremely difficult. (Baxter Magolda, 1999, p. 133)

Professor Snowden's reflection revealed that he used the grant proposal as a process for exposing students to the nature of scientific research. Despite the fact that they had insufficient time and experience to produce a high-quality proposal, his goal of having students understand the complexity of defining questions was met. In the process, the three core assumptions and three principles were clearly evident.

This zoology course helped students learn to think like scientists. They learned how to critique primary scientific literature, identify the next step in research, prepare a professional presentation, and write a grant proposal (the learning goals specified on the syllabus). More important, they learned how to think about and interpret scientific data and construct new knowledge. Thus, the learning goals of the course were met simultaneously with promoting self-authorship. Most students in the class reported that they were actively involved in the course and were able to envision their future role in science. The course promoted their ability to internally define scientific beliefs and themselves as scientists. Students in this course were generally open to the challenge for self-authorship because they used ways of knowing at the outset of the class that were not completely dependent on authority for knowledge (Baxter Magolda, 1999).

Similar outcomes occurred in the mathematics course, where students initially used authority-dependent ways of knowing. Melissa's report of her reaction to the course shows that the Learning Partnerships Model is useful for those who have further to travel toward self-authorship:

> With Math, up until now for me, in my own personal experience, there has always been one answer and how you arrive at it. [Sam's] trying to [help us] see that there is more than one possible answer or one possible solution. It gives you an opportunity to be creative and to try things. Sure you may be discouraged at times but I think it is very rewarding when you do come up with something and get excited and a lot of times the ideas just start flowing and you don't want to stop or put it down so it's kind of exciting. (Baxter Magolda, 1999, p. 160)

Although Melissa did not achieve self-authorship at the end of the semester, she was moving in that direction and excited about trying new things in math. Most students reported increased confidence in their ability to understand mathematical structure and generate mathematical ideas. They also succeeded in achieving one of the course goals: developing their personal (as opposed to memorized) understanding of the structure and functioning of mathematics. Most held more complex perspectives about knowledge construction at the end of the course than they did at the beginning (Baxter Magolda, 1999).

The Learning Partnerships Model promoted the journey toward self-authorship in a large education class as well. At the outset of this course, the majority of students used transitional knowing—the belief that while some knowledge is certain, other knowledge is not yet known (Baxter Magolda, 1992). The goals of the course included learning to interpret, critique, and judge educational practices. The objectives of *recognizing* positions in educational discourse and *interpreting* educational practices as they related to the purpose of schooling required that students value their own perspectives or have a "mind of their own." Cheryl described coming to value her perspective in the course:

> I feel more like a part of this class. I feel less than the professor in a lecture where he is telling you his knowledge. I feel equal in this class because it is based on my experience. The students and teacher share experiences. I have something to contribute. I am usually quiet and don't speak in class. I feel like I can in here. (Baxter Magolda, 1999, p. 196)

Cheryl also reported that sharing her perspective prompted more internal self-evaluation and questioning. She noted that her family offered what she called a "one-way" background and that the class introduced her to alternative ways to think.

Critiquing positions in educational discourse and *evaluating* educational practices required going beyond an awareness of new perspectives. Elaine, who on a questionnaire at the outset of the course expressed interest only in students explaining material to each other, said in her interview at the end of the course that she was learning to critique:

> Hearing opinions is important to deciding my own. I read, take my opinions, ideas that have been put forth, look further into it, compare to my ideas, and think about what we should do. I combine different things, get the main idea, compare it to my idea. I become a better person by changing my views as I learn about others' experiences. (Baxter Magolda, 1999, p. 197)

Elaine's more recent view assigned greater value to what her peers think, and their views sometimes affected hers in a positive way. Elaine said that she had learned to critically analyze through the assignments and felt that the course offered a chance to evaluate her opinions.

Judging educational practice and *defending* positions in educational discourse required taking a stance on what information and beliefs to endorse. Hugh was confident that he could judge educational practices on the basis of the course, saying,

> I think I can make judgments about educational practice. I will be able to make judgments in the classroom setting. This class has helped me by giving me different ways of seeing things and thinking about things. My judgments will be my own; not other people who told you you should think or do this. I appreciate this. I try to make decisions that say I've examined this situation and from past experience and what I've learned—what is the best way to handle this? (Baxter Magolda, 1999, p. 198)

These comments are an indication of contextual knowing in which one decides on the basis of appropriate evidence that particular approaches are better than others, thus representing a shift from Hugh's valuing all opinions equally at the outset of the course to deciding what he believed at the end of the course. Hugh thought that his classmates had helped him decide on a viewpoint and that the instructor had allowed him to make his own judgments. These stories reinforce the value of learning partnerships for helping students move toward self-authorship.

The next story illustrates that the Learning Partnerships Model can be effectively implemented early in college. A college sophomore participating in a panel on productive learning experiences shared this story about her first year in college:

> Good Evening, My name is Erin and I am a sophomore at IUPUI. I am majoring in Social Studies Secondary Education. It was my first day in

college, my first course, I was terrified. I was in a room full of people I did not know. The professor walks in wearing a sweater that says "Question Authority." I was somewhat shocked; coming from a small private school I was not expecting that to be the teacher's first statement. I was overwhelmed as he began to go over the syllabus. I just knew that I was doomed. Would college really kill me? I can remember asking myself that question as I slouched into my couch that night at home; little did I know that the next semester would hold the answer to my question. This particular professor's course would change my outlook on college and learning in general. Presenting new and thought-provoking information, creating an understanding atmosphere, and by altering the class routine this professor gave me the opportunity to gain a new perspective on learning and interpreting information.

The professor would present thought-provoking information, most of which was new to me. He went about telling the story or giving the facts without drawing conclusions. This gave me the opportunity to come to my own conclusions about the situations that he presented. My entire educational background to that point told me exactly what to think but now I had the opportunity to decide for myself. At first I looked for clues from the professor so I would know the "right" way to think, but he was very good at hiding and disguising his personal beliefs. Because I was not directed by the professor I became eager to find information on my own. I wanted to read the class text and even searched for articles that addressed our topics outside of the classroom.

The atmosphere created inside his classroom was one of understanding. Dividing the class into small groups the professor would initiate discussions. The small groups helped break down some of the barriers such as not knowing others in the class and allowed everyone to participate without feeling threatened. I was timid at first and I remember being reluctant to talk about my ideas and interpretations, but I quickly warmed up to group discussions. I found myself openly expressing my opinions. I always felt that my opinions were respected, not only by my classmates but also the professor. The lines of communication were always open between students and the professor. He seemed to enjoy our input and when we had error in our line of thought he never talked down to us. Through the discussions I gained new ideas and perspectives from other students. I began to have the ability to see issues from all sides of the argument. This not only helped in the classroom setting but in all other aspects of my life.

The class structure would vary. There were times when the professor would lecture and on other days our group discussions filled the entire class session. This continual change kept my interest. I looked forward to going to his class. I wanted to know what type of new and controversial information he would present and what my classmates and I would discuss.

I am thankful that I enrolled in this class my first semester even though it was not recommended. It didn't kill me but much rather made me a more responsible student. I walked away at the end of the semester with a new attitude toward learning. I no longer take things as I hear them but I compile information from many sources to evaluate them in order to apply them to my life. Because of the thoughtful information, the open atmosphere, and stylistic changes in the class structure I was able to gain a new perspective on learning. I learned to question authority. (Hillenburg, 2002)

Erin encountered knowledge as complex and socially constructed through her instructor's approach to teaching. She was invited to bring her own mind and opinions to the class and felt respected as a thinker even when she and her peers had error in their thinking. The instructor organized the course in ways that invited Erin and her peers to mutually construct knowledge. Because the instructor invited and supported her in exploring ideas, learning excited Erin. Connection with her instructor and peers made questioning authority possible and educational. Her ability to question authority at the end of her first year suggests that the Learning Partnerships Model can be useful early in college with students who have not previously experienced questioning authority as a component of learning.

Employment Setting Exemplars

The components of the Learning Partnerships Model were evident, although not usually an explicit part of the culture, in employment settings. Employers were most likely interested in maximizing employee performance to achieve success relevant to the work setting. However, in their desire to maximize employee performance or perhaps in conveying the nature of their work settings, many employers provided the conditions to promote self-authorship.

Even in highly technical fields, ambiguity, complexity, and social construction of knowledge were common. Ned accepted a position selling paper chemicals on completing his paper science degree. His job involved analyzing extensive technical data to make decisions to address complex problems occurring at the paper mill that had contracted for his services. He explained,

> There are probably several hundred people working at a mill, making thousands of tons of paper a day using millions of gallons of water. So within that system there are many things that can go wrong on a day-to-day basis. So when I go into a mill, I never know what to expect. I start with a process engineer, and say, "What are the problems that you're encountering?" Then the problem-solving process starts really by asking lots of questions and just getting the feel for what their process is like. A lot of it is by drawing simple diagrams at first and just getting comfortable with "What are they doing

from start to finish there?" From that point I have to, on a rough scale, judge whether we can make a change or not with my chemicals. (Baxter Magolda, 2001, p. 246)

Ned had to understand the complexity of the mill operations before he could even offer a preliminary judgment about whether his chemicals would benefit the mill. This preliminary judgment was made in the context of his experience learning that particular mill's operation. If he judged that his chemicals might help, he then conducted laboratory tests in the mill to help determine the necessary changes. But the testing did not resolve the complexity. As Ned explained, "This test by itself might be extremely complex and require a lot of interpretation because they're not always exact science." The interpretation led to physically testing potential changes by using the new chemicals in the papermaking system and gathering data about the process for a week. This data served as the foundation for Ned's recommendations to the mill:

> I am responsible for deciphering—based on everything I know about the mill, all our tests that we did in the lab, based on the objections or problems the mill might have or the mill's limitations—take the data that we recorded and assimilate all that to say, "Did it work or not?" And it's not always easy to say that it did work. A lot of it is textbook kind of work—there's a certain way of running laboratory tests. But there's also a knowledge base background for knowing "How do these classes of chemicals fit into this kind of paper making and how are they going to affect what happens at the end of the machine?" You read a couple of lines in a book saying this class of polymers should do this, but it never happens that way and there's always some good reasons why it doesn't. If you've seen the reasons enough times in different applications or different situations, you're going to be alerted or aware of the potential problems before they occur or look for those opportunities when they're there. (Baxter Magolda, 2001, pp. 246–247)

Conducting laboratory tests and then physically inserting the chemicals into the paper machine further situated learning in Ned's experience. He used previous experience to analyze and interpret the tests and outcomes. His experiences, framed in a context where knowledge was complex and socially constructed, enhanced his judgment. He was responsible for conducting the tests, interpreting them, and making his own judgment, illustrating the challenge of making self central to knowledge construction. Ned also mutually constructed these interpretations with others, including his supervisor and employees at the mill. Ned's experience eventually led him to develop what he called a framework for problem solving and decision making. Developing this framework was part of the self-authorship required of employees to effectively deal with the complexity of their work. Ned found the framework useful in the challenge of bringing self to knowledge construction. He shared,

> I'm acting more like myself. The more I like the job, the more my customers like me and want to do business with me. I'm developing my own style. You might have the title of whatever—there's this preconceived image of what that person should do. After a few years of doing it, you realize you aren't that stereotype and are more successful if you don't act that way. Self-actualization, self-confidence—maybe that's it. Coming out of school I was worried about what people thought of me, how would I make the best impression. In retrospect, you say be yourself, you can be more motivated and do the best job. People judging you hopefully aren't so self absorbed that if you aren't identical to them its okay; hopefully they judge you on results. You figure out the stereotype is wrong but play that role until you change it. (Baxter Magolda, 2001, p. 257)

Ned's story illustrates movement toward self-authorship on all three dimensions. He became increasingly comfortable with the complexity of knowledge construction and adept at bringing his own experience to bear on decisions. His success led him to value his own style (i.e., intrapersonal complexity) and to be less concerned over what others thought of him (i.e., interpersonal complexity).

Complexity and social construction of knowledge were also prevalent in fields that combined artistic and technical skills. Dawn's experience in the restaurant business exemplified the Learning Partnerships Model in action. She reported,

> I'm one of the line cooks. I'm working with a certified chef—a brilliant woman—food is second nature to her. When you are cooking food, it's easiest to just watch. I've learned so much in five months that I never knew before. I pick up things in conversation, but the easiest way to pick up this skill is to watch someone who knows how to do it. Also experimentation—make this, taste it, have chef taste it, and she knows what to do with it. I thought of myself as one who learns by doing or watching rather than actively pursuing knowledge by questioning. I notice now that I ask questions. There is a wealth of information at my fingertips and I want to learn as much as I can while I have this opportunity. I never had a job like this—outside of theater—where I can actively pursue an art or craft. Acting is more of an exploratory thing—no right and wrong. That is true to some extent in culinary arts. But there are rights and wrongs—4 tablespoons rather than 2. But you taste, create, explore putting flavors together to come up with a final product that you present. It is experimentation like in theater. It is set up very much like theater is set up—work with a group of people, creating a product, give it out to the masses. Every night we look at elements

we have, and we have to make something. The job appeals to my frame of mind. (Baxter Magolda, 2001, pp. 244–245)

Cooking in this setting centered on a combination of knowledge and experimentation to create flavorful foods, reflecting the social construction of knowledge. Engaging in this experimentation situated learning in Dawn's experience. Sharing expertise and authority were evident in the openness to questions and she and the chef tasting food to determine the next step. The chef validated Dawn as a contributor rather than asking her to follow a recipe. Dawn's experience of creating something with her colleagues in the theater made her appreciate the mutual construction taking place in the kitchen. Her acting experience clearly reflected the notion of self as central to constructing characters, as she reported:

I have had opportunities to play more than one type of character. The thing that's involved in that is exploring different parts of yourself, learning about how many different types of people you are within yourself and being able to apply that to a script that someone has written. And along with your imagination, you create these different personas. As far as the character aspect—I think there's a lot of self-learning that goes on continually. And that's one of the things that I think that always fascinates me about this business is you never stand still. You're always progressing; you're always moving forward, learning new things about yourself, learning new ways to present your ideas to a group of people. Then that kind of melts into your technique. Oftentimes you have to get to a certain emotional level that you can't just create. So there's a process that you have to go through, self-disclosure, to some extent. You combine yourself with what you're given, what you interpret about a character. The technique comes in as transferring all that is within you to this character, your abilities to speak the character's truth from, probably, your truth. There are a lot of techniques in acting that not everybody can use. You pick and choose the ones that are right for you. (Baxter Magolda, 2001, p. 151)

Dawn's description of creating the truth of a character revolves around making herself central to the task of knowledge construction. The multitude of techniques available reflected the complexity and social construction of knowledge; actors and directors shared authority and expertise. Thus, Dawn encountered conditions to promote self-authorship in both her acting and her cooking contexts, contributing to her self-authorship described in chapter 1.

Barb, a new attorney, encountered learning partnerships in her law practice. She described translating her law school education into practice:

People are understanding. They know we are just starting out. They give samples and point you in the right direction to get started. With corporate work, I like it because it is new. You are drafting things you have no idea how to do, so you use samples. A lot of times, I'll be confident enough to know it is common sense. If there is no sample, I have friends that have worked on it so I ask them. Or look it up in reference books. Confidence is key. There is no right answer; with law you can argue both sides. You have to state your position with authority so people perceive you as knowing what you are talking about, to put clients at ease. Sometimes I tell clients both sides, but then you say which way we should go. This is all new; you don't learn everything in law school. Practicing law is doing it off-the-cuff; I have no idea how to wing it. (Baxter Magolda, 2001, p. 245)

Complexity and social construction of knowledge permeated Barb's work, as is evident in her statement that no right answer exists. She was responsible for using her resources, both written and human, to craft arguments for both sides and choose one to recommend to her clients. She relied in part on her own training and common sense and in part on mutual construction with her colleagues. Practicing law was clearly situated in her experience, and her colleagues were willing to construct arguments with her knowing she was new at corporate law.

These stories, and many others like them, demonstrate that diverse employment settings required self-authored employees. Regardless of context, these work settings required employees to be able to analyze situations, use appropriate data, interpret it effectively, develop solutions to problems, and produce some type of product. Employers required employees to use the expertise of those around them yet also required them to develop and use their own expertise. Although degrees of support varied widely, very few of the longitudinal participants found themselves in work settings that did not demand self-authorship.

Community Life Exemplars

Similar to employment contexts, longitudinal participants' community life experiences were not intentionally structured to promote self-authorship. The conditions for promoting self-authorship were present, however, in many contexts in which participants chose to engage. One such context was Lydia's choice to live abroad for 2 years. She reported,

It has made me more independent of what I know—more willing to try new experiences and not be so hesitant about it. I was so shy when I started college; not anymore! Because if there is one thing that living in an area that is not yours teaches you, it is that you have to get out there and speak up for what you believe in and what is right. To not let others roll you over to their ideas and roll you over to their ways. (Baxter Magolda, 2001, pp. 289–290)

Living in another country challenged Lydia to express herself and her beliefs. Although she expressed not letting others "roll her over," her openness to new experience led to reinventing who she was:

> It was a fabulous experience. I did things I never would have thought I would do. It makes you feel small; there are so many other people out there! If you have experienced this much, how much more is out there? I have a thirst for more. If you stay in the same place, you get in a rut. It is so exciting! You don't know what you are capable of; you reinvent yourself as you gain new experiences. We had earthquakes; we got used to it. We had [electrical] power-sharing there. There were 6 months when between two and four hours a day you had no power. It is fun to teach when the power goes out; 85 degrees—it gets overwhelming. It got to be a joke. Everybody accepted it. Here, the power goes out and people are beside themselves. I learned to be more flexible. When you experience other things and see other people deal with things, it puts your life into perspective. The more people you know and more experiences you hear about, you get stronger. I am a strong person now; we move and redo everything. I'm fortunate; I've stumbled onto things. I'm like a cat; land on my feet. Life is too short to be bothered by little things like moving and being uprooted from job and friends. There are other jobs and friends. (Baxter Magolda, 2001, p. 290)

New experiences to use to put her life into perspective introduced Lydia to multiple ways of living. Interacting with people who responded to life differently than she had been accustomed to doing helped Lydia reinvent herself. Her story reveals that she realized that she played a central role in constructing her view of life yet openly entertained others' ideas through mutual construction of knowledge. She reported gaining strength, flexibility, and security through this process. Regarding being uprooted from a job and friends as "little things" suggests that Lydia internally defines her beliefs, identity, and relations with others such that external changes do not shake her foundation.

Anita chose to volunteer after college in both a Big Sister program and a switchboard for runaways. Her story illustrates that learning partnerships were present in both these contexts:

> The little girl I have is 9. She has very difficult problems. She was taken away from her mother, who has AIDs. The chances of her going home are nil, but she doesn't know it. We went out for her birthday and she picked out some clothes. When I took them over, she didn't want to see me, she just wanted the gift. Her therapist said I should tell her how I felt, so I did. It went over poorly, she got angry, and now she doesn't want to see me. I also work for the national runaway switchboard. On the switchboard, you have to let

them figure things out for themselves; try to turn the conversation around to steer them in a direction without giving them an answer. I'm getting used to not knowing at the switchboard. Nothing you can say is wrong, as long as you are trying to help. The same call could be handled differently by different people. Like with my little sis, I feel like I shouldn't have brought it up, but others said I had to do it. I'm learning to let things go. I'm better at realizing and admitting when I've made mistakes. I'm more humble. Sometimes I hear other calls and I wouldn't have done something that way. I'm trying to figure out for myself if I have the right to an opinion. Like if someone hits them, I have a hard time saying it is wrong. It can lead to an arrest, and make a bigger mess. I have a hard time being as directive as I should. I have to figure out for myself what my own beliefs are. I do have the right to an opinion. I know molestation is wrong, but what will life be like if I make the call? (Baxter Magolda, 2001, p. 298)

Anita's struggles with her little sister and the callers to the switchboard stemmed from the complexity of making sense out of the events that were reported and deciding how to respond. There were no sure answers or no proven solutions to these complex situations. Anita mutually constructed knowledge with others in these settings yet worked hard at defining her own beliefs. Mutual construction was also expected in how she dealt with callers: she was to guide them yet let them figure things out for themselves. Learning was clearly situated in Anita's experience, and others validated her as capable in these contexts. Anita was still struggling at the time of this story to sort out her own beliefs in the face of the serious consequences of her actions for others.

The Learning Partnerships Model's Potential for Transforming Higher Education

Following learners longitudinally from their college entrance to their mid-30s provided extensive interview data from which to conceptualize the Learning Partnerships Model. The observation study contributed to conceptualizing the model through observing learning partnerships in action in various disciplines. Interviewing learners about how these learning partnerships affected them augmented the outcome data emerging from the longitudinal study. The assumptions and principles that constitute the Learning Partnerships Model are consistent with scholarship on how to promote student development and learning. They are also inherent in scholars' descriptions of culturally inclusive pedagogy. As a result, the model holds substantial promise for transforming higher education to promote self-authorship during college.

The chapters in part 2 of this book reveal that potential by reporting specific uses of the Learning Partnerships Model in multiple contexts. Each chapter describes the implementation of the model in detail and the particular goals it is designed to achieve. Use of the model in these diverse contexts illustrates its flexibility to blend with other models and particular practice goals. Because the Learning Partnerships Model consists of a set of assumptions and principles to shape practice, it is intended be used creatively rather than prescriptively. The authors report assessment data to indicate the model's effectiveness in promoting self-authorship in their particular contexts, adding to the growing data that support the model. We invite you to reflect on your own educational practice as you explore these exemplars.

References

Baxter Magolda, M. B. (1992). *Knowing and reasoning in college: Gender-related patterns in students' intellectual development.* San Francisco: Jossey-Bass.

Baxter Magolda, M. B. (1999). *Creating contexts for learning and self-authorship: Constructive-developmental pedagogy.* Nashville: Vanderbilt University Press.

Baxter Magolda, M. B. (2001). *Making their own way: Narratives for transforming higher education to promote self-development.* Sterling, VA: Stylus.

Belenky, M., Clinchy, B. M., Goldberger, N., & Tarule, J. (1986). *Women's ways of knowing: The development of self, voice, and mind.* New York: Basic Books.

Hillenburg, E. (2002, November). *Response to transforming pedagogy to transform learning.* Paper presented at the Association of American Colleges and Universities Faculty Work and Student Learning Conference, Indianapolis.

Perry, W. G. (1970). *Forms of intellectual and ethical development in the college years: A scheme.* Troy, MO: Holt, Rinehart and Winston.

Piaget, J. (1950). *The psychology of intelligence* (M. Piercy and D. Berlyne, Trans.). London: Routledge & Kegan Paul.

3

PROMOTING SELF-AUTHORSHIP THROUGH AN INTERDISCIPLINARY WRITING CURRICULUM

Carolyn Haynes

When I first became a faculty member 10 years ago in Miami University's School of Interdisciplinary Studies, I (like all my colleagues) was assigned a handful of seniors to mentor through the nerve-wracking process of writing a thesis. It took me only a few short weeks to grow intensely frustrated with my advisees. Not only did I find them to be intellectually unprepared for a year-long original body of research that blended two or more disciplines, but I also perceived them to be exceptionally immature—unwilling to muster the necessary dedication and perseverance, continuously attempting to manipulate me into writing the thesis for them, and stubbornly refusing to accept and incorporate feedback on their writing.

What made this process even more challenging was that many of these seniors were addressing interdisciplinary topics and utilizing disciplines and professional fields with which I had very little familiarity. During any given year, one student might be writing on the literary and anthropological influences in the novels of Zora Neale Hurston, while another might be analyzing domestic violence legal cases in a certain county in Ohio. One of the oddest combinations of disciplines came from a student who wanted to bring together pediatrics, child development theory, and theater to create skits and magic acts to help terminally ill children displace pain. Gaining a PhD in 19th-century American literature had hardly prepared me to advise such a project. To make matters even knottier, each student came to the project with a different set of insecurities, past experiences with writing teachers, and stylistic idiosyncrasies. Some of them combated an extreme fear of writing; others had never conceived of themselves as original thinkers or scholars. Still others were battling outdated conceptions of writing that may have been suitable for the high school setting but were inappropriate for college-level thesis writing. Oftentimes, I felt like the circus clown whose task it is to balance this thesis project like a glass ball on the end of a long pole, continuously dancing around in a vain attempt to keep the ball from shattering on the cement floor. I never knew which way to move in order to keep the ball perched on the pole, and I had little time to stop and figure out a system for operating the apparatus I was given.

Fortunately, I quickly discovered that I was not alone in my frustration. Beneath their breaths, my colleagues also groused and grumbled about the daunting task of advising senior theses. Finally, after several years of further frustration, I decided to address the problem. Through reading interdisciplinary studies professional literature, student and adult development theory, and compositional theory, I discovered that the problem did not really rest with the students themselves. After all, they were behaving in ways fully in keeping with the learning assumptions held by most undergraduate seniors.

Studies on undergraduate cognitive development suggest that the majority of traditional college seniors hold either "transitional" assumptions of knowing in which they believe knowledge can be separated into certain and uncertain categories or "independent" assumptions in which they perceive knowledge as being open to many interpretations and thus uncertain (Baxter Magolda, 1992). Transitional and independent knowers do not yet view knowledge in the context of a particular situation and generally are unable to comprehend that they must make decisions on the basis of their own values. Moreover, as Robert Kegan (1994) has pointed out, most college students have difficulty distinguishing themselves from their relationships or organizing their relationships or the internal parts of the self into a coherent value or belief system. In other words, they are not yet authors of their own psychological life, making it difficult to author their own original body of scholarship. In addition, the approximately 50 students admitted annually into our program are required to take a 4-year sequence of core interdisciplinary courses (team-taught by our faculty) as well as to design their own course of interdisciplinary study supported by continuous, ongoing advising by one of our 14 faculty members. Thus, if students were poorly prepared for the thesis, then we as faculty had to accept some of the responsibility.

Once I began to accept greater responsibility for students' inability to succeed at thesis writing, I took a closer look at the required skills and abilities needed to write an interdisciplinary thesis. The thesis requirement in our program stipulates that students must answer a question, solve a problem, or address a topic by drawing on "disciplinary perspectives and integrat[ing] their insights through construction of a more comprehensive perspective" (Klein & Newell, 1998, p. 3). To do this effectively, students must understand critically the differing aims, assumptions, and tasks of two or more disciplines while simultaneously possessing considerable proficiency in diverse forms of academic writing. In addition, they need a range of critical thinking skills fundamental to good writing and interdisciplinary inquiry: comprehension, application, analysis, synthesis, and evaluation. Thus, students must operate in and understand critically the limitations and strengths of at least two disciplinary fields, and, additionally, they must attempt to take the additional steps of synthesis and application—that is, creatively exploring ways in which insights from those fields can be combined or synthesized productively to respond to a real-life issue or problem. In short, in order to achieve the curricular demands of the senior thesis, they need to be self-authored, contextual thinkers.

The question for me was how to help students—who typically are not at this phase of development—reach or come closer to it so that they could succeed at the thesis assignment. I decided that it would be best to use the wisdom and guidance of my colleagues in the School of Interdisciplinary Studies. Each of us was trained in a different disciplinary or interdisciplinary field, but we planned and taught almost all our courses in teams of two to five persons. Using insights from my own experience and that of my colleagues as well as professional literature from interdisciplinary studies, composition, and adult development, I devised a 4-year writing curriculum, one that helps students move toward self-authored, interdisciplinary inquiry and scholarship (Haynes, 1996). In this chapter, I describe the conceptualization, implementation, and assessment of this developmentally attuned writing curriculum that was created in 1996. To prepare for this discussion, I reviewed all the syllabi (numbering over 120) created by interdisciplinary faculty in my program since 1996, and I interviewed three faculty members (one from the natural sciences, one from the social sciences, and a third from fine arts and humanities) who have taught regularly in the program for the past 15 years as well as five students currently in the program. The writing curriculum of the School of Interdisciplinary Studies helps students progress steadily through three phases, from engagement with expressive modes to an increasingly critical awareness of and proficiency in disciplinary forms to interdisciplinary scholarship. Underlying this plan are the core principles of Marcia Baxter Magolda's Learning Partnerships Model —validating learners' capacity as knowledge constructors, situating learning in learner's experience, and defining learning as mutually constructing meaning—as well as the assumption that writing is a social, emotional, and cognitive process.

Overview of the Writing Curriculum

When the faculty first came together to discuss how to better prepare students for the thesis, we decided that a good place to begin was to articulate our basic assumptions about how writing gets done and how faculty may ensure the best writing from our students. We all agreed that writers operate best in a supportive environment, one where trying new styles and ideas and making mistakes are accepted and where the various members of that community work to support rather than compete with one another. As a result, writers need some opportunities to experiment in new ways and to talk openly and honestly about their writing obstacles and fears without fear of judgment or penalty. Faculty can promote this atmosphere by offering some ungraded and creative or nontraditional assignments, speaking candidly about their own writing process, and encouraging tactful but frank discussions of one another's writing. These strategies work to affirm the Learning Partnerships Model assumptions of the self as central to learning and the construction of knowledge through interpersonal interaction.

The faculty also agreed that students need to be prompted to view writing as a process that includes brainstorming and planning, writing (we hope multiple) drafts, receiving feedback, and revising work as needed. Many of the faculty members complained in our discussions that far too often students operate under the misperception that they can wait until literally hours before an assignment is due, plunk themselves down in front of their computer, and hammer out an acceptable piece of writing. For them, writing is not a means of constructing and reconstructing meaning but rather a means of recording one's ready-made thoughts. They have not yet come to recognize that revision is the conduit through which thinking and writing develop, mature, and improve. In other words, they had not accepted the Learning Partnership Model principle that knowledge is complex and socially constructed. Research on college writers affirms this point. According to Nancy Sommers (1982), one of the crucial differences between experienced and novice writers is the level and amount of revision they are willing to conduct. As Toby Fulwiler (1995) puts it,

> For novice writers, learning to re-write is an alien activity that doesn't come easily. In fact, many college students, first year and graduate alike, assume that writing is essentially copying down what they've already been thinking—well, maybe with a little spell checking, editing a few awkward statements,

adding a transition or two, and throwing in (get it, throwing in) a few supportive examples. (pp. 71–72)

Thus, we decided that in every course we offered, a revision-friendly pedagogy would be used. Faculty would assign multiple revisions of at least one
assignment and confer individually with students to discuss work in progress.
Peer reviews, individual conferences with students, and written comments on
drafts all can assist in supporting this view of writing as a process of constructing knowledge.

During these faculty discussions about teaching writing, many also con-
fessed that they felt a tremendous burden in each course they taught—from
first-year courses to junior seminars—to try to cover in one semester every
conceivable aspect of writing that students would possibly need to know
throughout their college careers. Toward this end, a number of my colleagues
assigned mammoth, complex research papers that were due at the end of the
term, and they often experienced abysmal results. Blatantly plagiarized
papers or boring, incoherent papers that read like a series of poorly
connected book reports on a common topic abounded. To eliminate these
problems, we decided that our students could be better served by a more
purposeful sequencing of writing experiences.

Since Miami's School of Interdisciplinary Studies offers students a 4-year
core curriculum, 95% of our students enter the program in their first year,
and almost 90% graduate from the program 4 years later, we decided to create a 4-year writing plan and assign a different set of learning goals for each
semester. For the first 2 years, students take three core interdisciplinary
courses each semester (a natural science, humanities/fine arts, and social science course). Because the learning goals would have to be applied to all three
cognate areas, determining the various goals for each semester took some in-
depth communication and negotiation. Faculty were understandably wary of
pinning themselves into a curricular corner or of being overly monitored by
the associate dean (the curriculum review authority). Thus, we made sure to
make the goals somewhat modest and pliable so that faculty might be creative in the ways that they meet them and might even incorporate additional
learning goals as they desire. Table 3.1 summarizes the stages we devised
(Haynes, 1996).

In addition to providing flexibility and creativity, we wanted each stage
to respond to students' developmental needs and to challenge these learners
to expand their worldviews and thought processes. Thus, we created a plan
where students would progress from engagement with expressive modes to an
increasingly critical awareness of and proficiency in disciplinary forms to the

Table 3.1 Stages of a 4-Year Interdisciplinary Writing Curriculum

Stage	Learning goals	Possible assignments
1. Reading and writing proficiency (first year, first semester)	• Acquire fluency and practice in interrelated actions of reading and writing • Improve one's critical and active reading skills • Gain practice in the fundamentals of writing (summary, definition, description) • Gain self-conscious awareness of one's writing process	• Academic journals • Summaries • Descriptive essays • Narratives • Commentaries • Definitional essays, fact sheets, informational pamphlets • Personal, exemplification essays • Self-evaluations, peer reviews
2. Critical analysis (first year, second semester)	• Gain practice in various forms of analysis (close textual analysis, evaluation, comparison, etc.) • Spend time reading and analyzing the rhetoric (purpose, evidence, organization, vocabulary, audience) of various disciplines	• Analytical essays • Interviews with disciplinary experts • Questionnaires, surveys of disciplinary thinkers • Imaginary dialogues between two disciplinary thinkers • Annotated bibliography
3. Learning and writing in the disciplines (second year, first semester)	• Write and analyze various disciplinary forms of writing and for different disciplinary audiences • Compare and contrast disciplines • Read and analyze conflicting disciplinary viewpoints on a single topic	• Disciplinary forms of writing (lab report, literary analysis, case study, policy analysis, theoretical paper) followed by some reflection or comparison and contrast on the differences and similarities among these forms of writing

Table 3.1 Continued

Stage	Learning goals	Possible assignments
4. Introduction to interdisciplinary writing (second year, second semester)	• Compare and contrast disciplinary and interdisciplinary perspectives on a given topic • Critically analyze the benefits and shortcomings of disciplinary and interdisciplinary approaches • Translate disciplinary knowledge for an audience of another discipline • Combine knowledge gained from various disciplines to address a given topic	• Analytic essays examining disciplinary and interdisciplinary writing • Handbook or guide on writing in the disciplines • Revision of a disciplinary piece of writing for an audience of another discipline or for a nondisciplinary audience
5. Inter-disciplinary methodology (third year, first semester)	• Gain practice in and a critical awareness of two or more research methods • Compare and contrast different methods and analyze their purposes within different disciplinary settings • Use two or more research methods to investigate an interdisciplinary topic	• Evaluation of a research method and its purpose for a given discipline • Comparison/contrast essay examining different research methods • Research paper using two or more research methods • Self-evaluation or reflection paper
6. Inter-disciplinary theory (third year, second semester)	• Study and analyze theoretical models of integration • Study theoretical writings that address interdisciplinary scholarship or topics • Analyze primary sources or topics using two or more theories	• Evaluations or analyses of theory • Comparison essay examining different theories • Research paper using two or more theories

(Continued)

Table 3.1   Continued

Stage	Learning goals	Possible assignments
	• Compare and contrast different disciplinary theories relating to a given topic • Use two or more theories to investigate an inter-disciplinary topic	• Peer review or self-evaluation of a research project that discusses its level of integration
7. Inter-disciplinary capstone (fourth year)	• Utilize and apply the knowledge and skills accrued in the previous six stages • Integrate in a self-conscious manner two or more disciplines to respond to an interdisciplinary topic or problem	• Senior interdisciplinary thesis that integrates disciplinary insights and uses theory and/or methodology

development of interdisciplinary scholarly inquiry. Such a progression would help students come to validate their own instincts and ideas (rather than relying too heavily on authorities), to understand that knowledge is never absolute but always under construction, and to see that understanding is dependent on the writer's context.

Underpinning this plan are the Learning Partnerships Model components and the assumption that writing is a process using a combination of cognitive, emotional, and social forms of intelligence. Unquestionably, writing demands all the cognitive abilities outlined in Bloom's (1956) taxonomy of educational objectives: knowledge, comprehension, application, analysis, synthesis, and evaluation. However, in order for writers to identify their own position on a topic, they must have what Mayer and Salovey (1993) have deemed "emotional intelligence," or "the ability to monitor one's own and others' emotions, to discriminate among them, and to use the information to guide one's thinking and actions" (p. 433). Although emotional and cognitive intelligence are often perceived to be at odds, the Learning Partnerships Model reveals their fundamental interdependence. How one understands knowledge is directly related to how one understands others and the self. In other words, interpersonal and intrapersonal awareness mediate the epistemological dimension of development. Learning necessitates both connection and autonomy.

This view is also underscored in Robert Kegan's theory of adult development. Those who hold assumptions consistent with Kegan's third order of meaning making (which is the majority of adults, including almost all college students today) are excellent at discerning others' points of view, but they do not possess a coherent sense of meaning making or self apart from those other people and viewpoints. By contrast, those who hold fourth-order assumptions—or those who have attained self-authorship—are able to differentiate their sense of meaning and the self apart from but in relation to other people and sources. Accepting this view of development, our faculty believed that by teaching writing as a complex interrelationship of cognitive, interpersonal, and intrapersonal processes, we would help students not only become more successful at thesis writing but also do much more—that is, become more proficient authors of their own lives. In the next section of this chapter, I outline more specifically some of the diverse ways that faculty went about using the Learning Partnerships Model to help students move toward self-authorship.

Implementation of the Writing Curriculum

Because we observed that most of our first-year students are absolute thinkers, believing that correct answers exist in all areas and are known by authority figures (Baxter Magolda, 1992), we decided to place an emphasis during that year on the Learning Partnerships Model principles of situating learning in the students' experience and affirming their capacity as knowledge producers. Put another way, we validated students' experiences and knowledge and encouraged them to identify their voice and position on various topics. Selecting course topics and readings that are relevant to first-year students' lives, assigning them writing that connects to their own experiences, helping them analyze and take a stand on various readings, and providing them comfortable opportunities to share writing are important ways of addressing their needs.

In the first week of a first-year natural systems core course for our interdisciplinary majors, faculty and students take a field trip to a local wooded area (Cummins & Myers, 1992). Students are counseled to walk through the park silently. They may spend the entire time strolling or find a quiet place to absorb the environment. Learners take notes on their experience, reflecting on what it means to them. Hays Cummins, one of the faculty members of this course, describes this assignment as follows:

> In the first year, first semester, we do a naturalist essay where the style is to let it free-flow. I provide a little structural framework about what the essay should contain, but I let the students take it from there. The idea is to help students gain a voice of their own because there is clearly no right answer to this assignment. I just want to hear their voices. Some people will write about clouds. Some people will write about grass. Some people will write about past campouts as it relates to this field trip experience. I don't really care about the content. I just want them to connect [the field trip experience] to themselves and to express their voice. (personal interview, April 9, 2003)

What this professor is emphasizing is the core Learning Partnerships Model principle of the self as central to knowledge construction.

In another first-year core interdisciplinary science course taught by Muriel Blaisdell and Hays Cummins, students' first assignment asks them to create a science autobiography in which they describe how their views of the natural world and science have evolved throughout their lives. This assignment encourages them to reflect on their own attitudes about math and science—including, in some cases, their own science phobia—and to imagine what they would like to do in the future that might contribute to the scientific or natural world. In short, it prompts them to see themselves as knowledge constructors and to begin defining their own belief system and identity.

In a first-year interdisciplinary humanities core course on identity development from adolescence to adulthood, students are asked to create a narration about a turning point in their own adolescence. After studying various theories on adolescent development and young adult literature for many weeks, they are then asked to revise the narration, fashioning it into a fairy tale of their own. The fairy tale assignment advises that the "tale should demonstrate an effort to put your life into metaphoric terms." Sally Harrison-Pepper, one of the faculty members for the course, says that she focuses on the metaphoric "in order to stretch students to complex ways of thinking so that they move from the particular to something larger, more representational and abstract" (personal interview, April 7, 2003). Often she assigns Alice Walker's novel *Meridian,* which focuses on a young African American civil rights activist attempting to find her identity in the Deep South who is struck by a paralyzing illness. Many of her students initially view this character as being literally ill, but after having engaged in this fairy tale assignment, they are able to think more symbolically, analogically, and metaphorically. This assignment sequence not only reinforces the Learning Partnerships Model notion that knowledge is constructed but also stresses the idea that knowledge is never static. It must be continually renegotiated.

Once these principles have been established through more personalized forms of writing, students in both the science and the humanities courses described previously engage in more traditional academic assignments—lab reports, literary analyses, biographies, and environmental case studies. Although most of these assignments are individual, each course also builds in some collaborative or group assignments to assist students in learning how to develop their voice within a community of learners. As one professor puts it, the goal throughout the year is to help students become "more conscious of writing as a rhetorical device" and "to develop their voice within an academic context" (Harrison-Pepper, personal interview, April 7, 2003). Faculty claim that by devoting time at the beginning of the year engaging in more personal forms of writing (narratives, personal essays, and autobiographies), students are more comfortable writing authoritatively in traditional academic pieces of writing. As Dr. Cummins remarks,

> The writing I teach to undergraduates is often kind of awkward. But part of the awkwardness is intentional ambiguity. I am trying to move them away from worrying about what I want to thinking more about their own ideas. I want them to come up with their own structure, to go to the library and look up other people's ideas, and finally to trust their own judgments and instincts. It is quite a struggle—full of ambiguity, but ultimately the journey can be pretty successful. (personal interview, April 9, 2003)

A third faculty member, William Newell, also comments on this struggle and its transformative power: "By the end of the first year, they have experienced interdisciplinarity in multiple courses, often with only modest discussion of what it means exactly. The experience is powerful to the point of being transformative. . . . The transformation is destructive—Piaget would say 'de-centering'—in the sense that the courses . . . challenge much of their world-taken-for-granted" (personal interview, August 6, 2003). The goal in the second semester of the first year is not so much to critique or compare disciplinary frameworks but to aid students in articulating their views within disciplinary forms. In short, in the first year, faculty members want to provide students with a solid introduction to the key principles of the Learning Partnerships Model: validating students' capacity to construct ideas, grounding learning in their own experience, and helping them to see learning as mutual knowledge construction. The second year's goal is to deepen their engagement with these principles.

Marcia Baxter Magolda's (1992) research on Miami college students suggests that as students progress into the sophomore year having already confronted in their first year an array of complex problems as well as a host of different disciplinary frameworks with which to view the world, they begin to move to transitional knowing, increasingly coming to the idea that absolute knowledge exists in some areas while uncertainty exists in others. For many of them, some disciplines offer more certain, definitive answers, while others are more open to interpretation and opinion. As one rising second-year interdisciplinary student whom I will call Don comments in an interview,

> Well, especially in a philosophy class, there really is no right answer. It's impossible to say you know the right answer. So, I think it's interesting to see, because pretty much nobody agrees in that area. I think it's interesting when somebody says something and you're just like wow, I agree with that, or I never thought of that before. And you see a different way. . . . But I think in the science area, it's usually pretty cut and dry, right and wrong. Our final [in my science course] had one-word answers; it wasn't like essays in our humanities class where we could write in different ways. (personal interview, January 10, 2003)

Don's view of knowledge is beginning to evolve away from what Baxter Magolda's (1992) research found and our faculty describe as the typical first-year student who seeks absolute knowledge in all areas toward someone who detects differences in the way knowledge and writing get framed differently in different disciplines. Although not all sophomore students are as advanced in their thinking as Don, faculty teaching sophomore courses nevertheless seek to reinforce and deepen this new development by helping students compare and contrast disciplinary frameworks, critically analyze the limitations and benefits of various ways of viewing the world, and begin to use various disciplines to think about their own questions. As one faculty member comments, "I try in the sophomore year to notch up the level of analysis and critique and the expectations of integration even more fully" (Cummins, personal interview, April 9, 2003). These more advanced expectations speak to the complexity and social construction of knowledge as well as the sharing of expertise and authority that are integral to the Learning Partnerships Model.

In a sophomore, interdisciplinary fine arts and humanities core course titled "Women and Theatre" taught by Dr. Harrison-Pepper and Rebecca Howard, students not only study the canonical works of drama, looking in particular at the relative absence of plays by women and minorities, but also use feminist theoretical principles and collaborate with one another to revise scenes from canonical plays to effect a more progressive vision (Magolda, 1997). Because the professors assume learning happens in multiple ways (cognitively, visually, kinesthetically, affectively, and so on), they continually prompt students to rework their ideas using various learning modes—intellectually in form of written assignments as well as visually in form of graphic representations and bodily in form of group and individual performances. Students create visual maps of scenes, theories, and arguments, and for their final solo performance they must integrate the various dramatic, feminist, anthropological, and philosophical theories they have read about women and the body and create their own 10-minute solo performance. Students write the script, block the scene, create the setting, and write any accompanying text or program on their own. These individual performances vary tremendously—from formally scripted monologues to highly abstract, risky performances—but all incorporate disciplinary forms of knowledge as well as an implicit critique of the traditional discipline of theater.

A sophomore interdisciplinary core course titled "Critical Reflections on the Life Sciences" focuses on the questions, What is biology? How did it come to be as it is now? What are its relationships to other disciplines, such as ethics? How do debates arise and get resolved in biology? and Which people and questions are given prestige and privilege, and why? (Blaisdell & Cummins, 1999). After studying the role of women and minorities in the life sciences and research on science education for children, students are asked to analyze biological textbooks, looking particularly at gender and race. Next, they are challenged to work in small groups to create a biological discovery-oriented lab or field experiences for middle and high school students, taking into account the research they have conducted throughout the course.

In a sophomore interdisciplinary social sciences and humanities core course titled "Law and Literature in U.S. Society" taught by Dan Herron and myself, students explore the question of how the narrative structures embedded in the disciplines of law and literature propel or constrain social justice, particularly justice relating to race, gender, and sexual orientation. Students begin the course by writing case briefs on historical Supreme Court cases relating to the course themes. They also create close textual analyses of literary works that address these same themes. These first two assignments are designed to familiarize students with the way legal and literary scholars approach and analyze narratives of social justice. The second half of the course pushes students to critique and then integrate these two disciplinary frameworks, first by creating and performing a mock trial using a legal case presented in a work of literature and then by creating a piece of legal fiction based on a historical case of law. The course ends by asking students to reflect on the limitations and opportunities that each mode of justice—the law and literature—affords.

In all these interdisciplinary sophomore core courses (required of all inter-disciplinary majors), faculty members are interested in propelling the Learning Partnerships Model principle of knowledge as socially constructed by debunking students' perceptions of disciplines as objective, value neutral, and absolute. Special attention is paid not only to highlighting the problems with the disciplines studied (the inherent racism, homophobia, and sexism as well as ethical concerns) but also to prompting students to see themselves as knowledge producers and potential agents for change in these disciplines. By engaging in performances and mock trials, writing pieces of literature, and authoring science curricula, students are put in the position of constructing knowledge within and among these disciplinary frameworks. These assignments also spur students to take a clear stand on the interdisciplinary topics at hand. It is difficult to create a closing argument in a mock trial, teach a science unit to middle schoolers, or offer a solo performance to your peers if you have no idea who you are or what you think. Moreover, because many of the assignments in these second-year courses call for collaboration (e.g., scene work, mock trials, and team-taught science curricula), students must learn to distinguish their own viewpoints from others, learn empathy, and co-create meaning within a group context. As a result, they are being continually challenged interpersonally, intrapersonally, and intellectually, and they are engaging in a unique integrative implementation of the Learning Partnerships Model. As one professor puts it,

> By the second year, students have so embraced the interdisciplinary approach that it becomes second nature to them. It's hard for them to imagine why people would ever limit themselves to a single discipline. Writing interdisciplinary papers as a means of thinking through a complex issue comes easily to most of them. (Newell, personal interview, August 6, 2003)

If the second year's primary goal is to teach students to think critically about disciplines, make comparisons between disciplines, and begin to understand interdisciplinary studies, the third year's goal is to help them understand more deeply the value of the Learning Partnerships Model and to engage more systematically in interdisciplinary inquiry. According to Baxter Magolda's research as well as our faculty's perceptions of students' writing, most students in this year are either transitional knowers (viewing knowledge as absolute in some areas but uncertain in others) or independent knowers (seeing knowledge as open to many interpretations and viewing themselves as equal sources of knowledge) (Baxter Magolda, 1992). As Bill Newell notes,

> The junior experience is epitomized by the academic advisee who replies to my query about how one of her disciplinary courses she is taking outside the

program is going by informing me that the instructor seems to know his stuff but is frustrating because he seems to feel that there is a single right approach to the topics covered in the course. (personal interview, August 6, 2003)

This instructor's focus on a single right approach frustrates this advisee because it does not acknowledge uncertainty and multiple interpretation. Because students are moving away from absolute forms of thinking, it is important to continue disrupting the notion that knowledge is universal, encouraging learners to identify their own viewpoints and worldview, and urging them to engage seriously with the ideas of others.

Junior-year interdisciplinary core courses in our program deepen the implementation of the Learning Partnerships Model by focusing pointedly on interdisciplinary theory and research method. Students study interdisciplinary scholarship, theory, and practice, and they typically undertake a somewhat lengthy interdisciplinary project of their own. Early in the course, many faculty assign students to create or take part in academic journals, annotated bibliographies, or electronic exchanges to cultivate the habit of engaging in dialogue with other scholars or, as spelled out in the Learning Partnerships Model, to define "learning as a collaborative exchange of perspectives" (preface). One professor claims that she seeks "a rapid give-and-take" in her junior seminars among students and between students and faculty members; her hope is that she will no longer need to facilitate the seminar but instead that students will co-facilitate it among themselves (Harrison-Pepper, personal interview, April 9, 2003). They will enter each seminar full of ideas and ready to share them with their peers. Another faculty member remarks,

> I am always trying to build a community around writing. Students write proposals and reports and post them on the website. Other students must respond to this writing. . . . Moreover, when we have students present their findings, we tell them we will interrupt them at anytime to ask questions, to push them to expand upon something. And I tell their classmates to do the same, and ask questions of the presenter. In the beginning, everyone is kind of fearful being up in front of the class and not being able to answer all of the questions posed. So, they are uncomfortable. But as the semester progresses, they become much more comfortable with being uncertain, with having to reason out questions and even saying they don't know the answer and asking their peers for help. Everyone is always asking questions and exchanging ideas. (Cummins, personal interview, April 7, 2003)

Along with fostering the learning partnerships principle that writing and scholarship is enhanced when done within a community, professors in the junior year also frequently assign more ambitious interdisciplinary projects. For example, in a junior interdisciplinary seminar on global climate change, students select a topic relating to a disruption in the modern-day or historical climate. The professors then assign primary source articles on the topics chosen. Students undertake further research and complete a set of sequenced assignments (a research proposal, oral presentation on the proposal, Web page, and final report), all of which culminate in a personal essay reflecting on how they integrated disciplinary insights and what they learned from the inquiry process. These projects entail multiple methods of research, various theories, and different forms of writing. Cummins notes,

> In this instance, [students] are right at the cutting edge. They are looking at primary, current literature about topics where there are no certainties. As in most things in science, there are a lot of ambiguities. We are asking them to address these ambiguous issues, collect data in articles that others have written, and then test their own questions as it relates to a larger topic in a scientifically sound way. They collect data, conduct statistical analyses on what others have found in order to see if what others are saying really makes sense. So the process is filled with ambiguity. But the third-year students are much more able to handle it [than sophomores]. They even seem to enjoy it because they have reached another level of thinking. (personal interview, April 9, 2003)

In an interdisciplinary humanities seminar for juniors, another faculty member, Curtis Ellison, collaborates with his students to create a social history of the Western College Program. The School of Interdisciplinary Studies at Miami was created in 1974, but its buildings and land were formerly part of the Western College for Women (founded in 1853). Although an archive of both institutions exists, no comprehensive social history of the Western College or the present-day School of Interdisciplinary Studies (also known as the Western College Program in honor of its predecessor) has been written. Professor Ellison saw the availability of numerous primary and secondary sources on the character of these two institutions in different eras as well as on the evolution of college life generally as an excellent opportunity for interdisciplinary inquiry. After studying some existing sources, students in his seminar select their own topics. The topics range from individual people, such as a past president, to a college ritual or tradition to a specific building or landscape. The class then draws on archival and museum materials (campus records, diaries, scrapbooks, artifacts, photographs, and so on) to produce one chapter or section in what will eventually be incorporated into a *History of Western College, 1853–2003,* created collectively by Dr. Ellison and his students. To do this, students must engage with theories of historiography as well as with multiple modes of research (archival, textual analysis, theoretical reasoning, and visual analysis) and disciplinary insights.

In these junior-level interdisciplinary courses, the interplay of connected and autonomous thinking that is integral to the Learning Partnerships Model is valued through open-ended projects and assignments and free-flowing conversations where differing opinions are allowed. Although fewer collaboratively written assignments are given, students are expected to view one another and the faculty member as colleagues and are given responsibility for leading class discussions, providing thoughtful feedback on writing, and playing the role of the expert in oral presentations and writing.

Although freedom of thought and expression is encouraged, faculty also continually challenge students to ground their ideas and pursue their inquiries in the academic context and to pursue their ideas by combining insights from multiple disciplinary lenses. Thus, not anything goes. Learners must now begin to view knowledge as complex and contextually situated by fitting their independent thought within a specific context. This move is not as easy as it may first appear. Because interdisciplinary thinking is drawn from multiple disciplines, interdisciplinary learners often must invent a new way of organizing their thoughts or a new audience for expressing their views. In other words, unlike students in disciplines who can follow decades or even centuries of tradition, interdisciplinary students do not often have an established set of assumptions, organizational structures, language, and use of evidence to draw on. They must cobble together notions and assumptions from other, more established disciplinary communities in order to convey their thoughts. This problem is especially present when students are not given accessible theories and models of interdisciplinary writing (or even when students are given them and are not able developmentally to digest them). As Bill Newell remarks, "In the absence of a coherent and explicit statement of the interdisciplinary approach, they start to develop their own idiosyncratic version through the papers they write" (personal interview, August 6, 2003). Thus, interdisciplinary students' initial steps into the playground of independent academic research are often very messy and unpredictable—filled with awkward transitions from one mode of thinking or analysis to another, weird combinations of seemingly contradictory theories and methods, and uneven forays into disciplinary and interdisciplinary professional literatures.

These messy steps, however, are not without important value. By introducing students to the process of interdisciplinary inquiry in the junior year (rather than the senior year as I and my colleagues did before the 4-year writing curriculum was instituted), students are able to gain more practice with

the inevitable pitfalls and unexpected challenges of interdisciplinary scholarship and a deeper awareness of the assumptions of the Learning Partnerships
Model, and thus they are able to better succeed in their senior year.

Although only a few students use the actual projects completed in their
junior year as the basis of their senior thesis, they all employ the knowledge
and the inquiry process they have cultivated over the past 3 years to
approach the senior interdisciplinary thesis. Julie Thompson Klein (1996) has
argued that interdisciplinary work

> gets done by moving across the vertical plane of depth and the horizontal
> plane of breadth. Breadth connotes a comprehensive approach based in mul-
> tiple variables and perspectives. Depth connotes competence in pertinent dis-
> ciplinary, professional and interdisciplinary approaches. Synthesis connotes
> creation of an interdisciplinary outcome through a series of integrative
> actions. (p. 212)

The process of interdisciplinary inquiry almost always begins with a problem,
question, topic, or issue, and it entails overcoming problems created by differences in disciplinary language and worldview (Klein, 1990). Beyond that,
however, scholars can take a variety of paths and individual steps, including
determining all knowledge needs, developing an integrative framework, specifying specific tasks or studies to be taken, reconciling conflicts in findings,
and integrating the individual findings into a more comprehensive view.
Indeed, interdisciplinary scholars must be ready to navigate through
uncharted waters and generate new ways of combining or making sense of
disparate pieces of information on their own. And in order to be effective, the
student must learn to recognize that within a given context, some knowledge
claims are more appropriate than others. Such a realization does not generally happen automatically with seniors; it is learned throughout the process
of creating the thesis and must be reinforced and sometimes prompted by
the faculty adviser. In short, students must embody all three of the Learning
Partnerships Model assumptions. They must construct knowledge in relation
to others, connect learning to the self, and understand knowledge as complex, contextual, and socially constituted.

The challenge of the senior thesis relates not only to the interdisciplinary
process of inquiry but also to the form of the thesis itself. Because the School
of Interdisciplinary Studies defines the thesis broadly, students must decide
what form their theses will take. It could be a case study, expressive product,
series of laboratory experiments, service-learning or internship project, portfolio of creative writing, exhibition or performance, documentary video, or
even the founding of a social movement organization. From the very beginning of the process until its completion, seniors are faced with a barrage of

decisions to make, each one affecting the others. This seemingly endless line of choices can often be overwhelming for the student.

As a means of support, these seniors confer weekly with a faculty adviser and meet as a group to share ideas, generate strategies for improving the writing process, and provide feedback on work in progress. Both settings—the individual conference with the faculty adviser as well as the group seminar with peers—are designed not only to reinforce the key principles of the Learning Partnerships Model but also to nurture students in all three dimensions of learning: cognitive, interpersonal, and intrapersonal. My experience in advising dozens of thesis writers is that the most difficult obstacles are not the cognitive ones. With some guidance, students will generally select topics that they can handle intellectually, and college life has generally prepared them to be ready for intellectual pitfalls and struggles. The far thornier problems relate to the intrapersonal dimension of learning. Of the three principles embedded in the Learning Partnerships Model, I have observed that the most challenging to foster in students is the first—validating learners' capacity as knowledge constructors (preface)—perhaps because most of their education has neglected to underscore the self as central to learning. As a result, the majority of my time working with senior thesis writers is devoted to helping them gain self-confidence, define their own set of values that will influence their study, and overcome bad habits and internal messages that impede their progress rather than collaborating with them to deepen their analyses or acquire new research skills.

Other faculty members in my program have experienced similar struggles with their advisees. Dr. Harrison-Pepper, for example, told me in an interview about a student she recently advised who was suffering from extreme writer's anxiety (personal interview, April 7, 2003). As a result of this stress, this senior doggedly perched herself at the computer for 5 or more hours each day, only to produce what seemed to be incomprehensible gibberish. The student complained that she had abandoned her friends and social life in order to indulge her steadfast obsession with the thesis. Hearing this, Dr. Harrison-Pepper ordered her advisee not to touch her computer for 3 days and instead to dance to her favorite CD for half an hour each day. Her theory was that if the student jump-started other aspects of her intelligence (in this case, the kinesthetic and aesthetic sides), she might be able to get her brain and emotions back into alignment and then become creative as a writer again. This faculty member's unorthodox advice worked, and by the time of their next advising session, the student's writing was once again prolific and lucid. This student had managed to put herself once again in the center of her work.

Although Dr. Harrison-Pepper's specific advice might not be applicable to every student, what is important about this example is that it underscores the Learning Partnerships Model implication that writing (as a primary means of learning) is a social, emotional, and intellectual process. If one dimension is not being nurtured, the other dimensions suffer. Faculty working with students in this year spend a great deal of one-on-one time with them to reflect on their learning, troubleshoot problems, offer much-needed assurances, and provide feedback on the writing in progress as well as the process of investigation. The senior workshop offers students additional support in the form of small writing groups in which students share drafts, exchange ideas, and support one another. Such a supportive structure appears to work because the program graduates over 90% of the students who entered as first-year students. Although many of our students are very bright and creative, they are not all "A" students. Even those students whose grade-point average may not be stellar do complete this yearlong ambitious project. Bill Newell describes the ways it is so ambitious:

> The two-semester, 10-credit senior project workshop walks them through all the research steps from identifying an appropriate topic to presenting their results in a professional conference format. Even when they've done a computer search or annotated bibliography or literature review in a previous seminar, it feels different in a project of this magnitude (80 pages of text split into anywhere from 5 to 8 chapters) and comprehensiveness (drawing explicitly and exhaustively on several disciplines or interdisciplines, making use of every key relevant book or article from each). Finally students confront issues of structuring an interdisciplinary argument with many steps, and establishing credibility in the eyes of each of the contributing disciplines. They complete the spring semester with a sense of mastery of the entire interdisciplinary process, empowered to undertake interdisciplinary research on whatever topic interests them, and ready for graduate work. After the senior project, a master's thesis is a breeze and even a doctoral dissertation has lost its aura of mystery and fear. (personal interview, August 6, 2003)

General Guidelines for Writing Instruction

When the faculty in Miami's School of Interdisciplinary Studies approved the 4-year writing curriculum in 1996, our hope was that it would help improve the quality of students' thesis writing through a carefully sequenced set of writing experiences and expectations. This curriculum has achieved our primary goal (which is discussed in the next section of this chapter), and implementing the curriculum has taught us a variety of important guidelines for writing instruction.

Although the curriculum focused most pointedly on cultivating students' intellectual development, we realized very quickly that little cognitive progress can be made if students are not encouraged to grow emotionally and socially. As is made clear in all the chapters of this book, learning happens best in partnership and in context. Learners must not only be encouraged to construct knowledge but must also learn to think contextually and in relation to others. In our original construction of the writing curriculum, we underestimated the amount of time and energy that would be needed to foster the interpersonal and intrapersonal dimensions of learning, and we did not clearly articulate those dimensions in the curricular goals.

In addition, although the writing curriculum effectively parcels out discrete writing goals for each semester over the course of 4 years, its own linear structure may at times defy the way students actually learn and faculty teach. In an article on writing in interdisciplinary courses, Marcia Bundy Seabury cautions against viewing the interdisciplinary writing process solely in terms of a linear, staged progression from simple forms of thinking to more complex forms such as integration. Seabury (2002) writes,

> "Moving toward synthesis" embodies a metaphor that deserves unpacking. It suggests a graph-like progression whereby students gradually move from lower forms of thinking on up to more holistic, abstract thinking, ending in the upper-right quadrant of the page. "Toward" involves a destination, a goal, an end. We hope students will "reach" a holistic understanding. But . . . the "goal" may be not a position but a motion: students' facility with moving among levels of abstraction and generalization. Integrative thinking means not just bringing together diverse data, diverse disciplinary perspectives in order to reach an overarching synthesis but also using and testing such a synthesis in relation to the more specific and concrete. . . . Thus, as we create assignments to encourage integrative thinking, the process and goal may be to build a synthesis but may also be to apply, evaluate, or break down a synthesis. (p. 47)

In other words, it is important not to use the writing curriculum and its goal of helping students achieve an integrated thesis or piece of writing as a fixed template or a "cookbook" for how to teach students writing. Too much structure can defeat spontaneity and creativity. Faculty members in our program have learned to veer away from the curriculum structure when needed—that is, to push students to further depths of the Learning Partnerships Model than the semester goals of the writing curriculum dictate or backtrack to earlier goals when the need arises. It is important to include opportunities for students to try entirely new modes of learning and expressing learning—whether they fit neatly into the plan's boxes or not. Teachers, like students, need to be encouraged to follow their instincts and to create their own unique style and framework for fostering a deep and rich learning environment. Thus, it is imperative that a writing curriculum such as this one not be followed too rigidly or monitored too closely. Faculty should meet, discuss, and revise it regularly in order to better serve their students' needs. In short, the curriculum should be in a continual process of flux and revision, enabling selected opportunities for serendipity and creativity without ignoring the developmental needs of students. Such flexibility models the Learning Partnerships Model both in faculty sharing authority and expertise and in staying with students in mutual construction.

Assessment of the Writing Curriculum

Although faculty members occasionally veer from the prescribed goals of each semester, a review of syllabi from 1996 to the present reveals a remarkable tendency to follow the curriculum's overall structure. Ninety-four percent (118 of 125) of syllabi reviewed contained writing assignments that were in keeping with the writing curriculum's stated semester-by-semester goals. Fifty-nine percent (74 of 125) of the syllabi made specific reference to the writing curriculum and its importance for student learning. In the audit of syllabi, some general trends were noted:

- As is evident in syllabi statements, faculty on the whole seem to value writing as a means for supporting the three principles of the Learning Partnerships Model.

- Overall, the curriculum evolves from personal essays and narratives in the first year, various forms of analysis in the second year, smaller research-based projects in the third year, and finally the senior thesis in the fourth year.

- Over half the courses (63%) include collaborative forms of writing and peer reviews, demonstrating faculty members' belief in the Learning Partnerships Model notion of writing as a tool for the mutual construction of knowledge.

- Over 66% of the course syllabi have statements that underscore the importance of gaining a personal or independent voice in writing, thus reinforcing the Learning Partnerships Model emphases on intrapersonal learning and complex intellectual functioning.

- Since the inception of the curriculum in 1996, the 14 full-time faculty members have met four times to discuss the overall goals and outline of the plan. On all occasions, they agreed to continue using the curriculum and expressed their general approval of effectiveness.

These findings suggest that our 4-year writing plan is an effective example of a curriculum structured as a learning partnership and seems to be successful in its goal of fostering self-authorship. However, the audit of syllabi also suggested some areas that could be further improved or reconsidered:

- Although writing was assigned in every course offered, the amount and length of papers and projects assigned vary. A few courses (less than 5%) assigned only one paper. Students in courses with few writing assignments thus miss some valuable opportunities for personal development and thesis preparation.

- Although all faculty assign writing (and some even make reference to the writing curriculum), the extent to which they articulate its goals to students varies. Many of their syllabi do not include assignments that explicitly mention the principles of the Learning Partnerships Model or the goals of the writing curriculum. Nor do they explicitly articulate the interdisciplinary nature of their learning.

- A few of the faculty members taught a course on the same topic to different levels of students (e.g., first-years vs. juniors); however, the writing assignments listed on both syllabi appeared to be the same. This suggests that not all faculty members are attuning their teaching to students' developmental needs.

- The information offered in a syllabi audit is limited. Faculty members do not often provide detailed information about the assignments or other forms of writing instruction offered in a course in their syllabi. Moreover, a syllabi audit reveals how learning is organized rather than what learning actually takes place in a given course or throughout a student's undergraduate career.

In order to find out what our students may have learned in our program, my colleague Christopher Wolfe and I (with sponsorship and advice from the Association for Integrative Studies) decided to create an instrument for assessing the level of our students' interdisciplinary learning that we termed the "Interdisciplinary Writing Assessment Profiles" (Wolfe & Haynes, 2003). We developed a scoring rubric that assessed four dimensions of students' learning: (a) drawing on disciplinary sources, (b) critical argumentation, (c) multidisciplinary perspectives, and (d) interdisciplinary integration. The first two dimensions focus primarily on elements that should ideally occur in disciplinary as well as interdisciplinary expository, research-based writing. The final two dimensions are more pointedly focused on interdisciplinary writing.

Because we wanted to know how our interdisciplinary students were learning similarly and differently from disciplinary students, we used the instrument to assess 10 interdisciplinary theses written by students in our program and 10 discipline-based theses by students in Miami's University Honors Program. Honors students were used as a comparison group because they have a senior thesis requirement and their academic profile is equal to and in some cases superior to interdisciplinary students. As a result, their projects can be presumed to be well written, thus reducing the chance of confusing good writing with interdisciplinary writing. The instrument requires 55 separate judgments, and each scorer independently scored each item. Each of the four dimensions had a list of positive source and negative source elements. A score was determined for each of the dimensions on the basis of the number of positive and negative source elements. Each thesis (with a mean of 55 pages in length) was scored independently, and the two scorers (Dr. Wolfe and I) agreed on 1,062 of 1,096 judgments, demonstrating a global interrater reliability for the instrument of .97. There were no significant differences between the interdisciplinary and disciplinary theses on two of the dimensions: Drawing on Disciplinary Sources and Critical Argumentation. However, statistically significant differences did exist on the other two dimensions. Interdisciplinary students scored higher on both of the dimensions of Multidisciplinary Perspectives, $F(1, 18) = 5.55$, $p = .03$, and Interdisciplinary Integration, $F(1, 18) = 5.50$, $p = .03$.

The positive source elements in all four dimensions are essential for cultivating the Learning Partnerships Model, but some are clearly focused on the goals of intrapersonal, interpersonal, and cognitive development. Among the elements where interdisciplinary students scored significantly higher are the following:

- Reflects self-consciously on the limitations and merits of the author's approach
- Reflects self-consciously on the insights and limitations of one theory, school of thought, or disciplinary approach
- Demonstrates an understanding of how each discipline would approach the object of study
- Identifies how at least one term is used differently or similarly in different disciplines within the context of the problem
- Draws on sources from two or more disciplines
- Presents a clear rationale for taking an interdisciplinary approach

- Makes explicit and compares assumptions from more than one discipline
- Creates new holistic understanding through a new metaphor, model, or theoretical understanding

In order to achieve these elements, writers must not only be able to construct new knowledge (e.g., combine disciplinary knowledge to respond to a topic, present a rationale for taking an interdisciplinary approach, and provide a new holistic understanding of the topic) but must also engage with other thinkers (i.e., exploring sources and requesting feedback) as well as have a clear understanding of themselves a scholars and thinkers. Moreover, because few models of interdisciplinary projects or process exist for students, a level of independence and creativity is necessarily demanded of interdisciplinary thesis writers that may not be required for disciplinary writers who can follow established patterns of scholarship. In short, the higher scores achieved by interdisciplinary students suggest that they are progressing toward self-authorship, perhaps even more than are the disciplinary-based honors students.

Conclusion

The 4-year writing curriculum instituted in Miami's School of Interdisciplinary Studies provides one model assisting students to achieve not only the more complex levels of interdisciplinary inquiry but also self-authorship. Evidence presented here indicates that interdisciplinary study may propel students toward deep engagement with the Learning Partnerships Model components. One possible reason for this finding is that interdisciplinarity may better reflect the way the human mind deals, every day, with life's challenges. And it may be better suited to addressing the highly complex global issues and problems—from environmental issues such as global warming to issues of world politics such as the Middle East crisis. As Peg Downes (2002), professor of literature and language at the University of North Carolina, Asheville, and director of the Key Center for Service Learning, puts it, "Disciplines are time-bound, changeable packets of knowledge and epistemologies, constructed for human comfort and convenience. In each, we buff a particular set of mental muscles. But they too easily can become mindsets, castles we defend, paradigmatic bastions." Interdisciplinarity forces us to dismantle these castles and often calls on all the dimensions of learning—cognitive, interpersonal, and intrapersonal—thus helping propel learners gradually toward self-authorship.

Although the interdisciplinary writing curriculum developed at Miami's School of Interdisciplinary Studies affords a unique and powerful venue for propelling the Learning Partnerships Model, it is a means of implementing writing curricula in other settings. The Association for Integrative Studies (the national organization for the advancement of interdisciplinary studies) has advocated this model in its national conferences and published it in its journal, *Issues in Integrative Studies* (Haynes, 1996). The founder and current executive director of the association, Bill Newell, affirms that the writing curriculum "is the most sophisticated and elaborated set of theory, guidelines, and concrete suggestions I've ever encountered in all of the interdisciplinary programs I've evaluated or served as a consultant to" (personal interview, August 6, 2003). In 1997–1998, I worked with faculty at the University of Southern Illinois, Edwardsville, to develop sequenced writing curricula that advance the components of the Learning Partnerships Model in a variety of different disciplinary and interdisciplinary departments. In 1999–2001, I served as the interim director of Miami's Center of Writing Excellence and worked with faculty in five different disciplinary departments to create similar writing curricula, and an Association of American Colleges and Universities task force on interdisciplinary learning is using this model to generate new strategies for advancing integrative liberal learning.

Promoting the Learning Partnerships Model in the college interdisciplinary or disciplinary classroom, however, is not easy or simple. Because it must be fostered throughout the curriculum, implementation on a program level requires a critical mass of faculty to pursue this model together. Because not all faculty members will immediately accept the Learning Partnerships Model, achieving the requisite "buy-in" from all stakeholders can be challenging. In addition, the differing disciplinary worldviews and past writing and teaching experiences of faculty can make the process of finding common goals and strategies time consuming, frustrating, and cumbersome. Yet this diversity of perspectives and expertise can also open up a valuable opportunity to enact the Learning Partnerships Model components with faculty. Through discussions about what learning we wanted to cultivate in our students and how we could use writing to achieve those outcomes, faculty members of Miami's School of Interdisciplinary Studies ended up recognizing the complex and socially constructed nature of knowledge, incorporating and validating our own identities as scholars and thinkers, and creating a new plan through the sharing of expertise and authority (for a model of faculty development utilizing the Learning Partnerships Model components, see Haynes & Watson, in press). Our intense discussions and debates helped us create a more coherent curriculum, a more uniform set of learning outcomes, and a greater sense of shared commitment and community than we had ever had before. Key to this process was the fact that we preceded our discussion about the actual curriculum with a shared set of readings on student development (including Marcia Baxter Magolda's research), interdisciplinary education, and composition pedagogy. These readings provided a solid theoretical foundation for our future discussions and planning.

Thus, with openness and patience, the many differences in viewpoints that exist among faculty members can also be opportunities for creativity and enlightenment. New models and new paradigms might emerge. With these new models, we educators can stop viewing ourselves as circus performers attempting to hold our students in perilous balance and reenvision ourselves as agents for effecting deep learning and lifetime change in our students.

References

Baxter Magolda, M. B. (1992). *Knowing and reasoning in college: Gender-related patterns in students' intellectual development.* San Francisco: Jossey-Bass.

Blaisdell, M., & Cummins, R. H. (1999). Syllabus for critical reflections on the life sciences: Lives in science. Available: http://jrscience.wcip.muohio.edu/courses/criticalreflections99.html

Bloom, B. S. (Ed.). (1956). *Taxonomy of educational objectives: The classification of educational goals: Handbook I, cognitive domain.* New York: Longmans, Green.

Cummins, R. H., & Myers, C. A. (1992). Incorporating sciences in a liberal arts education. *National Honors Report, 13*(1), 2–5.

Downes, P. (2002). 16 reasons for interdisciplinary studies, created for the University of Missouri–Kansas City campus conversations, 2001–2002. Available: http://www.umkc.edu/conversations/Downes.htm#Bio

Haynes, C. (1996). Interdisciplinary writing and the undergraduate experience: A four-year writing plan proposal. *Issues in Integrative Studies, 14,* 29–57.

Haynes, C., & Watson, S. (in press). Preparing liberal arts faculty to teach writing: A contextual-developmental model of faculty development. In J. Castner & J. A. Inman (Eds.), *Teaching writing in the liberal arts.* Creskill, NJ: Hampton.

Fulwiler, T. (1995). Provocative revision. In C. Murphy & S. Sherwood (Eds.), *The St. Martin's sourcebook for writing tutors* (pp. 71–82). New York: St. Martin's Press.

Kegan, R. (1994). *In over our heads: The mental demands of modern life.* Cambridge, MA: Harvard University Press.

Klein, J. T. (1990). *Interdisciplinarity: History, theory, and practice.* Detroit: Wayne State University Press.

Klein, J. T. (1996). *Crossing boundaries: Knowledge, disciplinarities, and interdisciplinarities.* Charlottesville: University Press of Virginia.

Klein, J. T., & Newell, W. H. (1998). Advancing interdisciplinary studies. In W. H. Newell (Ed.), *Interdisciplinarity: Essays from the literature* (pp. 3–23). New York: College Entrance Examination Board.

Magolda, P. M. (1997, May/June). Life as I don't know it. *About Campus: Enriching the Student Learning Experience, 2,* 16–22.

Mayer, J. D., & Salovey, P. (1993). The intelligence of emotional intelligence. *Intelligence, 17,* 433–442.

Seabury, M. B. (2002). Writing in interdisciplinary courses: Coaching integrative thinking. In C. Haynes (Ed.), *Innovations in interdisciplinary teaching* (pp. 38–64). Westport, CT: American Council on Education and Oryx Press.

Sommers, N. (1982). Responding to student writing. *College Composition and Communication, 33,* 148–156.

Wolfe, C., & Haynes, C. (2003). Assessing interdisciplinary writing. *Peer review: Emerging trends and key debates in undergraduate education,* 6(1), 12–14.

4

CREATING A CONTEXT TO PROMOTE DIVERSITY EDUCATION AND SELF-AUTHORSHIP AMONG COMMUNITY COLLEGE STUDENTS

Anne M. Hornak and Anna M. Ortiz

Designers of multicultural education intend their efforts to produce significant changes in the students who participate in their programs and courses. Although outcomes research concerning multicultural education is relatively sparse, findings do indicate that students learn more about other cultures (Robinson, Wolffe, Hunt, & Hoerr, 2002), begin to broaden their worldviews through the reduction of prejudice (Chang, 2002), show an emerging capacity to critically examine society (Chizhik & Chizhik, 2002), are more likely to enter high-risk situations with more confidence (Dunlop, 2000), and experience positive changes in identity (Allen, Floyd-Thomas, & Gillman, 2001). For students to achieve and demonstrate these outcomes, it is absolutely necessary for them to internally coordinate beliefs, values, and loyalties and act on them consistently as they interface with varying segments of their lives—all keys to self-authorship. These outcomes are internalized and strengthened when they are context bound for students or when they are grounded in their own realities. Thus, students best learn about other cultures when they experience them directly rather than simply reading about them in class. Similarly, critiques about social justice issues in society are more effective when witnessed firsthand. Situating multicultural education in the lived experiences of students is a hallmark of the Multicultural Education Framework (MEF; Ortiz & Rhoads, 2000). This framework shares many of the characteristics of the Learning Partnerships Model. This chapter describes the MEF and the ways in which it exemplifies the assumptions and the principles of the Learning Partnerships Model through a discussion of both the model and of a community college course where it was implemented.

Multicultural Education Framework

The MEF pays particular attention to the challenges in working with White students in multicultural education endeavors; however, the focus on culture and its creation can be used with students from other racial and ethnic backgrounds. The MEF is composed of five steps with specific educational outcomes and cognitive goals. Each step builds on the previous step. However, the framework does not make the assumption that people progress through steps, as they might in a linear, developmental model. Mastery of one step is not required for progression to the next. Individuals may revisit steps as they progress through the framework and realize that additional work needs to be done in a previous step. The framework is both practical and theoretical. My (Ortiz) work with multicultural education in the college setting suggested that this framework is effective in anticipating and confronting White students' resistance to "diversity" training and the presence and ownership of White privilege. The framework is theoretical in that we (Rhoads and Ortiz) made assumptions about the order of the steps and their connection to basic tenets of cognitive development theory. For example, one of our basic assumptions is that multicultural education often begins at a place that is too challenging for students without significant experience with culturally different people. When programs or training begin early with the topic of White privilege, students resist and "tune out," often because groundwork has not been established to help students ease into the topic of White privilege. The framework addresses this problem by beginning with an examination of culture and one's place in the evolution of culture. We assume that this is a more favorable, less threatening place to begin multicultural education. The steps of the framework and the cognitive goals associated with each are outlined in Table 4.1.

The cognitive goal of each step is directly related to the achievement of multicultural outcomes and self-authorship. In the first step, students are asked to gain an understanding of the concept of culture, both a definition and the process of culture development and change. A key to this step is helping students see that culture is dynamic, composed of the past, present, and future. Here, students not only learn about culture from a broad, anthropological perspective but also are given the opportunity to examine ways that society and its members create culture. Because the cognitive goal of the first step invites

Table 4.1 Framework of Multicultural Education

	Step 1: Understanding culture	Step 2: Learning about other cultures	Step 3: Recognizing and deconstructing white culture	Step 4: Recognizing the legitimacy of other cultures	Step 5: Developing a multicultural outlook
Cognitive goal	To develop a complex understanding of culture (culture shapes people's lives, and people shape culture).	To develop a more advanced understanding of diverse cultures.	To develop an understanding of how White culture has been universalized as the norm and to begin to question its privileged position.	To recognize that culture other than one's own is just as valued to another individual.	To recognize that all cultures within a given society shape each other and that the inclusion of all cultures requires the reconstruction of U.S. society.
Beginning problem statement	"I see culture as something a society creates."	"I know that differences between cultural groups exist, but the differences are only superficial."	"I see culture as something that some have but others do not."	"I understand that there are many cultures, but we should agree on a common culture."	"I value living in a society that is multicultural."

(Continued)

Table 4.1 Continued

	Step 1: Understanding culture	Step 2: Learning about other cultures	Step 3: Recognizing and deconstructing white culture	Step 4: Recognizing the legitimacy of other cultures	Step 5: Developing a multicultural outlook
Ending problem statement	"Culture is something I create but that also creates me."	"I understand that many cultural groups exist within the United States, and each reflects deeply held norms, values, beliefs, and traditions."	"I see culture as something that all people have."	"I see that many diverse cultures can coexist, including my own, and that this is a good thing."	"I can work to make society an equitable place for people of all cultural backgrounds because our vitality is intricately tied to one another's."
Activity	Understanding Culture—observing and critically analyzing everyday events.	Exploring Cultures—attending cultural events and reflecting on their meaning as well as dialoguing with culturally diverse others.	Analyzing White Culture—learning to recognize White culture and to begin to challenge its normalization.	The Impact of Culture—students identifying aspects of their own cultures that play important roles in their lives and sharing these with other students.	Multiculturalism Leads to Action—discovering how institutions shape the ways in which culture is expressed.

Source: Ortiz and Rhoads (2000). Reprinted with permission.

students to grasp how culture shapes their own lives and how they shape culture, ultimately, they learn that their own actions, beliefs, and connections contribute to the perpetuation of culture. Once this is learned, its corollary becomes evident—that students' actions, beliefs, and connections have the capacity to change culture. This step gives students an opportunity to critically examine the culture in which they live and their own place within that culture, which serves to promote both multicultural outcomes and self-authorship.

Step 2 of the MEF focuses on the values, traditions, and practices of different cultures. While many of the cultural awareness activities that are a staple of campus diversity programming are similar to the learning activities associated with this step, the theoretical knowledge gained through Step 1 helps students develop more complex understandings of the cultures that are explored. For example, with a theoretical understanding of culture, traditions such as food, music, art, and dance go beyond artifacts to be admired and demonstrate complex relationships between history, group identity, self-worth, and individual and group empowerment. Admiration, accompanied with a deeper understanding of why groups do what they do, helps dispel stereotypes and is an early step in prejudice reduction. The activities recommended for this step require students to enter into different environments, giving them the opportunity to construct knowledge on the basis of their own observations. Again, the personal interaction with subject matter and people makes this a qualitatively different experience that has greater potential to promote self-authorship.

The third step in the MEF focuses specifically on the exploration of White culture. Although there is wide-scale discrepancy on whether a White culture exists, Rhoads and I maintain that even this discrepancy is evidence of its universal nature. We steadfastly hold to the assumption that White culture must be recognized and deconstructed before White students can realize that they are culturally positioned. Step 3 takes the cognitive goal of Step 1 (that all culture is complex) and asks White students to apply that to themselves. This application requires critique because a central feature of the step is the recognition of White privilege on both personal and societal levels. The activity associated with this step asks students to list 10 characteristics of White culture. Rhoads and I have witnessed a number of approaches students use to complete this activity. Often students reflect on their own families and communities and identify elements that may represent a common culture, some students use terms that reflect knowledge and ownership of White privilege, and other students identify elements of U.S. society that are assumed to be "American culture." White students often have difficulty completing a list of 10 characteristics, while students of color often complete the list fairly quickly. This step holds the greatest promise for critique of self and society as well as the challenge to define and own values related to White privilege and multiculturalism.

Step 4 prompts students to recognize that cultures are of value to the individuals who are a part of them and that individual cultures are important to U.S. society. Some students believe that if we "fix" White (or American) culture, making it less oppressive and less privileged, then it is more likely that a single, common culture can be achieved. The learning activity associated with this step focuses on the importance of culture to individual identity and how culture affects an individual's worldview. The emphasis on the individual reinforces the personalization of culture and the development of respect for culturally different people. The respect is based on a complex understanding of both culture and the importance of values and beliefs to individuals. With this understanding, it is then impossible to advocate for the amalgamation of cultures.

The final step in the MEF takes the individual understanding that is fostered in Step 4 and broadens it to the societal level. The cognitive goal is to recognize that all cultures within our society shape each other and that the inclusion of all cultures would require the reconstruction of U.S. society. On a personal level, students may incorporate elements of other cultures into their own lives, perhaps through behavior, values, or educational activities. On a societal level, students may act to oppose inequity and work toward the inclusion of our society's multiple cultures. The blend of the personal and the societal ideally results in students seeing that they can take action to create a more multicultural society. They can not only take ownership of their own beliefs, actions, and relationships but also take ownership in societal transformation.

A multicultural outlook and the acknowledgment and ownership of White privilege calls for the assumptions and principles of the Learning Partnerships Model to be met (Baxter Magolda, 1999, 2001; chapter 2 of this volume). In a community college diversity course, described later in this chapter, students expertly demonstrated that developing a multicultural outlook is a *complex process that is socially constructed.* Students needed a number of experiences and cognitive challenges to achieve greater understanding and appreciation of others, including exposure to people and communities that were ethnically or racially diverse. The curriculum and the instructor wanted to provide challenges to worldviews that reflected limited experience and exposure. The students also looked for the guidance and confidence to begin to deconstruct the childhood messages from family and communities that negatively valued ethnically and racially diverse people. Students also came to know that their ability to broaden their perspectives and change the way they perceived the world required that *self be central to knowledge construction.* No matter how hard the instructor and the materials that she used may have tried to provide information that was contrary to what the students *knew,* it was the experiential activities that helped students come to know about race and privilege. The opportunity for students to place themselves at the center of knowledge construction was critical. Similarly, some students began to understand and value that fundamental changes in themselves were necessary to own White privilege and to work to end its effects in their lives. This process of moving away from a way of being and understanding that is limiting and largely defined by external forces to a way of being and understanding that is self-defined based on carefully chosen values and beliefs is part of the essence of self-authorship. This was enhanced by the decision of the instructor to encourage students to *mutually construct knowledge with authorities and peers.*

The MEF also meets the principles of the Learning Partnerships Model. When this framework was integrated into the curriculum of a course at Midwest City Community College, we (Hornak and Ortiz) created the opportunity to *validate learners' capacity to know, to situate learning in learners' experience, and for the mutual construction of meaning.* The focus on experiential activities of each step, such as different culture immersion, observation and interpretation of campus cultures, the use of popular media, and so on, helps students develop their own knowledge about the construction of culture and their role in culture maintenance and change. These activities fundamentally rely on situating learning in the students' experiences. We have found that too often multicultural education and diversity training asks students to reflect from an outsider perspective rather than from their own lived experiences. When training and education is intellectualized or taught from a "special" culture perspective, students learn that culture is outside themselves and that there is a formula for success in race relations that they can learn from being an involved participant. However, developing a multicultural outlook and taking subsequent action for social justice requires that students begin to understand and claim their role in constructing the racial climate in our society. As they learn to deconstruct the racial scripts that have been a part of U.S. culture and society, they can begin to develop self-authorship in multicultural understanding.

Implementing and Assessing the Framework of Multicultural Education

Context

The opportunity to implement a theory into practice is a chance to test the underlying assumptions driving the theory and to provide assessment data to the larger research community. Such an opportunity arose when the MEF was implemented in a semester-length diversity course, "Diversity in the Workplace: A Domestic and Global Perspective," at Midwest City Community

College (MCCC). This particular business course, a requirement for the associate degree in general business administration, was taught at a branch of MCCC, approximately 35 miles from the main campus, in a rural, primarily White community.

The content of the course was managing diversity, specifically addressing issues managers need be aware of to work successfully in a variety of business environments. The students not only were exposed to other racial and ethnic groups but also had the opportunity to look at their own racial and ethnic identity, prejudices, and internal stereotypes. The students were challenged to critically reflect on the implications of their identity, prejudices, and stereotypes as aspiring supervisors and managers. This focus, in addition to the study of racial and ethnic groups, helped students prepare for management in culturally diverse work environments. For many students in the course, the work environment was the primary location of their experiences with racial and ethnic diversity.

The course was taught in the fall of 2001, with an enrollment of 18 students. There were 10 women and 8 men in the class, and the ages of the students ranged from 18 to late 40s. More than half the students worked in full-time jobs and attended school part time. All of the students were from the local area and had a short commute to the MCCC branch campus. The racial composition of the class was all White, with the exception of one female student who was multiracial and self-identified as White, and one male student who was of mixed heritage and also self-identified as White. Socioeconomic characteristics of the class were primarily lower-to middle-class backgrounds, with many students attending school with the assistance of governmental grants and other financial aid packages and programs.

Course Goals

The MCCC course description of "Diversity in the Workplace: A Domestic and Global Perspective," Management 234, reads,

> Explores cultural, gender/sexual, and physical diversity experiences in the workplace and in the world. The management of human resources is examined from a global perspective. The emphasis is on educating both majority and minority students to become aware of each other's opinions, feelings, and perspectives and on encouraging decision-making in the workplace free from prejudice. The students are exposed to a variety of cultures, through panel discussions, readings and a minority experience. The emphasis lies in looking at cultures that are different from their own ethnic and racial identity.[1]

---

[1]The citation for the course catalog was omitted to protect the anonymity of the MCCC and students enrolled in the course.

The MEF was used to structure this particular section of the course. I (Hornak) worked closely with the faculty member teaching the course to incorporate the framework and to ensure that proper care and attention was paid to all five steps. Together, we completely revised the curriculum to blend the framework with the management information that was required for the associate's degree.

Overview of Class Sessions and Activities

A brief description of the activities designed to address the cognitive goals in each step of the MEF are included in this section. The MEF was integrated into the course curriculum from the onset of the course and continued throughout the 16-week semester.

STEP 1: UNDERSTANDING CULTURE

- Students watched film clips from movies in which a ceremonial event took place that is familiar to a wide audience (e.g., a wedding in which the bride and groom are introduced as a married couple, a funeral procession and the process of saying good-bye, graduation ceremonies, and birthday parties). The students were encouraged to critically examine how participants shaped the events and followed the cultural norms already in place. Additionally, students were challenged to think about how these events are taught to generations of people and incorporated into one's culture.

- Students wrote down greetings they received for 1 day from people they knew. The students then examined the differences in the greetings and identified possible themes.

STEP 2: LEARNING ABOUT OTHER CULTURES

- Weekly class sessions were devoted to learning about other cultures. This was done in a variety of delivery methods, including film clips, articles, and guest speakers. The cultures included Asian American, African American, Latino American, Arab American, and Native American in addition to women, gay/lesbian/bi/transgender, and people with disabilities. The films included *The Laramie Project: The Matthew Shepard Story* (Kaufman & Baldwin, 2002), *Smoke Signals* (Eyre, Estes & Rosenfelt, 1998), and *Raise The Red Lantern* (Zhang & Chiu, 1991). Clips from newsmagazine shows and history documentaries were also used. The films, news clips, and documentaries were used to illustrate how events shape relations between cultural groups and to learn different aspects of the culture being studied.

- Students attended an event in which they were not the majority. It could be cultural, religious, or gender related as long as it was a meeting of a group in which they were not a member. The key criterion for this assignment was that students were strongly encouraged to challenge themselves. Following the experience, the students were required to write a paper reflecting on the experience.

STEP 3: RECOGNIZING AND DECONSTRUCTING WHITE CULTURE

- Students were asked to analyze White culture by listing on paper 10 items that describe White racial identity or White culture.
- Students first drew a picture of what is was like to be White in their community and then drew a picture of what they believe it is like to be a person of another racial group in their community.
- The instructor used Peggy McIntosh's (1989) work on privilege by reading privilege statements (e.g., I can watch television and see individuals from my race widely represented, I can send my children to any school) in class and asking students to think about whether they felt they had this privilege. The instructor then linked this to noticing racial privilege and the fact that most White people do not notice it because it is so much a part of their lives and American culture.

STEP 4: RECOGNIZING THE LEGITIMACY OF OTHER CULTURES

- An activity used to illustrate this step was looking at aspects of students' culture that are important to them and comparing those among students in the class. The students completed a worksheet with three columns: the first column invited students to list a cultural attribute that was of value to them, the second column invited students to explain how that attribute contributed to their sense of self, and the third column invited students to explain how this attribute affected how they see the world in their particular way.
- Students put together a business plan for an assigned region of the world. The students had to sell the business plan to the class, which meant not only learning about the other culture but also embracing its cultural attributes.

STEP 5: DEVELOPING A MULTICULTURAL OUTLOOK

- Students conducted an analysis of different institutions in U.S. society looking at how multiculturally oriented the institution is based on print media, year-end reports, and other media shared with the public. The students examined the items during class and in small groups reported how they viewed the commitment of the company to multiculturalism based on policies and the public image. The instructor encouraged groups to explore ways in which different cultural group's views are expressed and what those expressions say about the organization in a multicultural perspective.

- The final activity (similar to the previous one but given at the conclusion of the course) was assigned to the students as an ongoing challenge in their lives. They were encouraged to conduct continuing analysis of the offices and institutions with which they frequently came into contact. The students were charged to look at the media that institutions are distributing, talk with staff, and look at ways the institution is enhancing multiculturalism.

Assessing Multicultural Outcomes

I used an ethnographic approach to capture and detail the effectiveness of the MEF and its effects on students over the 16-week course by attending every session (3 hours per week) and taking field notes of what took place, including how students responded to the instructor, the activities, and to each other (Hornak, 2003). I augmented my participant observation by analyzing all documents created by and for the course, such as course documents (e.g., the syllabus and handouts) and student assignments (e.g., papers, reflective journals, and class presentations). I read and analyzed students' work throughout the semester for patterns and themes to consider with those that were simultaneously emerging through the participant observation.

In order to understand how the MEF may work differently for students at various cognitive levels regarding multicultural education, I invited students in the course to complete the White Racial Identity Scale at or near the beginning of the course. I also interviewed six students who represented the range of Helms's (1990, 1995) White racial identity statuses (i.e., contact, disintegration, reintegration, pseudo-independence, immersion/emersion, and autonomy). The interview process included three separate interviews. The first interview, conducted at the beginning of the semester, was designed to elicit background information in the context of the participant's life. The goal of the second interview, done at midsemester, concentrated on the details of the course and how the students were experiencing class activities and discussions. The final interview was conducted 4 to 5 weeks after the class was finished to allow for additional reflection. The purpose of the final interview was for the student to reflect on the impact of the class and the meanings this particular course had on their understandings of multicultural-ism and their own racial identity development. Conducting interviews over a 5-month time span, in conjunction with the participant observation and document analysis, yielded a comprehensive assessment of the impact of the course.

The six students who participated in the interviews were Boats, Madeline, Noah, Lucy, Chloe, and Tatiana (all pseudonyms). Boats is a White male in his late 30s who took classes part time and worked in a factory in a large city. He took classes to earn an associate's degree in general education and hoped to someday get a bachelor's degree. He worked the night shift and supervised a large, diverse crew of men. He is married and has two older children. Madeline is a White female in her early 20s who is engaged to be married and worked in a retail job. She took classes on a part-time basis and hoped to earn a bachelor's degree in business and become a retail store manager. She is planning to marry in a few years but currently lives at her mother's home to save money for the future. Noah is a single White male in his early 20s. He took community college courses near his home because he was dismissed from a 4-year school at the end of the last semester. He worked a part-time job and was unsure of his future educational plans. He described himself as an "easygoing, go with the flow kind of guy who likes to have fun." Lucy is a divorced female in her late 20s with two children. She described herself as half White (Italian) and half Native American. Her primary racial classification is White because, she said, she "feels more White and looks more White than Native or Italian and everybody thinks I am White. . . . I also pretty much act more White as well." Chloe is a married, White female in her late 20s who took this class because diversity and issues of diversity fascinate her. She described herself as "completely open minded and I actually have never lived in such a nondiverse area. It is very strange and I am not sure I like it here." Chloe attended two other schools and was unclear about her future career goals. She is a musician and also loves to draw and paint. "I am not sure I could make any money so I need something to fall back on." Tatiana is a female in her late 40s and took this class for fun. "I am recently divorced and also loved to learn . . . this class was right up my alley and so I decided to take it." She works full time as an administrative assistant and takes classes only every few years. She has a bachelor's degree in education and taught school for many years. She is retired from the public school system and described herself as a "lifelong learner." These six individuals represented a range of Helms's racial identity statuses, ages, gender, socioeconomic conditions, and reasons for pursuing higher education.

Moving Toward Self-Authored Multicultural Perspectives

The journey to a self-authored multicultural perspective took on varied meanings for participants. Many struggled with the concepts of identity and the multiple meanings of identity in their lives. The cognitive development levels of the students in this study, based on informal assessment, appeared to vary greatly, and their willingness to take risks in this journey was wide ranging. Some of the students viewed multiculturalism as an issue between Black and White people and tended to think in categorical (either/or) terms. Others in the class had the ability to view multiple perspectives and were willing to explore new ideas about diversity.

Based on personal statements, most students in this class were pursuing higher education more for career advancement purposes than for the excitement of engaging in higher learning. This affected their willingness to take risks and to challenge themselves fully in this pursuit of multicultural education and self-authorship. Despite these dynamics, growth was evident in three arenas: revisioning one's past, taking responsibility for learning about difference, and showing glimpses of culture creation.

Revisioning One's Past

A part of the MEF and the course activities encouraged students to explore their own cultures through exploration of their families and communities. When students were asked to reflect on the influential people and events in their lives that helped shaped their perspectives on race and multiculturalism, they conveyed responses that reflected a range of critical understanding about how racism is perpetuated and how their own attitudes and beliefs were developed. Nearly all students were able to identity just how their negative attitudes and beliefs were developed, but they varied in how they were anticipating that the work could be undone. For example, one woman wrote in her journal,

> I guess I understand how my parents have had such a strong influence over who I am. I really believe they are solely responsible for me and my attitudes. It is hard to change what you think when you have heard it for so long.

The immutability of this student's unwillingness to explore and challenge what her parents taught her represented an extreme perspective in the class. Her lack of agency, denial of personal responsibility, and reliance on external authority for knowledge creation was a major obstacle in her growth toward a self-authored multicultural perspective. However, most students showed definitive movement toward a critical assessment of their own views and their origins and were making plans to change.

Lucy's comment is a good example of an emerging critical perspective. Like the previous woman, Lucy's mother also communicated negative racial attitudes, but her mother used fear as way to reinforce her beliefs. Lucy said,

> I did not go to a school that was diverse and I could have in the neighbor-hood where I lived. But my mom sent me to a different school that was not very diverse. I think she was afraid of the school in my neighborhood. I also could have gone to a school on the reservation [where] my dad lived because I am Native American. But I feel like I grew up White.

Lucy referred to this decision by her mother as "her way of keeping me away from my father's heritage since they hated each other." She went on to say, "This class has made me think about how evil my mother made colored people[2] out to be. . . . She could and can say some mean stuff." At this point, Lucy paused; it was evident that talking about this was painful for her. As she became visibly uncomfortable, she quickly changed the subject and began talking about how being White can be scary. She said,

> Actually sometimes I think . . . it is scary being White; like I can't go in a "tough" neighborhood, where it's predominately other cultures and feel free to be myself and not worry about my safety. My mom said I should always be leery of, she uses the word "those" people. I guess it was a learned thing for me.

The class gave Lucy an opportunity to reflect on the lessons her mother taught her, and through that reflection, Lucy was on the verge of re-visioning her past. She was evaluating it and its lessons in another light.

Her discomfort reflects the pain involved when students are faced with critiquing parents whom they love. For Lucy, it was the start of understanding that authorities can be faulty but that love and respect for authorities is not reliant on their infallibility. As she works to deviate from the cultural lessons that have shaped her and to achieve a multicultural perspective, Lucy will need to recognize and claim her own values and beliefs and assert them consistently despite how much they may deviate from her mother's.

Other students also attributed the development of racist attitudes and beliefs to their parents. Boats understood how his parents communicated racism both explicitly and implicitly. He said,

> I wouldn't say I was brought up a racist, but back in 1976 I lived in the city and a couple of Black men moved in so my mom and dad . . . packed up

---

[2]The term "colored people" is retained in these direct quotes to maintain the original language of the students.

and moved to the . . . [country]. Why we moved from our friends because these Blacks moved in I am not sure. I was 12 at the time. That's all I ever knew. I didn't know any Black people. I just knew when they moved in, we moved out and I still do not live around any Blacks . . . I do work with some though.

When his parents moved out of this neighborhood, they sent an implicit message to Boats. He continued, "My father is extremely racist and to this day [he] chooses not to associate with or be friends with any Black people." He continued, "I am not proud of my father's racist attitudes and feel that raising my children differently will help." Another man had similar experiences with his father. He wrote in an assignment,

I myself [saw] racism and grew up with White privilege. When I was young, I met a young Black man named Prince. For fun, I brought him to my house to ride dirt bikes. My dad's reaction was what I expected. He didn't want him there. That pissed me off; he was a good guy. I [saw] nothing different between us but our skin [color]. My father only looks skin deep. I informed him how ignorant he was being. Till this day he has not changed, my brother [also] still has the same views, because he is around him all the time and my sister [even] shows racist views. I have stopped her [from] using the N word. [I think] people should interact no matter [what their] skin color, religion, or political views. The world would be a better place.

This student clearly was not internalizing his father's racist feelings but was well aware of where those feelings originated. In fact, he saw himself as a learner who was willing to be different than his family. In another assignment, this student wrote,

I think I am more accepting of others' differences because I attended a school with some diversity and have had a little bit of interaction with people who are not White. I do realize my exposure is not that great but I am willing to learn, unlike my family.

Lack of exposure to culturally diverse people and communities made it more challenging for students to more fully develop attitudes and beliefs different from those of their families. Boats faced similar challenges and began to realize how his lack of exposure had affected how he views being White. He said in the final interview,

I think the most important thing I learned in this class was that White is so much a part of who I am and who my family is I cannot see it. Everything is important when you are talking about race. To me that has never been important but it is now that I know being White is important and that I do have a race.

As the semester progressed, the students became more aware of how their communities and families helped shape their beliefs. Even Chloe, whose family influence would be considered much more positive and racially tolerant as compared to other students, understood the importance of unspoken messages:

> It is fascinating to me that my parents worked so hard to talk about other's differences and how those [differences] should be valued. But [they] were unwilling to move to a diverse area or take us to festivals and other events where we [my siblings] could actually experience firsthand some of what was unique. I hope that someday I will take my children to actual events instead of just paying lip service to the notion of difference.

Chloe's ability to assess her parents' behavior as inconsistent with their teachings shows that she has learned that authentic multicultural perspectives include both behaviors and attitudes. Her ability to discern this inconsistency from her childhood memories shows that she is becoming thoughtful about how she was raised. A male student went one step further and turned the critique on himself. In his final paper, he wrote,

> I think of colored people as inadequate a lot. I know that comes from my lack of exposure to them. I realize the power in actually becoming part of their life. I think the minority experience [activity in class] really helped me see how ignorant many of my beliefs and false impressions of colored people and people in general who are different came from. I really need to work on this aspect of my life and learn to not make snap judgments about people. I would not have known that without this class.

This student also demonstrates how difficult multicultural education can be with students who have little experience with those who are culturally different, coupled with home and community environments that create and reinforce prejudice and racism. Although the growth he experienced is evident, the fact that he continues to use the term "colored people" shows that his sensitivity to language issues has yet to develop.

The students quoted here both accepted and struggled with notions of their past and how it affected their current thoughts. The student's community of origin and parental and family attitudes toward individuals of color had a strong impact on their present attitudes toward diversity and multiculturalism. The activities and lessons in the course helped these students see how others' prejudiced attitudes have shaped their own attitudes about differences. The voices represented in this theme show how the students worked between the first two steps in the framework: understanding culture and exploring other cultures. As they were involved in learning about and experiencing other cultures, they were able to see their own more clearly. Because the activities and assignments asked students to situate their learning in their own experiences, they were able to see the interconnections between their past and their present and to deconstruct their present racial attitudes, prejudices, and identities. This theme illustrates important components of self-authorship. Breaking away from the negative influences of families and communities required that students develop their own beliefs and values rather than rely on external beliefs and values. However, in these cases, the challenge is for self-authorship to develop while maintaining the interpersonal loyalties of family, which often proves to be painful, as evidenced in Lucy's story. Students found support for this struggle in each other because many of them shared similar backgrounds and experiences. With their peers and instructor, students were able to construct meaning out of these common experiences. Through their reflections, students began to develop new possibilities for their own identities and destinies. They wanted to be more embracing and tolerant of differences than their parents, and, more important, they realized that they could begin to change society and culture through the lessons they planned to teach their own children.

Taking Responsibility for Learning About Those Who Are Culturally Different

Embedded in all five steps of the MEF is an understanding of culture, including students' own culture, and an understanding of those who are culturally different. All five steps required the students to examine and take responsibility for their beliefs about those who are culturally different. This was challenging for many students because it meant taking responsibility for long-held stereotypes and prejudices about individuals who are culturally different. Some students also realized that the learning had to be sustained, that it was easier to remain diligent with the structure and frequency of the class, but that they had to make a personal commitment beyond the semester. This student explained this realization:

> I just hope I will always remember all the issues we have learned about. I just hope that in 6 months down the road I don't just brush off issues of women's rights, religious rights, and minority problems of being accepted, etc. . . . . I never looked at it like that; I just really didn't care what people thought, which I know I can do most times as a White male. But some

people just . . . [cannot ignore the situation] because their battle really hurts their everyday life, and I was never aware of that before. I think it is important to learn about others and to educate my children about differences.

Additionally, this student's ability to admit that individuals from diverse populations struggle on a day-to-day basis shows that he was willing to critically examine his environment. He was also showing the motivation to apply what he learned in this class to daily situations and the ability to question knowledge he previously viewed as absolute.

Other students were also motivated to learn about culturally diverse others once they were exposed to the challenges diverse individuals face. Another male student wrote,

I can see how it is hard for a minority to voice their opinion in a group that is different than the one they are from. I could understand how afraid a minority would be when criticizing the majority group that they are around and I can see how being uncomfortable around a majority group can make a minority feel contempt for the people of the majority. . . . Around here darker skinned people can't even go get a drink without people saying something rude, staring or worse. This is the biggest thing I've learned so far. I learned that I need to be more tolerant of others, even if we have different viewpoints or different skin color and to be forgiving of others even if they have wronged or upset me.

Not only did this student develop a deeper understanding of the experience of skin-color discrimination, but he also began to understand his role in the mistreatment of those individuals. He was beginning to take responsibility for those actions and to question his attitudes toward diversity. In an interview, Noah expressed a similar understanding of his role in learning about differences. In response to a question about the changing face of diversity in the United States, Noah said,

You . . . need to be open-minded . . . and consider that they [individuals of color] may have come from different religions or grown up a different way than you have. Therefore if they say something and you think it's wrong, you'll have to go along with them and try to . . . make them understand how you feel. . . . I think that is easy for me to realize as a White person because usually what I say is alright and my whole race is not on the line.

Noah was also willing to admit that an action by one individual should not then be blamed on the entire race. This was a substantial step for Noah in his journey because he began the process resistant to challenging long-held beliefs and assumptions. He began the course believing that everyone was treated the same regardless of skin color and that he treated everyone the same. The acknowledgment that this is not true is a big step in his journey to a self-authored multicultural perspective.

Although many students came to own responsibility for learning about culturally diverse others, others demonstrated the challenge in reaching this goal. Students had to come to an understanding of their own culture in order to accomplish this goal, and at times their inability to understand the implications of Whiteness was a stumbling block in owning responsibility for learning about other cultures. A female student said,

> I know my skin is White, but that does not mean anything to me that is meaningful. I had a hard time thinking of things that are associated with being White in class the other day. I guess being White means being White. . . . I do not think of myself as White everyday or really ever until you made me think about it. I do believe that I have a hard time talking about being White because it is all around me. I live in a White town, [have a] White job, watch White TV, and all the other things we talked about in class. I can understand that so maybe I do get it.

Her understanding of the implications of being White is not yet developed but shows her willingness to move toward a deeper level of understanding by "getting it." She does not quite know what to do with her new discoveries, but she appreciates that simply understanding Whiteness and its role in her life is a dramatic change in her perspective. This represents a dramatic first step in her journey to a self-authored multicultural perspective.

These students' ability to personally begin to take responsibility for learning about differences and other racial and ethnic groups was rooted in the MEF curriculum. A powerful activity generated by the framework is the exploration of other cultures and immersing oneself into a situation where one is a minority. One of the most important aspects of promoting self-authorship is grounding learning in students' own reality. Since many of these students live in an area that is racially homogeneous, simulated exercises like the minority experience were extremely thought provoking. Through journaling and reflecting on their experiences, real and simulated, the students were able to see that they were not taking responsibility for their own beliefs about others who are different. As the semester progressed, the students began to accept that multiple truths exist and that their own values about multiculturalism are important in the journey. In addition, their ability to examine knowledge and how it had evolved became more complex.

Glimpses of Culture Creation

This theme reflects students' discovery of their ability and desire to shape and change culture (Step 5). This appeared to be a two-part process, where students first needed to explore the notions of White privilege and then develop a multicultural perspective that included action. The notion of White privilege has been explored in other themes. In glimpses of culture creation, White privilege was something that was explored in relation to diverse others rather than owning White privilege. Students whose comments reflected this theme were able to see how their own actions and beliefs could begin not only to change their own perceptions but also slowly to change their families, communities, work environments, and ultimately society around them. Tatiana reflected on the skills and tools she needs to thrive in the diverse world in which she lives:

> I think you need experience and exposure to [diverse] others. I think the experience with different people in [a small town] is difficult because it is so White, but why not get out and experience the world around? Even traveling to a larger, more diverse city and spending some time [would help]. I loved the minority experience because it forced me to see what it was like to not be part of the majority. It made me grow as a person and see the privilege I have.

Tatiana not only admitted her privilege but also acknowledged that living in a small town was inhibiting in her desire to live in a multicultural society. She was willing to travel beyond the safety of her small town to experience diversity. Her desire to engage in activities that put her in contact with culturally diverse people helped her make choices based on multiple truths rather than relying solely on the instructor's knowledge.

While Tatiana was reflecting a change in her perspective that was likely to change the ways she would interact in community settings, Madeline was already changing the way she interacted with customers in her store. She said,

> I think it is negative to be part of another racial group because they are treated differently. A lot of times they are treated badly because of the way they look. I don't think it's fair. I try not to make fun of them when people come into my store. I have to admit that sometimes I treat and watch colored people more because of their color. That is wrong and I have learned that is part of me being White, but not right. I guess I was never aware that I did that before this class. The sad part is, I think I was acting like this in the store and hurting others, because I was taught that and it is just part of my life. I can . . . say that I know lots of others who think this way and I want to challenge them to think and act differently. Why are we hurting people because of the color of their skin? It is not fair.

Madeline's ability to question the external authority figures she has relied on for so long shows she is beginning to make meaning of her actions on the basis of her own values and identity. She is moving toward an understanding of how her thoughts direct her actions and the acknowledgment that these are rooted in past assumptions. She also said, "Just because I did not know I was doing this does not make it right or an excuse to keep doing it." Her confidence in this understanding of her own behavior and its impact led her to the realization that she has responsibility in educating others. Similar to Madeline's comments, Noah talked about how people in society get treated:

> I guess sometimes I do get special treatment because people look at me differently because I'm huge and much larger than the normal White male. So when I walk in a place I'm usually the tallest White man in the place. I think I have learned that I should not be taking advantage of the fact that I am a very tall White man. I know I have used this to my advantage on more than one occasion.

Noah's comment reflected a pattern of advancement that materialized throughout the semester. At the time of the first interview, he was unwilling and unable to address notions of White privilege. As the semester progressed, both in interviews and in written work, Noah began to not only acknowledge White privilege but also address ways in which he could give up some privilege. He said, "I know I can be more inclusive in who I hang out with, but also I need to begin broadening my horizons in terms of education and where I choose to take my classes." The discovery that he could give up some of his privilege by "broadening his horizons" and interacting with diverse individuals is a significant step for Noah. He began the semester unwilling to engage in class discussions, but in one-on-one interviews, he had strong opinions about what was going on in the class. When challenged to speak up in class, he embraced the challenge and began to share his thoughts with the class.

The notion of White privilege was a topic that many of the students feared and were unwilling to acknowledge. The goal of the MEF in addressing White privilege was not to punish the students for having racial privilege but to help students come to the realization that all cultures and races should be valued. Students who initially appeared to place knowledge creation and truth solely on external authorities (e.g., Noah and Madeline) showed major cognitive growth. Along the same theme, Tatiana talked about being a middle-aged White woman, saying,

> White privilege makes me sad because I have to wonder how many things have been given to me just because of the color of my skin. Not because I

was so worthy of them, but because I am White. It makes me very sad. . . .
I wish I could do more but I am just not sure what to do and if one White
woman would really make a difference.

Tatiana was willing and able to acknowledge her White privilege, but she
was also willing to think about ways of reshaping her White identity. She
recognized the complex level at which she was thinking about White
privilege and her willingness to relinquish some of the privilege. In the final
interview, she said, "I guess I was unaware that I could become so close to self-
actualization in terms of racial identity. I always thought of myself as a higher
level thinker, but now I believe I truly am because of this class." Tatiana's
ability to see how this class has changed her perspectives on diversity is an
important step in her journey to a self-authored multicultural perspective.

Tatiana also talked about wanting to "become an activist for racial and
cultural change." When asked how she would pursue this agenda, she said, "I
am sure there are ways to become an activist for social change, like rallies
and other big events but it takes a very long time. . . . I am not sure I have
the energy or time to make that commitment." She did say that she would be
getting more involved with groups that represent people who have been historically discriminated against and said, "Hopefully I can make some good
connections to people who are well connected." The desire to become an
activist for racial and cultural change shows Tatiana's desire to take action
on an external level in addition to the ability to recognize that developing a
self-authored multicultural perspective requires a reflection of self and
personal actions.

Challenges in Developing a Self-Authored Multicultural Perspective

Whereas the previous section recounted growth in developing a multicultural
perspective, this section outlines the challenges students faced in this journey.
These challenges indicate the difficulty of achieving a self-authored multicultural perspective, particularly in the areas of owning White privilege, lack of
exposure to diverse others, and failure to see the applicability of a multicultural perspective to their own lives.

Owning White Privilege

Owning White privilege was a constant challenge for students and became a
significant barrier to developing a self-authored multicultural perspective.
Many times, differentiating racial and other privileges, especially class privilege, proved problematic. When students grew up in poor, working and

lower-middle-class households, they often had a difficult time understanding issues of White privilege because they perceived themselves as having less than many other people in this society. Additionally, in the initial phases of learning about White privilege, many students had difficulty because they perceived it as something that made them a bad person and was something they could not change. This became uncomfortable for participants in class and in interviews because, as Tatiana reported, "feeling like this [feeling aware of White privilege] makes me feel like a bad person and my skin color is out of my control." Nearly all the students in the class shared Tatiana's comments. The struggle to accept and own White privilege shows students' intrapersonal dilemma with self-authoring a multicultural perspective because recognizing ownership of White privilege causes them to reconsider their own identity and their own relationship to both society and individuals within society. The common response of guilt and feeling bad about oneself often stifles students from further education on multicultural issues and truncates the critical reflection necessary to come to terms with privilege and determining personal and social action.

In addition to feelings of guilt, students also perceived a contradiction in applying White privilege to all Whites, viewed as parallel to stereotyping, as this was just the type of behavior they were being encouraged to change in themselves. A male student articulated this well in his journal:

> I feel that the White privilege is a stereotype. I've been tagged this name and I don't want it. I'll earn the title that I want to have. I feel that a Black man can earn any title that he wishes to have. In fact, we all earn whatever we want and go wherever we choose to go.

After the same class session, another male student wrote, "I work three jobs to get better and still am going to school—it does not matter that I am White." The intersection of race and class was the most difficult for students to differentiate. Although the few students who came from higher socioeconomic families also wondered about the reality of their own privilege, students from lower socioeconomic backgrounds not only refuted their own privilege but also applied a meritocratic perspective to their analysis of privilege and opportunity in U.S. society. In a written response to a class session about power, a male student challenged the notion of unearned power:

> I'm not exactly sure what . . . [the instructor] meant by saying Whites had the power, because power is used in so many ways. As individuals Whites don't have any more power than any other colors. Any American can vote, find a job, or even start a business. Anybody colored or not can find a job; it

takes a little hard work, ambition, and determination. Any African American person can work where I'm employed; I wasn't hired based on my ethnicity. The most ridiculous thing I heard the entire class was "Why is it when you watch the news you see more people of color being convicted of crimes than Whites?" That statement was absurd. More of them are convicted because they commit more crimes. The court system is not racist; people just need to quit breaking the damn law. . . . To sum up my thoughts, a high crime and African American populated city like Detroit may never be even a middle class city but the people and families that want to get out and further their lives have the possibilities. It is not in Omaha in 1963 anymore and people of color may buy a house wherever they may please. I am aware that it is not only people of color that are located in Detroit. White people and White families are located there also, but to make something out of themselves people need to get jobs and stop committing crimes. Anybody can further their own lives if they want to, I don't care what color they are!

His strong belief in meritocracy, that all opportunities are open to all if individuals work hard enough, clouded his ability to see White privilege as a viable lens for explaining class difference between racial groups. This focus on meritocracy and lack of ability to critically consider the intersections between race and class highlights the complexity required in the cognitive dimension of self-authorship in developing a multicultural perspective.

Similarly, women in the class also struggled with the intersection of White privilege and sexism. Some felt that their negative experiences with sexism far outweighed any White privilege that may have accumulated. A female explained this:

By the way, I do not feel I have the power you speak of because I am White. I am also at the mercy of the White man, and I really don't care if this is considered less of a problem than an African American woman because *my* life has been made much more difficult due to my gender. Who is to say whose hardships are less important than others?

In reviewing students' assignments and their participation in class discussion, it became apparent that students who operated from a more simplistic perspective were unable to perceive the distinct contributions of multiple avenues of oppression. If they claimed an identity that they perceived to lack privilege (e.g., being female, of lower social class), they were unable to consider how one oppressed identity might be qualitatively different than another and how multiple oppressed identities might increase the impact of White privilege. These students struggled because of their cognitive assumptions, which limited their ability to critically examine and deconstruct their racial lives. Students who could consider the impact and distinct contribution of multiple identities showed cognitive complexity and flexibility, which are indicative of self-authorship. Additionally, as some students moved closer to ownership of White privilege, their ability to critically examine and deconstruct their racial lives increased. The challenge of differentiating types of privileges persisted throughout the semester, but as the course progressed, many were able to move closer to ownership of White privilege.

Lack of Exposure to Diverse Others

Lack of exposure to diverse others was common among many of the participants in the course. Many students lived in the small, rural, and racially homogeneous community where the campus is located. Despite limited exposure to diverse others, students were challenged to think about the ubiquitous nature of Whiteness; their lack of exposure caused challenges for the instructor in moving them toward an understanding of multiculturalism. Many struggled early because of their limited exposure to diverse others, but as the course progressed and they were intentionally exposed to other racial and ethnic groups, students were more willing to learn about and embrace the differences.

Lucy was asked in an interview to think about being White and what that meant to her as a college student. She said,

> I do not really think about being White, but am beginning to realize that White is all around me. I guess it is so much a part of my life that I cannot see it. Is this a bad thing? What can I do about that? I am just now beginning to realize my lack of exposure to colored people has tainted me being White or rather what it means to be White—wait I guess I am trying to say it has tainted even the notion of being White. I need to think about it and how it is all around me.

Developmentally, Lucy was beginning to internalize what it means to be White in America and to recognize the impact that has on her life. As Lucy became more aware of the ubiquitous nature of Whiteness in her world, she became more accepting of this because she realized this discovery was not a threat to her identity.

It was clear that many students struggled with notions of diversity because this knowledge and exposure challenged their sense of identity. Step 2 of the MEF is learning about other cultures. This occurred throughout the semester as the students were exposed to many different ethnic and racial groups. Many of the students had limited experience interacting with individuals from other racial groups. As the semester progressed, it became clear that having authentic relationships and interactions with diverse others was valuable. A male student wrote in a journal response paper,

> When we first started learning about people who are not White I cared but not really. I figured I would get through this class and be done with it. As I have learned about other people I see how cool people who are not White are. They do really neat things on holidays, cool clothes, and languages are neat. I sometimes wish I had more interaction with non-White people.

This is a good example of how learning about others can minimize personal biases. He describes his own struggle with the cognitive dimension of multiculturalism and how working through those issues paved the way for accepting diversity.

A male student who read about Arab Americans during the class also highlighted the importance of exposure and also the necessity for students to take advantage of opportunities for exposure. He wrote,

> I also noticed that as I was reading I was skimming the paragraphs and sentences that broke down their culture and religions. Maybe subconsciously I was trying to stay the same and not expand my point of view, in turn keeping me biased. After I noticed I was doing this, I made a conscious effort to read and understand every word and sentence before I moved onto the next and I am glad that I did.

This student emphasized that mere exposure is not sufficient for substantive multicultural learning. He caught himself minimizing other cultures and understood the danger in that. Removing bias requires the conscious effort that this student demonstrated and the diligence to develop independently. Students need to discover that there are benefits to building relationships with people different from themselves in order to sustain the effort. A female student said, "Stereotypes set restrictions on me; I was setting limitations on myself. I could have met a number of new and interesting people, if I hadn't restricted my interactions with the people I had stereotypes against." These students confirm the necessity of developing self-authorship in order to make significant progress through multicultural education. Movement toward a self-authored multicultural perspective required the students to reevaluate what they knew about diversity and contemplate what life might be like as a member of another cultural/racial group. While some students were able to make more progress in creating a self-authored perspective, many were unable to challenge or question the knowledge they had gained from their families and communities.

Failure to See Applicability of a Multicultural Perspective to Their Lives

When students are unable to make meaning through multiple lenses, they are trapped in a unidimensional view of the world. Many were unwilling to question their respected authorities and were unable to understand that their own worldview was capable of adaptation. For them, knowledge was fixed, and social constructions could not be reconstructed. The failure to see the applicability of a multicultural perspective to their lives embodies these struggles. Although students came to understand how their lack of exposure prohibited them from embracing differences, many were unwilling to see its importance since they did not plan to live or work among diverse others. In addition, the students were unwilling to admit that their lives or their communities may change in unforeseen ways. A male student in class said,

> I have a great job in this town. I work with pretty much all White people or people who act White and I am going to stay. I guess I do not see why it is important to think about these issues.

Similarly, a female student said on her final exam, "I am not going anywhere and I would bet that not a ton of colored people are moving in so what is the big deal?" These two students represented an extreme position, but many other students made comments like Noah did in our second interview: "I have taken a class like this before and it is going the same way. I feel like since I will never live in a huge city that is mostly diverse this does not matter to me." When asked to think more broadly about the global nature of multiculturalism and living in a world where White is not the majority, he said, "I think people have been saying that for so long that many do not believe it to be true. I think White will always be the majority."

Failure to see the applicability of a multicultural perspective in changing one's behavior was a challenge that was left unfinished at the conclusion of the course. At the conclusion of the course, an interview with the course instructor was conducted to gather data on her perspective of the course. Having taught the course several times previously, she had outcome information on other classes that was not available to the researcher. In the follow up interview, the instructor commented on this. She observed,

> I think some of that comes from the course being taught at a community college. I also believe that these students are many times such dualist thinkers that to embrace diversity and multiculturalism with limited exposure is very foreign to them. I also believe developmentally this class has made an advance that many other classes have not and that is a direct reflection of the

incorporation of the framework [the MEF]. In previous classes some of the same information was presented but the organization really differed. Having the direction and guidance of the [five-step] model was a major reason for these outcomes.

These students were not unlike other college students who fail to see the value of learning to improve self and expand one's perspective. The belief that a college education should have definitive utility often interferes with the development of self-authorship, as was evident in the comments of some of the students in this course. However, the incorporation of the MEF did move students closer to both a more complex understanding of multicultural education and self-authorship. It was evident in their written and oral stories over the semester and in the interviews. It is tempting to dismiss some of these challenges by focusing on the fact that the course was offered at a rural community college; this would be a mistake. The candid nature of this assessment, which was possible largely because of the quality of the rapport developed between the observer, instructor, and students, allowed valuable insights to be gleaned about the attitudes and experiences students have, no matter how surprising or even distasteful these attitudes may be to others.

Conclusion

The development of a self-authored multicultural perspective is an extremely complex process that requires the reconstruction of knowledge, beliefs, and values that arise from living in a racist society where privilege is based on skin color. It is a lifelong journey that includes introspectively developing one's own identity cognizant of the elements in life that reinforce a closed perspective on multiculturalism. That identity is intricately involved in the development of a multicultural perspective is key to both understanding the struggles students (and all people) have in this arena and the difficulty in creating change through educational interventions such as the Learning Partnerships Model. Since the elements that reinforce a simplistic perspective on multiculturalism often permeate one's life span, students need to learn to question the values and beliefs associated with their upbringing and in the process disavow some of the teachings of parents and families they love and respect. They may have to judge the idyllic small town where they were raised as insufficient experience for living in a multicultural world. These two tasks require that students learn to follow their own paths in developing an identity that is unique and relevant to the challenges they will face in their future. Their cognitive structures need to routinely accommodate ambiguity and critical thinking. Their strength of self needs to weather instability in interpersonal relationships that may arise as they seek congruency between their values, beliefs, and loyalties.

Approaches based on the Learning Partnerships Model that seek to help students develop a self-authored multicultural perspective need to help students stretch cognitively while simultaneously giving them emotional support to allow intrapersonal and interpersonal stretching. In our work with students around multicultural issues, when students began to discover that the formulas they were given were flawed, deep emotions came to the surface. Because it is difficult to confront family members and friends about their racist beliefs and expressions, students may need practice making these confrontations through role plays or scripts. However, they more often need to be given the space to cry and express the sorrow and disappointment that results from more realistic appraisals of their own beliefs and actions and their origins. One woman in the class wrote about the pain that she experienced in the class:

> I understand that diversity awareness is important but it is also very painful to learn about. I spent many nights not sleeping after this class. Sometimes because I was mad at how evil some people are but other times because I was trying to think of ways that I could help make the world a better place for others.

Although she does not directly acknowledge that her pain was derived from the critique of her own beliefs and actions, she is beginning to place herself within the context of change by showing that she suspects a link between that pain, evil, and herself. We believe that the emotionality inherent in a curriculum seeking to promote a multicultural perspective makes it more important that the educational approaches are true partnerships between teacher and learner. In this partnership, what is taught is not only the content but also a way of being and a way of responding to the challenges of living a racist society. The teachers, whether they are peers or instructors, need to share the struggles in their own experiences in developing a multicultural perspective and the fears they encountered along the way. Perhaps the personal support that students require needs to be more explicitly outlined in the MEF in order to achieve its goals. Of course, this call for personal support resonates with the foundational perspective on student learning that Sanford (1962) offered—that students need both challenge and support to achieve cognitive, interpersonal, and intrapersonal learning goals.

The story of the diversity management course at Midwest City Community College clearly showed the challenges that students encountered in developing a multicultural perspective. The MEF helped provide the support for students' construction of knowledge by grounding learning in their own experiences and by leading them through a step-by-step process of increasing cognitive complexity and in increasing personalization of key constructs. The MEF asked students not only to learn about multicultural issues from an outside perspective but also to become insiders—to understand how their own culture and perspectives came to be and how, through their actions and choices, they can change themselves and the culture around them. That some students were able to achieve the goals of the MEF while others struggled may be related to the fact that students came to the class with varying experiences with both the topic as a subject matter for a college course and varying degrees of lived experiences with cultural difference. We are left to wonder if providing greater challenge and support to those with less experience, as suggested by Sanford (1962), would have helped them achieve more of a self-authored multicultural perspective during the course. Indeed, if this were the case, we would strongly recommend that providing the personal support discussed in the previous paragraph be incorporated as a strategy of the MEF.

When the instructor compared the class using the MEF to the general curriculum she had used for the past 5 years, she felt that a curriculum intentionally designed to address culture and White privilege from students' personal perspectives increased their ability to change the way they thought about culture and society. Although this change was subtle in some students and more evident in others, the constant reframing of culture, its creation, and students' roles in maintaining and changing culture helped them reconsider the ways in which they viewed their experiences and the world. The instructor used examples such as wedding rituals, religious ceremonies, holidays, and family gatherings to encourage the students to think about culture, which helped students construct their own knowledge about culture and to see themselves as cultural beings. A student who attended a religious ceremony that was outside her faith tradition, observed,

> I felt stupid not knowing what to do at certain times during the service and everyone else seemed to understand what was going on and what to do. I felt like people were staring at me and knew that I did not belong. I really think I view some of my cultural . . . [attributes] differently having experienced this. I see that I am just as big a part of the creation of my culture as my parents and family are in dictating to me what we will do at certain events. When [the professor] talked about weddings and the rituals of introducing the bride and groom for the first time, I realized that yes, White people may look the same but are all very different, but nobody really has to learn how to be White. It is just ingrained in us socially . . . very interesting.

Through this assignment, two things were accomplished. This student began to understand what it was like to be a cultural outsider, and she began to see how culture is created and that she plays a role in this creation. The instructor's ability to communicate the importance of rituals as cultural constructions, coupled with the student's own experience, created mutually constructed knowledge that proved to be powerful in broadening the student's perspective.

Ultimately, the ability to take the perspective of another is a key prerequisite to achieving a self-authored multicultural perspective. This ability requires the cognitive flexibility to be reflexive about previously held beliefs, the identity strength to prevent a sense of loss of one's own importance while placing another's position as paramount, and the interpersonal complexity to do this in a way that communicates respect and compassion without patronizing and making assumptions. The following student demonstrates the changes in thinking necessary for perspective taking:

> Once we had a drill and four men did not finish because they were tired. I was one of the four. Another guy was a Black man who did not finish. Well, when we got into trouble by the drill sergeant the Black man acted like it was a big deal and that he was being singled out because he was Black. Well at the time I thought, "Get over it, we all got into trouble." Well now 10 years later as I think about that event, it was about being Black, at least for him. I made a judgment as a White man and did not even think that his [interpretation] was about being Black and that I could not understand that. It is like being followed in a store. I can be followed and it would not be a big deal but it may be if I were looking at the situation from a different color lens my interpretation would be different.

As a result of the change in perspective, this student can now apply a "color lens" to his analysis of both past and future situations. Because the course and its use of the MEF validated students as knowers, situated learning in their own experiences, and encouraged a mutual construction of meaning about those experiences, the tools and abilities that students gained in the course can be transferred to their lives outside class. The focus on culture as a lived construct gives students an opportunity to apply these lessons on a daily basis.

The fact that diversity or multicultural education happens early and often in a student's college experience reinforces the use of the Learning Partnerships Model in any multicultural education intervention. Whether it be in orientation, in student staff or leadership training, in the classroom, or in service-learning activities, if diversity educators incorporate the assumptions and principles of the Learning Partnerships Model in their multicultural education efforts, students would be more likely to see themselves as intimately involved in culture as it is perpetuated and culture as it is changed. Much of the ineffectiveness of diversity or multicultural education can be placed on the common practice of placing the student outside the issues relating to multiculturalism. When we teach about the culturally different, we promote the notion that the students themselves are not cultural beings. When we fail to include students' own experiences as learning opportunities, we communicate that they should learn only from others' lessons. Providing educational experiences that situate learning in students' experience, allow for the mutual construction of meaning, and validate students' capacity to know encourages them to use their own life experiences (or lack thereof) as lessons for multicultural understanding. The assumptions of knowledge as complex and socially constructed, the inclusion of self as central to knowledge construction, and the sharing of expertise and authority in knowledge construction helps students understand that they can create knowledge and that their peers are also valid knowledge constructors. These assumptions are absolutely necessary for students to gain the most from multicultural education. Without a community of knowledge constructors in the setting, the expertise of the teacher or leader (or the tools they use) becomes the sole source of knowledge, invalidating the notion that we all have culture and placing the teacher's culture and experiences as central. This discounts what students have to offer, which would be a critical mistake to continue to make as U.S. student populations continue to become more and more diverse.

References

Allen, K. R., Floyd-Thomas, S. M., & Gillman, L. (2001). Teaching to transform: From volatility to solidarity in an interdisciplinary family studies class room. *Family Relations, 50*(4), 317–326.

Baxter Magolda, M. B. (1999). *Creating contexts for learning and self-authorship: Constructive-developmental pedagogy.* Nashville: Vanderbilt University Press.

Baxter Magolda, M. (2001). *Making their own way: Narratives for transforming higher education to promote self-development.* Sterling, VA: Stylus.

Chang, M. J. (2002). The impact of undergraduate diversity course requirement on students' racial views and attitudes. *Journal of General Education, 51*(1), 21–42.

Chizhik, E. W., & Chizhik, A. W. (2002). A path to social change: Examining students' responsibility, opportunity, and emotion toward social justice. *Education and Urban Society, 34*(3), 283–297.

Dunlop, N. (2000). Teaching and learning with the seventh generation: The "Inward Bound" experience. *Journal of Experiential Education, 23*(3), 150–156.

Eyre, C. (Director), & Estes, L. & Rosenfelt, S. (Producers). (1998) *Smoke signals* [Film]. (Available from Miramax Films)

Helms, J. E. (1990). *Black and white racial identity attitudes: Theory, research and practice.* Westport, CT: Greenwood.

Helms, J. E. (1995). An update of Helms's white and people of color racial identity models. In J. G. Ponterotto, J. Manuel Casas, L. S. Suzuki, & C. M. Alexander (Eds.), *Handbook of multicultural counseling* (pp. 181–198). Thousand Oaks, CA: Sage.

Hornak, A. M. (2003). *Implementing a curricular framework in the exploration of White racial identity.* Unpublished doctoral dissertation, Michigan State University, East Lansing.

Kaufman, M. (Director), & Baldwin, D. (Producer). (2002). *The Laramie project: The Matthew Shepard story* [Film]. (Available from HBO)

McIntosh, P. (1989, July/August). White privilege: Unpacking the invisible knapsack. *Peace and Freedom,* 10–12.

Ortiz, A. M., & Rhoads, R. A. (2000). Deconstructing whiteness as part of a multicultural educational framework: From theory to practice. *Journal of College Student Development, 41*(1), 81–93.

Robinson, H., Wolffe, R., Hunt, P. S., & Hoerr, N. A. (2002). Creating cross-cultural connections. *Urban Education, 37*(4), 533–547.

Sanford, N. (1962). Developmental status of the entering freshman. In N. Sanford (Ed.), *The American college* (pp. 253–282) New York: Wiley.

Zhang, Y. (Director), & Chiu, F. (Producer). (1991). *Raise the red lantern* [Film]. (Available from Metro-Goldwyn-Mayer)

5

AN URBAN LEADERSHIP INTERNSHIP PROGRAM

IMPLEMENTING LEARNING PARTNERSHIPS "UNPLUGGED" FROM CAMPUS STRUCTURES

Katie Egart and Melissa P. Healy

"FEELS LIKE SOMETHIN'S ON THE WAY"

Certain moments in life quickly come and are quickly replaced by subsequent steps in life's endless dance. Other moments become immortalized in memory as events, feelings, or understandings that influence every other step that is ever taken. This summer seems to be filled with those glimpses of the past that lead directly into the future. The first foreshadowing moment in time took place on I-90 as I steered my neatly packed car north towards the Carnegie Exit and Case Western Reserve University. My stomach was doing cartwheels that were somewhat reminiscent of those that I felt . . . as my parents and I neared Miami University for the first time. This time, all responsibility would be falling on my own shoulders, and I was both grateful and wary. A tough school year left me drained physically and emotionally, and it was both difficult and exciting to leave the safety of home to strike out completely alone. Suddenly, the Cleveland skyline appeared in my windshield and I pulled myself away from my thoughts to catch the unfamiliar lyrics playing on the radio, "I hear a sound and turn to see a new direction on that rusty weathervane. And my breath is snatched away, and a chill runs up my spine. Feels like somethin's on the way." (Barbara)

Each summer, 25 Miami University students set out from their rural Ohio campus to one of five destinations: Dayton, Columbus, Cincinnati, Cleveland, or Chicago. They are Urban Leadership interns, set to immerse themselves in a 10-week paid full-time internship combining professional practice and service in an urban setting. The students engage in work that encompasses many disciplines, including medicine, law, social work, speech pathology, psychology, education, and architecture. The Urban Leadership Internship Program (ULIP) is designed to challenge these bright students through work, service, and urban exploration. At its best, the program can act as the "crossroads" between "following formulas" to "becoming the author of one's life" (Baxter Magolda, 2001, p. 189). For most, it is a critical step on the journey to self-authorship. The structure of the program encourages interns to leave the security of their identities as students with identifiable teachers and fairly certain answers to become urban explorers, full-time employees, and city dwellers.

The teachers in this new setting are not so easily recognizable as such: the homeless man passed by on the same corner every morning, the supervisors and coworkers at the job, the clients at the service site, and the urban context itself. The educational assumptions of the Learning Partnerships Model do not have to be manufactured or manipulated in such a setting; they are givens. In students' urban environments, knowledge about the work, the community, and one's own role and responsibilities is complex and socially constructed. As the intern negotiates her new identity and environment, she is central to the process of making meaning out of her own experience, finding herself on a peer level with others in the workplace and sharing mutually in learning and doing. The Urban Leadership Internship Program consciously implements Baxter Magolda's three pedagogical principles: validating learners' capacity as knowledge constructors (encouraging conscious reflection through writing and group process), situating the learning in the learner's experience (having jobs and engaging in community service in urban settings), and defining learning as mutually constructing meaning (working closely with coworkers, roommates, internship coordinator, supervisors, and role models). The goal of growth towards self-authorship is made explicit. As will be apparent from in-depth assessment of the experience of interns from the summer of 2002, indeed, "somethin's on the way."

Program Description

The ULIP is administered through the University Honors and Scholars Program. Students with grade-point averages of 3.3 or higher may apply to participate. About 25 students (usually 75% to 85% female participants) are selected each year for a paid full-time internship in an urban setting. The program is educationally focused on a holistic learning experience, not mere résumé building. The students participate in a 10-week "sprint course" prior to embarking on the internship. In this course, students meet once a week to explore themes of learning through experience, contemporary urban issues, and keys to active engagement and reflection to develop a focus on conscious learning and growth. During the internship itself, each student writes weekly guided journal entries that cover topics ranging from daily work schedule and routines to service models, critical incidents, and one-on-one interviews with professionals. They also compose a final journal reflection that allows them to consider the entire experience and incorporate a personal assessment of their initial goals, how they learned, and their perception of overall challenges and growth in personal values and interests that developed through the course of the 10-week period.

Miami University provides a stipend of $3,500 for the 10-week internship. This allows the internship selection process to begin with the student's own ideas of what he or she would like to do with the opportunity rather than a "choose from this list" type of placement. The student is required to give at least 1 day of service per week to an urban nonprofit organization during the 10 weeks of full-time work at an internship located within the urban center. This student-centered, urban-focused learning experience is meant to provide students with challenges on many levels to develop as knowers—epistemologically, intrapersonally, and interpersonally. Often, the first challenge for a student selected into the program is narrowing down the universe of possibilities for work. This process of deciding for oneself what to do launches the journey to self-authorship.

Navigating this initial task presents the students with a significant challenge at the outset. This process directly calls on the student to determine her goal for the internship. Because the student is both challenged and supported by the coordinator's experience and internship resources, she has the freedom to investigate, fail, succeed, question, and ask for help. In the end, each student should feel she has secured her opportunity through her own effort and initiative. The student owns her experience as well as takes responsibility for her choices. Through this process, the student must take into consideration her own abilities and readiness for a particular opportunity; this situates learning in the learner's experience and shows how self is central to knowledge construction. Moreover, the process demands that the student communicate with diverse others, including her family, friends, faculty, internship providers, and the program coordinator, in determining the best fit for her interests; this illustrates the principle of learning as mutually constructing meaning and sharing expertise and authority.

The preparatory sprint course, held during the 10 weeks prior to beginning the summer internship, focuses on identifying each student's personal starting point as well as personal, professional, and academic goals for the summer. The syllabus includes readings and discussion on topics of learning through experience, internship preparation, urban issues, and service learning. Guest speakers involved in urban issues join the class frequently. By the beginning of the internship, students should have a heightened self-awareness regarding values, identity, and personal career interests and familiarity with at least one urban issue. Knowing their "starting point" allows students to assess their own growth on a variety of dimensions at the end of the internship experience. This solidly places the student in the category of "knower." In this way, the preinternship preparation utilizes the Learning Partnerships Model in an effort to prepare students for a further journey in self-authorship through the actual urban internship experience.

Guided reflection is an integral component of the program. As students proceed throughout the internship, they are given weekly journal "prompts" to reflect on a variety of aspects of work, supervision, service, urban living, self, and learning. Students ground and construct their new knowledge in their direct experience as well as in relationship to others through these journal writings and with the support of reflective group gatherings during the internship. In my (Katie) initial attempt to assess student learning in the internship program in a qualitative way, I reviewed student journal documents with basic questions in mind, such as, What did students learn, and how did they learn it? As I perused journal entries and feedback from the program archives, I discovered some remarkable illustrations of developmental growth in the students' own words. Students reported on learning that took place in many contexts, including the professional internship, the service component, and the urban environment, and through interpersonal relationships in all these sites.

On exploring these contexts for learning, I found myself reflecting on Baxter Magolda's (1999, 2001) writing on constructive-developmental pedagogy and the notion of self-authorship. Her development model seemed to be a useful template for the *cognitive, intrapersonal,* and *interpersonal* learning in which the interns engaged. Students reported learning about objective topics (cognitive), such as the urban environment, career options, and work habits. They also wrote, often profoundly, of learning about self (intrapersonal), such as values, interests, abilities, and decision-making and learning styles. And in characterizing how they learned, many described learning in and with others (interpersonal), such as work in collaborative groups, living with others, and interaction with clients and with diverse others in the urban environment. All the elements of the internship (job, living situation, transportation, the city, and the service) are considered the "texts" for the learning. But it is each student's integration of activities, concepts, assumptions, and questions that results in making meaning of her own experience. This process of making sense out of the actions, thoughts, conversations, and, indeed, the totality of their new environment closely resembled steps on a journey to self-authorship.

Assessing Internship Outcomes

The assessment of outcomes for the summer 2002 interns consisted of a thorough review of students' journal entries, the "your calling" paper, and 12 one-on-one student interviews. The "your calling" paper is a preinternship assignment in which students are asked to write a brief paper describing their "calling" in life. To give students an opportunity to ground this assignment in their experiences, directions are intentionally left vague and open for interpretation. Students were asked to write a page or two on what they think their calling in life is; this document could guide us in capturing the essence of each student's aspirations. During the internship, students respond to a weekly journal prompt that asks them to describe, interpret, and question their experiences. Specifically, they are asked to describe a typical workday, to walk around the urban area and reflect on what they see, to describe the values and mission of organizations that they work for, to interview a professional in their field, to describe and analyze a critical incident, to write on how they think others view them, and to comment on the urban environment itself. The two journal entries that we reviewed most closely were responses to the prompt during week 9 of the internship experience, "What helped you learn the most this summer?" and the final journal reflection, which asks students to reflect on their goals, calling, and overall learning experience. The interview questions focused on how the student sees himself and how he has changed over time, relationships that have influenced his life, powerful learning experiences he has had, his overall impressions of his ULIP experience, and a description of how he determines what is right and true for him and what he views as his purpose in life.

As we examined students' journal entries, "calling" papers, and interview transcriptions to interpret their stories over time, it became apparent that the meaningful and substantive experiences offered through the ULIP exposed students to a new way of thinking about themselves, their relationships with others, and the world. Underlying this development is the unique situation of a learning context that takes place far from the traditional classroom, "unplugged" from the familiar structures and fairly standard expectations of mainstream campus and community life.

Experiential Learning

> The learning that I have previously done before was mainly in the classroom, where there is little opportunity for hands-on experimentation. Books are read and teachers are listened to; however, there is very little time allotted for application. Most classes are designed to describe how to do something or what a particular thinking is, but they seem to lack the critical step taking "words" and converting them to objects, pictures, actions, etc. In addition, the unspoken philosophy that the professor's beliefs are true is present. Both internships have presented me with many controversial issues all of which I was allowed to decide for myself what I agreed with and what I would support. Yet in both situations, I did have guidance from a professional (professor, doctor, or social worker) through their experiences and values. In Dayton, I simply got to take the next step on my own. (Anna)

An underlying thread woven throughout the ULIP experience was that the way students learned through experience was qualitatively different from classroom learning. Arthur Chickering (1976) defines experiential learning as "the learning that occurs when changes in judgments, feelings, knowledge, or skills result for a particular person from living through an event or events" (p. 63). Working in an inner-city hospital emergency room and at a domestic violence organization, Anna was challenged by controversial issues and guided by professionals in her field, yet she *got to take the next step on her own.* She was challenged to yield to the authority of her inner voice to make her own judgments about these issues. One of the most noticeable contrasts that students identified regarding the classroom experience and the internship experience was the expectation that they be the knowers—that what they thought had significance and that their point of view was respected.

Kendra, who worked at a public health clinic in Chicago, noted that in the real world right and wrong are not so clearly defined as they are in a traditional classroom:

> As mentioned previously, there is much more emphasis on experience and independent discovery here than anything that I've experienced in a classroom. To a certain degree, most courses indicate what to believe or which theories are the "best." At the clinic, I am on my own to develop my own impressions and beliefs. Most of these are rooted in observation and experience, which also makes this experience different than the average classroom experience. There is not "right" or "wrong" nor is there anyone present to decide if your perceptions and ideas about a particular situation are accurate. This inherently places more responsibility on the observer (myself), as I am obligated to look at all aspects and sides of a situation carefully on my own before making a decision about a certain idea. This is occasionally difficult

because I find it necessary to look at situations from a standpoint I have never experienced.

Kendra's challenge was to take in the contextual complexity of various situations and consider for herself her own beliefs. This development of an internal foundation for knowledge claims helped move her toward self-authorship on the epistemological dimension.

Through active engagement in a real-life career, students were often reinvigorated regarding their studies. Barbara wrote,

> By the second week of the internship, the passion had returned. I had been reminded that my book knowledge was the foundation that I needed but that the precious children that I saw each day were the real richness of my career. Each day was a new opportunity to effect change—a subtle transformation that can easily become an entirely new existence for a child. Exposure to real children who lived the lives I read about in my speech-language pathology course. My career quickly became less about term papers, presentations, and research, as it was about the little girl who loves to shop, a teenager who will play Uno for hours on end, and the infant who absolutely can't stop smiling. I learned that the worst sound imaginable is the silence of a baby crying with a tracheotomy, and I discovered that hearing the same baby babble for the very first time has the ability to reduce an entire room to tears. I discovered the awesome power of 5 minutes spent with a patient between sessions, and I witnessed the results of connecting with a lonely individual's culture.

Barbara acknowledges the importance of her school studies but, through interactions with clients, begins to feel the empowering possibilities for herself as a professional in the field of speech pathology. What was missing in her prior courses was the opportunity for the development of interpersonal abilities necessary to integrate the essential competencies for her career. Her direct experience synthesized her learning through texts (epistemological), through clients (interpersonal), and through her emotional connection (intrapersonal).

ULIP students also had the self-affirming experience of being able to make a positive contribution to their city or to particular clients at their internship site. Amy, who worked with a university law school clinic on research on police brutality, commented,

> While I did enjoy reading about theories on the court system the realities of its operation hit me with full force. The pragmatics of how both juvenile and adult court systems work forced me to stare down the harshest realities I have ever faced, and I wasn't even the one directly affected by the corruption

and mismanagement. I spent considerable time working in issues surrounding police brutality in Chicago. Not the theory of why police beat others, not the theoretical civil rights objections to such brutality, but the nuts and bolts of how to fight such actions and remove the officers associated with them. Helping to write a presentation to teach others about their recourses and, in particular, creating a database to actually log information [about] police who commit acts of brutality allowed me to take very real and pragmatic steps to combat this almost overwhelming problem.

Amy's obvious passion about this problem was ignited through her research and through the action she could take to effect change. She felt personally empowered by her ability to create something that will be used by real people in a real situation in a real city. This actualization of her beliefs gave her a sense of participation in the larger whole of society, offering her own talents and abilities to make positive change. She donned a new identity, moving from "learning student" to "contributing professional." This is the realized potential of experiential learning. As Weil and McGill (1989) noted, "Making sense of ourselves in relation to the world is at the center of experiential learning" (p. 246). It is an ideal environment for the implementation of the Learning Partnerships Model.

As we examined the dimension of self-authorship in the development of each student through participation in the ULIP, several of the program components emerged from the students' stories as distinctly effective in promoting developmental growth. The program components that had significant impact were the following: interaction with the supervisor, the experience of independence, encountering dissonance, and engaging in reflection. These four points of critical impact correspond directly with the three assumptions of learning partnerships. Validation and sharing authority relate to the supervisor–intern relationship, self as central to knowledge construction corresponds with the experience of independence and autonomy, encountering dissonance leads to knowledge that is complex and socially constructed, and engaging in reflection is critical to the process of seeing self as central to knowledge construction, validation of the student as knower, and situating learning in the learner's experience. Each of these program components is described in more detail here.

Supervisor–Intern Relationship

She wanted me to—she was so "*yes!*" And that made me feel like "*yes!*" (Laura)

It was evident in our work that the students were highly influenced and motivated by supervisors who validated them as knowers by treating them as knowledgeable and trustworthy from the onset of their internship experience. Most students began their work feeling unsure about their professional capabilities, yet many ended their 10-week experience with a view of themselves as competent and confident, able to contribute as a professional in the real world, and capable of making sense of the world around them. As Emily shared,

> I was just like, whoa, I'm never going to be able to do anything. I'm just going to be a huge disappointment and I'm not going to come out of this with anything substantial but I did—I did figure it out and you know, the first couple of weeks I asked a million questions and the next I kind of did it on trial and error and, you know, I just acquainted myself to all of the different materials and machines and stuff in the lab and I just did it on my own and I was just really surprised. You know, when that much confidence is given to you and that much responsibility is given to you—I just didn't think I'd be able to step up to the plate and actually get stuff done but I did. So I was pretty pleased with myself by the end of it because I mean, they're publishing a paper about the stuff that I did this summer and I'm going to be one of the coauthors for that. They presented a poster at a conference and my name was on the poster. At the end of the summer, I was like "wow, I kind of did important things, you know?" This stuff's for real—so that's cool.

Emily began her experience feeling unsure of herself and doubting her abilities. Her supervisor shared his confidence in her by offering her substantial responsibilities, trusting her judgment, and providing an opportunity for her to "step up to the plate" in the research lab. Over the course of her experience, Emily encountered an internal realization that she was fully capable of accomplishing tasks that were important and meaningful in her professional field of study. This realization transformed the way she viewed herself as an individual and also allowed her to cognitively construct her world from a new frame of reference. Emily's interpersonal development was equally enhanced through the ongoing interaction with her supervisor.

Similarly, Anna, working at a domestic violence organization, expressed how her supervisor's confidence in her abilities allowed her to grow over time:

> I think I got more confidence, no doubt, throughout my experience, because at the beginning I was like, "whoa, I can't do the hotline, no, no, no" because anyone could call with any situation and I was supposed to be versatile and deal with it, you know? But yeah, I was really surprised that they

gave me as much responsibility as they did because I've never really gotten that kind of responsibility here at Miami, you know? You don't, you know, get much responsibility. But um, that they really treated me like an equal—that really kind of, that was refreshing to say the least. Their encouragement was always positive encouragement—you know even when I messed up they'd say "well, we'll fix this" and "this is the way you do it—I'll help you work on it" that kind of thing. And, it was OK to mess up.

As Anna's supervisors validated her abilities to work effectively in the workplace, they also situated the learning in her experience by offering ongoing encouragement and supporting her growth despite mistakes or errors. She viewed her internship site as a place where it was safe to learn and grow. There was substantial challenge within her experience, yet the support provided by her supervisors allowed her to embrace the challenges that might have otherwise proven to be obstacles that she was unable to overcome. By viewing her as an "equal," her supervisors also defined the process of learning in the workplace as a mutual construction of meaning where learning was a "joint effort to develop new perspectives and apply these new perspectives and structures to everyday life," as Baxter Magolda (1999, p. 27) states. This process provided yet another foundation of support for Anna to grow developmentally in her mentally and emotionally demanding work environment. Unlike her experiences at Miami, where individual responsibility seemed to be lacking for her, Anna received consistent messages from external sources (her supervisors) that she was competent and capable of doing exceptional work. Over time, Anna internalized these messages and began to see herself in the same light.

In the context of the ULIP, it is clear that many supervisors care about the student's developmental process. Laura described the power of such an experience with her supervisor at an organization providing services to children who were in the foster care system:

My supervisor, she was awesome. She was all about getting me engaged in everything and sometimes I was worn out because she would want me to do so many things and do this and do that, and write this up and that up, and look up files—it was awesome, but wow. She was such a people person. Plus she was a teacher, so I think her demeanor was really different because she wanted me to learn and she wanted me to make sure I was learning, engaging, and interacting and stuff and getting a realistic picture of social work and things like that. She wanted me to—she was so *"yes!"* And that made me feel like *"yes!"* It was great. We made really good connections because we spent a lot of time together. She was so, I guess, praising me all the time and complimenting me—and they actually valued what I said. Like in the foster care team meetings, we would go in and they would say, "Laura, what did you think?" And it really mattered what I thought about these foster parents. Whether I thought the kids would be safe there, whether I thought this was a good match, and that was kind of shocking again—like, wow, they really want to know what I think and they really value it. I mean I was a student intern, but they also saw me as like, a coworker.

The confidence Laura's supervisor instilled in her abilities allowed her to grow intrapersonally as she began to see herself as an effective professional. As her interpersonal relationships formed over time, she also grew in her understanding of herself as a team member who was capable of interacting with others not as a student intern but as a coworker with a real contribution to make.

Supervisors such as Laura's not only serve as a source of extrinsic support and motivation for the student, but also encourage a way of taking responsibility for learning in the context of a particular career environment (epistemological development) in which the student views him- or herself as capable of making choices, negotiating with others (interpersonal development), and choosing and acting on his or her internal belief system (intrapersonal development). By asking the question "What do *you* think?" on a regular basis, these supervisors reinforce the notion of situating learning in the learner's experience and the mutual construction of knowledge with others.

In the real world, not all supervisors provide the kind of mentoring and support that would be ideal, and unfortunately that was true of some of the supervisors of our students. The critical role of the supervisor can also be seen in the unsettling effects created by an unsupportive supervisor on a student's sense of self, view of others, and view of their entire internship experience. As Raymond described,

I was very intense about getting work done—and my supervisor kept giving me small tidbits of work to get done. I felt like I wasn't trusted to tackle any big tasks, like really getting my hands dirty and doing the job. I did report back to her on stuff I did for the other department and she would say things like "Well, as your supervisor, I ultimately have control over you and you must report back to me at all times" and I'm like, whoa—that doesn't make me feel great. It was just a really strange relationship. I think she thought that I was just a weakling and she could just push me around. I just felt like she didn't consider me—and she even said this in our exit interview—she said, "You're not a staff member, you're not a member of our team. You're just here to see how things work" and I was like, "Oh—I kind of got the idea that I was going to be treated as part of the team, or like a staff member"—I really thought that was what I was there to do. I came ready to work and do good things and I felt like she really didn't take me seriously or think that I had the skills to do anything. I constantly wanted to prove to her that I could do good work—but she never gave me anything big enough to do that with.

Unlike many of his peers in the program, Raymond did not receive the external support from his supervisor that he needed and desired. As a result, he felt devalued and unsatisfied with this professional side of his internship experience. The actions of his supervisor led Raymond to feel uncomfortable about himself and to question his abilities. Despite the impact on his overall professional experience, however, Raymond viewed this as a powerful life lesson:

> However, the lessons I learned from what I perceive as a less than ideal job environment in the end were more valuable lessons than I could have imagined when I first scrawled out my goals (in the sprint course). . . . I feel like the most important and useful development I made, falling under the category of personal goals, was becoming more assertive and aggressive. This wasn't a goal I had planned on achieving, but I felt like it was the greatest lesson I learned as a result of this internship. . . . As a result of my experience, I have decided that I will no longer allow anyone to push me around and take me for granted as [my supervisor] did. Reflecting back to my life before this internship, I can see now in hindsight that I have often allowed other people to use me and walk all over me, taking my hard work and friendship for granted. Now, after a 10-week experience of being held down by my supervisor, I am ready to be assertive, aggressive, and confident in my own abilities.

Through his own reflections and processing with the program supervisor, Raymond learned to value his own assessment of his abilities over those of others, even authority figures. Raymond revealed his intrapersonal development in leaving behind the definition of self by external others and realizing the need to define for himself an internal identity. This realization affected his interpersonal relationships by allowing Raymond to begin to move beyond gaining approval to acting in a manner that was true to himself. This illustrates movement from the "crossroads" phase in the journey toward self-authorship to "becoming the author of one's life." Raymond's experience clearly reveals how, despite the challenges that existed, when given sufficient opportunity for reflection and support, even a seemingly negative experience can be integrated as a significant developmental opportunity.

Experiencing Independence/Autonomy

> Looking back now—I'm like "Oh my gosh, I was out, like really by myself and I was OK." (Jessica)

Throughout the spring semester sprint course, students are provided with a framework of knowledge to prepare them for their urban experience. The ULIP intentionally offers educational resources (e.g., readings and guest speakers) to expose students to urban issues and allow them to learn about the setting that they are preparing to enter. It is clear that one of the most powerful lessons learned by the ULIP students is that they are able to be independent in an urban setting. Leigh described being surprised by herself in the city of Chicago:

> I think the whole summer surprised me really, because I didn't necessarily think that like, I didn't expect to be as independent as I was when I went. I thought I would hang out with my roommates more and after being there a couple of weeks, I just realized that I didn't want to—I was like this is my summer, I'm going to get as much out of it as I can. It surprised me that I didn't—I've always known that I was independent—but it just surprised me that for two and a half months I was pretty much on my own and I loved it.

Leigh began her experience with the assumption that she would depend on others yet found that she "loved" being alone and exploring the city independently. By viewing herself as a person who was capable of making her own decisions and embracing her independence, Leigh's way of making meaning shifted from being preoccupied with external definition through peers (i.e., hanging out with roommates) to one that was more comfortable with and comforted by an independent internal definition of self: "I was on my own and I loved it."

Caroline described her urban experience in a similar way:

> Just being completely on my own—I'd never been to Cleveland before, didn't know what to do, didn't know anything. So going up there, just kinda, like, figuring it out on my own, it was just real extensive independence I didn't think I would ever have. And now that I am going to graduate in May, I always thought I would go back home just because it was, like, the easy, comfortable thing to do. But I'm not ready to go back home anymore, like, I want to go to a bigger city, and I want to do something new, not just go back to the familiar.

Caroline entered the ULIP never having had the opportunity to live on her own. However, she returned from her ULIP experience with an inner confidence and a willingness to explore further options outside her comfort zone. By taking this step to release herself from depending on external others (i.e., her parents at home) for security and validation, Caroline was exposed to the possibility that she was fully capable of functioning independently. Through this process, Caroline's view of her relationship with others, her self, and the world also began to change. She became more willing to see herself as capable of acting on her instincts, trusting her own judgment, and making decisions for herself. Caroline's new construction of the world allowed her to begin the process of understanding her own internal identity—which, over time, will ultimately enable her to function as the author of her own life.

By allowing students to select the city in which they will work and providing structure and a network of support that they can tap into as needed, the ULIP situates learning in the experience of each individual student and opens the door for students to test the waters of "extensive independence." Throughout our assessment, students expressed the intensity of the realization that they were challenged to face as they functioned entirely on their own. This realization was often coupled with an infusion of confidence that extended beyond the ULIP experience into their perceptions of the future. As Jessica explained,

> Looking back now—I'm like "Oh my gosh, I was out, like really by myself and I was OK." That's good to know that I can do that and I'm fine. So, just being confident in the fact that I'll be able to go anywhere and I'll be OK by myself and I know what to do—that has been a benefit—that I can do that. That helped a lot.

As Jessica reflected on her overall experience, she shared her initial surprise at her own ability to live on her own. This experience allowed her to grow intrapersonally by enabling her to view herself as a capable and confident woman who can manage life in an urban environment entirely on her own. Interpersonally, Jessica grew to see that although she can have relationships with others, she need not depend on them entirely to meet all her needs. This, in turn, allows her to negotiate relationships more effectively and to better understand when the help of others is needed and when it is not.

A strong sense of autonomy also played an important role in Shannon's ability to learn in the workplace, as she shared in describing her work for a large health care provider:

> At my site, what helped me learn the most was the freedom I was allotted. I was the project manager for two of the projects I worked on, and had a

fairly independent role doing research for the large capital improvement project we worked on. I liked being able to explore and pursue whatever aspects of a project particularly intrigued me, and I liked having the independence to work through the challenging parts of the project on my own.

Shannon uses the word "freedom" to describe her independence. Her ability to play an independent role helped her to see herself as someone capable of understanding a complex system of health care, managing tasks responsibly, and interpreting the projects she was assigned through her own frame of reference and understanding. This autonomy allowed her to process information "on her own," and as a result she was more equipped to confidently embrace the challenges that she faced on a daily basis.

This new experience of independence promoted a sense of true autonomy that the majority of our students fully and readily embraced over the course of the summer. Students who experienced this feeling internalized the belief that they were not only able to be independent within the context of the 10-week ULIP experience; this opportunity also provided them with the ability to view themselves as capable of being independent from this point forward in a world that now appears to be far more manageable than ever before.

Encountering Dissonance

I learned more from the shock of moving out of the socioeconomic ivory towers of Miami into the crumbling red brick walls of the Cabrini Green projects of South Side Chicago than I could ever learn reading files in an office. (Amy)

As individuals were immersed in the urban experience throughout the summer, many found themselves in settings that they had not previously encountered. By assuming the role of urban explorer and city dweller, students were able to see other realities that existed outside their own privileged life experiences up close and personally on a weekly and, in some cases, daily basis. Through their experiences in cities, students often came face to face with the realization that their privileged upbringings had given them opportunities and benefits in life that the adults and children with whom they worked in the urban setting did not share. The reaction to this realization provided a critical moment for many students that allowed them to reflect on their own privilege, whether race, socioeconomic status, or both infused it. These experiences provided challenge in the form of dissonance that granted students the opportunity to reconsider their multiple roles and their personal identity in the big picture of life. The dissonance that resulted from such experiences

opened the door to a new view of the world as complex and socially constructed. Sandy, working with a homeless children's summer educational
enrichment program, commented,

> If anything, my passion has been heightened. I think that this summer defi-
> nitely played a part in that. I just really think everyone should do this.
> Because, to get in there and actually see it, and just to be a part of it, you
> probably could never have imagined what homeless children are going
> through, and I could never have imagined that all my life's belongings were
> in trash bags, and I was just being moved from home to home, and I'm sup-
> posed to be OK with that. I cried really hard, and the kids were looking at
> me like, not like I was crazy, but they were just so [pause], this was just
> normal for them. It broke my heart so much for them just to think this was
> normal. Little things like that have made my drive and my passion to do
> whatever I can to make some kind of change that much stronger for me.

Sandy described the intensity of her experience and the dissonance that resulted
from her interactions with homeless families who lived lives drastically different from her own. This personal experience opened the door for deeper intrapersonal exploration for Sandy as she was challenged to consider her core
belief system and how these beliefs were (or were not) displayed in her everyday behaviors. Epistemologically, this dissonance also challenged Sandy to
reconsider her construction of the world and the complexity of the society in
which we live as she learned about the realities of homelessness. Through her
constant interaction with homeless families and children, Sandy learned how to
develop and maintain interpersonal relationships with diverse others.

Similarly, Amy described the contrast in her experience that opened her
eyes to a new world in the urban environment:

> The aspects of my internship that helped me learn the most were oddly
> enough the most hands-off this summer. Attending the meetings of grass-
> roots organizations and a public housing rally were invaluable in opening
> my eyes to the personal aspects of the injustices in the city as well as to see-
> ing a culture that I had no idea existed. I learned more from the shock of
> moving out of the socioeconomic ivory towers of Miami into the crumbling
> red brick walls of the Cabrini Green projects of South Side Chicago than I
> could ever learn reading files in an office.

Amy's experience in the Cabrini Green projects allowed her to see a culture
entirely different from the one in which she was raised. By engaging fully in this
experience, Amy was able to embrace the new and different culture and learn
more about herself and the urban environment by attending local meetings on

a regular basis. By experiencing the reality of diverse others in her world, Amy was able to learn more about herself. In transforming her initial shock into learning to view the world with new eyes, Amy grew in powerful and meaningful ways.

Raymond, a White student from suburban Ohio, described a particular encounter with racial and socioeconomic class difference as one that "tested boundaries" for him:

> I kind of tested the boundaries this one time when I ran into a park in a Hispanic neighborhood that didn't have the best reputation—and I really got a couple of people yelling at me. I felt like I really wanted to cross boundaries for myself and that was one way I was able to do it. I felt really uncomfortable in this park, because as soon as I walked into it, this guy said, "get out of here white boy" and then he just continued yelling and other people looked at me funny—others were yelling but I couldn't hear what they were saying. It was the first time I really felt discrimination. I think that was like, one incident where I really think I broke some boundaries and did something I wasn't supposed to do. I took some liberties that my mother and others probably wouldn't approve of—but it was worth it, because I kind of felt good about it.

Raymond made the conscious decision to go running in the Hispanic neighborhood near his apartment in downtown Chicago. As he describes, he wanted to learn about himself and challenge assumptions within society as well. By doing something that he "wasn't supposed to do" and that his "mother wouldn't approve of," Raymond asserted his ability to make his own decisions and determine for himself how he would behave in such a situation. Even though Raymond acknowledged that he considered the external influence of his mother, it is telling that he also felt "good" about choosing his own way and testing his own internal boundaries as well as his sense of the external boundaries within society. This experience allowed Raymond to recognize racism and to make choices about his own course of action. As he made this decision and broke these boundaries for himself, Raymond was able to see himself in a different light. Again we see Raymond moving through a "crossroads," this time a self-imposed challenge to experience dissonance, in order to develop his own definition of self.

Engaging in Reflection

> How all these events kind of shaped your entire experience, and I think it's good because now I can look back on it and see kind of like a road map of all of the things that happened to me and I look back and reflect on how this has benefited me personally. (Nancy)

Engaging in the assigned written reflections played a critical role in the lives of students and in their ability to make meaning of the ULIP experience. These weekly entries are a fundamental component and requirement of the ULIP. Rhoads (2000) argued, "Reflection is key to promoting the self because it forces students to give serious thought to their experience and their overall lives" (p. 43). After reviewing all the journal entries, assignments, and interview transcriptions, it was clear that their reflective writing reminded each of them that "deep change demands the time and energy of serious thought" (p. 43). As Sandy shared,

> Each week, I would sit down to do my journal and one prompt would just pop out at me because I was just, like, that totally applies to my experience yesterday or the day before! It just, it really made you reflect, and I think it made the experience more powerful because I think you absorb your experience on your own, but to have to sit down and think about it and write, like, write out your thoughts and to really organize them just, like, helps you even more—it really helps you learn from it even more. I mean, you notice things, but to take the time to organize them on paper organizes them in your head more too.

Sandy benefited a great deal from her journaling and reflection time because it allowed her to organize her thoughts and process them more deeply. She was also able to situate this process in her own experience and truly share what was on her mind. This process allowed her to reconsider all the things she had "absorbed" in her experience and articulate the meaning of these experiences in her own words each week. Similarly, Nancy commented,

> Actually, I mean, you think about things a lot in your head but when you write them down on paper it just seems like all like the jumbled thoughts that are going around in your head just somehow become clear when you try to express them in words on paper. It just kind of helps you collect your thoughts and clarify, like, how you feel about the different experiences that you've been faced with over the summer you know, and how you reacted to this person or that person. How all these events kind of shaped your entire experience, and I think it's good because now I can look back on it and see kind of like a road map of all of the things that happened to me and I look back and reflect on how this has benefited me personally.

Nancy used her writing as a way to clarify her thoughts and express her feelings. The process of journaling also enabled her to reflect on her experiences and to consider how much she had grown and changed over time. This allowed Nancy to develop intrapersonally as she continually expressed her personal thoughts and feelings and then reflected on her life. The structure of the weekly journaling assignment within the ULIP provided Nancy and the majority of students with a supportive outlet for their personal expression and reflection.

As Kendra said, the weekly reflection component provided an opportunity for students to examine the meaning of experiences during and after the time that the actual experience took place:

> For me, engaging in the learning process meant being open to and aware of learning experiences at all times. I found that being prepared to experience and reflect on that experience helped me to glean more from my time in the city. This internal reflection helped me to immediately consider what I had seen or experienced. This method helped me to reflect on things without distorting what I had observed. If something had a more powerful impact, I often found myself thinking about it and reflecting on the experience even more later on.

Kendra viewed her reflection as a way to examine the true meaning of her experiences. By journaling her thoughts, she was able to engage in an active process of considering the meaning of her own actions and responses long after they occurred. This allowed her to grow in her ability to make decisions that reflect her true inner feelings and desires. Active reflection also allowed her to approach life from a critical and analytical point of view and to make meaning of her world as a place where she can make decisions, consider the course of action that was taken, and reflect on and learn from these decisions so that she will have the power to make more informed decisions in the future.

Students who were not initially comfortable with the journaling assignment admitted that they were able to ultimately embrace this task and learn from the activity over time. As Anna explained,

> I'm not really into processing my feelings—but for the most part what I think I got out of the writing was an understanding of what was going on, what was happening, what I was learning from it. Because otherwise I wouldn't have really thought about it. So I think the writing really helped in that it pushed me to process what I was learning and see what my strengths and weaknesses were.

Though Anna did not enjoy processing her feelings, she shared that she would not have given much thought to her ULIP experience if the structure for journaling as an assignment had not been in place. By being encouraged to reflectively examine her experience, Anna was challenged to think more deeply about her engagement with active learning. She was also able to reflect on herself and consider strengths and weaknesses in her interpersonal behaviors and interactions. The ability to actively reflect on one's life, one's relationships, and one's view of the world is fundamental to the development of self-authorship. The weekly reflection component in the ULIP influenced students' ability and desire to engage in this practice and started each of them toward more active and ongoing reflection in their daily lives.

Outcome: Making Meaning of Self as Citizen

> All of my experiences [through the summer] have changed me and molded me into a new person. I feel that I am more confident about who I am as a person, and I now have a focused idea of what my calling is. (Jessica)

Through our assessment, we found that students had integrated a view of themselves and the world that was larger and more complex than they had had before the internship began. This shift in perspective encompassed a new view of self in relation to others, to knowledge, and, inwardly, toward self. The critical program components that emerged as catalysts to development (the supervisor–intern relationships, experiencing independence and autonomy, encountering dissonance, and engaging in reflection) challenged students to develop a more thoughtful and complex approach to understanding their experience. By stepping outside their comfort zones into unfamiliar urban settings, students not only learned to embrace challenge with the help of a number of fundamental support systems in place but also created a new definition of what it could mean for them to become engaged citizens in the larger world community. As Maria, who spent the summer working with the American Civil Liberties Union and on a political campaign, reflected,

> I really want to do something that advances some belief I have and some cause that I believe in. I don't want to just sit back and let other people decide how this country and how this world is going to turn out. I want to be active in that. I'm definitely dedicated to helping do what I can to make the world better in some small way, however much I can.

Cognitively, Maria has grown to view the world as a place where she can contribute and where she has the power to make a difference. As a result of her summer experience working both on constitutional legal issues and on a gubernatorial election campaign, she is grounded in her own acquired knowledge to take an active role in determining the future. Intrapersonally, Maria feels new confidence in herself as a person committed to, as well as capable of, creating change.

Raymond also shared his thoughts on being an active contributor to society:

> I really feel that my purpose in life is to help people. Much has been given to me in the form of good family and good socioeconomic status and access to resources and um, the strong work ethic that I've gotten from my family, and I feel like since I've been given—"[those] to whom much is given, much is expected." I just feel like it's my duty and my responsibility to find things that I feel the need to change and to change those things. I can't imagine just pursuing money in my life—I think that's the quick and easy way out. I feel like I want to be on the front lines in life.

Based on his work on affordable housing in Chicago, Raymond wanted to take an active role in helping others. Much like Maria, he does not want to wait for others to create change; he wants to be "on the front lines in life." He has seen his own ability to be independent in a new and challenging environment, and he has experienced ways of life and realities that were entirely different from his own. Raymond came to the realization that he has been a privileged member of society. This acknowledgment led him to question more deeply the core of his internal sense of self and purpose. Consequently, his view of his place in the world changed, and he committed himself to giving back to society and focusing his energy on the needs of others less fortunate than himself.

Several students expressed their reaction to this internal paradigm shift by voicing their frustrations about their peers who did not participate in the ULIP experience and do not see the "big picture" that they had grown to see. Natalie shared,

> This is the whole Miami bubble thing. Like, think outside of yourself and your 12 friends, please! There is a greater world going on outside of Oxford and someone somewhere is going to expect you to be able to talk about it or something. You need to eventually contribute, give back, or make it better. I really felt this way when I came back from Chicago this summer. I just want to say, you guys don't even know the half of it, like you don't even, you're missing, you're not seeing the big picture! You're not seeing that there is so much more out there besides, you know, the little things that you do here that are directly affecting you. There is so much more!

Her internship experience exposed Natalie to a way of life outside her community of origin and the Miami University community. When she returned to campus, back in her preinternship environment, her own changes were set in stark relief against the "status quo" of the perspective of her friends.

Natalie's frustration with her peers illustrates the intensity of the transformation in her way of making meaning about the world and a new sense of her own capacity to be a contributing member to it.

Laura shared a similar frustration:

> Sometimes I just get the urge to tell people that there comes a point when you have to take responsibility for your own education beyond the books, beyond, you know, your 15 hours of bannerweb [course registration]. Something else needs to be going on because someday, somebody's going to depend on you for something more than fashion advice. Someone's going to need you to make some decisions that affect their life.

Through her experience, Laura internalized a new definition of educational responsibility, in fact, a new definition of learning, one that involves the active self-directing of the meaning making. Much like Natalie, she viewed the world as much larger and more complex than the campus of Miami University. She saw herself and her peers as people who are capable of serving as leaders who will be depended on to make big decisions that will affect the lives of others in the future. Her frustration with her peers shows that she wants them to "see the light" and make sense of the world as she has come to see it so that they can join her in her commitment to creating change and making a difference.

A new sense of self also emerged from the overall summer experience. Students frequently referred to this different "me" that evolved over the activities of the internship, service, and urban living. Jessica expressed this development of passions and sense of purpose:

> Through my work with Legal Aid, I quickly found that benefits law is not for me, and through my work with the National Underground Railroad Freedom Center (NURFC), I have found that I have a passion and deep interest in constitutional and civil rights law. . . . All of my experiences [through the summer] have changed me and molded me into a new person. I feel that I am more confident about who I am as a person, and I now have a focused idea of what my calling is. Although I enjoy events planning, I have found a passion to pursue constitutional civil rights law. I feel that I would be happiest and best utilized in the world working to eliminate racism, discrimination, and other social tragedies that have caused the need for the formation of organizations such as the NURFC.

Jessica's voice captures the enthusiasm of self-discovery, especially self-discovery that leads to a commitment to making a contribution to the common good that is personally satisfying as well. Her journey to self-authorship is under way with this sense of confidence and focus based directly on her own experience.

Similarly, Greg reflected on the integration of his experiences and the new direction he found through them:

> However, as a result of my summer experience, not only in politics, but also volunteering with inner city children, I was able to focus in on my vision. This focus was achieved with the help of a leadership camp I attended (LeaderShape). . . . I was able to even more intensely reflect on my summer experiences, beliefs and passions to create a clear picture of my future. Combining my love of politics with my love of world travel, as well as my desire to help children, I have decided on going to law school and focusing on International Law so that I can coordinate international adoptions, as well as be a voice to defend the rights of children throughout the world. All the children working sweatshops, all the children dying of AIDS in Africa, these kids need a voice; and I know now that I could be that voice.

The sense of empowerment that comes through this statement is brought on by the intense reflection that made meaning from his experience—an intrapersonal direction, a vision of active engagement in the world, and a sense of purpose beyond self-satisfaction.

It is clear from these student reflections that the development of intrapersonal, interpersonal, and cognitive complexity promoted a sense of citizenship or connection to others that refined their sense of "calling" and their engagement with the world around them.

Conclusion

> It makes you sort out what's important, what's not, how you felt about it, what you think, how you've changed, how you've grown, and then you just look back and figure out okay, now who am I now, what am I planning to do later and how has this affected me? (Jessica)

The ULIP provides a rich and unique experience for students that incorporates the basic principles and assumptions of the Learning Partnerships Model. It encourages students to view themselves as equal partners in the ULIP journey, as competent professionals, and, finally, as responsible and active citizens who have the ability to interact effectively with diverse others and ultimately make an impact on our greater society. The critical program components for learning that emerged through our assessment were the supervisor–intern relationship, experiencing independence and autonomy, encountering dissonance, and engaging in reflection. The Learning Partnerships Model promotes a pedagogical framework that "is a means of blending guidance and enabling responsibility to promote self-authorship" (see preface). The blend of challenge and support that existed within each of these components invited students to transform their notions of self, other, and knowledge itself, allowing them to express a powerful new view of self and world.

Contrasting her on-campus experiences with her internship experience, Jessica put it this way:

> I guess, I mean, like, granted college is like a bubble where you can go and you can get in trouble but there's not a whole lot—you can fall down without really killing yourself, you know. You pretty much, it's like [pause] it's kind of like when you have a baby and you put up a little guard rail in front of the stairs and they can wander but they won't really hurt themselves. So I think college is kind of like that, but in terms of getting ready for the next step, the next level, that's what this program is—you get to go pretty much for free and just try out stuff. And see what you like and what you don't like and you come back and you sit down and figure it out. It makes you sort out what's important, what's not, how you felt about it, what you think, how you've changed, how you've grown, and then you just look back and figure out okay, now who am I now, what am I planning to do later and how has this affected me?

Jessica compared her experience in college to living in a protective "bubble" of safety and comfort. The "next level" that she described further illuminates the challenges and supports that exist within the ULIP experience. The ULIP students learned to make sense of themselves (intrapersonal development), their relationships with others (interpersonal development), and the world around them (epistemological development) by sorting through the experience in the manner that Jessica describes. The teachers in their urban settings—the homeless man whose face became familiar, the supervisors and coworkers at the job, the children at the shelter, the city itself—were not easily identifiable as teachers at first sight; yet, over time, it was the individual experience with these teachers that challenged students to reconsider their ways of making meaning in and of the world. Through this unique experience outside the college "bubble" in real work situations in real cities, students were able to see their world and their role within it in new and meaningful ways—and take significant steps in the long journey toward becoming the authors of their own lives.

It is clear from our assessment that paying special attention to the supervisor relationship would enhance experiential learning environments. This relationship forms a critical component of student learning and may have the greatest effect on student development in work settings. Students demonstrated that getting out of the classroom environment, living on their own as working adults, and experiencing independence served as great catalysts in intrapersonal development. In addition, we learned from the students that encountering situations that challenged their values and beliefs (dissonance) propelled them to critically analyze previously held views and decide for themselves what they valued and believed. Finally, the principle of engaging in reflection, an essential element of all learning through experience, was validated here. The journal writing on a regular basis encouraged students to evaluate and probe their activities and contexts to make meaning of these new experiences.

"Unplugging" from the relative safety and predictability of campus life, though often formidable, can offer a rewarding opportunity for growth and learning. As the ULIP students expressed, their experiences in typical campus-based learning contexts are limited by a lack of willingness and ability by educational institutions to offer programs that provide hands-on, real-life experiences that remove students from the sheltered collegiate atmosphere and place them in an environment where the lessons learned come from engagement with unorthodox yet powerful teachers, contexts, and self-imposed challenges. With the support of the Learning Partnerships Model, students can be guided to self-authorship through the challenges of experiential learning—challenges that promote the transformation of other-directed students to self-directed citizens who are engaged in their communities.

References

Baxter Magolda, M. B. (1999). Engaging students in active learning. In G. S. Blimling & E. J. Whitt (Eds.), *Good practice in student affairs: Principles to foster student learning* (pp. 21–43). San Francisco: Jossey-Bass.

Baxter Magolda, M. B. (2001). *Making their own way: Narratives for transforming higher education to promote self-development.* Sterling, VA: Stylus.

Chickering, A. W. (1976). Developmental change as a major outcome. In M. T. Keeton et al. (Eds.), *Experiential learning: Rationale, characteristics, and assessment* (pp. 62–107). San Francisco: Jossey-Bass.

Rhoads, R. A. (2000). Democratic citizenship and service learning: Advancing the caring self. In M. B. Baxter Magolda (Ed.), *Teaching to promote intellectual and personal maturity: Incorporating students' worldviews and identities into the learning process. New Directions for Teaching and Learning,* No. 82 (pp. 37–44). San Francisco: Jossey-Bass.

Weil, S. W., & McGill, I. (1989). Continuing the dialogue: New possibilities for experiential learning. In S. W. Weil & I. McGill (Eds.), *Making sense of experiential learning* (pp. 245–272). Philadelphia: Open University Press.

6

A LEARNING PARTNERSHIP

U.S. COLLEGE STUDENTS
AND THE POOR IN EL SALVADOR

Kevin Yonkers-Talz

A few months before she was murdered for working with the poor in El Salvador, Maryknoll Sister Ita Ford wrote to her niece Maria in Brooklyn,

> I hope you come to find that which gives life a deep meaning for you. Something worth living for—maybe even worth dying for—something that energizes you, enthuses you, enables you to keep moving ahead. I can't tell you what it might be. That's for you to find, to choose, to love.

We have high hopes for the students who come to live with us at the Casa de la Solidaridad (House of Solidarity), the Jesuit study-abroad program in El Salvador. Our hope—like Ita's hope for her niece—is that our students discover their vocation, that special call that gives life deep meaning. We also hope our students undergo a transformation at a variety of levels, especially in their heads, hearts, and hands. We want to expand our students' horizons and exercise their imaginations to include the realities of people who live in poverty. We want students to think more critically and contextually about the world around them. We want them to learn to analyze information from a variety of cultural perspectives and use it to make wise decisions for themselves but also for the common good. We want students to recognize the power of academic research when it is placed at the service of those most in need. We hope that as they come to better understand the struggles and hardships of the poor, students become more compassionate. In addition, we hope to affect students' future commitments. We want them to become global citizens who act consistently with their beliefs and values. We want students to become, each in their own way, collaborators in promoting global solidarity. All these hopes require that students become the authors of their lives—that they develop the capacity to internally define a coherent belief system and an identity that will enable them to effectively engage our world.

Our students are not our only focus. Living and working in the context of a developing country like El Salvador, one recognizes the urgency of the current global situation. The statistics are startling:

- 2.8 billion people live on less that $2 per day (World Bank, 2001).
- 2.4 billion people do not have adequate access to water, which is one of the main reasons why 6,000 children die each day from preventable diseases (United Nations Educational Scientific and Cultural Organization, 2003).
- One percent of the world's people receive as much income each year as the poorest 57% (United Nations Development Program, 2002).
- Two thirds of the 876 million illiterate adults are women (United Nations Development Program, 2003).

Our hopes at the Casa de la Solidaridad extend to embrace our wider global community. We hope for a more peaceful and just world, one where all people, but especially the poor, can live with dignity.

Working with college students in this context raises two important questions: (a) how do we best assist our students to develop the capacity for self-authorship, and (b) how can we best respond to the current global situation?

This chapter explores how the Casa de la Solidaridad addresses these questions by simultaneously supporting and challenging students as they are immersed in the realities of the poor of El Salvador. I describe the Casa and show how it has drawn from the wisdom and insights of Baxter Magolda's Learning Partnerships Model. In addition, I share initial results of how this experience has affected students' development, specifically in relation to promoting self-authorship. My experience in El Salvador has convinced me that engagement with poor people and their struggle to survive, when combined with personal and academic reflection, can help students become the authors of their lives and contribute to addressing the global situation.

Jesuit Higher Education in the United States and El Salvador

Casa de la Solidaridad is an opportunity for students, especially those from Jesuit colleges and universities, to study for a semester in El Salvador, where they integrate direct immersion with the poor and rigorous academic study and reflection. This opportunity is set in the context of Jesuit higher education in the United States and at the University of Central America, the Jesuit University in El Salvador.

Jesuit Higher Education in the United States

Jesuit higher education is rooted in a philosophy of education that emphasizes academic excellence, education of the whole person, and promoting service to others. Ignatius of Loyola, the founder of the Society of Jesus (Jesuits), did not intend to start colleges and universities when he formed the Society of Jesus in 1540. He and his companions put themselves at the service of Pope Paul III to go where they were most needed. The pope asked Ignatius and his companions to begin teaching theology and scripture. Subsequent requests for schools indicated that this work was an effective way to correct ignorance and corruption among the clergy and the faithful, to stem the decline of the Catholic Church in the face of the Reformation, and to fulfill the motto of the Society of Jesus, "Ad Majorem Dei Gloriam"—to the greater glory of God (O'Neal, 2003).

For the next four centuries, the overriding mission of the Society of Jesus was "the service of faith," which tended to focus Jesuit works primarily on pastoral activities, personal religious development, research, and education. In 1975, 10 years after the closing of the Second Vatican Council, Jesuit delegates from around the world gathered at the 32nd General Congregation to consider how the Society of Jesus was responding to the deep transformation of the Catholic Church at the time, a transformation that began to look more closely at the connection between faith and life. After much prayer and deliberation, the Congregation decided to set out in a new direction; "the service of faith," it concluded, must also include "the promotion of justice." This change has significantly influenced not only the Society of Jesus and the 28 Jesuit colleges and universities in the United States but also the over 100 institutions of higher learning that Jesuits administer throughout the world. Although not actualized at each institution, the promotion of justice is now intricately embedded within the mission of Jesuit education.

Peter-Hans Kolvenbach, S.J., superior general of the Society of Jesus, identified dynamics crucial for promoting justice and solidarity for Jesuit colleges and universities in the United States. After a conference in which he spoke, the presidents of each of the 28 Jesuit colleges and universities endorsed his speech in a sign of support for the renewed commitment of Jesuit higher education in the United States to educating for justice and solidarity. Excerpts of Kolvenbach's talk are shared here to demonstrate this commitment within Jesuit higher education. The Casa shares the perspective on education that Kolvenbach expressed that day:

> Students, in the course of their formation, must let the gritty reality of this world into their lives, so they can learn to feel it, think about it critically, respond to its suffering and engage it constructively. They should learn to perceive, think, judge, choose, and act for the rights of others, especially the disadvantaged and oppressed.
>
> . . . students need close involvement with the poor and marginalized now, in order to learn about reality and become adults of solidarity in the future.
>
> We must therefore raise our educational standard to educate the whole person of solidarity for the real world.
>
> All professors, in spite of the cliché of the ivory tower, are in contact with the world. But no point of view is ever neutral or value free. By preference, by option, our Jesuit point of view is that of the poor. So our professors' commitment to faith and justice entails a most significant shift in our viewpoint and choice of values. Adopting the point of view of those who suffer injustice, our professors seek the truth and share their research and its results with our students. . . . To expect our professors to make such an explicit option and speak about it is obviously not easy; it entails risk. But I do believe that this is what Jesuit educators have publicly stated, in Church and in society, to be our defining commitment. (personal communication, October 6, 2000)

These are radical challenges to Jesuit higher education. While some might think it impossible or even undesirable to use the perspectives of the poor as a pedagogical starting point, the Jesuits put it into practice in El Salvador.

Jesuit Higher Education in El Salvador

Historically, El Salvador has been controlled by a small number of families; at their bidding, the military, the police forces, and army-linked death squads repressed any civil or religious movement toward a more just society. A civil war broke out in 1980 and ended in January 1992, when the government signed peace accords with the FMLN, a coalition of guerrilla groups made up mainly of peasants. During the war, until the killing of the six Jesuits in 1989, the United States strongly backed the Salvadoran government by funding and training the military.

In the early morning of November 16, 1989, members of the Salvadoran army's elite Atlactal battalion, recently trained by a team of U.S. Green Berets, entered the University of Central America (UCA) and brutally assassinated its president, Ignacio Ellacuria, S.J., and his five Jesuit companions, including a housekeeper and her daughter. Ellacuria had been a critical voice throughout the war because, to the consternation of the U.S. and Salvadoran governments, he had long called for dialogue and negotiations to end the conflict.

A renowned philosopher, Ellacuria believed that the university's role was to be a social force at the service of the people. In a country where the majority lived in poverty and where those who tried to speak the truth were often tortured or killed, this vision had serious consequences. In the 1970s, the UCA began conducting academic research of the Salvadoran social, political, and economic conditions. It began analyzing the government's land reform proposal as well as the construction of a controversial dam. In response, bombs were set off inside the communications building at the UCA where the analysis was printed.

Today, the Jesuits and their colleagues at the UCA in El Salvador continue conducting rigorous social analysis of the social, political, and economic realities in the country. It is this same legacy that inspired the creation of the Casa in 1999 on the 10th anniversary of the killing of the Jesuits. Its aim is to commemorate their lives and continue their commitments of promoting justice and solidarity.

Casa de la Solidaridad

The summer of my junior year at Fairfield University, I had the opportunity to travel to Kingston, Jamaica, on an international volunteer experience offered through campus ministry. The idea was to experience and immerse ourselves in a different culture. Suddenly, I went from my parents' comfortable home outside Chicago to a dirt floor eating with two Jamaican children, Zane and Kayla. As they ate rice and beans, cockroaches whizzed by me on every side. The shock was dramatic. As night fell, the electricity in our shack went out, and we were surrounded by darkness. As the kids cried for more food, Camille, the 19-year-old mother, was noticeably upset that she could not provide for her children. I sat there completely overwhelmed. "Where am I?" I thought, "What is going on here?" One moment I was packing my bag for the adventure of experiencing another culture, and the next my world was being blown wide open as I tried to grasp the reality of this poor Jamaican family. This was the beginning of my journey to the Casa de la Solidaridad. Although I did not recognize it at the time, it was the place where I started to ask a variety of important questions: Why are there so many poor people here? How do these people survive? Why do they live like this while others possess such wealth, including my own family? What is my role in all this?

Who am I in this context? These questions (and others) had a significant impact on my own transformation as well as on my vocation. Thirteen years later, Trena, my wife, and I are the codirectors of the Casa.

Trena and I studied for 2 years in the College Student Personnel Masters program at Miami University, where we were introduced to student development theory and Marcia Baxter Magolda's longitudinal research. We incorporated these theories, especially Baxter Magolda's Learning Partnerships Model, into our subsequent work with college students, and they have directly influenced our work at the Casa. After graduating from Miami, we enrolled in master's programs at Boston College, where Trena focused on feminist theology and I on liberation theology. On graduation, we decided to seek out an extended experience of working with the poor in a developing country, so we went to Belize, Central America, for 2 years with an organization called Jesuit Volunteers: International. This gave us a chance to develop deeper relationships with the poor and further reflect on life from their perspective. Throughout these experiences, we were asking life's big questions: Who am I? What is my place in all this? What are my hopes and dreams? What kind of relationships do I want? How can I make sense of all this?

By the time we returned from Belize, it was clear that Trena and I had a common vocation: a passion to work directly with the poor and with college students from the United States. After 10 months of searching for meaningful work, we received a message from Dean Brackley, S.J., a Jesuit theologian from the Bronx who had gone to work in El Salvador after the six Jesuits were killed in 1989. He had an idea for a study-abroad program in El Salvador and wanted to talk to us about it. Dean suggested we contact Steve Privett, S.J., then provost of Santa Clara University, to explore his interest in supporting the idea. The four of us—Trena, Dean, Steve, and myself—met in El Salvador in February 1999 and over beer and pupusas (tortillas stuffed with cheese and beans) began to talk about the prospect of a Jesuit study-abroad opportunity focused on issues of justice and solidarity. Dean had the contacts in El Salvador and at the UCA, Steve and Santa Clara University had the administrative resources and were willing to endorse the program, and Trena and I were willing to carry it out. That night, the Casa was born.

Mission

The mission of Casa de la Solidaridad is the promotion of justice and solidarity. With our students, this is expressed through the creation of a meaningful learning experience where students integrate direct immersion with the poor of El Salvador with academic and personal reflection. With the Salvadoran community, it is expressed in a variety of ways: through supportive and mutual relationships with individual Salvadorans and Salvadoran communities, through the exchange of needed resources, through financial support for scholarships at the UCA and in rural El Salvador, and through meaningful and dignified employment opportunities.

There are four main objectives for the Casa:

(a) Education for transformation—to expand students' imaginations, broaden their worldviews, and challenge and support them to think more complexly and critically

(b) Education for global citizenship—to foster global understanding and peaceful cooperation between citizens of North and Central America and challenge students' perceptions about global justice and human liberation

(c) Education for self-authorship—to challenge and support students to reflect on their system of beliefs, values, and commitments in order that they become the authors of their lives

(d) Institutional solidarity—to foster academic and institutional links between North and Central America

Key components of the Casa include the praxis course (field placement in poor communities), the relationships with the Salvadoran community, the integrated curriculum, the relationship with the UCA scholarship students, the emphasis on personal and academic reflection, the intentional living/learning communities, the campo experience, and the Casa staff. These components are described in the following sections.

Praxis Course: Engagement with the Poor

The primary point of entry into the Salvadoran way of life is through the praxis course, which integrates praxis in local communities, social analysis, and personal reflection. Based on academic background, personal interests, and professional goals, each student is paired with a fellow classmate and assigned a praxis site in a poor Salvadoran community. Each praxis site has an on-site educator to ensure that students are exposed to realities of the people in their community. The on-site educators are generally social workers. Students attend their praxis site 2 full days a week over the course of the 4-month semester. In addition, they spend at least 2 long weekends living with families in order to gain a better understanding about life's daily rhythms. This learning environment cultivates an awareness of and sensitivity to the realities of those living in poverty. The praxis site is also the place where students develop meaningful relationships with poor Salvadorans. It provides the opportunity for students to develop friendships with people who are struggling to end social injustices while working to promote human dignity.

Students enter these communities as learners, not as volunteers. They are there as students and, as part of the curriculum, are required to analyze the social-political-economic situation within the community. At the same time, the relationship with the community is one of mutual service. Students are expected to be helpful and participate in a variety of activities, such as helping out in day care centers, translating letters from children to their financial sponsors in the United States, working with at-risk youth, helping in soup kitchens, and working in women's cooperatives.

A weekly seminar complements students' experiences in the field and provides them with opportunities for personal and communal reflection. Students are required to conduct a social analysis of their community in attempts at uncovering the root causes of the social-political-economic realities.

Relationship with Salvadoran Community

Although students are fundamental to our work, they are a part of a much larger context. Another fundamental aspect of our work is the well-being of our Salvadoran companions. Through the Casa, we work very closely with eight poor communities around San Salvador: Mejicanos, Tepecoyo, San Ramon, San Antonio Abad, La Chacra, Jayaque, El Cedro, and Las Palmas. Over the years, we have developed a great deal of *confianza* (trust) with these communities; in this postwar context, such trust is the basis of friendship. We are committed to supporting them and their work in a variety of ways. According to Salvadorans, this support is most directly felt by our presence in their communities. We are constantly told that our presence is seen as an act of solidarity. Often, this brings hope to people whose voices, unfortunately, are rarely heard. Our presence and that of our students give Salvadorans hope that the voices and concerns of the poor will be heard. In every community, people say, "We hope you share with others in your country about our reality." Given the fact that the policies of the United States toward countries like El Salvador greatly influence the lives of Salvadorans, this hope contains within it the possibility for future change.

Another means of supporting these communities is through employment. The individuals in the praxis communities are considered the professors of our students. As mentioned, our students are not volunteers. They are learners entering a different type of educational environment—the "classroom of the poor." In exchange for the communities' work of educating our students, the communities are paid. This money is often put to the service of communal projects and initiatives. In addition to the praxis sites, the Casa employs approximately 15 Salvadorans (professors, support staff, and so on). In a country where unemployment is approximately 50%, job creation is certainly a positive factor.

A third way the Casa supports the Salvadoran community is through scholarships. Each semester, two full 5-year scholarships are given to the UCA for its scholarship program that targets students with the greatest need. In addition, we support a scholarship program in rural El Salvador.

Integrated Curriculum

Students choose five out of six courses offered through the Casa. Those courses are Latin American theology, political science, Salvadoran literature, praxis seminar, Spanish, and sociology. Each of the professors is aware of the praxis site placement and attempts to relate the subject material to the students' experiences in these communities. For example, in the sociology class, students gather data from residents in their praxis communities on their perspectives of current events. This information is then analyzed in light of the messages sent by mass media (national newspapers and television). This curricular integration is systematically emphasized in a meeting at the beginning of each semester with the Casa staff, professors, praxis site directors, and UCA scholarship students. At this meeting, these linkages are conceptualized and concretized.

Casa Students

The Casa combines rigorous academics with a heavy emphasis on immersion with the poor and, therefore, tends to draw students who are open to this kind of an experience. Generally, we receive applications from students who have had short-term immersion experiences or have volunteered in a soup kitchen and wish to have an extended experience learning more about those who live in poverty. The students, most of whom are juniors, are required to have an intermediate level of Spanish, be in good academic standing, and be open to the experience of studying in a developing country. Although the Casa is open to any interested student in the United States, the invitation is especially extended to the 28 Jesuit colleges and universities in the United States. Students come to us studying a variety of academic disciplines, including economics, theology, political science, Spanish studies, sociology, and literature. We receive fewer students who study physics, chemistry, or biology because their core curricula are often less flexible. Students from diverse backgrounds, including different faith traditions, are highly encouraged to apply. Although the program is rooted in the Ignatian tradition of education, it is not designed exclusively for Christians.

Scholarship Students at the University of Central America

Casa de la Solidaridad collaborates closely with a group of 30 scholarship students through the Monseñor Romero Pastoral Center at the UCA. These students come from poor communities around San Salvador and receive a scholarship to study at the UCA through the Romero Center. Without this assistance, they would not be able to continue their higher education. Given that scholarship students come from poor communities, they have a great deal to teach our students about the hopes and struggles of average Salvadoran citizens. Although many of them have heartbreaking stories of the hardships they have endured throughout their lives, they are full of life and hopeful about the future. Among other things, this makes them excellent companions for our students.

Eight scholarship students live in community with our students at the Casa. Their presence in the community makes a significant difference in the learning experience of our students because of the power of peer relationships in our students' lives. As significant friendships develop with these scholarship students, our students' perceptions of the world often get challenged. For example, last semester, Patty (a scholarship student) shared how her family struggles when there is not enough rain to water her father's crops and how, in times of drought, the family has no safety net. Students visit Patty's family farm to work in the fields. These experiences bring the reality of Patty's family into the immediate imagination of our students. It makes their situation more tangible, more real.

Reflection

We assign meaning to our experiences through the process of reflection. Therefore, since we wish to foster students' development, it is essential that they have opportunities to reflect on their experiences at the praxis sites and on their relationships with the other students (Casa and UCA). These reflection opportunities offer great potential given that they invite students to question their own beliefs and values.

How does substantive reflection occur? At the Casa, students are invited, formally and informally, to reflect on their experiences both communally and individually. A prerequisite for successful communal reflecting is, of course, the level of confianza (trust) shared among the group. The degree to which students develop an "ethic of care" within the community is the degree to which reflections will be authentic and meaningful for students. Therefore, much attention is given at the beginning of each semester to the creation of a positive group dynamic. Students participate in team-building exercises to develop a positive community atmosphere. Students also participate in an exercise where they communally articulate hopes and expectations for their living/learning community. This list is then revisited throughout the semester. These community development activities are the building blocks of a community that can then be of service to students, encouraging them to authentically reflect on their experiences and their own beliefs and values.

A few examples demonstrate how formal communal reflection occurs. During orientation, students travel to all eight praxis sites so that each student has the opportunity to see where her or his classmates will be studying. In traditional Salvadoran style, the praxis sites plan activities to welcome our students. Students are introduced to many of the community's activities and then are often invited to visit the homes of some residents. These experiences tend to be very powerful for students given that many of them have never before witnessed such poverty or such generosity. Each evening during orientation, time is dedicated for students to share what has affected them during the day. Students find this time essential because it allows them to start to make sense of the experiences as well as recognize that they are not alone in their questioning. Given the circumstances, simply creating the space and inviting feedback is enough to get students reflecting. While Casa community facilitators and program directors are always present to ensure that all students have the opportunity to reflect, they are never required to do so.

Another example of formal communal reflection is through the praxis course, the weekly seminar connected to the students' experience in the communities. Every other week, students are invited to reflect on two broad questions: (a) What has struck you in the praxis site? and (b) How is what you are learning connected to your other classes? Again, given the nature of the student's experiences, meaningful reflection occurs simply by providing the outlet. Since I teach the course, I am able to follow up with other questions given students' feedback.

Individual formal reflection is also essential at the Casa. In the praxis seminar, students are required to keep a journal about their experiences in the communities. The questions are the same as the communal check-in questions listed previously. In this context, however, because students do not share these journals with their peers, they are able to write about thoughts and/or feelings that they may not feel comfortable sharing in the large group. I read these student reflections and give feedback. In addition to the journals, students have a personal development assignment where they reflect on how the Casa experience is affecting their own development. Students reflect on questions such as the following: What are you learning about your central beliefs? What are you learning about yourself? What questions are you asking yourself right now? and What are you learning about the world around you? This assignment offers students the chance to individually reflect on the effects of the experience on their development.

The student interviews I conduct in an attempt to better understand how students make sense of the experience over time offer another individual formal reflection opportunity. I interview the students at the beginning and the end of the Casa experience and annually afterward (2 years to date). Questions revolve around the three dimensions of development: interpersonal, intrapersonal, and epistemological. Examples include, What is your sense of yourself? What are characteristics of your relationships? What are your central values and beliefs? How do you make decisions? Some of the results of this investigation are shared in the following sections. It is important to highlight the value of asking these questions. Although students often find them quite challenging to answer, they report that it is very meaningful to have a space to reflect in such a way. Their reactions to the interview process itself suggest that many students lack opportunities to reflect on these fundamental questions.

Informal reflection happens quite naturally and often at the Casa. Students live in community with other Casa students from the United States and UCA scholarship students. This learning/living community offers many opportunities for spontaneous reflection, for example, over shared meals.

Living/Learning Community

In addition to living in community with UCA scholarship students, students also live with other students from the United States who are participating in the Casa. This intentional communal living arrangement is a key component to the Casa and is important because it offers students a supportive living/learning environment where they can deal with the challenges inherent in the program. Communities also offer the potential for conflict, which, provided that it is dealt with appropriately, can serve as a learning experience for our students. Living in each community is a Casa community facilitator whose responsibilities include assisting in the development of a positive community experience.

The Campo Experience

Another significant aspect of the Casa is the campo experience, where students travel to Arcatao, a town in the northern province of Chalatenango, and spend a week living with rural Salvadoran families. Donald Ballinger, S.J., the Jesuit priest in Arcatao, coordinates the experience. He matches our students with individual families who live in the mountains close to the border of Honduras. This experience tends to be rated on evaluations as one of the most significant for a variety of reasons. Students are struck by both the immense generosity of the people and the extent of the poverty in which they live. Campesinos (rural farmers) open their homes to our students for the entire week—unconditionally. They share the little they have and do so joyfully without expecting anything in return. Most of the communities lack electricity, adequate sanitation, and running water. Common health problems, such as diarrhea, present high risks to the campesinos, especially to the children. Given that they are subsistence farmers in an area of frequent droughts, they often suffer from malnutrition. The Casa supports the development of the community through supporting a local scholarship initiative.

Casa Staff

Students are vulnerable when they arrive at the Casa. They leave behind their families, their friends, the familiarity of school, and even their language and come to a country with a totally different cultural context. At the same time, students come asking many questions: Who am I? Where do I fit in? What is my vocation? What kind of relationships do I want? They have rarely reflected on these questions—and not from this unique context. In addition to these customary college student questions, the Casa raises others: Why all this poverty? Why are these people smiling? What is my role in all this? How did this happen? How am I going to respond? Given all these challenges, students need the best kind of support to begin to answer these questions for themselves. This support is systematized in a variety of ways.

The fundamental role of the codirectors is to ensure that the Casa fulfills its mission. This takes place most directly by accompanying students as they journey through the experience. As directors, we try to assess when and how individual students can be best supported. Through individual meetings, we are able to identify those students who may need a little extra support (e.g., those who are extra homesick or too challenged by the experience). This extra support can be as simple as taking the student out for ice cream and asking how he or she is doing. If students are really struggling, we set up more frequent meetings to ensure that we are aware of the student's condition. We invite students to meet more often if they feel the need. This open-door policy is an essential means for providing student support.

Given the nature and intensity of this experience, it is necessary to have a qualified staff to accompany the students. At the beginning of each academic year, the entire staff (professors, central staff, UCA scholarship students, and support staff) meets in order to review the mission, history, and future direction of the Casa. The staff consists of 34 individuals. This number is quite remarkable given that there are usually only 20 students studying during any current semester. In addition to the two codirectors, there is a Salvadoran assistant director, three community facilitators, nine UCA scholarship students, a Jesuit adviser, eight praxis site supervisors, and five professors, all of whom are ready to assist the students. The assistant director teaches two Spanish courses and coordinates the campo experience as well as other field trips. The community facilitators live in community with students and are responsible for promoting community development. The scholarship students serve as peer educators. The Jesuit adviser supports the directors and serves as a liaison to the Jesuit community as well as the UCA.

Learning Partnerships Model and the Casa de la Solidaridad

When Trena and I began the master's program at Miami University, we attended a graduate student retreat to kick off the academic program. After the introductions, the faculty began by asking all of us about our previous experiences with learning environments. They asked us which environments we thought assisted our learning and which did not. Then they invited us to have a say in creating our own learning environment. This one event symbolizes for me the key aspects of the Learning Partnerships Model. They validated that we as students had something to contribute to this learning environment, situated the question in a way that invited us to draw on our own experiences, and encouraged us to be co-creators of our own learning. The combination of having *experienced* the Learning Partnerships Model in graduate school while simultaneously studying student development theory has influenced the way I see learning as well as how we have structured the Casa. All the basic assumptions of the Learning Partnerships Model are deeply embedded within many aspects of the Casa program. A few specific examples of each are described next.

Knowledge as Complex and Socially Constructed

Soon after students arrive in El Salvador, they are faced with many complex and challenging questions: Is the current process of globalization helping or hurting the citizens of El Salvador? What are the root causes of poverty here? What led up to the 12-year civil war? What impact do the policies of the

U.S. government have on this small developing country? Through their classes, in their praxis sites, and in conversations with the UCA scholarship students, Casa students encounter these and other complex social problems. The praxis seminar and the political science and sociology classes all emphasize gathering data and conducting analyses of the current social-political-economic situation in the country. At the same time, students are required to develop their own interpretations given the data. Addressing these topics provides students the opportunity to view knowledge as complex and socially constructed.

The living/learning community presents students with another level of social complexity—that of living in community with others. Communal living provides students the opportunity to connect their knowledge with the knowledge of their peers. For example, once a week students have a community night, a time when the whole community comes together to participate in a group activity. Some examples include discussing a topic of interest (e.g., the intricacies of significant relationships, the art of yoga, or the problem of deforestation), communal reflecting around a particular question (e.g., what is justice? what does it mean to live in solidarity?), reviewing the highs and lows of the previous week, or a community development exercise (e.g., ropes course or learning how to make pupusas). During these activities, students are able to share their values, beliefs, and interests with their peers and have the chance to listen and learn how their community mates construct knowledge. From these experiences, students learn that we construct knowledge within a complex context.

Authority and Expertise Are Shared in the Mutual Construction of Knowledge Among Peers

The educational philosophy of the codirectors and the practice that flows from it is an essential aspect of this assumption. Our educational philosophy owes a great deal to Paulo Freire, the Brazilian educator who developed his classic work, *Pedagogy of the Oppressed,* from his experience of teaching peasants in Brazil how to read. Freire (1970) describes how peasants are not objects to be filled with already existing knowledge but rather are the subjects of their own learning; that is, they play an active and essential role in the development of knowledge. We have a similar educational view with our students. Certainly not all perspectives are equal; however, it is important that students' perspectives and knowledge base are respected. Of course, professors do have expertise in a certain field as well as an added responsibility to ensure that learning takes place in the classroom. This learning is accelerated when we recognize that students bring with them a valuable perspective to the classroom.

At the Casa, students are strongly encouraged to "take the reins" of their own learning. That is, they are encouraged to be active players in their own educational process. During the weeklong orientation, students are informed that they should frequently reflect on how the overall program could be improved in order to make the experience more meaningful for students. Three weeks into the experience, a program evaluation is conducted that solicits the students' feedback in all areas of the experience (predeparture material, orientation, praxis sites, classes, and community living). On the basis of this feedback, significant changes are often made in the Casa program. For example, some students may have a desire to focus more in depth on women's issues in El Salvador or on the situation of the gangs in San Salvador. These wishes can then be shared with praxis site directors, professors, and UCA scholarship students in order to target students' specific learning needs. While it is time consuming, the evaluation process is important because it gives students a chance to see that they are an important part of the process in which knowledge is constructed. Because of this, students often comment that they feel respected as active participants in the Casa. At the end of each semester, a final programmatic evaluation is conducted. Before students depart for the semester, they are given a copy of the overall evaluation as well as the changes to be made in the upcoming semester based on their input. Taking students seriously is central to validating their capacity to know.

Self Is Central to Knowledge Construction

At the beginning of each semester, students participate in a weeklong orientation in order to prepare them for the upcoming 4 months of study. During this time, Casa directors share suggestions from experiences with other groups and some of the general findings of the research we have done with previous Casa students. One important finding is the centrality of the "who am I?" question for students. We share with current students how for many of their peers who have gone before them, this was a central, if not the central, question they were struggling to answer in this context. Sharing this at the beginning of orientation highlights right away the importance of coming to better understand ourselves. Through interviews and in the praxis seminar, students are continually invited to reflect on the question of identity.

The point of departure for students' learning is their personal experience with the poor in their praxis sites. The curriculum as well as the majority of students' reflection time tend to revolve around the many elements of this central experience. As mentioned previously, the students' personal experience with the poor is intentionally integrated into their other classes. For example, in the Latin American theology class, students are encouraged to investigate theological questions from the perspective of the people in their praxis sites. Students are then invited to reflect on how their experience in the praxis site is contributing to their own personal theology. Similarly, the political science professor ties class material to students' real-life experience. For example, students study electoral politics and are required to learn about the perceptions of the people at their praxis sites in regard to upcoming elections. Then students serve as monitors in the national elections. Students value the connection between academics and their real-world experiences. Situating their learning in their own experiences with their praxis sites makes learning and academics more appealing.

Effect of the Casa on Students' Development

On the basis of past research describing environments that successfully promoted students' development, Trena and I decided to make the assumptions of the Learning Partnerships Model operative in the Casa program. The question remained, however, as to how the Casa experience, given its unique educational context, would affect students' development. We decided to pursue the question, What effect did the Casa experience have on students' epistemological, interpersonal, and intrapersonal development?

I conducted a series of interviews with Casa students: during the first week after they arrived in El Salvador, at the end of their experience, and each year thereafter (2 years to date). The interviews, which lasted for approximately 1 hour, revolved around the different dimensions of development. Among other questions, students were asked about their beliefs and values (epistemological), their sense of themselves and who they are becoming (intrapersonal), and their relationships (interpersonal).

As with any assessment process, there are advantages and limitations to the method of data collection and analysis. Because I am the codirector of the Casa program, I have the advantage of daily contact with students. This enables me not only to develop positive relationships with them but also to establish a basic level of trust, both of which are important factors in obtaining honest data. When students feel a confidence in the relationship, they are more likely to share authentically what they are feeling and thinking. However, the same codirector—student relationship could, at times, be a limitation if, for example, students tried to give responses they felt I wanted to hear. Second, although the insights from this assessment can be useful to educators working with similar students in similar contexts, it is important to emphasize that these outcomes are particular to this context.

Drawing from over 96 interviews with 42 students over the past 3 years, I identified two broad themes. First, exposure to the realities of people living in poverty while living in a different culture created dissonance, challenging values and beliefs (cognitive), sense of self (intrapersonal), and relationships (interpersonal). Second, support for students' transformation came via opportunities for personal and communal reflection, community living and experiences with poor Salvadorans, and assignments that integrate students' experience in marginal communities with academic disciplines. Maturity in all three dimensions of development occurred when students experienced the optimal combination of challenge and support.

These themes and their interconnectedness are evident in Jackie's story. Through Jackie's reflections, we get a glimpse of how she made sense of her time at the Casa and of the impact the experience had on the different dimensions of her development. Jackie's story and the voices of the other Casa students are summarized to further explore the dynamics of their growth and transformation toward self-authorship in the context of the Casa.

Jackie's Reflections

Jackie is a former student at a Jesuit university in the Midwest who had been out of the United States only one other time in her life. Her experience at the Casa fostered growth in each of the dimensions of development. Jackie began to think more critically and contextually (epistemological), to develop her own internal belief system (intrapersonal), and to become more interdependent with others (interpersonal). This was due to the fact that she experienced a special blend of challenge and support within the context of El Salvador.

Exposure to the Realities of Those Living in Poverty Creates Dissonance

During Jackie's time in El Salvador, she spent a significant amount of time learning and teaching in a public school located in Las Brisas, a poor community outside San Salvador. In this community, Jackie encountered the realities of people living in poverty. These comments about her participation in the Casa reveal the cognitive growth she experienced:

> Everything I have done here has been a challenge, but a good challenge. It has forced me to look at the way that I live and what I want to do with my future. Now things are not as cut and dry as I thought they would be because now *I have been exposed to the reality of the poor* [emphasis added] which I have never experienced before which is wonderful. It has been a

huge challenge and a huge struggle and it had its fun parts too. But now I have a lot of thinking to do about what I am going to do with my future. I know I still want to teach and my praxis site really reaffirmed that I still want to be a teacher. I loved being in the classroom setting. But I just don't know whose kids I want to teach anymore. It has been a challenge and a wonderful challenge and life changing—all the things that people said it was going to be but that I did not believe. It really was life changing.

When asked to expand on how she has changed, she commented,

> The way I look at things. Before, I read the newspaper but I didn't take into account my part into it. Now I realize I do have a say, for example, in the policies of our government. I never really took an interest in it. Now I look at things through different eyes. Things I do and even things I buy, things I say, even just talking with people. And on the big level to what I am going to do with my life. One of the big things I have learned is that I am not going to solve all the world's problems. No matter how hard I work—how many lives touch me and how many lives I can be a part of—this world is a big place and seeing some of the neighborhoods that we have seen, it is depressing but at the same time, after you have individual conversations with the people who live there, you realize there still is hope. So looking at the big picture it is hard not to be depressed by these realities but then the individual contact we have had with Salvadorans has been just an amazing learning experience in and of itself. Like I have been saying over and over, that the people are not just numbers anymore. The poor are no longer just statistics. They have names and faces. They are friends. So I am going to look at that differently when I hear statistics about poverty. I am going to remember what I have seen here. I will remember my friends.

Jackie's view of the world broadened during her time in El Salvador, as did the way she made sense of it. It was larger and more complex than before, and knowledge was not so "cut and dry." Her experiences with the poor gave her a new set of eyes with which to see the world. Trying to see the world through the perspective of the poor encouraged and even "forced" Jackie to rethink her old assumptions about herself, the world, and her role within it. She started asking life's big questions (about identity, vocation, and relationships) from a totally foreign context, a context where the poor are struggling to survive. From within this context, Jackie began to think more contextually, to reexamine her own set of beliefs and values and her relationships with others. Asking these questions in this context created a great deal of cognitive dissonance. As she said, the experience was "a huge challenge and a huge struggle." Fortunately, Jackie found the support she needed in order to meet these challenges.

Community Living Supports Transformation

For Jackie, the Casa living learning community was one of the central factors that supported her transformation. It provided an environment where Jackie felt comfortable about questioning her values, beliefs, and relationships. When asked about her relationships, Jackie said,

> The relationships I have formed have been one of the best parts of this experience. And coming down here it was very scary because I was coming down here, not knowing anybody. But it has been unbelievable. I mean, the individual relationships with people. You go through such a meaningful experience with somebody and then you are bonded to them. Whether it is just between you two or a few of you . . . a bond is formed and I think throughout this whole trip, we have been individually experiencing this with each person. So we have our individual bonds, close personal bonds and then the whole community has been very open to not judging each other and laughing at our mistakes and teasing each other. It has really been a wonderful experience. . . . The deepest relationships have been through our Casa community, but the fact that we were exposed to so many other people outside of our community, even if they were brief encounters, helped so much. . . . I have learned so much from them. And in many cases there was a relationship formed. I think there are three levels, the people you meet for 5 minutes, and then people like Lillian and Daisy [UCA scholarship students]. . . . But the community relationships have gone way deeper than that, just trying to struggle through who we all are together and individually.

The support Jackie needed came primarily from the Casa learning community, the community of other students from the United States. This learning community provided a safe, reflective space where Jackie did not feel judged when she expressed her viewpoint. This environment helped her honestly reflect on her experiences and begin to answer some of her questions. This support helped Jackie mature in the three dimensions of development.

Promotion of Self-Authorship

This unique combination of experiences that simultaneously challenged and supported Jackie also prompted transformation of her identity. Asking life's big questions from the context of the poor in El Salvador, given the supportive environment of the Salvadorans and the Casa community, created a fertile environment for Jackie to begin the process of becoming the author of her life. One year after Jackie left the Casa, she had this to say when asked the questions, Who are you? What is your sense of yourself?

I started discovering this when I was at the Casa . . . that I'm not what other people think of me. . . . I am what I am, and how other people perceive me doesn't worry me as much anymore. . . . I realize that life is very individual, and I don't have to depend on other people to figure out who I am. That I can figure out who I am. I already am. I just need to. . . . It is a process, an individual process of finding out who you are. It is not always just people telling you who you are. You have to do it on your own.

In addition to better understanding the perspectives and *realities of people living in poverty,* Jackie came to discover that she can and indeed wants to be the author of her life. Her realization that she could "figure out who I am" was key to the whole process of defining for herself who she was and, in turn, how she thought and how she viewed her relationships with others. Her comments suggest that she started the process of no longer being authored by the beliefs and values of others but instead began to discover her own voice and subsequently start exploring her own integrated internal belief system.

When Jackie was asked about the changes in her central beliefs, she responded,

Beliefs about what is important are now more focused for me on seeing the needs of other people. I realize that people are coming from very different backgrounds, very different places. People have different ideas and I am more willing to listen and be open to things that I have never experienced before especially where I don't have any background.

Inquiring into Jackie's hopes and dreams for the future revealed her level of *intercultural maturity* as well as her desire to continue to grow and develop:

I hope that I never get tired of learning about new things, new places, new people . . . that I never get stuck in one way of thinking or thinking that just one way is right . . . that I am going to continue to change and that my ideas will continue to change . . . that I am going to continue to challenge myself to meet people that are going to challenge what I believe and what I think because that is the only way we can grow. I want to be comfortable, but never so comfortable that I am not challenged.

Jackie's experience in El Salvador and the growth she experienced have motivated her to search out environments that simultaneously challenge and support her. One year after her time in El Salvador, I asked Jackie how that experience affected her thinking. She responded,

In general, I have been surprised. I thought I would come back from El Salvador and think a lot about it and not that I would just move on, I knew it would play a part in the decisions that I make, but I did not realize that, a year later, it would come up in my mind about 200 times a day just about different experiences that I had and people that I met. And so, the Casa experience definitely influenced my way of thinking. Previously I had never had to make decisions on social justices types of things. I didn't really read the newspaper. I was interested in world events but they didn't concern me because they didn't seem all that real. You could read about them but it did not affect me. But then after the Casa, I realize how world events need to play a role in my life because I am responsible. I have a responsibility to be aware of what is going on. . . . I think the personal connection with people in the Casa really influenced this.

Jackie was surprised at the degree to which her experience with the people of El Salvador continued to influence her thinking. This degree of thinking about social justice, which began in El Salvador, continued to develop 1 year later. Characteristic of a mature global citizen, Jackie felt personally responsible to be aware of what is happening to others in the world. Her contact with the people in El Salvador gave new meaning to the statistics and numbers she read about in the newspapers. The statistics now had names and faces.

Jackie's experiences with the poor in El Salvador fostered growth in each of the dimensions of development. She started to discover the complexity of knowledge and began to recognize the need to think contextually when analyzing different situations. She also developed a respect for different ways of knowing based on different experiences (cognitive maturity). Simultaneously, she started to discover her own role within knowledge creation. She began to recognize her responsibility in developing who she was becoming and began rethinking her set of values and beliefs in light of her own experience (integrated identity). Simultaneously, Jackie started to recognize that her relationships were important for helping her along the journey but that they did not define who she was becoming. She developed a deep respect for people different from herself.

Maturity in all three areas is leading Jackie toward becoming a global citizen concerned for others, especially the poor. Her desire to seek out new and challenging environments continued after the Casa. At the time I completed this chapter, Jackie decided to travel to Nicaragua through Jesuit Volunteers: International, which is an international volunteer organization in which she is working with the poor as a schoolteacher.

Reflections on the Dynamics of Challenge and Support

The stories of additional Casa participants provide more details about the dynamics of challenge and support with each theme. Exposure to the realities of people living in poverty while living in a different culture created dissonance for students. These challenges called and at times "forced" students to rethink their values and beliefs (cognitive), sense of self (intrapersonal), and relationships (interpersonal). Support for students' transformation came from opportunities for reflection, community living, and assignments that integrated their experiences with academic disciplines. The combination of these challenges and supports enabled them to think more critically and contextually, to reflect more deeply on their internal beliefs and values, and to develop a better understanding about their relationships with others.

Exposure to the Realities of the Poor and Cognitive Dissonance

While in El Salvador, Christina spent a great deal of time in the community of Tepecoyo, a rural village outside San Salvador, working in a soup kitchen for malnourished children. She commented on her experience:

> It is an eye opening experience for me. It has turned my world upside down and has made me more aware of things in the world. Spending time in the communities in Tepecoyo [praxis site] and really talking to the people and hearing what they have to say about political issues, their beliefs, and their spirituality. It opens your eyes, seeing how other people live, and the atmosphere and the setting, but also the Casa students have been a key aspect of my learning, because I looked at them and what they say, and they have a lot of views and have so many wonderful things to share. I'd get so much more out of what they had to say than out of any class. . . . The classes helped solidify it all.

Christina's comments again demonstrate how the experience turned students' views of the world upside down and encouraged them to critically reflect from different contexts. Seeing the way the people live in Tepecoyo opened Christina's eyes to the way others live in the world. This encouraged her to further reflect on her life, as is evidenced in the following comments:

> I feel like I have been inwardly trying to figure out what this experience means to me and how I'm going to take that back, and how that is going to shape what I do in the future. So I feel right now I am more inwardly focused on myself and on my own development of ideas and thoughts and stuff and political thoughts and things along those lines. I am trying to make sense of the experience to myself and figure out how I am going to share that with others—starting inward and going outward is my biggest thing in my life right now. I am eager to understand things down here and in the world and reading more about it. I have gotten my feet wet. I feel like learning more is a huge part of my life right now. I'm really motivated to do that.

She continued to talk about the challenges she currently faces:

> Having my mom here really made me realize how much I want to go home. She was the person I keep in the best contact with and I have been telling her about everything. And she told me that she had no idea how this was until she came and saw it and I feel like that is going to be how it is with everyone at home. That is a huge challenge: figuring out how I'm going to deal with that and dealing with the people like my grandma. I spoke with her last night for Thanksgiving and she asked if I had Mexican food for dinner and I said we had turkey. She said, "Oh, that is civilized. I didn't know people were civilized like that there." I feel like I'm going to get a lot of that.

Christina's concerns about returning to her relationships in the United States were shared by many students. As students make the shift from defining themselves on the basis of other people's beliefs and values toward becoming the authors of their lives, they experience dissonance in many areas, including the area of relationships. Christina's values and beliefs, indeed the way she views the world, are changing. At the time of her departure from El Salvador, she worried about how that is going to play out in her relationships. This fear gets expressed in her wishing, at one level, that she did not even have the experience. Here is what she said when asked how the experience is affecting who she is becoming:

> This is a hard question. Sometimes I wonder why I am so grateful for this experience. Now I can never ever again be the same person I was. Sometimes I think it would be so much easier if I didn't know that people live like this and could go on living in my happy little world, thinking everything is perfect, doing the service project and not questioning things. That is kind of what I did before. I would work in homeless shelters, but I never cared to think and ask why people are homeless. So life would be easier without this experience, but now I am forced in the best way possible to go down a different road. I am forced to see things differently, but there are times I wish that this did not happen. Things would be so much easier. It has affected what I'm going to do. It affected every action that I take. I'm forever dedicated to these people that I have met here. I am dedicated to them and their struggle for justice. In a way I am pushed to figure out why people are living so awfully in the United States. There is still so much poverty in the United States. I feel like I have an obligation to get to know the immigrants in my own neighborhood. It has influenced what I want to do. I thought I would go into nursing and be a missionary but now I feel drawn towards education—to learn about the realities of the world, to do education. That is one of the major ways that things could change is through education. I don't see things changing any other way beside people realizing what is going on. I could

become a nurse and administer medical aid. But now I feel like I need to try and change things. Now I know I can't change the world but I can get people's eyes opened. I am more aware of how my little decisions affect the greater population, and how things in the U.S. affect smaller countries like El Salvador. My train of thought is changed, asking questions that I would never have bothered to ask before. When we don't know a lot of this stuff [poverty], you don't think about it. You just think about if there are people living like this here, how are people living in the rest of the world and what is the way to deal with that?

Christina's story provides an overview of the different dynamics within the challenge-and-support continuum. Like many others, her perception of the world is much larger, more complicated than before. Her experience with the poor has, in her words, "forced" her to see things differently. Awareness of this perspective made her question a great deal about her life to the extent that she is considering changing her vocation from nursing to education.

At the end of Miguel's time in El Salvador, he commented on the most important aspect of his learning. He said,

The most important thing for me was getting a better understanding of what poverty is. I knew it was inequality, and I went to Mexico for a week, and I remember being surprised then, seeing that contrast with Tijuana. It has been just so much more powerful here because the experiences of being in such extremes going in the same day from the campo [rural El Salvador] for a week and going for a run the next day and being in one of the richest neighborhoods in El Salvador.

The contrast between being exposed to the extremes of wealth and poverty created a dissonance within Miguel and was one of the most important aspects of his learning in El Salvador. Similarly, Sophia highlights the dissonance this reality created for her:

The most important one is that everyone really is equal—is created equal. That is a thing that is easy to say, but a lot of people don't understand, and I don't know if you can understand until you hold hands with a poor child.

Sophia suggests that this dissonance came primarily through contact with the poor symbolized by her description of holding the hand of a poor child. Many students commented on the dramatic difference between studying statistics on poverty and actually meeting people who live in such conditions. The latter tended to create more dissonance. In this next statement, not only did Tim see the dissonance the experience created, but it led to a new perspective for him:

> It has pushed me over the edge. I have always been socially conscious just being in my family. My dad, I shared this with you before, and my mom are involved as well, more on the local level, so I have always been aware. I have always been and had these strong feelings of devotion to the poor, but I see it now has more of a personal challenge as well. "If you have come here to help me, you are wasting your time. . . . But if your liberation is bound up with mine then let us work together."[1] We are struggling in the United States in a different way and I needed this experience to completely expose me to these kinds of realities and feel them, and it has changed . . . my eyes will see the world from the perspectives of the Salvadorans and from their reality.

The dissonance Rosie experienced led her to be more open to different realities. She said,

> This experience has been the most life-changing experience I have had in my life where I can see that I have changed. My heart has been opened and my eyes and my mind have been opened to a reality I did not know existed before. I can say this has been the most amazing experience I have had in my life. I was so sure in what I was going to do with the rest of my life. But I've never been so challenged to think outside of the box of what I was going to do and to go out of my comfort zone. It has been worn thin. I have faced many fears and have had faith that I am going to make it through certain things. I feel I have grown in that way a lot.

After Alex finished his semester at the Casa, he was asked, What gives your life meaning? What are you passionate about? He answered,

> What really moves me is when I go to places like La Chacra and Las Palmas, when we went down to the squatter communities [where people live in cardboard boxes]. I couldn't even go down there. I went down there, but then I left. . . . Those are two experiences that were like . . . they make you want to cry. What really gets me going is when I can take an experience like this in a place like that and come back and say to people look at what is going on and to try and plant some seeds. I'm trying to be a witness to the loss of dignity of lives here, because there are just countless people that have no dignity to their lives. It gets me going to try to be present and then be a witness to other people to bring some awareness of the dignity of their lives here.

---

[1]This popular phrase is attributed to a Brisbane-based Aboriginal educator and activist.

When asked to reflect on his central beliefs 1 year after his time in El Salvador, Brian commented,

The way I live my life is connected with the way others live their lives. The decisions I make have some bearing on the lives of other people. I don't want to put too much importance on me as a selfish person, but the way I choose to act and the things I choose to buy and what I choose to do with my free time really does affect other people's lives. There is definitely an interconnectedness and based on that interconnectedness I feel a responsibility to do something about that, to improve it. Certainly that is why I do human rights work. I've spent all year working on the [domestic service] program here [his university], because there is an interconnectedness, whether it be domestically through the [domestic service] program or internationally with victims of human rights abuses. For me this is very real and it makes sense. I could not doubt it after going to El Salvador and spending time in San Ramon and feeling very connected to the folks that were there and realizing the only real difference between them and me is the chance of where we were born. As we began to open up to each other and understand each other's stories, I began to understand how that interconnectedness is so urgent in the way I live my life, in what I pursue and my vocation. So more than anything, the Casa program reaffirmed that.

Brian's experience with the realities of the poor at times moved him to tears. But it also moved him to think about his life, his vocation, and the interconnectedness of us all. He developed a deep respect for the lives of others, especially the most vulnerable. His experience with the people in San Ramon, his praxis site, enabled him to learn the stories of the people there. This led to a new understanding of the connectedness of people even through great distances.

Reflection and Community Living Support Transformation

Julia's opening comments during her second interview captured the dynamic many of our students' experienced during their time in El Salvador:

The experience has been totally impossible to sum up in words. The most encompassing thing I can say is that it has changed my life in so tangible a way. It has changed my life, the way that I feel about everything. Things have changed, that I kind of expected, but you can never know to what depth things like this are going to happen. It has been an extreme experience of the extreme emotions, extreme thoughts, if you will, thoughts that go very deep. At the same time it has been very peaceful. It has shaken me up. But taken me to this place where I feel more solid than before.

Julia's experiences with the people of El Salvador turned her world upside down. Fortunately, she obtained the support necessary to deal with these challenges and emerged from the experience feeling more solid than before. When asked how the experience affected her thinking, she commented,

> I feel I have received a revolutionary education here. There is a much more secure and peaceful person in Julia in general. I have been a pessimist ever since, I don't know, third grade probably. I feel that loosening. It has been helpful to be out of the States as long as I have, because it has made me look much more critically at things. And when we were on retreat, I had a revelation about the whole U.S. consumerism culture. I think it [retreat] has influenced me to take more time for my self. I realize how nourishing that time was and how peaceful it was. I feel like a much more stable person. Just happier in a certain way.

Julia noticed herself changing in El Salvador into a less pessimistic person. She also noticed herself becoming a more critical thinker. Being outside the United States enabled her to think critically about U.S. culture particularly in regard to the level of consumerism. Having this distance from the United States provided many students the opportunity to further reflect critically on their own U.S. culture. On retreat, where students spend a good deal of time reflecting on their experiences, Julia discovered the value of taking time for reflection and even noticed herself feeling happier. At the time of publication, Julia had received funding to write a story about the Salvadoran immigrants.

During Beth's time in El Salvador, she reflected a great deal on her own identity. She said,

> I am embracing the idea that it is a process of becoming me. Today Beth is Beth and tomorrow she will be someone different and you can never fully capture who someone is. Who I am becoming has gone in two different directions. One sense, I have come to realize that who I am becoming is completely shaped by all my experiences, but mostly the relationships and people that have been in my life. So I am not just Beth but I am also all these Salvadorans now, like that is a huge part of who Beth is, but the other side of it is a lot of aspects of this experience have been on my own, especially when it comes to processing things and that sort of thing. It has only been me. It hasn't been anyone else. None of my mentors or anyone from back home saying, hey, what do you think about this? What do you think about that? So, I feel like I have definitely found my own voice in a different way. So going in those two directions but understanding that they can't work without one another.

Beth's reflections on the power that mentors have had over her and her ability to become the author of her life elicited a follow-up question about the significance of this distance. She said,

> I definitely have grown a lot more confident in myself, in what I say. . . . So being able to be away in another country, where I do not need to see them the next day has given me a lot of freedom to just really show the real Beth and just explore that. But there is a core to Beth that no one else has seen at this point in this moment today. I think Beth is, she has been broken open. She is broken here in El Salvador by the love and hospitality of the Salvadorans. So she is still a young woman searching but knowing that this whole life is a search. I am no longer searching for one thing in one direction. Just rather taking everything as it comes. So Beth is a woman searching. I put a lot of stock into authority and what their impressions of me are, what their idea of me is and that sort of thing, and being away from that has been really, I think healthy for me. To not have to be what I think people expect me to be. So, not having that constant presence. I have been really able to just be Beth, who Beth is. . . . So I have been able to be more of who I want to be myself and not to have anyone judging that or critiquing that right away.

Beth found the distance between her and her mentors freeing. This enabled her to more authentically discover her true identity and find her own voice.

Whereas Beth benefited from personal reflection, Matt appreciated the communal living arrangement at the Casa. He comments on why this was so important:

> I think it was just how real it was. We were all going through the same experience; we were all experiencing it in completely different ways. And if we weren't living together, I don't think necessarily we would have known that. It helped in the sense that I think we would have all been friends but I don't think we would have known each other as well as we did. And I don't think our experiences in terms of praxis sites would have come together so perfectly. We would not have had that interplay as a result of living in community. I think the community setting sort of facilitated that process almost. And when I say how cool it was the disagreements and everything were kind of frustrating at times, very frustrating, but if that didn't happen, there wouldn't have been that realness. I think it enabled us to better let our guard down in a good way to really experience the Casa inside and out. I don't think it would have been possible without that community setting.

Matt explained how the distance helped him become a more critical thinker:

> I like to critically distance myself once in a while, it helps me just understanding more about it and what I want to be doing, and physical distance for me at least is often times a critical portion of that and that is what El Salvador or

the experience there was to a large degree. We were all able to completely step out of what was normal for us and try and make sense of the situation, our decision-making process. I would go back to that—my thoughts and feelings there—because it was one time when I was really able to physically distance myself and expose my real self. I have a renewed excitement as well to start answering my own questions, to start really. I have always crumpled with these before they start, especially in regards to spirituality. Writing your paper has helped me to begin to look at these questions.

Like many other students, Matt appreciated the distance between himself and the U.S. culture because it enabled him to more authentically reflect on himself. Matt also expressed his enthusiasm for beginning to answer his own questions, citing his theology assignment, which asks students to integrate their experiences in El Salvador with their own theological beliefs.

Reflecting on Dissonant Perspectives

The generosity of the poor in El Salvador often takes visitors by surprise. Maria alluded to this when asked about the impact the Casa experience had on her thinking:

The things that have impacted me the most have been my experiences with the poorest people of the poor. I feel like back home, we complain about tight economic situations. We can't get this and we can't do that. But here being with the poorest of the poor, I have had the opportunity to walk into their houses. They know that they are poor, almost to the level of misery, but they open their doors with their arms wide open. They offer what they have even if that directly affects them, their dinner for the night or for the week. Their ability to be accepting and nonjudgmental is incredible. I have learned a lot of things about the United States' role in this country. And the role in the history of this country has made me feel embarrassed a little bit. I have been told by so many Salvadorans, "It is not you that we are disappointed in" and that "we are grateful for you being here and your presence means a lot." I don't know if I have experienced that kind of forgiveness or acceptance in the States before, and it has made me look at my forgiving of people and my allowing people into my life.

She continued to talk about the new role of reflection in her life as of late:

I have been reflecting a lot lately, thinking outside of my life in the States and what I knew there and what I experienced there—thinking globally about other people and the way my actions affect other people and thinking. I think a lot of times I just went through the motions without thinking, without reflection. So reflecting on my experiences, reflecting on my actions, reflecting on how everything is intertwined or whether it is intertwined has been important lately.

Maria was affected by the generosity of the poor in El Salvador, which made her rethink her ability to forgive others as well as her willingness to let other people into her life. Her comments on reflection demonstrate the value many students discovered in taking the time to make meaning of their experiences.

One year after Marcus left the Casa, he described how the experience affected his thinking:

> It had an incredible impact on my thinking. I came into the experience with my lens and left with an entirely different set of lenses of analysis and understanding of realities and I think that the community experience of the Casa and the way in which we learned together, discussed together, and came out of an experience together led me to realize that there is so much more to analysis and to looking at an issue rather than simply reading a paper on it. There are so many contexts, especially in the case of everything we studied. It led me to be much more critical of all of the experiences and led me to be so much more critical of every little nuance that we are led to believe or gets written. I think absolutely a lot of the realization of that came out our experience in El Salvador. Without my experience, I don't think I would be so engaged and interested in really looking into things, and really asking the questions.

Marcus's comments indicate that he is thinking more critically and reflectively in light of his experience in El Salvador. He was exposed to different lenses, which invited him to see knowledge as more contextual. This occurred especially in his course work of conducting a social analysis in his praxis site, where students are required to explore some of the root causes to the social-political-economic climate in their communities.

At the end of Tom's experience in El Salvador, he commented on how the experience broadened his worldview. When asked about the overall impact the experience had on him, he said,

> If there is a mosaic and you're looking at the mosaic and you're standing an inch away, you can see a couple of colors. They are there and they are true. But when you back up, you see more colors. Those colors you saw initially are still true, but you have to compare and see how they are different from the other colors around them. I still believe in Christianity. It is very truthful. I just have a much larger, more complicated world now.

Tom highlighted the importance for him of reflecting on his experiences. He said,

> I think reflection is like incredibly important because if you just kind of ride through life without reflecting you can miss life. . . . But if you are truly reflective and you're honest with yourself—you avoid putting up walls, and start looking at everything. How does that get played out? Through my academic stuff, obviously, through papers and assignments.

Assignments

The assignments were designed to integrate students' real-life experiences in the praxis sites with academic study. The students said they found this very meaningful. Tina commented on the difference between this and her previous academic experiences:

> Finding my own voice—I am definitely struggling to do that right now. Especially I think there is something in the way that I had a lot of success in the academic realm before and I think a lot of that has been knowing how to reflect back the teacher's voice back to them, if that makes sense. And it is a rewarding system academically. So I think that has been a big struggle. It has become easier as I disagree more and more with authority and am not willing to compromise as much. The type of education here is different. It really encourages you to use your own voice. I have not had the moral dilemma to just say what I think the professor wants me to say, versus voicing my own opinion.

Through her academic assignments, Tina was encouraged to use her own voice and experiences. This was something new for her in the academic realm. Pam also commented about the convergence between her compassionate side and academics. One year after Pam's experience at the Casa, she said,

> I had been going to a prestigious university and they have a big focus on thinking analytically and critically and being able to rationalize and reason and have arguments. It is a very certain style of academic thinking. And I had gotten better at that from writing my papers and participating in class and along with that I had always cared about poverty and justice issues. But it was more just from a compassionate emotional intuitive thing, and I think in the Casa, from the things we were reading and the people we were talking to, I started to see those two converge. Like applying the tools of analysis and academic thinking to the issues we were looking at in El Salvador and seeing the immense importance of that and seeing how often it doesn't happen in higher education, and how those issues are often brushed aside and

not looked at. So I think, more than anything, just applying these academic tools to what was happening in El Salvador and also at the same time, recognizing the values of different ways of thinking. How you can know things from your experience. You can know things from your faith and spirituality and those ways of thinking should be just as valued, and just as respected as the academic intellectual type of thinking. So ideally, to work on issues like the ones we saw in El Salvador. There should be a convergence of different ways of thinking and they should all be valued.

Pam saw value in integrating her academics with the real-life situation of the people in El Salvador and therefore decided to focus her senior thesis on women and progressive Catholicism in postwar El Salvador. Researching this topic brought her back to El Salvador one year after she left the Casa:

> Coming back from El Salvador, I have a lot more confidence, especially after this summer living on my own for 2 months and traveling around El Salvador and doing crazy things by myself. It taught me that I can do this kind of thing—I can be my own person. I can do what I want and so coming back I have a lot more confidence in who I am and that makes a tremendous difference in relationships, because you are not worried about having other people's approval or doing what makes you fit in the best. I just do what I want to do because it is who I am and the rest falls into place among my own group of friends.

As exemplified in her comments, the process of researching her thesis led her closer to being the author of her life.

Francine's experience at the Casa prompted an interest in international events. It also raised her awareness of the connectedness between herself and others. One year after her Casa experience, she said,

> I am a lot more interested in international events, and I think a lot more, I think about the relationship to everything. So, like just thinking, if you are going to buy clothes or whatever, like, where do they come from? Who is making these and what conditions are they under? Like that different equality issue between men and women. It comes up so many times, like I mentioned to you guys in an e-mail about our finance class and a couple of kids picking topics that were socially responsible and one of them having a huge effect on the pipeline in Colombia so it is obviously affecting the campesinos down there. It makes me think a lot more about the effects of things and makes me realize a lot more about the things that I say and that impact that they have. It makes me want to read a lot more. That is my favorite thing to do right now. There is just so much to know out there.

Conclusion

I began this chapter with Ita's quote expressing her hope that her niece would find that which gives life deep meaning. Ita and many others found and continue to find deep meaning amidst the poor in El Salvador. Certainly not everyone needs to have an immersion experience in El Salvador to find her or his way. Our bias at the Casa, however, is that the poor, those who struggle to survive and suffer unjustly, have a great deal to teach us about ourselves and our world. Encountering the realities of the poor is challenging at many levels. When provided with the optimal amount of support, however, these experiences can effectively foster students' development, enabling them to find that which gives life deep meaning. Doing so enables them to participate in creating a more peaceful and just world, one where all people, especially the poor, can live with dignity.

References

Freire, P. (1970). *Pedagogy of the oppressed.* New York: Continuum.

O'Neal, N., S.J. (2003). *The Life of St. Ignatius of Loyola.* Available: *http://www.stignatiussf.org/himself.htm*

United Nations Development Program. (2002). *Human Development Report 2002: Deepening democracy in a fragmented world.* New York: Oxford University Press.

United Nations Development Program. (2003). *Human Development Report 2003: Millennium development goals: A compact among nations to end human poverty.* New York: Oxford University Press.

United Nations Educational Scientific and Cultural Organization. (2003). *Water for people, water for life—The UN world water development report.* New York: UNESCO Publishing/Berghahn Books.

World Bank. (2001). *World Development Report 2000/2001: Attacking poverty.* New York: Oxford University Press.

7

COMMUNITY STANDARDS MODEL

DEVELOPING LEARNING PARTNERSHIPS IN CAMPUS HOUSING

Terry D. Piper and Jennifer A. Buckley

Residential life professionals have used a variety of analogies to explain their unique role and function. One of these is the pressure cooker. One could argue that a residence hall is like a pressure cooker: one mixes together a variety of ingredients (students and staff), puts them into the pressure cooker (residence hall), fastens the lid (imposes rules, regulations, policies, and procedures), and slowly turns up the heat (provides programming, conflict mediation, and so on) until the optimal cooking pressure is achieved (a balance of challenge and support). After a predetermined amount of time (two semesters), the pressure is released (summer vacation), and the food is prepared (development has occurred). However, there is one important caution: if the pressure in the cooker becomes too high, then the lid can blow off and splatter the food everywhere. During the 1991–1992 academic year, the lid came off at the University of Nevada, Las Vegas (UNLV). In the fall of 1991, UNLV doubled its on-campus housing with the addition of three new residence halls, bringing the total occupancy to 1,100 students. By the end of the spring semester those students did $90,000 in damage, initiated scores of false fire alarms, and drove away many of the resident assistants.

The Residential life staff was at a loss to explain what happened during the year. They worked hard to develop community and promote student development. They provided activities and programs. They structured a student government. They fairly enforced the rules and regulations. They did everything they could think of to create a healthy living environment. They did all the things that they thought good residential life professionals should do. Then, during one of many discussions about how to prevent a reoccurrence in the coming year, an important insight occurred to them. They had not truly invited students into a partnership in developing the residential life experience. They had defined, created, and imposed a residential life experience without the participation, willingness, or understanding of students. This insight began a commitment to develop a new approach to residential life, one that would not dictate and control the experience but that would allow students to be the creators and managers of their experience. The new approach became known as the Community Standards Model (CSM).

Residence Hall Living as a Context to Promote Self-Authorship

Residence hall living has long been viewed as a context to promote student development and learning (Schroeder & Mable, 1994). In order to intentionally promote self-authorship, the internal capacity to define one's beliefs, identity, and relationships with others (Baxter Magolda, 2001), residence hall living must be structured to create a context through which students are engaged in the three dimensions of development: epistemological, intrapersonal, and interpersonal. This residence hall context must allow students to explore and define how they know or decide what to believe, how they view themselves, and what kind of relationships they want with others.

As noted in chapter 1, the developmental trajectory moves from a reliance on external authority to internal capacity on all three dimensions. Students' ways of knowing—that is, how they acquire, analyze, and judge knowledge—moves from a view that knowledge is certain or absolute and obtained from authorities to a view that knowledge is contextual and judged on the basis of evidence (Baxter Magolda, 1992). Students' sense of self evolves from one defined primarily by how others articulate who the individual is to one based on self-reflection and self-definition (Chickering & Reisser, 1993). The evolution of interpersonal relationships moves from dependency, where the self is defined by the relationship, to interdependency, the ability to be in yet separate from relationships (Kegan, 1994). Collegiate experiences that involve substantive peer contact appear to be a particularly salient context for this evolutionary process.

The peer group has been defined as the "single most potent source of growth and development during the undergraduate years" (Astin, 1993, p. 398). Astin defines a peer group from both a psychological and a sociological point of view. He suggests that a collection of individuals, such as roommates and floor mates, may be viewed as a peer group if the student identifies and affiliates with and seeks acceptance and approval from them. This implies some element of comparable status as well as a desire to be perceived in the same manner as he or she perceives others in the group. From a sociological point of view, a peer group would have the same elements—identification, affiliation, acceptance, and approval—but *assumes* that members seek these from each other. Group membership is based on having at least the minimal characteristics of the group and being viewed as conforming to group norms and expectations. Residence hall communities do not automatically form a peer group. Individuals in the community may not see themselves as like others or seek acceptance from others in the community. Likewise, the members of the community may not recognize, accept, or be willing to adapt to the group. However, residence hall communities possess characteristics that can be used to increase the likelihood of peer group formation, that is, a potential for a high degree of interpersonal interaction, opportunities to gain interpersonal knowledge, and mechanisms to increase the salience of the group.

Theories of peer group effects in college (Astin & Panos, 1969; Feldman & Newcomb, 1969) suggest that the direction of change in development of a student's values, beliefs, and aspirations is toward those dominant in the peer group. Kegan (1994) suggests that during the teenage years, individuals become self-reflective, develop the capacity to subordinate their view to include others' views, and form a sense of themselves based on their relationships. The primary interpersonal motivation during this period is to maintain relationships. This may explain why many college students seem unable to think for or act by themselves. They have yet to develop the capacity to stand separate from the peer group and make choices based on self-defined values, norms, and beliefs. As Baxter Magolda notes in chapter 2 of this volume, higher education is increasingly being called on to produce graduates with cognitive maturity, an integrated sense of self, and mature relationships. Residence hall living, as a subunit of the educational milieu, can contribute to this transformation from an external to an internal orientation. The residential life experience can assist students in learning to create internal standards to regulate behavior, establish a personal ideology, and separate their identities from their relationships.

Transforming from an external to an internal orientation requires that the student experiences confirmation of his or her sense of self as well as experience contradiction or challenge that stimulates new meaning making (Kegan, 1982). The residence hall community can be structured to provide both support for this current sense of self and challenge that stimulates growth, thus creating a developmental bridge, "a holding environment that provides both welcoming acknowledgement to exactly who the person is right now as he or she is, and fosters the person's psychological evolution" (Kegan, 1994, p. 43). The developmental bridge can be constructed by applying Baxter Magolda's three principles to promote self-authorship: validating the learner's capacity to know, situating learning in the learner's experiences, and mutually constructing meaning (Baxter Magolda, 1992). Treating students in ways that affirm the experience and knowledge they bring to residential living and trusting them to expand that knowledge on the basis of their experience of living in a community validates them as knowers. Utilizing the day-to-day reality of residential living as a focal point for dialogue, problem solving, and decision making among students situates learning in the student's experience. Staff and students mutually construct meaning by working together to understand, make sense of, and respond to the myriad events that occur in residence halls.

Baxter Magolda's principles serve as the framework for the CSM. However, their effectiveness is grounded in three key assumptions: knowledge is complex and socially constructed, self is central to knowledge construction, and authority and expertise are shared in the mutual construction of knowledge among peers (see chapters 1 and 2). These principles are not simply tools or strategies to apply; they require a philosophical orientation that views learning and development as a highly relational activity. The success of the CSM depends on the staff's ability to adopt a partnership orientation rather than maintain a more traditional authority-oriented approach.

The Community Standards Model

Historically, residence hall community development has been thought of as a goal, an end state achieved through individual contributions to the formation and maintenance of community (Anchors, Douglas, & Kasper, 1993). In the CSM, community is process, a means to an end emphasizing the individual and his or her development within the group context. Community development and individual development are interactive and best illuminated through the Community Progression Model (Peck, 1987). The artificial or pseudo-community that typically exists when groups form transitions to healthy community through a process of open communication and recognition of the personal benefit of contributing to the community. Members of healthy communities acknowledge their differences, seek to understand each other's perspectives, clarify roles and responsibilities, participate in group decision making, and authentically communicate their needs.

The CSM is a structured and guided process that emphasizes civility, responsibility, and accountability among students living in a residence hall or specified unit within a residence hall. Community standards are shared agreements that define mutual expectations for how the community will function on an interpersonal level, that is, how members will relate to and treat one another. On one level, developing community standards is a task for the community to complete. On a more significant level, the process of developing community standards provides opportunities to promote intrapersonal and interpersonal understanding and development. The process of using community standards is never finished, as the standards themselves, their refinement, and their implementation continuously evolve and the community interactions shape and reshape individuals' understanding, expectations, and behavior toward others. The CSM is comprised of three phases, described next.

Phase I: Establishing a Foundation for Community

This phase begins prior to and continues through residents' arrival at the beginning of each academic term. Residents are introduced to community standards through a newsletter that provides information about the residence halls and residential living. Community standards are mentioned in the context of differing expectations students may have for their residential life experience and the resulting potential for conflict. The newsletter states that "it is important that residents discuss compromises *before* problems arise," and continues by defining the process: "You will have the opportunity to participate in floor discussions, called Community Standards meetings, during which your floor members will talk about issues that may become problems." Additionally, the desired outcomes of the CSM are expressed: agreement on how floor residents will treat the community and each other, acceptance of personal responsibility, and the obligation to uphold the standards and hold each other responsible for the standards.

Phase I concludes with the setting of community standards during the first 2 weeks of the semester. The floor's resident assistant (RA) facilitates the community standards development meeting. The meeting outline contains seven elements:

1. Individual introductions and an acquaintanceship activity to begin establishing interpersonal relationships.

2. An explanation of the meeting's purpose and an explanation of the meaning and purpose of community standards.

3. An explanation of the process to be used to set the community standards.

4. An explanation of the rules of group discussion; that is, one person speaks at a time, introduce yourself before you speak, comments should be positive and build on what someone else says, critique ideas instead of the person offering them, and do not repeat.

5. Soliciting residents' ideas for specific community standards. Residents are asked to write down the issues, concerns, and expectations they have for the floor and their relationships with floor residents.

6. Review of suggestions and agreement on community standards. Residents are asked to discuss the various ideas and to consider the implication of accepting or rejecting the suggestion. Only those ideas accepted by consensus become community standards.

7. Discussion of accountability. Accountability is defined as the responsibility to adhere to the community standards and to seek cooperation from those who fail to abide by the standards. Strategies for approaching each other to discuss community standards issues are considered and agreements made on how and when individuals will approach each other. The role of the RA is also discussed with emphasis being placed on assisting residents rather than enforcing the community standards.

While residents are likely to focus on the task of setting community standards, it is the dialogue generated by the process that is more important. Some floors reject the idea of community standards as unnecessary. Dialogue focused on the assumptions and rationales that underlie rejecting this process can lay a foundation for an eventual return to discussing the need for community standards as the semester progresses. Phase I encourages residents to begin understanding and adapting to the residence hall context and provides the framework for the next phase.

Phase II: Community Problem Solving

Phase II commences when residents realize that community standards alone will not guide everyone's behavior. This realization typically occurs after an incident that is perceived by a member or members of the community as violating a community standard. Community problem solving is initiated by a resident requesting a meeting to discuss the alleged violation. The meeting, referred to as a Critical Incident Meeting, allows each community member to voice his or her perspective on the alleged incident, specifically whether the incident violated a community standard and how he or she was affected by the incident. It is fairly typical at this point in the CSM to not identify the offending party, although he, she, or they may be known to the individual(s) requesting the Critical Incident Meeting. Without identifying the alleged violator, the dialogue typically will focus on the need to further define the meaning of or the need for additional community standards. The result of this dialogue may be to reaffirm, modify, remove, or add a new community standard.

An important dimension of Phase II is the RA's preparation of the community for the Critical Incident Meeting. Most communities will experience the need for a Critical Incident Meeting within the first few weeks of the year. Residents are unlikely to know each other well and hesitant to speak out about the alleged community standards violation. The RA's role is to speak with as many community members as possible before the meeting to encourage their participation and to inquire about their reaction to the incident and pending meeting. This helps residents clarify how they feel or think about the issue and assists them in preparing what they would like to say at the meeting.

Phase III: Accountability to the Community

This phase begins when the alleged violator(s) of a community standard is (are) identified and called before the community to discuss the offending behavior. This meeting is known as an Accountability Meeting and is intended to determine if the community considers the behavior to violate a community standard and, if so, to have the individual(s) understand how the behavior affected the community. The desired outcome of the Accountability Meeting is an agreement to modify the offending behavior. Accountability Meetings are not judicial procedures. Sanctions or other forms of punishment may not be imposed. The "consequence" for violating a community standard is to listen to its impact on one's peers and to become more aware of what one's peers expect in the future.

The RA's role is similar to that in Phase II. He or she prepares the community for the dialogue and facilitates the meeting. Unlike Phase II, in which the alleged violator is unknown, in Phase III the RA must also prepare the alleged violator by assisting him or her to reflect on the offending behavior and to determine how he or she will present his or her point of view.

As this description shows, the CSM shifts the role of staff from taking actions that are authority based to those that are facilitator based and shifts the role of the student from recipient to creator of his or her experiences. The primary function of staff members is to guide the community toward an understanding and implementation of individual and group responsibility and accountability based on mutual expectations and desires. It would be inaccurate to view standards as shifting the authority structure to students for them to implement themselves, as is done with some community-based disciplinary committees; doing so maintains the philosophy of control and differential power/status relationships. Community-based disciplinary committees simply empower selected community members to exercise the authority typically held by RAs or hall directors; that is, they are able to make disciplinary decisions and impose them on members of the community. The exercise of this authority creates differential status among community members—a differential not unlike that between students and residence hall staff. By contrast, the CSM replaces the philosophy of control with a philosophy of individual and group empowerment. It is also important to note that the CSM does not take the place of the residence hall disciplinary system. A significant challenge in implementing the CSM is differentiating behaviors that are appropriately addressed through the CSM versus those more appropriately addressed through disciplinary procedures. At UNLV, formal rules concerning legal mandates, safety, and security are maintained and violations thereof adjudicated through the disciplinary system. In addition to judicial procedures, the alleged violator can be called before the affected community to address the community standards aspect of the formal rule violation.

Community Standards as a Learning Partnership

Residence hall living has inherent within it the three assumptions of the Learning Partnerships Model: knowledge is complex and socially constructed, self is central to knowledge construction, and authority and expertise are shared in mutually constructing knowledge among peers. Students bring their prior experiences, assumptions, and expectations into the residence hall context and use these to guide their interactions and to make meaning of their experiences. These interactions, mediated by staff interventions, form the basis for constructing new insights and understandings about oneself and others. Daily residence hall living requires students to resolve issues with roommates about visitation, study hours, cleanliness; to negotiate with neighbors over noise and use of common space; to interact with others from different ethnic, racial, and values backgrounds; and to make choices about drugs, alcohol, and sexual behavior. Most traditional age college students have not yet achieved the internal capacity necessary to effectively respond to these complex challenges (Kegan, 1994). The CSM uses the Learning Partnerships Model to support students as they learn to function in more complex ways.

The CSM is designed to validate the student as a knower and thus promote epistemological complexity. The summer mailings that inform students of the standards process are designed to do this. Inviting students to think about what they expect from their residential living experience communicates that they have a perspective on this experience and that their ideas and feelings are important. This is reinforced through establishing the standards. Community standards are proposed by, discussed among, and eventually enacted by students. As the CSM unfolds over the course of the year, students share with each other their perspectives, points of view, and information about occurrences in their community. The expression of what one knows is fundamental to the community's ability to function effectively, reinforcing the importance of participation as a further means to validate the student as knower.

Situating learning in the student's experience occurs by engaging students in ongoing dialogue about the day-to-day reality of community living. Initially, students ground their expectations for the community standards in their precollegiate experiences and/or prearrival information. These early expectations are mediated by actual experience once they move into the residence hall. The CSM provides a means through which students become aware of their needs as well as the needs of others, relationships are negotiated, decisions are made, and consequences are experienced. Dialogue concerning community standards violations focuses on the impact of the behavior, and students are assisted to arrive at their own decisions about obligations associated with group living.

In order to have community standards, students must mutually define how they will relate to and treat each other. Students typically will need to learn how to work collaboratively with peers to mutually construct meaning of the residence hall experience. Residence hall staff, particularly the RAs, facilitate the learning process and share in the construction of meaning. This occurs through group process (i.e., leading the community standards meetings) as well as through individual interactions (i.e., conversations with students in advance of Critical Incident and Accountability Meetings). The RA is critical in the CSM because he or she promotes dialogue among students that allows for free expression yet affirms civility. The RA is also instrumental in creating a caring community, one that values and recognizes each member's experiences and promotes his or her participation in the CSM.

The CSM promotes the student's ability to develop his or her own point of view through self-reflection. Engaging in dialogue with peers allows the student to hear and reflect on the views of others. Commonality of perspectives serves to confirm the student, and different perspectives serve to stimulate new meaning making and thus promote epistemological development. Concurrently, this emerging sense of self as different from one's peers contributes to the student's self-confidence and ability to express his or her views as different from the peer group (intrapersonal development). The students' awareness of themselves as unique individuals who are independent from the

peer group contributes to their ability to define the nature of their relationships with peers (interpersonal development).

The Development of Self-Authorship Through Community
Standards: Survey Responses

To understand the impact of the CSM, all UNLV residents were offered the
opportunity to complete a year-end quality-of-life survey. This survey was
created at UNLV to measure self-described behavioral outcomes associated
with the interpersonal, intrapersonal, and cognitive growth that the CSM
intends to foster. This survey also measured students' reactions to residential
life activities and general housing services. The survey was administered to
1,880 residents through hall-closing floor meetings in the final week of April
or the first week of May. In 2003, 730 surveys were completed, tabulated,
and analyzed representing over 50% of the residential population. In this
administration, 54% of respondents identified themselves as women and
46% as men. Fifty percent indicated they were first year students, 25% were
sophomores, and 25% were juniors, seniors, or graduate students. Ethnically,
48% identified themselves as Caucasian, 13% as Asian or Asian American,
9% as African American, 9% as multiracial, 6% as Pacific Islander, 6% as
Hispanic, and 1% as Native American. The following section summarizes
results from the 2001–2003 administrations of the survey.

In all phases of the CSM, students are encouraged to share their thoughts
and feelings, consider others' perspectives, and resolve issues as a community.
Because this process is not determined for students but required students'
active engagement and open communication, they needed to state their opinions, stand up for their desires, and express their objections. As the CSM
encouraged all to participate in community dialogue, students had increased
opportunities to listen to and consider their peers' perspectives. These experiences created a context that fostered students' interpersonal growth, as outlined in Table 7.1.

The CSM required a significant personal commitment from students and
created multiple opportunities to foster self-awareness and intrapersonal
growth, also identified in Table 7.1. Because accountability to the community
standards is managed through resident-to-resident discussions and facilitated
floor meetings, students are encouraged to consider their reactions to issues
and to voice these to each other and the community. Students also make
choices about responding to these situations and must live with the consequences of these choices. Additionally, the RA's role in asking students about
their thoughts on how the community should function and soliciting their

Table 7.1   Items That Reflect Interpersonal and Intrapersonal Issues

Item	% Agreeing
I am more comfortable making my own decisions.	73
I am more understanding of others.	73
I am more aware of how I affect others.	72
I am more open to ideas different than my own.	72
I am a more responsible person.	71
I learned to appreciate others' uniqueness.	71
I am more willing to state my opinion.	70
I am more able to stand up for what I want.	68
I learned to appreciate my uniqueness.	68
I am more aware of my values.	67
I understand myself better.	67
I am more aware of my strengths.	67
I am more aware of my weaknesses.	67
I am more willing to object to activities or actions I think are wrong.	65
I have changed in a way I like.	64
I am more able to develop close relationships.	63
I am more concerned about others.	63
I am more confident.	59

reactions to community issues could serve as a catalyst to support students' increased self-awareness.

When asked about specific residential life interventions and services that contributed to creating a positive experience, a high proportion of respondents (74%) indicated that their "interactions with RAs" created a positive experience, which may reflect the facilitative approach that RAs utilize in the CSM. In addition, most respondents indicated that the following factors created a positive experience: quality of relationships on the floor (67%), informal discussions among floor mates (65%), community standards meetings and discussions (55%), floor programs (54%), and floor meetings (53%).

Table 7.2   Items That Reflect Overall Conclusions About Residential Life

Item	% Agreeing
Living in the residence halls added positively to my overall college experience.	73
I am satisfied with my residence hall experience.	72
I felt safe and secure in the residence halls.	71
I would recommend living in the residence halls to a friend entering college.	70
I had a positive experience living in the residence halls.	68

The focus on facilitated floor discussion, peer dialogue, and consensus decision making within the CSM may have contributed to these factors being positively related to students' residence hall experience.

Having such high expectations for student involvement and participation in the CSM might cause concern about diminishing students' overall satisfaction with their residence hall experience; however, the results of this survey contradicted this assumption. The reactions, summarized in Table 7.2, indicated an overwhelmingly positive student response to living in residence halls that used the CSM.

In addition to data on student perceptions, other evidence also suggests that the individual and group empowerment philosophy inherent to this model has dramatically improved residents' experiences. During the first year of implementing the CSM (1991–1992), the unbillable common area damages decreased 80%, the number of judicial hearings decreased 66%, and the false fire alarms decreased 80%. These levels have been maintained in subsequent years (Piper, 1997). Thus, implementing the CSM changed the culture of the residence halls to improve residents' day-to-day living conditions while simultaneously creating a developmental context to support students' learning and growth.

The Development of Self-Authorship Through Community Standards: Interview Responses

To better understand students' experience in the CSM and its impact on self-authorship, a yearlong qualitative study was completed at UNLV in the 1999–2000 academic year. Informal conversational interviews were conducted with 15 residents from three floor communities at three separate times during the academic year. The first interview occurred in late September, the second interview occurred in late November, and the final interview took place in late April. These videotaped interviews typically lasted from 30 to 45 minutes and focused on students' reactions to and understanding of the CSM and their expectations for their RA, their peers, and themselves in this process. Grounded theory methodology was used to interpret students' interview responses. Interview transcriptions were reviewed and analyzed for themes and patterns that created distinguishing categories. Including a second analyst[1] for reviewing the interview data enhanced the validity of the themes, patterns, and categories (Merriam, 1998).

The collective interviews revealed three states from which students made meaning of the CSM experience. Table 7.3 describes these states and the expectations students held within them. The table provides an overview of students' assumptions that illustrate their cognitive, interpersonal, and intrapersonal development at three states. The cognitive assumptions were determined by considering students' interpretations of the CSM, the role of their RA, and their reactions to their RA. Interpersonal assumptions came from how students interpreted and were influenced by their peers. Finally, intrapersonal assumptions described the role that students thought they should play and how peers and the RA affected views of themselves in this experience.

Overview of the States of Development

Concrete participants saw community standards as synonymous with floor-created rules that residents should follow. These students saw their RA as an authority to provide direction and as the only person responsible for addressing community standards violations. They believed they should report their community standards issues to their RA, who then addressed these concerns with the floor. Peers had very strong influence on concrete students, but students did not seem cognizant of this influence. It was most obvious when these students recalled times of potential conflict and violations of community standards. Concrete students were very concerned about their peers' opinions and as a result very apprehensive about peer conflict. These students seemed to lack the internal confidence to articulate their wants and needs when these differed from those of their peers.

Transitional students, in contrast, saw community standards as more of a process than of rules. They thought all students should express concerns in

---

[1]The second analyst was Tracy Bobertz, who served as a UNLV residential life coordinator.

Table 7.3   States of Development Derived from the CSM

Concrete state of development in the CSM

Cognitive: Assumptions about the CSM and the role of RA	*Interpersonal: Assumptions about the role of peers in the CSM*	*Assumptions about the role of self in the CSM*
Standards—Rules that the floor creates. Students should follow standards as if they are rules. RA—Seen as authority. RA provides direction and guidance in the CSM. Residents report concerns about standards to RA. RA addresses these problems with peers and community. Self/peers—Should listen to and abide by RA, who is authority. Students benefit from answering to authority.	Peers—Have strong influence on participation in the CSM. Self—Avoids conflict with peers. Finds it too risky to publicly acknowledge differences in what self and others want in community.	Self—Avoids conflict with peers and RA. Lacks internal confidence to articulate needs as different from peers and RA. Believes that RA should address issues with peers and community. Peers—Strongly influence individual's behaviors, attitudes, and beliefs.

Transitional state of development in the CSM

Standards—Have become more of a process than rules. RA—Facilitates and assists with the CSM because of knowledge and prior experience. Offers support with problem-solving and accountability interventions.	Peers—Should participate in community standards discussions. Peer group acceptance is still important.	Self—Participates in community standards discussions. Standards process promotes self-reflection. Peer group acceptance is still important. Individual experiences dissonance during peer confrontation and conflict.

Table 7.3 Continued

Self/peers—Should participate in community standards discussions. Should consider advice from RA because of experience.	Self—Acknowledges that peers have own ideas and listens for understanding. Recognizes the need to address community standards violations with peers. Chooses less direct confrontation.	Peers—Individuals prefer direct communication about needs through standards conversations to prevent surprises. RA—Assists with peer accountability conversations and provides general support.

Advanced state of development in the CSM

Standards—A process to manage floor community functioning. RA—Has same power and influence as self and peers in the CSM. RA is equal to self and peers.	Peers—Seen as separate from and equal to self. Peers should equally engage in the CSM and accountability discussions. Peers are equal to self and RA.	Self—Less dependent on peer group approval. Thinks for self and expresses needs for community living. Self should equally engage in the CSM and accountability discussions. Self is equal to RA and peers.

Source: Adapted from Buckley and Bobertz (2002).

the community standards discussions. They saw the RA as providing assistance because of prior experience and support during accountability interventions but did not depend on their RA to address all issues. Acceptance from the peer group was still important and affected how these students approached conflicts. They recognized the need to address community standards violations but chose less direct confrontation. The transitional students could easily reflect on their participation in the CSM and seemed more self-aware than concrete participants.

Advanced students saw community standards as a process to express views on how the floor should function and a way to address community problems. They did not distinguish their RA as having any more influence or power than themselves or their peers. They expected students to actively engage in the community standards and accountability discussions. They seemed much less dependent on peers for approval. They could also easily reflect on their participation in the CSM and seemed most self-aware.

To explore the interconnection of these three states, the CSM, and the Learning Partnerships Model, we offer a detailed description of three participants from the same mixed-age floor community, each demonstrating a different approach to the CSM: concrete, transitional, and advanced. Interview excerpts are provided that highlight how these students interpreted their experiences in the CSM. For each state examples are offered for what students experienced as guidance, a learning partnership, and empowerment.

Concrete State of Development

Leslie is a first-year student whose interviews reflected the concrete state. In her first interview in late September, she shared the following reactions about her first community standards meeting:

> Actually I like the idea of floor standards because if I have a problem, without floor standards, then it's up to one person to delete the problem. But this way, if I have a problem then we all build on it kind of like a team and we can change it. Also if I'm the only one with a problem, and everybody doesn't just agree with me, nothing's changing for just one person.

It is clear that Leslie valued the opportunity to collaborate and mutually construct meaning with her peers. She described the philosophy of working as a team in community standards further:

> Sometimes people aren't as strong as others so if you're a strong person and you say, "This is how I want it." And you're like, "Does anybody disagree?" and people are, "Well, no," when they in fact do. They just don't want to be the first person to say, "I do," and then have everybody jump up and say, "Me too, that's stupid." . . . When people aren't strong, they just go with people and with the group. But when it's one-on-one, they tend to express their ideas more. And most of the time, they express it to one person who is stronger and then that person adapts and makes up for them in the next meeting or just in life in general.

In these passages, Leslie identified some supportive elements that reflected concrete-level assumptions. These students lacked confidence to express themselves directly if they disagreed with peers. Concrete participants valued that the group addressed problems together, alleviating the responsibility for individuals to do so alone. In addition, because the CSM allowed for issues to be reconsidered, those who felt less confident could later talk individually with others to gain support to reconsider an issue in the next floor meeting.

In the following passage, Leslie explained how RAs could support students in this process and articulated more concrete-based assumptions about peers and authority:

> Interviewer: Did you see that play out when you guys were establishing your standards, that some people were stronger than others?
> Leslie: Definitely. . . . In the meeting, "Well, I want this." "OK, who doesn't?" And of course nobody does. No one person is going to be, "No, that's wrong." And then other people are going to be like, "OK." And have that person later on, the person who changed the rules or didn't agree, then they have a conflict there, immediately. So as soon as somebody says, "Well, that's fine with me," then everybody says, "Oh, that's fine," "Fine with me, too." If it's not meant to be, then it usually works out. Especially if you have a good RA and you talk to them. Like Emily, she's my RA, she would probably bring it up in the meeting again, "Are you sure this is the way you guys want it? Because some people have come up to me and said that this isn't the way they want it. Does anybody agree with that?" Instead of putting them on the spot.

As outlined in Leslie's passage, peers strongly influenced the concrete students. These students were threatened by the potential of peer conflict and so dismissed their concerns, accommodated to the predominant opinion, or sought support from their RA as a perceived authority. They seemed to want their RA to advocate for them when conflicts or disagreements arose. However, it is important to note in Leslie's previous interview passage that her RA did not directly speak on residents' behalf but more generally stated that some students expressed dissatisfaction and asked if others felt similarly. This is an important distinction in the RA's facilitation in that she provided validation for students' concerns and invited those concerns to be expressed. Leslie shared more about what she valued in her RA's facilitation of the CSM:

> Leslie: She organized our ideas. . . . We didn't know what floor standards should be like. She made it where it was appropriate. We could have had scary floor standards, but we didn't. She gave us some examples from last year, maybe problems that she saw last year so that now we can make a floor standard in the beginning so we don't have to go through that again. So it was experience on her part that did us good.

Interviewer: She helped organize other people's ideas?

Leslie: Yes. Like if we had an idea and we didn't know how to say it, she would say, "Well, maybe are you guys meaning it this way?" Or maybe, "That won't work because this will happen if you do that." Or "Does everybody agree or is that just yourself?"

Leslie appreciated her RA's direction and guidance so that the floor did not create something disastrous or, as Leslie indicated, a "scary floor standard." For Leslie and other concrete students, support meant that their RA provided previous examples, identified weaknesses and offered suggestions, asked clarifying questions, and encouraged group consensus. Leslie was empowered when her RA said, "It's your floor. You're living with each other. You do it." This resulted in Leslie's realization that "we are living with these guys all year long . . . so by using the floor standards, you're doing this for everybody, for living conditions." Leslie's last comments offered examples of the Learning Partnerships Model's assumptions in that her RA communicated that their floor needed to collectively determine their standards, that this process involved sharing authority and expertise, and that Leslie and her peers played important roles.

In Leslie's second interview in late November, she described her RA's role in the CSM as, "She doesn't say much about it. . . . Unless it needs to be enforced, then she comes through. She's there for enforcement." When asked to expand on this, Leslie indicated,

If something's wrong, then she brings the floor standards up as a reference to why you should be acting one way or the other. And if it's a floor standard, she makes sure that everybody's going by that standard. Because we decided as a floor that's what we'll go by. And she's there to make sure that everybody does. Kind of like a parent.

This interview excerpt demonstrated Leslie's understanding that the floor should determine their standards but shows how she abdicated responsibility for holding peers accountable to these agreements. Like Leslie, all concrete participants struggled in the peer accountability phase of the CSM. They either expected their RA to hold peers accountable or dismissed the impact of issues.

For concrete participants, the RA provided a learning partnership by mutually constructing meaning among residents when establishing standards. Students were expected to be active participants in these discussions, providing validation to share their perspectives. Because openly disagreeing with or directly confronting peers presented too great a challenge for concrete students, they benefited from expressing these concerns to their RA or other peers, who could raise such concerns generally in subsequent floor meetings. Thus, the structure of the CSM that allowed for revisiting and revising community standards became a source of empowerment.

In the final aspect of her second interview, Leslie reflected on her learning in the CSM. Her response demonstrated increased self-awareness and indicated that she was moving toward the transitional state. She shared,

> I've learned to compromise, kind of. I've learned to listen to others. . . . It's kind of like respect . . . I mean if you're at your house and you want your radio loud, it's OK. If no one's home, you can just blast your radio. But through the noise and the quiet hours you have to compromise. You have to do something that you wouldn't normally do because of someone else. . . . I mean, I wouldn't turn my radio off at 11 P.M. if I was listening to it. But I do, because it's a floor standard. . . . Because I'm an only child, I've never really had to live with anybody else. I've never had to live by a set of rules that are only rules because they mean something to someone else. I've never had to deal with that before, so it's kind of neat.

In this passage, Leslie realized that community standards exist because these issues were important to other community members. This seems to indicate that she saw the CSM as a way to manage competing demands among residents rather than as rules external to the community and enforced by authority. This excerpt also demonstrated Leslie's development of greater intrapersonal and interpersonal awareness in that she articulated how she learned to compromise and listen (intrapersonal skills), and she described applying these skills by turning off her music because of its negative impact on others (interpersonal skills). This revealed that she was forming a sense of herself on the basis of her relationships, as she could subordinate her wants and needs to include others. Furthermore, it is an excellent example of how the CSM situates learning about these issues in students' everyday living experiences.

Transitional State of Development

Transitional students saw the CSM as a way to communicate and compromise about different community issues and expected active participation from themselves and their peers. They saw the RA as providing assistance, particularly when establishing standards and during community problem solving. Peer group acceptance affected how these students approached conflicts. They recognized the need to address issues but chose less direct confrontation. Finally, they seemed more self-aware than concrete participants.

Kelly, a first-year student from the same floor community, exemplified more transitional assumptions (see Table 7.3). In her first interview in late September, she shared the following reactions to the CSM:

> Kelly: If you don't want trash on your floor, you have to say that. Because if it happens and you didn't write it down, you can't complain about it. It's just the things that come automatic, you write them down. Things that you would expect other people to do or that you need to make everything comfortable with your environment.
> Interviewer: Why do you think that is valuable, expressing those things that are significant?
> Kelly: So that we can make our floor standards work. There are some schools that just can't and I think it's great that we can make our environment the way that we want. And if we want to be loud all the time, then it's our floor and we can do that. I mean, we have to live there the whole year. So I really like that. . . . It's ownership of your rules and you and everyone individually puts effort into it and it's even more yours instead of just sitting there and agreeing with everybody else. I mean, if you do that you're still helping because you're agreeing. And of course, everybody had to agree. Everyone got to clarify, everyone got a chance to change this or that, and I like that. Just a good team effort. I like that it was one of our first meetings together, so we were still learning about each other in the process.

Kelly, like other transitional participants, saw the CSM as a process to clarify group expectations. She particularly valued having ownership to develop her community standards and shared more about this:

> I have a friend from another campus who called this weekend and they set their rules before they come to school. And that's it. No ifs, ands, or buts about it. I know that when any child or any person is given a set of rules and you didn't make them up, it's hard to follow them because you probably don't understand them or you don't care about them. But I just think when you have your own rules and your own environment, it makes things a lot easier because they're our own. I have a big thing about ownership and I think people take pride in their own things rather than other people's things. I think it's an ongoing project. I think that people also know that if they want to change something, to come to that meeting once a week and most of the time at meetings, we change it.

Clearly forming community standards empowered Kelly. Through the CSM, she appreciated that her community could express what they wanted from each other and that this could evolve to reflect changing needs. This interview excerpt further demonstrates how the CSM is grounded in the three assumptions of the Learning Partnerships Model. Specifically, the floor socially constructed their community agreements, authority and expertise were shared among participants, and students' experience was central to creating these agreements.

When asked more about her role in developing community standards, like other transitional students, Kelly described herself as an active participant.

> Kelly: Well, I was writing them on the board, so I would have them clarify exactly. I remember a couple of times I asked them, "Are you sure?" Or "Do you want to switch this?" Because I was up there writing it down, I had a lot of extra suggestions, like after-suggestions. . . . They would say it, and I would be like, "Wait, do you really want this? Do you want to add this part to it? Or do you just want to put it like that?"
>
> Interviewer: So building on what was offered?
>
> Kelly: Yeah, to make things stronger because people just threw things out there and we worked together to make a long standard.

She also described how her RA provided support to establish the community standards because of her previous knowledge. This was a similarity among the transitional and concrete participants:

> Because none of us had ever done standards before, she [the RA] gave us suggestions on how it's done and what standards were done last year, just to kind of get us on the right track. . . . Because everybody on our floor is a first-year student. If they're not freshmen, then they're first-year students here at UNLV. So we're just kind of left with, "Well, what do you want us to do?" . . . Emily [the RA] kind of gave us a couple of suggestions so we knew what she wanted of us. And she explained what floor standards are. That really helped.

Transitional participants also thought their RA could assist with accountability interventions but did not rely on them as heavily as the concrete participants. Should someone violate a community standard, Kelly clarified her expectations as, "I would hope that they go to the RA. And then I'm sure the RA would go and tell the resident that was in violation. Or I hope they would go up to them and say, 'You know, that's against one of our floor standards. I would like to ask you to please stop it.' Or, 'Can you not do that? It's a common courtesy.'"

When asked how to handle a situation that personally affected her, she replied, "I would take a stand because it is my personality. I would say 'Please stop it,' or 'Don't do that.' I would probably also incorporate the reason why that's a floor standard if I had to." This demonstrates a significant difference in students with transitional assumptions as compared with those with concrete assumptions. These students were not opposed to peer confrontation and accountability discussions. When describing how they would confront a peer, they utilized a particular community standard as supportive rationale, which made this experience seem less risky. Rather than abdicating responsibility for peer confrontation to the RA as a perceived authority, transitional students relied on the agreed-on standard as an external support.

In Kelly's second interview that occurred in late November, she demonstrated greater familiarity with the CSM because of her leadership role in Complex Council (a volunteer-based student governance board for the complex). In that interview, she shared the following impression of the CSM:

> Kelly: It's weird, because now I'm in Complex Council and we have standards there. So now, standards are kind of going farther with me than just my floor. Our floor hasn't really had any problems. We obey the standards about noise and trash and things like that. . . . In Complex Council we made them there and they come up in almost every meeting and we'll say whether it was done or what hasn't been held or what hasn't been done. . . . I see how it works now, because you can take out your feelings without hurting someone because you're telling them that they didn't uphold a standard. Not that they didn't do this and you think it should be right. I think it's a good thing.
> Interviewer: What do you feel like you gain?
> Kelly: I feel like I gain almost like . . . confidence to back up what you think. Because there's something there that thinks almost the same way you do. You know what I mean? Because I think the standards for our floor are the way a floor should be. So when someone doesn't do one or when there's something wrong with one of them, then I feel like I can tell someone what they're doing is wrong, not because it's what I think. . . . It's what everyone thinks and it's documented.

In these excerpts, Kelly appreciated the opportunity to mutually construct meaning with her peers about the group's functioning. Her depiction of accountability discussions as expressing her feelings without hurting someone else is intriguing. Perhaps this is because she perceived her feedback as less personally critical and more directed toward helping achieve the group's goals. Again, Kelly and other transitional participants benefited from having the group's support via their agreed-on standard to express concerns.

When asked to reflect on her learning in these experiences, Kelly declared,

> It's helping me mature. Because if we learn now what standards we want to live by then it'll be easier when we get older. Like with a roommate in an apartment, a spouse, a neighbor, or a person you work with. Or any kind of

colleague you might expect the same things, so you could tell them right up front, "I like people who are responsible and I don't like when you litter." . . . It's just, you know what things you want as a person.

Through Kelly's experiences of forming and upholding standards, she learned more about her values and beliefs, another excellent example of learning being situated in students' experience throughout the CSM. This represented building blocks in Kelly's intrapersonal and interpersonal development in that she realized her values and imagined using this insight to articulate her needs in future relationships and situations.

Transitional students welcomed the opportunity to mutually construct meaning in forming standards with their peers. They felt empowered to express themselves and wanted to know about their peers' concerns. During accountability discussions, guidance came from the expectation that residents should address standards violations because these represented a failure to uphold a shared goal. During these situations, students found support in the agreed-on group norms and were more comfortable confronting peers using the standards as rationale. Transitional students described developing greater intrapersonal and interpersonal awareness through community discussions, by observing the community live according to their standards, and by managing the consequences of when standards alone did not guide everyone's behaviors.

Advanced State of Development

Advanced students viewed themselves as equal to the RA in their sense of authority. Like their transitional peers, they thought the CSM helped manage community functioning. However, in contrast to their transitional peers, those with the advanced framework expressed almost no anxiety about accountability discussions. They relied less on agreed-on standards as a reason for confrontation and seemed more comfortable weighing in their feelings and thoughts as equal to peers. In the following passage taken from Kelly's third interview in late April, she characterized herself as having the same authority as her RA to address standards issues and contrasted her participation with other floor members:

I think there are groups of people that uphold standards, people who try to uphold them, and people that don't come to floor meetings, aren't involved on the floor, don't try to enforce them. . . . The kind of people who are sleeping and they get woken up and it's quiet hours they just go back to sleep. They don't get up and do anything. There are people who come to floor meetings who are interested in our floor and interested in our floor standards and they uphold them. And then sometimes they will, if one of them is being broken, they will go to the source. Our whole Floor Council (a volunteer floor governance group) that I am on and my RA are student leaders on our floor, are the ones you really see at the meetings saying, "I didn't like what you did this weekend, it is a standard and I told this person and they stopped," which is really good.

Evidently, Kelly internalized her leadership role and saw herself as fully capable of addressing community standards violations. In this interview, Kelly also demonstrated more advanced assumptions when clarifying what she learned from the CSM:

> You learn how to problem solve with people, that is something that I learned this year. To mediate and to play devil's advocate with conversations. . . . Something that I think we all get from floor meetings and floor standards is compromising and working together. Because when you have to make rules for your whole floor and you have 40 residents, or even more than that, and it's hard. One person wants this, one person wants that, one person doesn't want this, so it's really hard.

Through the CSM, Kelly had opportunities to mutually construct meaning with her peers about effectively living together. As her comments indicate, this was not an easy process, but it resulted in the development of compromise and negotiation skills that she used to assist her community. In all these experiences, Kelly's role as a community member was central, authority and expertise was shared, and the challenges of living in an interdependent community were not ignored.

Diamond is another first-year student who lived on the same mixed-age floor as Kelly and Leslie. In her first interview, she demonstrated advanced assumptions and shared that she would approach a peer about a standards violation and, if unsuccessful, would bring up the issue in a floor meeting. She indicated, "I don't have a problem with that because I'm outspoken about certain things. I've done it a couple of times where I'm trying to study and someone's music gets too loud. . . . If I want to get it done, I have to go to the person; I can't be shy or scared."

Diamond's confidence to directly address noise issues was also demonstrated in her desire to influence the establishment of community standards. When asked for her reactions if someone dictated what their standards should be, she replied,

> I don't think that's the way to do things. . . . Because if someone says, "You have to do this," then most people are going to be like, "I'm not going to do this." Because we're all adults and it's just being placed on us like you

have to do this. Well, I wouldn't like it. I'd abide by it, but I wouldn't like it. So, I feel comfortable where we have a say-so and if we want to change it, we can go ahead and do that.

Like their transitional peers, the advanced students wanted direct influence in developing community standards. Diamond saw value in the floor community creating their standards together because these represented mutually agreed-on compromises. In the absence of such agreements, Diamond expressed concern that "if we didn't have floor standards and somebody was playing their music extremely loud and somebody went to them and asked them to turn it down, they'd be like, 'Yeah, right. I don't have to.'"

A majority of Diamond's second interview addressed her frustrations with the floor's quiet hours. She questioned their relevance when individuals did not follow through with the agreements. This demonstrated the realization noted earlier in the description of community problem solving that standards alone would not guide everyone's behaviors. Diamond's interview ended with her sharing what she learned from this dynamic.

I'm learning how to respect the fact that everyone's not the same. That we are all different, and I am learning that right now. At times, I expect others to react the same way that I would or do something different. But then I have to realize that everyone is not like you, Diamond.

Perhaps having her peers fail to follow through with their community standards in the way she would resulted in this awareness. Although this insight stemmed from something bothersome, this realization situated in her experience marked an important step in Diamond's intrapersonal and interpersonal development. Understanding that not everyone will react equally provided important insight about her preferences and values. In the future, she could use this understanding to communicate her expectations to others.

In her final interview in late April, Diamond continued to share reactions about the floor's quiet hours. When she had issues with others loudly playing music, she explained she would nicely ask them to turn their music down. She indicated that every time they would apologize and turn their music down or close their door. She thought this worked well during the spring semester because people became more open and friendly, and this resulted in the community running more smoothly. When asked about her RA's role in these quiet hour situations, she described Emily's approach:

If something's wrong she doesn't just jump in. She let's us handle our problems on our own and if it doesn't get settled that way then we can go to her. Like with the nighttime thing, she doesn't get up because if we have a problem with it we should get up and go to whoever is making the noise. . . . She's just there to listen to us; she's like one of us and it's cool.

Diamond was asked how she felt when her RA said, "If you have a problem, go and talk to them." She replied,

> I think it's good because we're all adults and we need to learn how to handle our own problems. She's not our mom, so we have to go do that first. I understand that if it gets to a point where that person just won't listen to you and you need a mediator or something. I think it's good that she does that.

Diamond's comments highlight a significant element that advanced students appreciated about the CSM. They saw themselves as capable as the RA to address community standards violations, so they did not want the RA to communicate for them. Assistance from the RA was sought only if a peer accountability intervention was unsuccessful and the assistance was to improve the communication process. The CSM was an effective intervention for the advanced students because it assumed that they were capable of addressing their concerns. The intervention was also effective for transitional and concrete students because it provided more support through the shared and flexible agreements, and the RA facilitated accountability discussions.

When asked what she learned from the community standards process, Diamond ended her third interview in late April by reflecting on the value of directly expressing her needs and recognizing everyone's uniqueness. She shared,

> I've learned how to be more open. I was always really open, but now I'm really blunt about certain things. I've learned that if you just try to beat around stuff certain people just don't get it, so you have to be straightforward with them. It makes things work out better if you have issues. Just sit down and talk about it and not try to hide that you're upset. . . . I've learned how to be more open to other people's ideas. I didn't realize that not everyone does things the same way as I do. So, living in that type of community I've realized that and I've become open to more ideas.

Because Diamond had to manage some challenges in community living, she could develop her interpersonal skills. As a result, she became more direct in her communication and more open to others' ideas and valued her peers' needs as equal to her own. This was a phenomenon shared among the advanced participants.

The advanced students considered the CSM as a way to manage their community and resolve conflicts. The RA provided validation for advanced students when they demonstrated a partnership attitude, shared authority for running the floor together, and trusted students' ability to handle issues independently. Advanced students were empowered through this intervention to express their needs in the mutual construction of their floor's standards and to resolve issues directly with peers.

Comparing Student Perspectives

It is informative to compare the differences among Leslie's, Kelly's, and Diamond's interviews, all of whom experienced the same RA (Emily), the same floor meetings, the same community dynamics, and the same floor issues. The variations among their interviews indicate the importance of being aware of the different assumptions that students brought to this intervention and how these assumptions affected their interpretations and experiences. It is noteworthy that the CSM intervention worked for students at multiple developmental levels and that all three individuals grew over the course of their reported experiences. Leslie, who began the year holding concrete assumptions, manifested some transitional attitudes in her second interview, when she saw standards as a process to compromise her needs with those of her peers. Kelly, transitional during her first and second interviews, clearly saw standards as a way to express individual needs within the community and began demonstrating a more advanced perspective when peer confrontation became less threatening in her third interview. Diamond, who entered holding advanced assumptions, saw the CSM as helping to manage competing demands on the floor and was comfortable with peer accountability from the onset of the experience. She seemed to gain more personal insight over the course of her interviews as she recognized more about her unique perspective. Thus, the CSM offered an effective learning partnership with students whose expectations and meaning making varied widely.

Conclusion

In the preface to this volume, Marcia Baxter Magolda invites readers to explore the space between guidance and empowerment through the Learning Partnerships Model. The CSM exemplifies the use of a learning partnership to promote self-authorship. It provides guidance through a structured process of focused dialogue. It provides empowerment through the application of Baxter Magolda's three assumptions and three principles. It is a partnership between residence life staff and residence hall students. The outcome assessment data from the CSM strongly suggest that this intervention can contribute positively to the transformation of students becoming masters of their own destinies. However, it is important to keep the CSM in proper perspective. The journey to self-authorship is a long one. It would be unrealistic to expect that the CSM would result in dramatic changes in maturity over the period of 9 months. However, Leslie's, Kelly's, and Diamond's stories, the results of the quality-of-life surveys, and the reductions in vandalism and student judicial issues demonstrate that the CSM provided many students with the guidance and empowerment they need to take steps along the bridge between adolescent dependence and adult responsibility.

References

Anchors, S., Douglas, K. B., & Kasper, M. K. (1993). Developing and enhancing student communities. In R. B. Winston Jr., S. Anchors, and Associates, *Student housing and residential life* (pp. 461–480). San Francisco: Jossey-Bass.

Astin, A. W. (1993). *What matters in college?* San Francisco: Jossey-Bass.

Astin, A. W., & Panos, R. J. (1969). *The educational and vocational development of college students.* Washington, DC: American Council on Education.

Baxter Magolda, M. B. (1992). *Knowing and reasoning in college: Gender-related patterns in students' intellectual development.* San Francisco: Jossey-Bass.

Baxter Magolda, M. B. (2001). *Making their own way: Narratives for transforming higher education to promote self-development.* Sterling, VA: Stylus.

Buckley, J. A., & Bobertz, T. B. (2002, March). *Hearing students' stories about community standards.* Preconference workshop presented at the Annual Conference of American College Personnel Association, Long Beach, California.

Chickering, A. W., & Reisser, L. (1993). *Education and identity* (2nd ed.). San Francisco: Jossey-Bass.

Feldman, K., & Newcomb, T. (1969). *The impact of college on students.* San Francisco: Jossey-Bass.

Kegan, R. (1982). *The evolving self: Problems and process in human development.* Cambridge, MA: Harvard University Press.

Kegan, R. (1994). *In over our heads: The mental demands of modern life.* Cambridge, MA: Harvard University Press.

Merriam, S. B. (1998). *Qualitative research and case study applications in education.* San Francisco: Jossey-Bass.

Peck, M. S. (1987). *The different drum: Community making and peace.* New York: Simon & Schuster.

Piper, T. D. (1997). Empowering students to create community standards. *About Campus, 2*(3), 22–24.

Schroeder, C. C., & Mable, P. (Eds.). (1994). *Realizing the educational potential of residence halls.* San Francisco: Jossey-Bass.

8

A COMMUNITY OF SCHOLARS

ENACTING THE LEARNING PARTNERSHIPS MODEL IN GRADUATE EDUCATION

Judy L. Rogers, Peter M. Magolda,
Marcia B. Baxter Magolda, and Kathleen Knight Abowitz

Everything about this program encourages critical thinking and self-authorship. Assignments and class discussions provide the opportunity for us to engage with material and make sense of it for ourselves. The development part of the curriculum encouraged me to reflect on how I make meaning of the world. When we talk about students, we talk about holistic development and helping students see how things connect. In much the same way, this has been my experience in the program. I consider consequences for others and myself before I take action. I recognize that my actions go beyond myself. In this sense, I see the connection between the world and myself. (2001 Miami University CSP graduate)

This student's reflections on her experience in the master's program in College Student Personnel (CSP) at Miami University manifest the interplay among the cognitive, intrapersonal, and interpersonal dimensions of development. She recognizes that her beliefs and identity also interact in mutual relations with the larger world. Her insights capture the complex blend of autonomy and connection that lies at the heart of self-authorship. What she expresses here is the learning outcome we purposefully strive to achieve with our graduate students: that they come to author their own perspectives. The majority of students we serve, like the one cited at the beginning of the chapter, attest to the fact that we are, indeed, accomplishing this goal. In this chapter, we tell the story of how the Learning Partnerships Model came to be at the core of our program, how our curriculum provides the structure that implements the Learning Partnerships Model, and how the pedagogical approaches and advising processes employed by the four program faculty are grounded in the model and enact it. Finally, we describe the ongoing critical reflection and evaluation that is necessary for the renewal, growth, and relevance of the learning community that is constructed as a partnership among teachers and learners.

A key assumption that grounds our work is that engaging the Learning Partnerships Model is a mutual process of transformation among teachers and learners. Teachers' stories intersect with students' histories as a learning community, grounded in this model, is created. The key argument here is that one does not just implement the Learning Partnerships Model in an objective, dispassionate, intellectual way. It requires of teachers a personal transformation, often a shift in paradigms, beliefs, and behaviors. Thus, in this chapter, the four authors (Judy, Peter, Marcia, and Kathleen, who make up the CSP faculty at Miami University) share the stories of our own transformation as the context for how this particular learning community has emerged. We use our first names throughout the stories to reflect the culture of our program and the Learning Partnerships Model. Our journey as teachers/learners continues to evolve as our lives intersect with those of our students. Therefore, we tell the story of this program by weaving together our own transformation and that of the students who engage with us in this educational project.

The Central Role of Explicit Core Values in Establishing and Maintaining the Learning Partnerships Model

Judy's story serves as the conduit for demonstrating how a set of explicit core values emerged as a result of the transformation she and Marcia experienced in the process of adopting perspectives of empowering education.

Judy's Story

"Those are the worst teaching evaluations I have ever given an instructor." I winced when I overheard this comment made by one graduate student to another as they filed out of my student affairs administration class on the last day of the semester. I thought to myself, "So much for my experiment in trying to create an empowering environment in my classroom" (i.e., giving students more voice in assignments and readings, minimizing lectures in favor of discussion, expecting students to take responsibility for their own learning rather than relying on me to tell them what was important). Implementing a more democratic approach in my course had been a colossal failure on all levels, or so it seemed. Clearly I needed to rethink just how to do this—that is, if I could ever force myself to enter the classroom again.

Thus began my journey into what I called at the time "empowering teaching." It was not an auspicious beginning. However, what I have come to see in retrospect is that this unsettling experience was a necessary and perhaps inevitable growing pain as I shifted my view of my role from "teacher as authority" to "teacher as partner." Wrenching loose from old paradigms is disconcerting if not downright painful. In this case, I was definitely flying without instruments, feeling my way as I went along. I had no map to guide me to my final destination, just the passionate belief that empowering education was better for teachers and learners. While I didn't have a formula for success to follow during this transition, what I did have was a companion on the journey, my colleague Marcia, who was simultaneously making similar changes in her teaching. Having company on this, at times, scary ride made all the difference.

My story begins in 1986, when I first joined the faculty of the CSP master's program at Miami. Having spent the first 15 years of my professional life as a student affairs practitioner, I was both excited and anxious about the prospect of teaching. The images of "good teaching" that I brought with me came from how I was taught. One of the expectations that I had for myself, if I was to be a good teacher, was that I had to know it all. I had to be "Answer Woman." My greatest fear was that students would ask questions that I couldn't answer. If that happened, then I believed I would be failing my students. This fear translated into obsession about class preparation. I could never be prepared enough. I read everything related to the week's topic that I could possibly fit into my 80-hour workweek. I developed interesting lectures, designed creative transparencies, and worked to distill for students what I believed to be the most important knowledge about the topic. My whole focus as a teacher in those first years was transmitting knowledge from my brain into the minds of my students.

The first chinks in this view of teaching came when I began to read about the empowerment movement that was occurring in leadership and management circles in the late 1980s (Block, 1987). The bureaucratic approach to management was losing credence in an increasingly fast-paced, global economy, and in its place were ideas about sharing power with employees, giving voice to the ideas of subordinates, and asking all organization members to take responsibility for the company's success, not just management. My own feminist views and belief in the value of collaboration resonated well with the empowerment literature, and I eagerly adopted these new ideas in my leadership and organizational theory courses. One day in class, as I was plowing through one transparency after another, it suddenly dawned on me that *how* I was teaching was not congruent with *what* I was teaching. I was still assuming the role of authority in the classroom with little space or respect for student voice. If I truly wanted to develop my students to be empowering leaders, then I had to model empowerment in the classroom. I had to create an empowering learning environment. Doing so proved to be a trial-and-error process.

I first decided to jettison all the transparencies and the accompanying lectures in favor of more discussion. I thought about the issues I wanted students to consider and the conclusions that I wanted them to reach, and then I carefully crafted questions that would lead students to the insights that I thought were important. I'm sure you can anticipate where this went. The students in my class who understood the concept of empowerment that I so passionately advocated and who were thus eager to truly engage in a more democratic form of education immediately saw the gap between what I espoused and how I taught. These students felt like they were playing a game, "Guess what Judy wants"—and they told me so. After receiving the feedback that this was definitely not an empowering experience, let alone a good learning environment, I decided that the problem was that I hadn't given the students enough voice. I was still holding on to too much authority. While I truly believed in empowerment, I hadn't moved yet from belief to action. Employing these new behaviors as an instructor involved a paradigm shift, and apparently I hadn't completely let go of my old worldview. Humbled and armed with this new insight, my next move was to jump all the way across the empowerment continuum and give students major responsibility in the course under question. At the beginning of the next semester, I entered the class with a half-developed syllabus indicating that the students could construct the rest. I had some ideas for assignments but wanted students to suggest others and then select what seemed most relevant for them. I told them that class discussions were their responsibility to design as they saw fit and assigned them in pairs to lead particular sessions. I am sure you can envision the student response to this power that I foisted on them. They were shell-shocked most of the semester and angry with me for "abdicating" my duty as the instructor. Students did not believe that I knew what I was doing or where I was going with this new approach, and they had no intention of following me. This was the disastrous class that I described earlier, and I did, in fact, receive the lowest course evaluations of my entire teaching career.

That summer, I retreated into introspection about why empowering education had not worked for my students and me. Frankly, I was at a loss. It was at that point that I acquired an important companion for the journey. My colleague Marcia had been prompted to change her ways of teaching and the nature of her relationship with students on the basis of what she was learning in her longitudinal study of student's intellectual development. Marcia shared that what was becoming clear from her conversations with students is that they learn best when three elements are present in the learning environment, specifically, when students are validated as knowers, when learning is situated in students' experience, and when knowledge is mutually constructed. I immediately noted that these characteristics had much resonance with the qualities of empowering environments that leaders and managers were espousing for organizations. Marcia and I began to see that though we were grounded in different theoretical frameworks, our vision for student outcomes was the same. We wanted to develop complex thinkers and multidimensional leaders, and to do so we needed to shift our paradigms about what constituted effective teaching and learning.

We then began to purposefully reflect on our initial halting attempts to transform our roles from teacher as authority to teacher as partner (Marcia had thrown away her transparencies, too). We assessed why our initial attempts to give students voice had not been completely successful. Student development theory was instructive here in helping us recognize that we had to start where students were. In traditional education, students are accustomed to being the passive recipients of knowledge. For students to adapt to the role of active partner with the instructor, they had to undergo a transformation right along with us as teachers. They would need time to learn this new role and to trust where it would lead them. Thus, I had to ratchet back what I could expect of students at first and then gradually introduce them to these new ways of teaching and learning. Marcia and I would try approaches in the classroom that enacted our new perspectives on teaching and then process our successes and failures with each other. Thus, we supported each other through the challenges of transforming ourselves as teachers. Of course, students' reactions, evaluations, and the learning outcomes they achieved also proved central to our growth in this new pedagogy. As we interacted with students as learning partners, their insights, victories and struggles helped us find the delicate balance between guiding them and empowering them to take responsibility for their own learning.

After a few years of continually and more fully adopting this new framework for teaching and learning in the graduate program, it became clear that what was emerging was a core set of values that truly guided and shaped all that we did. The values were implicit at the time, evolving out of our gradual transformation. Marcia and I decided it was important to make these values explicit for all members of the learning community and to let these core values be the beacon for who we were, what we did, and how we related to each other in our graduate program. At an opening retreat in 1992, we put our values into an explicit statement and offered them to our students for their consideration. Over the years since that retreat, we have collectively revisited the values annually and as a result of these dialogues added some values to the original list. This critical reflection process in itself is a product of our commitment to working with students to decide which values are most appropriate for our community of scholars and in this sense mutually construct what it means to be a community of scholars.

The Core Values of the CSP Program

The values of the CSP program, depicted in Table 8.1, frame the nature of our community of scholars. The core values are embedded in the three assumptions of the Learning Partnerships Model. Specifically, the values of integrating theory, inquiry, and practice and creative controversy manifest the assumption that knowledge is complex and socially constructed. The values of self-authorship, self-reflection, and situating learning in learners' experience (also one of Baxter Magolda's principles) are grounded in the assumption that self is central to knowledge construction. Finally, the values of inclusiveness, constructive collaboration, and significant challenge, coupled with adequate support, are grounded in the assumption that in empowering learning environments, authority and expertise are shared in the mutual construction of knowledge. In essence, the Learning Partnerships Model is at the heart of the CSP core values. The following student reflection indicates the significant role the core values played in his development during his 2 years in the program:

> I feel that there are common beliefs that bind all of us together and helped to strengthen my personal and professional goals. To learn with 40 other people who have decided to continue their learning and devote their lives to working with students has strengthened my commitment to my career choice. When I entered this program I thought I had a fairly good grasp on why I was entering Student Affairs, based on my undergraduate experiences. However, I have been challenged through the common values and connection among the members of our community to develop and focus my philosophy. I believe that this program establishes the environment for this type of exploration and development to occur. (2002 Miami CSP graduate)

Table 8.1 Core Values of the College Student Personnel Program

Core value	Description
Integration of theory, inquiry, and practice	Theory, inquiry, and practice inform each other. Their interaction is necessary for knowledge construction. Theory generates possible ways to understand and can be generated from putting together the particulars of practice, inquiry is the continuing quest for new or more in-depth understanding and can be conducted in the context of ongoing practice, and practice is the application of theory and inquiry in working with students and informs theory and inquiry.
Creative controversy	Community members engage in respectful dialogue and exchange. They employ active listening as they learn from multiple perspectives. Members recognize that out of disagreement comes new information, another way to look at something, a more complex perspective.
Self-authorship	Community members engage in exploration, critical analysis, and synthesis that contribute to informed judgment. Authoring one's own perspectives leads to engaging in lifelong learning.
Self-reflection	Community members analyze their own experience in relation to knowledge explored. Members understand their own development and how it affects practice. Members connect professional preparation to their personal beliefs.
Situating learning in students' experience	Community members' experience is used as a context for learning. Members' own lives and beliefs serve as a starting point for exploring the knowledge and practice of the profession.

(Continued)

Table 8.1   Continued

Core value	Description
Shared commitment to inclusiveness	Community members appreciate and include multiple forms of diversity through the recognition that multiple perspectives exist and should be acknowledged. Members create an inclusive atmosphere that respects each individual's background and perspective in the context of sustaining the learning community. There is a celebration of the differences and similarities among members of the community. Members participate in the complex struggle of balancing respect for diverse perspectives while sustaining an inclusive learning community.
Constructive collaboration	Community members help each other explore and express themselves. They build on each other's knowledge, form opinions, and work with others to explore multiple perspectives. Through mutual construction of meaning, they actively contribute to the collective learning effort. All members are viewed as teachers/learners.
Offer adequate challenge and significant support	Community members strive to create an environment that is committed to a balance of challenge and support. They provide challenge in course work, professional settings, and real-life situations while encouraging risk taking and situational learning. Members create support networks through mentoring and advising, faculty and student interaction, and a noncompetitive academic environment.

Constructing a Curriculum Grounded in the Learning Partnerships Model

Peter's arrival as a new CSP faculty member and his expertise in curriculum development served as the impetus for us to integrate the Learning Partnerships Model across the academic program.

Peter's Story

In 1992, because of a sudden illness on the part of a CSP faculty member at Miami, Judy and Marcia approached me one week before the start of the fall semester inviting me to teach a seminar. At the time I was in the midst of my doctoral dissertation fieldwork. I did not seek out any distractions, but this opportunity seemed too good to pass up, so I accepted.

On the surface, teaching the practicum seminar appeared relatively easy. The already-established seminar goals published on the syllabus were to "assist students in the integration of their knowledge of organizational and student development with practical experience; provide appropriate guidance for class members' practicum experiences; and assess and evaluate each student's practicum experience in terms of goal attainment, skill development, and professional development." These goals, especially goal 1, reminded me that the CSP curriculum centered on two areas: student development rooted in developmental psychology (Marcia's area of expertise) and organizational development rooted in sociology, management, and social psychology (Judy's area of expertise). Neither area intersected with my primary research interests, which included educational anthropology and qualitative inquiry. At the time, I wondered, is this going to be a good fit?

As I prepared for my role as substitute teacher, I studied the curriculum, which often symbolically represents core values of the program. Required course offerings included an introduction seminar to student affairs/student personnel, student development, organizational theory, counseling, inquiry/research, group interventions, the history of higher education, and campus ecology. Students also enrolled in numerous practicum experiences to augment their in-class learning. This curricular framework was almost identical to the master of arts curriculum I completed at Ohio State University in the late 1970s. No doubt, Judy and Marcia's doctoral work at OSU influenced the curriculum they had co-created at Miami University.

A cursory review of syllabi suggested that CSP faculty exposed students to contemporary scholarly readings and theories and required students to complete a multitude of writing assignments (e.g., journals, research papers, self-reflection essays, and argument papers). The curriculum appeared comprehensive, theoretically grounded, practical, rigorous, and relevant. Also embedded in these syllabi were clues about the program's pedagogy. The faculty embraced a community-of-learners orientation, which favored collaboration more than competition. Students learned not only from faculty but also from each other. Faculty and students favored both theory and practice as they both challenged and supported each other.

During my doctoral studies, I had honed my critical analysis skills, learned to deconstruct social scenes, and better understand foundational beliefs on which individuals and organizations base their actions. I applied this learning to this context as I prepared to temporarily join the community. This CSP curriculum looked like so many other CSP programs across the county. It was not distinctive, nor did it have an integrative thread. The discrete parts (i.e., individual course offerings) of the curriculum were stronger than the whole. The curriculum favored breadth, not depth; advanced courses (requiring prerequisites) were the exception rather than the rule. The curriculum privileged academic disciplines such as developmental psychology, management, and history while ignoring disciplines such as anthropology and philosophy. The curriculum also included an arcane research seminar that appeared detached from students' professional aspirations. Despite these concerns about the CSP curriculum, initiating change was not a priority since my involvement in the CSP program was a one-time opportunity (so I thought).

A year later, that same professor again fell ill at the outset of the term. I accepted Judy and Marcia's invitation to again teach the practicum seminar. Later in the semester, the professor's health problems worsened, and he retired. The next term, I agreed to teach a doctoral qualitative research seminar and an educational anthropology seminar to fill the department's unexpected teaching void. I relished the opportunity to teach these two courses because unlike the practicum courses I had taught, these two seminars intersected with my professional research passions. I felt more like a college professor than a substitute teacher.

The CSP faculty encouraged me to modify the seminars on the basis of my professional judgments. I heeded this advice. In the educational anthropology seminar, I encouraged students to view higher education through an anthropological lens; students mostly responded favorably. In the qualitative inquiry seminar, I concentrated on philosophical and paradigmatic foundations of research, not simply research methods and procedures. I also created research readings and assignments that were relevant to students' everyday assistantship/practicum work life. Despite being a temporary outsider, CSP colleagues encouraged me to be myself and renovate parts of the curriculum that were not necessarily broken.

Later that semester, the department initiated a search for a tenure-track, CSP assistant professor. At the time of the announcement, I had already taught three CSP classes and one doctoral seminar. I also had a dissertation defense date set, so the timing seemed right to apply for a job I had come to appreciate and enjoy.

The department invited me to interview for the vacancy. During this process, students could not say enough good things about the CSP faculty, the pedagogy, and the curriculum. The faculty accolades sounded right based on my past experiences with Marcia (my spouse) and Judy. Theoretically, the program's constructivist pedagogy was ideologically compatible with my views, but I wondered if these teaching practices were simply techniques (e.g., small seminar discussions and students teaching students), not philosophical foundations for the program. The curriculum worked and satisfied students, yet it did not directly intersect with my scholarly interests. During the interview, Judy assured me that once a candidate accepted the position, the CSP faculty, in conjunction with students, would review and modify the curriculum to make optimal use of the talents of all faculty. This news pleased me, but still I wondered, would this close-knit CSP learning community with a beloved faculty, a progressive pedagogy, and a functioning curriculum be inviting to a new faculty member and open to change?

During my interview, discussing the CSP program's core values and seeing these values in action tempered my apprehensions about the fit between the existing curriculum and my scholarly interests. Not only did students and faculty articulate the importance of the core values, but the interview process was a quintessential example of the application of these values to practice. Students were *self-reflective* as they talked about their graduate experiences and their dreams for the future. Students *integrated theory with practice* as they talked about how their assistantships informed their classroom learning and vice versa. Students modeled *constructive collaboration* as they jointly interviewed me. The *support* CSP faculty provided to students and the support students provided to each other was obvious and genuine. The interview schedule was *inclusive,* involving faculty, students, alumni, and student affairs colleagues. The program enacted the values it espoused, which surprised and intrigued me. The openness with which students and faculty talked about the program's weaknesses offset my skepticism and cynicism— qualities I perfected while growing up in New Jersey.

In early 1994, I accepted the department's invitation to join the faculty. Later that term, the CSP faculty, as promised, initiated in-depth discussions about curriculum. This initiative was unusual because the curriculum was not broken. Students were not complaining, nor were external accreditation boards clamoring for changes. The CSP faculty initiated this review because they did not simply want me to assimilate the existing ways the program did business. They wanted to engage in a reflective process that would build on the existing framework, maximally showcase the unique talents of the three faculty members, and, more important, benefit students.

During these meetings, my colleagues did not treat me a junior faculty member; instead, they encouraged me to openly express my views (an invitation I am certain they have regretted numerous time during the past 11 years). Not surprisingly, I readily accepted their invitation and expressed several curricular concerns (e.g., narrow disciplinary focus and not-so-integrated course offerings). From these discussions, the faculty co-constructed six objectives for the curricular overhaul: (a) make optimal use of the faculty's talents and passions; (b) integrate course offerings; (c) help students understand the interrelationship among courses more effectively (once the faculty figured this out); (d) strengthen students' preparation in a particular area by focusing on depth, not breadth; (e) strengthen the links between the academic program and the Division of Student Affairs (where most graduate students held assistantships); and (f) align the curriculum with the Preparation Standards and Guidelines at the Master's Degree Level for Student Affairs Professionals in Higher Education (Council for the Advancement of Standards for Student Services/Development Programs, 1994).

I assumed the roles of chief architect and facilitator for this process, which unfolded as four phases. During Phase I (March–April 1994), the CSP faculty brainstormed curricular possibilities and conducted three focus group sessions with current students and alumni. We also surveyed over 600 alumni and interviewed student affairs practitioners. During Phase II (July–August 1994), we compiled and analyzed syllabi from each CSP course. We sorted the objectives from those syllabi on the basis of the new national preparation standards and guidelines. Faculty integrated student, alumni, and student affairs staff feedback into this emerging framework, which we continued to share with constituents to collect additional input. During Phase III (September–October 1994), the CSP faculty studied curricular frameworks and syllabi used in other CSP programs and reached a consensus about which objectives to include in the revised curriculum. The faculty then translated these objectives into a master plan. During Phase IV (November–December 1994), the CSP faculty solicited feedback on the draft proposal from three primary constituents: current CSP students, university practitioners in student affairs, and faculty within the Department of Educational Leadership (EDL). The CSP faculty incorporated these groups' feedback into the final proposal presented to and approved by the EDL faculty in December. I found the curricular revision process occasionally challenging, contentious, confusing, conflict ridden, but, most important, always collaborative and creative.

This process yielded an integrated 48-semester credit hour curriculum that exceeded our stated aspirations. The revised curriculum was theoretically driven; blurred the in-class and out-of-class learning environments; blurred the traditional roles of teachers and learners (i.e., students are teachers and vice versa, depending on the specific context); focused on the past and present so that students can adequately prepare for the future; provided opportunities for students to become better consumers of the professional literature, thinkers, team players, writers, orators, and reflexive practitioners; fostered a climate where pluralistic ideas are introduced and critiqued; and instilled in students an ethic of lifelong teaching and learning. This process was reflective and reciprocal; through a deliberative and contemplative process, the curriculum review process changed me as I changed it.

In the new CSP curriculum, six core courses remained that addressed the nature of students' professional work and provided them a foundation from which to construct their graduate studies. Faculty transformed the two original foci (i.e., student and organizational development) into three thematic sequences (i.e., student development, organizational development, and student cultures). This new framework made optimal use of each faculty member's talent and passions and gave each explicit responsibility for taking the leadership in each sequence. Each thematic sequence included a core course, an advanced course, an inquiry seminar, a special topics offering, and a practicum experience. This framework provided the scholarly depth (lacking in the previous curriculum) and integrated the parts into a seamless whole. Placing the inquiry seminars within the thematic sequences situated the inquiry process in context (e.g., program evaluation for the administrative sequence), which greatly improved students' understanding of the centrality of inquiry in student affairs work. This thematic sequence framework also helped students better understand the interrelationship among courses and strengthened the links between the academic program and the Student Affairs Division. Finally, this revised curriculum was better aligned with the national graduate preparation program standards for student affairs professionals in higher education (Council for the Advancement of Standards for Student Services/Development Programs, 1994). The revised CSP curriculum better prepared student affairs professionals to create conditions for student learning in all areas of campus life and provided new forums for faculty to work with students to achieve these goals.

The benefits of this new curriculum that is rooted in this notion of self-authorship (particularly linking one's life with existing knowledge and organizing a value system and using it to guide practice) is evident in the reflections of two graduates of the program:

> The focus in the program on leadership styles and personal self-definition (see most classes and many papers) has been a huge influence in my work. I am able to define what I am doing and why I am doing it. (Miami CSP Alumni Survey, 2001)

> One of the most important things that I learned through the curriculum in each and every one of my classes was the importance of an underlying set of values, or a mission, or goals, whether they are personal or of the institution. I find that, although the professionals around me may not be as committed to reflecting upon values as myself, it is helpful to try to ground my experiences or my ideas in either my own personal values or the values of the institution. It is a way for me to continually connect with what I have learned, and a way for me to stay committed to the ideals of the profession and to my own personal goals. In addition, reflecting upon the larger purpose of my work helps me to deal with many of the more challenging aspects of the position. Instead of being stuck inside of the challenge, I try to step back and understand the experience as part of the overall scheme of what we are trying to accomplish. (Miami CSP Alumni Survey, 2001)

It was hard to believe that during the course of my first year as a faculty member, my colleagues provided me an opportunity to spearhead this curriculum renewal process. Many of my initial apprehensions about fitting in seem like a distant memory. Yet I continue to pose questions and critique while listening to questions and accepting criticism. Being part of a collaborative organization that practices what it preaches, constantly strives to lessen the gap between the program's espoused and enacted values, and not only conceptualizes new plans but also implements them is simultaneously exhausting and invigorating. This graduate concurs:

> The one thing I take away from this program is the value of questioning. From myself, to my position, power and experience, to the organization and individuals I interact with, I have been instilled to consider it all. This program constantly pushes their students to look at the personal, professional, organization, institution, society and culture on everything from doing to learning. The faculty, curriculum and program scores off the chart on this one. (2001 Miami CSP graduate)

This quotation from a recent graduate student not only accurately characterizes my early experiences as a substitute teacher and curricular reformer but also captures the ways I experience my contemporary work life as I cowrite this chapter, 11 years later. I questioned the program from the moment I joined it, and I invited others to do the same. I have pushed students and colleagues to understand, integrate, and synthesize the personal and the professional, organizations, institutions, society, and culture. Fortunately, students and faculty colleagues have returned the favor. No doubt the CSP community has been *doing and learning,* one of its greatest assets.

I recount these particular stories about my professional life for several reasons. On an instrumental level, the short stories introduce readers to me, present an overview of the CSP curriculum, and exemplify the ways faculty and students interact beyond the classroom. But most important, the stories illuminate the program's Learning Partnerships Model values in action. The Learning Partnerships Model was in action in 1992, when the CSP faculty and students interviewed me to join them and later when they hired me on a full-time basis. Through student and faculty colleagues' socialization efforts, I learned to adapt my teaching, research, and administrative practices. Most members of the CSP community recognized issues such as how to teach, what to teach, and the curriculum as complex social constructions. Faculty and students invited me to incorporate my own theoretical constructions and inquiry into my practice as a teacher. They "let Peter be Peter," which pleased and relieved me. The CSP community members embraced creative controversy as we integrated and synthesized our collective talents and perspectives. We all engaged in self-reflection and programmatic reflection on a daily basis. Students and faculty supported me as I introduced new classroom expectations and practices and critiqued and initiated changes to the curriculum. As both a substitute teacher and later as a full-time faculty member, others valued what I brought to the dialogue. The program allowed me to use my past experiences as a context for teaching and learning and as a starting point for exploring my knowledge and practice in the profession in general and the program in particular. I, in turn, attempted to provide students and colleagues similar opportunities.

This continual sharing of expertise and authority has afforded me the autonomy to influence the classroom experience and the curriculum while I remained connected to others in this collaborative (and sometime contentious) process. The combination of autonomy and connection that characterizes self-authorship was ever present among my colleagues—and a distinctive aspect of the program.

The CSP curriculum models the Learning Partnerships Model. The program faculty, students, student affairs colleagues, and alumni collaboratively created and offered ongoing learning partnerships for the entire community. Course offerings present knowledge as complex and socially constructed. The self-reflection and self-authorship core values invite students to infuse themselves in this process of knowledge construction. Faculty members support students by situating learning in their experiences and offering support and challenge. Creative controversy, constructive collaboration, and integrating theory, inquiry, and practice enhance learning and sharing authority and expertise. The curriculum solicits diverse perspectives both in course content and dialogue. The Learning Partnerships Model is a foundation on which all community members express themselves and build on each other's knowledge. Simply stated, the Learning Partnerships Model is alive and well and remains a mutual process of transformation among teachers and learners. The program's inquiry quest for new or more in-depth understanding as well as authoring our own perspectives leads to lifelong learning. Appropriately, I close this section of the chapter with a student's reflection on her experiences that illustrate self-authorship and the Learning Partnerships Model in action:

> I have always appreciated the program's insistence that students dream big, that they create for themselves a clear vision for *how things should be*. Why are we here, why do we do what we do, why is it important? We learn a lot about "the world's deep hunger," and are challenged to think about how we can contribute to addressing it. In a similar way, we are treated to many "stories and images of truth and goodness" through our study of important philosophical texts from within student affairs and from outside the field. We are encouraged to dream about how to bring these theoretical frameworks into reality in our practice, through our work with student development, organizational development and cultural analysis. (2002 Miami CSP graduate)

Constructive-Developmental Pedagogy as the Process to Enact Learning Partnerships

Constructive-developmental pedagogy involves creating the conditions for learners to construct knowledge in the context of their current assumptions about knowledge, themselves, and their relations with others. Coming to a full understanding of this process was a challenge that paled in comparison to living it in our daily work, as is illuminated in Marcia's and Kathleen's stories.

Marcia's Story

Earlier in this chapter, Judy recounted our initial teaching experiences and explorations leading to the articulation of our core values. Although I, too, had been influenced by the pressure to teach students particular knowledge, I relied heavily on my student affairs background of experiential learning.

I transferred key components of experiential learning to my classes—experience, reflection, sharing reflection publicly, and collaborative processing to make meaning. By the time of my first sabbatical in 1990, I had grown confident in my ability to engage students in rigorous learning, keeping their development in mind. Having studied and taught student development theory for a decade at this point, the constructive-development approach was firmly entrenched in my mind. Unfortunately, as I would discover during sabbatical, it was not firmly entrenched in my teaching.

My sabbatical project was completing *Knowing and Reasoning in College*, the synthesis of my longitudinal study of college students' intellectual development (Baxter Magolda, 1992). Immersion in the interview transcripts reminded me how often I had heard my own teaching behavior in students' stories of ways teachers intimidated them or dismissed their ideas. One good example was my ability (of which I was quite proud) to take what appeared to be a wayward comment, rephrase it 180 degrees (or more), and bring it directly into the core of our discussion without embarrassing the student who made it (for a more extensive discussion, see Baxter Magolda, 1999a, 1999b). Other students' stories helped me understand that this behavior underestimated students' capability by immediately judging comments as tangential and controlled the discussion to make sure it stayed on the track I found most useful. Reflecting on my teaching through the course of identifying and articulating themes to synthesize the longitudinal data led me to realize that I held deeply embedded assumptions that were contrary to my espoused teaching philosophy, my constructive-developmental foundation, and the emerging core values of our program.

These assumptions stemmed from socialization as a learner and educator—educators are responsible for transferring knowledge to students, educators know what is best for students, and educators maintain control in the classroom and ensure that the material is covered. Although I initially tried to convince myself that I validated students, situated learning in their experience, and mutually constructed meaning with them, it was apparent that I did so superficially with the foundational assumptions intact. Returning from sabbatical with my new discoveries, I announced to my student development class that I would be changing my teaching completely. Their trepidation was warranted. Having erred on the side of too much guidance for the previous decade, I abandoned it completely in favor of empowerment. One example was explaining to students that I wanted them to create theory prior to our studying existing theories. The first sign of trouble came when students acquired the previous year's theoretical charts from students who had taken the course earlier, hiding them in their binders to use in class discussion to avoid my seeing them. In retrospect it is clear that I imposed my new pedagogy, failing to recognize its true implications.

I recount this story to emphasize the difficulty of the transformation to learning partnerships. One might think that a veteran teacher and student development expert could easily implement constructive-developmental pedagogy. One might expect that she would at least recognize the discrepancy between her thinking and actions. Yet constructive-developmental pedagogy is not a set of skills or techniques. It is a particular way of making meaning of ourselves as educators, learners, and authorities. Just as the journey toward self-authorship requires learners to reconstruct their beliefs about knowledge, themselves, and relations with others, the journey toward learning partnerships requires educators to examine and often to reconstruct their beliefs about knowledge, themselves, and relations with others. To live the core values of our program and the Learning Partnerships Model that was emerging from my longitudinal study meant reconstructing my belief system about how people learn, my identity as an educator, and my role in mutual learning relationships. These reconstructions were central to my ability to find and dance in the space between making things happen (guidance) and letting things happen (empowerment) that Dawn described in this book's introduction.

Finding this space and dancing in it are ongoing challenges. I am learning more about it from the continuation of my longitudinal study into the participants' adult lives (Baxter Magolda, 2001). My partnership with these participants is one source of mutual learning that helps me balance guidance and empowerment. Another source that sustains this space is the learning partnerships we craft with our graduate students. Examples of mutual processes in my student development courses illuminate various ways to act on the three core assumptions and three principles of the Learning Partnerships Model.

At the outset of each course, I engage the class in crafting a public agreement (Kegan & Lahey, 2000), a process of determining how we will work together and what we expect from each other. This agreement generally produces particular expectations for preparation, active participation, mutual respect, risk taking, support, and how to address problems that arise among the group. As Kegan and Lahey point out, the purpose of a public agreement is not to prevent violations but to create a context in which groups can learn to address the conflicts that inevitably occur. As we encounter struggles in our work together, we have a system for analyzing them and maintaining our integrity with members' expressed learning needs. This agreement is revisited minimally in midsemester and more often as issues arise. The public agreement reflects the three core assumptions because it exposes learners to the complexity of socially constructing knowledge, highlights the importance of our individual identities in that process, and offers a mechanism to guide our mutual sharing of authority and expertise. The agreement validates learners' perspectives on learning, situates learning in their experience, and is a mutually defined agreement.

In a similar vein, I strive for the balance between guidance and empowerment in organizing and facilitating each class session. My pedagogical philosophy and the Learning Partnerships Model are articulated on the syllabus. Following each class session, I post a proposed agenda for the next session on our class Web site. I propose goals for the session and ways we might go about achieving them. Class members are invited to respond over the course of the week to revise or refine the agenda. We touch base about the evolving agenda at the outset of class and make decisions about how to proceed. Our public agreement, to which I contribute my perspectives, usually calls for joint responsibility in class facilitation. With our mutually constructed agenda to guide us, we proceed as a working group. Although I might be the one to redirect conversation or get us unstuck early in the semester, everyone takes this role as we settle into our work. At the end of a session, we synthesize our progress and identify ideas to pursue during the next session. These help me craft the following week's proposed agenda.

Assignments and their inclusion in class dialogue also contribute to learning partnerships. For example, the first assignment in the initial student development theory course is to write one's own developmental story. I hand out my story in the spirit of initiating the mutual trust and respect necessary in sharing personal stories. I also invite those who would rather not engage in this personal reflection to craft an alternate assignment. Students write their story the first week of class. We then explore the process of identifying themes in a story and organizing themes to form a theory. They then use this process to write a theory based on their developmental story. These portions of the assignment are complete prior to our reading any developmental theory to avoid the theory creation being influenced by existing theory. The remainder of the assignment is to compare students' theories to existing theories over the course of the semester. This places students' stories in the foreground, helping them see how particular experiences affect theory creation. For another assignment, teams of three class members interview students from populations that are underrepresented in the student development literature (e.g., students of color and gay, lesbian, bisexual, and transsexual students), create theories on the basis of those interviews, compare those theories to existing theories, and present their findings to the class. Our focus on theory building enables students to craft theory in particular contexts and familiarize themselves with existing theory simultaneously. These assignments rely on existing theory for guidance yet offer empowerment for learners to craft their own thinking in the context of existing knowledge, multiple frames of reference, and relevant evidence. Peer exchange of assignments to gather feedback and share ideas is also common. It is not unusual for a final exam to involve a critique of a peer's paper.

Balancing guidance and empowerment occurs in how we evaluate our work as well. I craft course assignments and include them on the syllabus. They often are improved or altered on the basis of previous students' feedback. Students may negotiate for different assignments if an alternative better suits their learning needs. We often collectively alter assignments as they evolve over the semester. Criteria for evaluating particular assignments are mutually constructed by the class. When a final exam seems useful in synthesizing our work, I offer goals of the exam and engage the class in constructing an experience that will meet those goals and their learning goals. Perhaps the most unique implementation of the Learning Partnerships Model in evaluating students' work is giving students responsibility for determining the grade percentages for assignments for the course (a process used throughout the program). Rather than faculty determining the weight of each assignment, students are asked to decide their individual weights for each course assignment in the context of their learning goals, learning preferences, and strengths. I usually include minimum critical specifications (e.g., percentages must be whole numbers, a major assignment might have a minimum weight) and offer to help students who want guidance determining their weights. These decisions are due a few weeks into the semester, prior to any grades being assigned but with sufficient time to get a feel for the course and the nature of the assignments. Each student has his or her own set of weights even if they are part of a team project. This process, along with mutual crafting of assignments and criteria for evaluation, exposes learners to the complexity of evaluating learning, emphasizes the role of their identities in learning, and models sharing of expertise and authority. It validates students' learning goals and situates evaluation in their experience. Evaluation of our learning environment and my teaching takes place in midterm processing conversations, discussion of issues as they arise, and closing evaluations for the semester. In the midterm dialogue, the process of identifying strengths, shortcomings, and strategies helps us determine what to keep, what to change, and how to proceed for the second half of the course.

All these dynamics of learning partnerships enable learners to practice self-authorship. Portraying the complexity of theory as socially constructed and simultaneously emphasizing students' own role in that social construction helped students internalize this body of knowledge. One student explained the result on a course evaluation form:

> Developmental theory is so diverse and complex and I felt we covered a large scope of the theories. This broadened my knowledge to include many different theories. Basing theory in experiences, specifically, my own, helped ground my understanding of the material in everyday implications.

This comment reflects a balance of understanding existing theory and an awareness of how it is constructed from and mediates everyday experience. Viewing developmental theory as contextual helps students gain the epistemological complexity needed for self-authorship.

The intrapersonal complexity needed for self-authorship is also a common outcome of these courses. Students routinely note that learning about themselves was the most valuable aspect of the course. One student included the following insights in one of his papers:

> Kegan's theory of self-evolution elegantly captures my own movement while I have been here, making its application all the more exciting for me to use and share with others. . . . Being a more self-defined person and having developed a clear sense of my own needs is also representative of my own growth a la Kegan. I am amazed at just how much clearer my sense of who I am is, what my needs are and how I am able to maintain my distinctness in relation to others. This growth is freeing. (Baxter Magolda, 1999a, p. 96)

Reflecting on one's values and organizing them into a coherent internal identity is supported through these learning partnerships.

Our partnerships also model and encourage the interpersonal complexity required for self-authorship. Sharing perspectives with others without being consumed by their approval comes from both content and process dialogues. Regarding content dialogues, one student wrote,

> The integration activity we did on the wall [mapping multiple theories on a wall chart to identify intersections] was *extremely* valuable. Mutually working on it made the theories come to life. That was when I made serious connections to theory and application. Class discussions were helpful as well. It is empowering when you turn the questions back on students to answer. It makes us work harder and learn more!

These experiences reveal the value of others' perspectives and of the intersection of multiple perspectives in constructing quality knowledge claims. Overcoming the need for others' approval is a continual challenge, yet students work diligently at it. It is routine in classes (and in meetings of the whole community) to engage in conversation about how we are functioning as a learning community. These conversations are sometimes initiated as a result of concerns particular students express or our observation that group dynamics have gone awry. Other times they are routine visits to check progress on the public agreements we have made. Commenting about one of these dialogues that occurred in a class where group dynamics interfered with learning, one student wrote, "I think what was most valuable, but also the hardest, was the conversations we had about our learning environment. I think that helped us to open the door to honest dialogue." Experiencing honest dialogue helps students work toward interpersonal mutuality.

This story both illuminates the personal transformation involved in adopting the Learning Partnerships Model as the framework for teaching practice and identifies specific ways the assumptions and principles are applied in a student development theory course. Kathleen's story offers another example of both teacher and student transformation, this time in the context of an applied ethics course.

Kathleen's Story

When I officially met my first group of CSP students on the first day of classes in the fall of 2002, there was much uneasiness all around. These students were the first to take the philosophy of education/ethics course that was a new core requirement in their program, and like most of the graduate students I teach in my education division, they were uneasy at best and terrified at worst of the often abstract and deadly dull discipline of philosophy. I, on the other hand, was acutely aware of my status of "new kid on the block" in the CSP community. Our semester together would be a process of mutual socialization. They would try to get me to fit into a framework of "CSP faculty member," and I would try to help them learn to speak the language of educational ethics.

My first official day of teaching in the CSP master's program was actually a career journey that I had begun almost 15 years prior to this day, when I was enrolled in the Higher Education and Student Affairs Administration Master's program at the University of Vermont (UVM). After graduating, I worked in service-learning programs at two campuses before returning to graduate school to study philosophy of education. Taking classes with Robert Nash at UVM had marked a pivotal point in my intellectual journey, and with Dr. Nash's guidance I enrolled in a doctoral program in the social foundations of education. My doctoral program work would mark the end of my "first" career in Student Affairs; my course work, my dissertation study set in a high school, and my primary teaching responsibilities in my current position at Miami University all focused on K–12 education. But after six years at Miami, an opportunity came for me to weave Student Affairs back into my intellectual journey as a teacher and learner. I began in 2002 to teach a required philosophy of education/ethics course in the CSP program.

I came to this first course in the fall of 2002 as a believer in Deweyan (1966) progressive pedagogy. I relied on my work in service learning and my studies of educational communities to construct experiences in which students can engage the subject matter of the courses I teach through cooperative, dialogical classroom structures. As Dewey (1963) advised, "It is not the subject per se that is educative or that is conducive to growth. There is no subject that is in and of itself, or without regard to the stage of growth attained by the learner, such that inherent educational value can be attributed to it" (p. 46). Even the topic of ethics, which in some senses is of intrinsic interest to most people whom I have encountered in my graduate teaching, is not inherently valuable to students unless they can connect with the material in some experiential way. And because ethics is an inquiry that is typically engaged through the study of philosophy, a discipline that often strikes fear in the hearts of students, the challenge to engage students is made more difficult. While I understood Deweyan progressivism and the challenges of teaching philosophy, I was only just beginning to understand how to put it into practice in the teaching of applied ethics.

With that first group of students in the fall of 2002, I was trying to socialize them into speaking the language of philosophy and educational ethics. In retrospect, I believe I was trying to get them to speak the language of ethics in the belief that they might be able to speak this language with their own authoritative voices as student affairs professionals. I wanted to engage them in the study of ethics, and I wanted to make ethics concrete and valid for their lives, but I also wanted them to speak *my* theoretical language. Their fluency in the language became my (misplaced) focus. I lost sight of the purposes this fluency might serve for them.

The conflicted and confused nature of my own goals for the class are, in hindsight, very apparent in the syllabus from that first semester. I wanted them to write "argument papers" in which they take an ethical issue in education and argue it through, attempting to exercise their logical and interpretive skills in making and defending a moral position. Yet I offered inadequate guidelines or suggestions for what topics they might engage and in class engaged them in few exercises designed to enable the students to generate topics or questions that would make the argument paper of interest to *their own* lives and concerns. I wanted them to use the language of ethics to help them articulate their own concerns, issues, and answers to complex educational problems.

The first text provided such an approach. As a first class text, I used *"Real World" Ethics* (Nash, 1996), understanding that my intellectual journey as a student affairs educator was still influenced by the work of Robert Nash. I valued, and the class also seemed to value, the way that this text clearly explains the complex process of moral decision making. Nash speaks of three moral languages that we all use in thinking about issues of morality: the first is a metaphysical language of ultimate truths and background beliefs; the second is a language of concrete communities, character, and virtues; and the third is the language of moral principle, designed for a world of "moral strangers" (p. 109) who do not speak the same first and second moral languages. Nash also introduces the assignments he uses in his own applied ethics classes to help students work through and understand the moral language analysis as a framework for thinking and acting. Nash's "moral briefs" (p. 67) are papers that are structured with concise, formal methods for "gaining access to important personal data in ethical decision-making" and to ask "simple, but essential, case-specific questions as preliminary to constructing a sound defense for taking a particular ethical action" (p. 117).

Following Nash, we read a series of texts designed to immerse the class in some of the current ethical debates in higher education and student affairs. We read books on in loco parentis (Hoekema, 1994), free expression and hate speech (Golding, 2000), and the moral and civic purposes of the liberal education curriculum (Nussbaum, 1997). I hoped that these philosophical texts would help engage the students to "speak philosophy" back to me. In hindsight, I suppose I believed that they would find ways to engage these issues through reading these texts and discussing them, but students found these texts to sometimes be off-putting through their use of theoretical language.

My uncertainty about how to engage the students in ethics was reflected in my limited use of Nash's moral brief assignment. While I used Nash's text as a first step in our inquiry into educational ethics that fall of 2002, I was uncertain about the centrality of the moral brief as an intellectual exercise and therefore offered it as a one of two options for their class final. It was telling to me that only 4 students out of 20 chose the moral brief final exam assignment; the others opted for a more standard essay exam, the questions to which we had collectively designed in class. My view at the time was that I could offer them different options for showing me how they had learned to speak in my language and that by using these different assignments I could glean how different students had engaged the content of the course. In hindsight, I found that my evasion of making the moral brief a central part of the class was a telling sign about my ambiguous visions for the course.

Students sensed my confusion about the class, of course. Many experienced the class in the same way one might experience a minor car accident: as an intense and engaging experience from which one walks away with a feeling of uncertainty about what exactly had happened. A few had vocalized early on their confusion about where I wanted the course to go, and my responses that I wanted them to learn a new language to identify and analyze moral problems in education somehow was not getting through to them. "I guess I just would have liked to know the direction the class was heading," stated one student. A few vocalized their displeasure with my feedback on papers—students rightly questioned some Bs and Cs that they felt were undeserved because of the lack of clarity in my assignment descriptions or the lack of clearly articulated feedback on the papers. Students also wanted more casework or 'real-life' examples to discuss in class. "There is a line between theory/philosophy and practice that we are working to define as soon-to-be professionals," wrote one student, implying that I was not helping students define that line for themselves.

I struggled with the theory/practice tension in this class because I have in the past interpreted this comment to mean that students wish to avoid the complexities of theory, particularly dense philosophical arguments, in favor of practice-oriented discussions that shed artificial clarity and cleanliness into real-life problems. But recently, prodded by further and deeper engagement with the Learning Partnerships Model that guides my colleagues in CSP at Miami and theories of caring (Noddings, 1984), I began to see students in a more generous light. What if their motivations were not to avoid theory but to read about theory without feeling stupid? What if their motivations for more casework were not to flee the ambiguity of philosophical arguments but to use these cases to grapple with the meaning of the philosophical texts? What if their motivations for me to provide vision for the course were not simply the simplistic desires of students to "tell me what you want me to learn" but rather the struggles of emerging professionals trying to find guidance in forming a strong moral voice as new professionals?

I was being socialized into the Learning Partnerships Model not so much by my faculty colleagues in the program as by the students. "Situate [the course] more in our experiences!" urged one student in her final evaluation. "Encourage more involvement," said another. "Do some work on the language of ethics—seems some students had trouble with the discourse," stated a third. I was, in a sense, learning to teach applied ethics to master's students who had been socialized into a partnership model of education. My struggle was understandable for someone who usually teaches a more theoretical, normative approach to ethics at the doctoral level and who was learning to teach in related but distinctly different subfield of ethics known as applied ethics (Nash, 1996). But I was also learning to teach within a learning partnership paradigm, a construction that my second-year graduate students were trying to teach me.

I can be a slow learner, but like most faculty, I am educable. The move from a Deweyan progressive pedagogy to the Learning Partnerships Model is not so much a conceptual or paradigmatic leap as a task of shaping my pedagogy to organize and invite the kind of engagement that I wanted to see students have with philosophical problems and texts. As I view the course now, my goal for students is to help them come to understand the skills, language, and dispositions necessary for self-authored ethical practice.

The goal of self-authored ethical practice relies on students' gaining confidence and skills in four areas: (a) the ability to discern and name ethical issues that confront them in their practice, (b) the willingness to judge and be judged as a person who must make decisions about moral problems or conflicts in their practice, (c) the ability to hear and to generously interpret the perspectives of those who are "moral strangers," and (d) the ability to arrive at a carefully analyzed decision that one can strongly and even passionately defend to others in a way that is compelling and creative, not rigid or dogmatic. A conception of self-authored ethical practice directs my insistence that students become familiar with the language (concepts and theories) of ethics but with the end goal being not to "speak my language" in an exercise of pedagogical narcissism but rather to use the language of ethics as a tool with which to articulate and defend their ethical decisions.

In shaping this goal throughout my teaching of the class in the spring of 2003, I experimented with new strategies. I brought in texts discussing the Elizabeth Shin case (Sontag, 2002) to help us dissect the debates about in loco parentis in a concrete way. Elizabeth Shin was a student at the Massachusetts Institute of Technology who committed suicide in her residence hall room in 2002, and this tragic case engages students with difficult questions of moral responsibility and freedom. The use of this one case unfolded in class and in on-line discussions as students shared their varied perspectives on parental responsibility, student autonomy, suicide, and the legal versus the moral obligations that universities have for students. I experimented with the selective use of videos to help elucidate the meanings of different ethical issues. For example, I used a provocative video, 'Secrets of the SAT,' on the use and abuses of the SAT (WGBH Educational Foundation, 1999) and related this video to our discussions on educational equity in higher education. I also kept the argument paper assignment as an important exercise in helping students learn to argue for their moral positions, though I provided much more detail in what I expected from these assignments and how students should approach the work required for an argument paper.

Most notably, my shift to a pedagogical goal of self-authored ethical practice is seen in the current final exam of the class: my own version of Nash's moral brief assignment. In this paper, students take a dilemma that arises out of their educational practice, either real or fictive. They analyze the dilemma using guiding questions that draw out more personal and subjective data about oneself as moral actor and questions that help the students think about the case from the perspective of the more publicly defensible language of moral principles. Nash does not think that this third language is more important than the rest. Indeed, he seeks to help students construct a "moral bricolage" (Nash, 1996, p. 146), a creative process of taking stock and weaving a new moral language out of older, existing languages of morality that the student has implicitly or explicitly learned up to this point. Nash states that his overall goal is "to help each of my students to create a useable ethics 'text': one that 'weaves' together a functional 'moral language' from among the 'bits and pieces' of traditional moral vocabularies" (p. 146). My goal for this moral brief assignment is to help students see themselves as moral bricoleurs who can author their own ethical judgments through a process of honest self-exploration, careful moral fact-finding, and thorough analysis using philosophical frameworks as conceptual tools.

Achieving success with the Learning Partnerships Model is marked not by the arrival at "the" perfect pedagogy or syllabus but with the sense that one has effectively communicated with a class and arrived at mutually agreeable destinations in regard to the course content. Some comments from the course evaluations of the spring 2003 class in philosophy of education/ethics affirmed for me that I had perhaps reached such a destination with a majority of this semester's students:

> I appreciated that Kathleen was able to present philosophical ideas and foundations in a tangible manner. The issues were pertinent and she encouraged us to personalize them, which led to rich discussion.

> The classroom dialogue provided meaningful ways to sort through complex ethical issues.

> The argument papers challenged me to consider an issue that I cared about enough to argue for/against.

The beauty of teaching for me is that the task of effectively communicating with students demands ongoing reflection on your philosophy and methods as your students change and as the world around you evolves. The demands of pedagogy based in the Learning Partnerships Model are usually rewarded with the satisfaction of having made a genuine impact with the way your discipline has been understood, received, and translated by students to improve their future practice.

Collectively, Marcia's and Kathleen's stories depict the challenges that are inherent when teachers engage in constructive-developmental pedagogy as the process to become partners with learners in the educational process. As teachers, they had to be open to hearing student voices and adept at grasping and interpreting what students were asking as they struggled to author their own perspectives. Marcia and Kathleen had to discern the appropriate mix of guidance and autonomy in structuring assignments, class discussions, and grading processes. They had to be purposeful in designing their courses as they used the three assumptions and the three principles of the Learning Partnerships Model in both content and process. Despite these very real challenges, the rewards are apparent. Perhaps the most gratifying result is that the CSP students owned their educational experience and actively participated in shaping it with both veteran and new members of the community of scholars.

Building Community Using the Learning Partnerships Model

The Learning Partnerships Model shapes our relationships with students outside the classroom as well. This occurs in a number of ways. For example, we incorporate students' perspectives in program decisions about the format of the comprehensive examination, curricular changes, and modifying the core values. We address students' needs for support and interpersonal growth by purposefully building community through the annual opening retreat and presentation of the core values, through the midyear assessment retreat, through the end-of-year "reflection on transitions" retreat, and through picnics, holiday gatherings, and celebrations in faculty homes. Professional development programs and individual coaching sessions address a number of values as we provide students with opportunities to polish résumé writing and interviewing skills, to develop expertise in conference proposal writing and presentations, and to edit and/or publish in an on-line student journal. Finally, the values inform the way we perceive our role as advisers. Rather than a peripheral aspect of our jobs, advising is considered to work in tandem with our pedagogical practices in promoting students' self-authorship. The assumptions and principles of the Learning Partnerships Model serve as the framework for our advising relationships with our graduate students.

Exit surveys conducted as our students graduate and alumni surveys administered after several years working in the field underscore how all these dimensions of the program affected their professional development. Specifically, alumni described the many benefits of the learning community focus, as defined by the core values of the CSP program. First, the learning community "created a model for graduates to work from when interacting with students on a daily basis." This was particularly significant since CSP graduates work primarily with undergraduates in student affairs settings. Second, alumni appreciated the opportunities that the learning community focus provided to "build working and social relationships" that were a "vital support network" during their education. The learning community also helped students develop, as they were "encouraged to not just accept but also challenge what they were learning." One alumnus stated that the community allowed him to "understand the importance and true meaning of lifelong learning." Another benefit of the learning community was the challenge to come together with "people from different walks of life to be open and not afraid to share their thoughts, experiences, etcetera with the group." Many alumni appreciated the sense of affiliation that was built during their time in the CSP program. They cited such events as the student-led retreats, CSP social events, dining at homes of faculty, and gathering in the resource room as contributing to building community in the program. The community was described as "safe," with shared "values and commitments to student learning," and helpful in conveying that "learning and teaching are shared responsibilities." Graduating students voiced similar perspectives as captured in this reflection:

> The first picnic helped acquaint new students with one another and to the change in professional relationships with professors from undergraduate life. The retreats provided community relationships and ideas to surface. It also allowed for a safe and open atmosphere to share and address relevant issues. (2001 Miami CSP graduate)

Graduating students also commented on the mutuality of their relationships with faculty as a significant part of their experience:

> I feel that I've learned so much about education, the development of young adults, the behavior of organizations and *a lot* about myself . . . and I feel as though I have studied with (not under) some of the greatest minds and spirits of my entire educational career. Working with the faculty here has been a gift . . . watching them enact their espoused values both in and out of the classroom has been such a nice thing to observe and see modeled. (2001 Miami CSP graduate)

In summary, our partnership with students occurs both within and beyond courses. We are more than an academic program; we are a community of scholars that encompasses and promotes the intellectual, intrapersonal, and interpersonal development of all members. Our students embark on the journey to self-authorship through their involvement in the learning community defined by the core values. The journey is represented in this student's experience:

> During my first semester of classes, I was challenged to look at who I was, what I wanted to accomplish, and what I needed to get there. I shared my experiences with my classmates and faculty and felt listened to and an active member of the community. Instead of being given the answers or validation to my fears, I was given the forum to explore the deep-down beliefs and principles that guide me. Also, I was able to hear from other members of the community that they felt the same way and we were able to support each other and learn together through these large questions. (2002 Miami CSP graduate)

In our interactions in the larger community, students are challenged to define their own perspectives and supported to voice them.

Ongoing Critical Reflection and Evaluation of the Learning Community

The process of mutual construction in our graduate program is ongoing, as teachers and learners (i.e., all members of the community) continually reflect on our experiences and make meaning of it together. The learning is never ending. Mutual transformation and learning occur in one-on-one advising conversations between faculty and students, in the dynamics of each course and class session, and in the context of all-community discussions. A good example of the latter is the community-wide on-line discussion that occurred recently in which members participated in a passionate dialogue over the issue of free speech versus harmful speech. Discussants engaged in creative controversy as they teased out community beliefs about diversity and its value in our program. The result of this lively and provocative yearlong dialogue was the adoption of a new core value: a shared commitment to inclusiveness. This event represents the very real partnership that faculty forge with students. The core values are always open for critique and modification if a reasoned and fully supported argument takes us there. Clearly, this kind of discussion, where students publicly stated their beliefs in the context of their relationships in the community, promotes self-authorship.

As described throughout this chapter, we collect both formal and informal data about the impact of our program on student learning and development on a continual basis. Anecdotal data is shared among us as a standard part of our faculty meetings. Quantitative and qualitative course evaluations are solicited for every class we teach. Annual exit surveys and advising evaluations are collected from graduating students and synthesized, and alumni surveys are conducted when we are debating major curriculum/program changes. These data are shared with students and faculty to shape every aspect of the program. In this way, we all continue to learn from each other and constantly transform our practice.

Conclusion

What we hoped to illuminate by telling the story of our graduate program is that the Learning Partnerships Model provides a powerful framework for promoting our students' self-authorship. We also hope it is apparent that graduate education can be life changing for students when the Learning Partnerships Model is enacted in a seamless way through multiple aspects of the learning environment. In our 10-plus years of using the Learning Partnerships Model, we have learned that when its assumptions and principles permeate all that we are and do as teachers and learners, we experience learning as transformation. We truly become a community of scholars. We close our story with the words of a graduating student who describes the metamorphosis to self-authorship as a result of participating in our master's program:

> In all, our CSP community has challenged me to evaluate my dreams, my hopes, and myself, to step back from various situations and truly explore the likelihood of creating a certain event or program, to learn to stand for my beliefs, and yet, to also respectfully question others'. My experiences at Miami have challenged me, but they have also helped me to see and to understand who I am to the core. I feel comfortable with the good and the bad, and feel at home with myself, something that may sound strange, but it is a welcoming feeling after all the questions, tears, struggles, hugs, and laughter of graduate school. Never did I expect to be on such a grueling journey of self-understanding and awareness, and never did I believe I would feel whole at the end of the experience. I am grateful to the community we have created, to the space I found for myself, and to the voice I found within me. And now, I am excited to go out, find a job and continue my journey. (2001 Miami CSP graduate)

References

Baxter Magolda, M. B. (1992). *Knowing and reasoning in college: Gender-related patterns in students' intellectual development.* San Francisco: Jossey-Bass.

Baxter Magolda, M. B. (1999a). *Creating contexts for learning and self-authorship: Constructive-developmental pedagogy.* Nashville: Vanderbilt University Press.

Baxter Magolda, M. B. (1999b). Learning-centered practice is harder than it looks. *About Campus, 4*(4), 2–4.

Baxter Magolda, M. B. (2001). *Making their own way: Narratives for transforming higher education to promote self-development.* Sterling, VA: Stylus.

Block, P. (1987). *The empowered manager.* San Francisco: Jossey-Bass.

Council for the Advancement of Standards for Student Services/Development Programs (1994). *Preparation standards and guidelines at the masters degree level for student affairs professionals in higher education.* Washington, DC: Author.

Dewey, J. (1963). *Experience and education.* New York: Colllier.

Dewey, J. (1966). *Democracy and education: An introduction to the philosophy of education.* New York: Free Press.

Golding, M. P. (2000). *Free speech on campus.* Lanham, MD: Rowman & Littlefield.

Hoekema, D. A. (1994). *Campus rules and moral community: In place of in loco parentis.* Lanham, MD: Rowman & Littlefield.

Kegan, R., & Lahey, L. L. (2000). *How the way we talk can change the way we work: Seven languages for transformation.* San Francisco, CA: Jossey-Bass.

Nash, R. J. (1996). *"Real world" ethics: Frameworks for educators and human service professionals.* New York: Teachers College Press.

Noddings, N. (1984). *Caring: A feminine approach to ethics and moral education.* Berkeley: University of California Press.

Nussbaum, M. (1997). *Cultivating humanity: A classical defense of reform in liberal education.* Cambridge, MA: Harvard University Press.

Sontag, D. (2002, April 28). "Who was responsible for Elizabeth Shin?" *New York Times.* Available: http://www.psc.uc.edu/news/Elizabeth_Shin.htm

WGBH Educational Foundation. (1999). *Secrets of the SAT.* Boston: PBS Video.

9

THE LEARNING PARTNERSHIPS MODEL

FRAMING FACULTY AND INSTITUTIONAL DEVELOPMENT

Terry M. Wildman

The power of any framing device is that it provides a way of interpreting and giving meaning to the events, large and small, that we encounter in any domain of interest. Frames, or frameworks, as in the Learning Partnerships Model proposed by Marcia Baxter Magolda (1999, 2001), also serve as generative tools in the sense of directing action, or suggesting ways of valuing particular actions, events, or outcomes. Frames have been shown to have a pervasive impact on meaning making (Bruner, 1990; Mandler, 1984; Minsky, 1975), where even the mere mention of a key word, such as *self-authorship,* evokes and activates a whole set of more or less commonly understood propositions about what makes a given phenomenon work. In the case of self-authorship, the word evokes important propositions about what makes students tick as learners. For teaching faculty and administrators, what is at stake is the accuracy and appropriateness of the course we set in designing experiences that will aid our students in developing their full intellectual powers.

In the domain of higher education, there are many competing frames, some of which are not made explicit but which nevertheless exert significant influence on perceptions and actions concerning students and their growth. In the long run, choosing and developing frames that both guide our work and inform the interpretation of results is a critical responsibility that we cannot afford to take lightly. The stakes are high because in complex communities we rely on particular frames, or story lines, to decide on courses of action, the distribution of resources, the roles and importance of various actors, and essentially what the enterprise is all about. The story lines may be in fact inherent or prescribed and thus not open to inquiry or debate. So, in the higher-education games we play, the competition is so often about resources or perhaps a particular project that is deemed desirable within the organization when the effort might better be spent in pursuit of a powerful and appropriate frame that could change everything.

Members of the Virginia Tech academic community are making such an effort by actively exploring how the Learning Partnerships Model might influence the educational opportunities available to our approximately 26,000 students. This chapter takes the form of a story that began about 5 years ago when members of the university faculty and administration took advantage of a single opportunity to discuss with Marcia Baxter Magolda the basics of her longitudinal work on adult intellectual development. What makes the work described here a potentially interesting story in the context of this book is that the single occasion of an invited speaker turned into an authentic quest for a new way of thinking about the educational goals and methods of a large and complex institution. The story provides a rich context for reflecting on how change works (or not) and how research can inform and guide the evolution of educational practice.

The institutional setting is Virginia Polytechnic Institute and State University. Virginia Tech, known for its historical roots in agriculture and engineering, made the transition to a more comprehensive status beginning in the late 1960s and quickly moved to the middle of the top 100 universities in terms of research expenditures. Eight colleges offer degree programs: Agriculture and Life Sciences, Architecture and Urban Studies, Business, Natural Resources, Engineering, Veterinary Medicine, and two recently restructured colleges, one oriented to the sciences and the other to liberal arts and human sciences. Undergraduate students may choose from among 60 degree options; graduate students participate in 110 master's and doctoral degree programs. Faculty who work at this university have grown accustomed to balancing the competing demands of being productive in research, effective in teaching, and also engaged in the outreach mission of this land grant institution. This is not an easy environment for change, particularly any change that may not align perfectly with the prevailing strategic directions and reward structures. Yet change exists: Restructuring of colleges, budget reductions, and a new strategic plan to vie for even higher ranking among research institutions describe some of the recent challenges. In the midst of this change, the university and its faculty continue to seek ways to better serve the undergraduate population of approximately 21,000 students.

This story begins about a year in advance of the second Baxter Magolda book, *Creating Contexts for Learning and Self-Authorship* (1999), which detailed the nature of constructive developmental pedagogy and implications for instructional practice. The author was initially invited to campus by the university teaching center to spend a day lecturing and talking with faculty about developmental concepts and how these concepts might influence our instructional practices. That visit led to another, and yet another, and soon a significant group began to ask, When will Marcia be back?

In the years that have passed since her first visit in 1998, the dialogue and the collaboration have continued and have become increasingly focused. The *framework* around which this book is organized is still at the center of these discussions. Evidence that the ideas are beginning to take root is beginning to appear in campus conversation and projects. Perhaps most important, a powerful story line about what we are trying to do with students is beginning to emerge. The focus on application is gradually shifting from individual faculty members working on their own courses to the much larger scope of the entire general education program. Faculty and administrators are recognizing in increasing numbers that a rich language is available with which we can talk about where we are going with the undergraduate curriculum.

The question addressed in this chapter is basically this: How did the process of introducing a new frame of reference work at Virginia Tech? Conceptually, we knew the work we were beginning was more than technical in nature and would extend well beyond a simple positivist interpretation where good science is expected to lead to nice clean solutions. As Donald Schon (1983) pointed out in his book *The Reflective Practitioner,* the problems of greatest interest to educators are most often found not on the high ground where technical solutions work best but in the swampy lowland where the problems we encounter and most care about are difficult to define and even more difficult to address in creative ways.

Situating the Story

The present story is clearly situated more in Schon's swamp than on the high ground and thus requires a more complex telling. The first question to address is one of preparation. How might an institution prepare itself to take on the challenges inherent in a model whose implications can be far reaching in terms of the design and enactment of instructional practice? In the Virginia Tech case, this *readiness factor* is discussed primarily in terms of the university's teaching center—the Center for Excellence in Undergraduate Teaching (CEUT). Established in 1993, CEUT was given the broad mission of serving as an advocate for teaching excellence and for providing various resources and development opportunities for the faculty. By the time we began exploring seriously the meaning of Baxter Magolda's constructive-developmental pedagogy and philosophy, CEUT had been in operation for about 5 years and had begun to reinforce the idea that there are interesting research-based alternatives to inform how we think about learning and student development. Moreover, CEUT had developed a range of strategies to support the institution's approach to implementing new ideas.

A second factor that figured prominently in this story was the introduction of a university initiative centered on the development of learning communities. The Learning Communities Initiative at Virginia Tech essentially opened the door to more explicit consideration of developmental concepts, the idea of self-authorship, and the notion of partnerships as a way of thinking about relationships among key players who participate in the education of our students. Funded by the university provost, the Learning Communities Initiative was implemented through CEUT and supported by a coordinating committee of faculty from the various university colleges. This emerging initiative in learning communities was in fact the context in which Baxter Magolda's initial visits to discuss student development occurred.

A key outcome associated with the initiative in learning communities was the development of several on-campus residential communities that accommodate entering freshmen in theme-related living and academic programs. One program in particular, the Residential Leadership Community, has developed as the flagship of our learning communities and is used here as a case to illustrate some of the complexities of building programs around developmental concepts.

I address also the more general question of how faculty come together to work on their teaching, extending the discussion of how a teaching center can foster dialogue, reflection, and partnerships among faculty. The Faculty Study Group program, begun in 1996, currently involves approximately 170 faculty members who have committed to working together in small groups organized around themes and objectives of their choosing. At this point only a few of the 27 groups are explicitly engaged in work related to the Learning Partnerships Model, but the ones that are provide good examples of how small-scale innovation occurs without top-down intervention. One group in particular will be featured in some detail.

The Learning Partnerships Model has also come into play as we have thought about larger-scale curriculum reform. Currently, the entire core curriculum has come under review, revealing a more elaborate context for consideration of student development concepts. The focus of this section of the chapter is to explain the way that frames for understanding student development are being utilized in the emerging reform effort. This work allows us to examine some of the daunting barriers to meaningful, large-scale curricula change.

The chapter concludes with an overall appraisal of how the Learning Partnerships Model is influencing our thinking about educational reform and the role that the model is playing in faculty development. We expect that the model itself will be shaped by the uses to which it is put and the contexts in which it is applied. Certainly for the people who work with the model over time, there will be different interpretations and understandings that will emerge.

The Institutional Readiness Factor

How does a large higher-education enterprise go about working on teaching? How do new ideas get into the system? What kind of ground can be prepared for the introduction of ideas such as *self-authorship, identity development,* and the *mutual construction of knowledge?* The answers to such questions do not necessarily lead to the door of the local teaching center, but there are preparedness issues that should be addressed through some formal structure. In the case of Virginia Tech, CEUT has in recent years played a key role in supporting and influencing educational change activity.

When I assumed the position of director of the CEUT a few years prior to Marcia's involvement with Virginia Tech, I proposed three general organizing principles that we used initially to think about the direction of the CEUT and how we would view our work with faculty and others who make up this large educational community. The first principle defined our stance on students, the second identified professional issues in teaching, and the third concerned our move from long-established habits and traditions to a more contemporary enterprise.

Principle 1: Students

We began with the idea that students must have legitimate participatory roles in the enterprise and that their needs as learners have to be recognized. This understanding can be articulated in terms of a general caring attitude for students, but the ways in which that general attitude is enacted have much to do with the frames we use to conceptualize the learning process. The problem, of course, is that our traditional frames for understanding learning and pedagogy have tended to leave the learner with an impoverished set of roles oriented mostly to compliance and reliance on external authority. When these older frames are combined with the pressures that faculty face in research institutions, the prevailing modes of instruction are certainly not in the direction of greater student centeredness.

Fortunately, properly established teaching centers can be licensed to promote and disseminate messages that run counter to older and/or out-of-date conceptions of the educative process. Also, fortunately, there are numerous ways to articulate such messages, and there are well-established conceptual frames that do give learners important roles to play, including ideas about how they can be supported in developing those roles.

Principle 2: Faculty and Professionalism

Most faculty, unfortunately, do not enter teaching in higher education with a great deal of specific preparation about anything outside the disciplines and professional arenas in which they will be teaching and conducting research. This leaves a lot of unexplored territory that must be learned on the job. In our initial description of CEUT's mission, we began to focus on and explain these missing pieces of the puzzle by defining teaching as a legitimate professional activity. By working from this fundamental assertion about the professional nature of teaching, we could then introduce and emphasize three key areas to develop and strengthen teaching, including (a) professional knowledge about teaching and learning that can inform teaching practice, (b) induction scenarios in support of new teachers, and (c) emphasis on reflection and assessment of teaching. All these considerations need to work together, and the process of moving toward a more professional and better-prepared teaching faculty creates a potentially huge agenda for the teaching center and its various partners throughout the institution.

The leverage in the promotion of greater professionalism in teaching, even if we take a softer, less technical approach and view teaching more as a professional "craft," is that, once we become confident about the validity of particular models of learning and teaching, it becomes much more difficult to justify inaction or complacency with regard to those principles. In the case of the Learning Partnerships Model, for example, it would be tempting to argue that the underlying principles are more *imperatives* for professional consideration than niceties to be considered if there is time, space, and interest. Indeed, the more the Learning Partnerships Model can be strengthened through supporting triangulation from related conceptual and empirical work, the stronger the case becomes. To make the point entirely explicit, educators should no more attempt to teach without detailed and explicit information about student conditions and needs than a doctor would attempt to administer drugs or treatment without detailed study of the patient's medical history.

Principle 3: Contexts for Learning

One of the first things we discover in our attempts to introduce new practices in institutional settings is that the *old designs run deep*. Indeed, they are embodied in the classrooms where knowledge is *delivered*, in the curriculum practices where requirements are *checked off*, in the space utilization policies where time is *parsed out* in small manageable chunks, in the textbooks where knowledge is carefully *scripted and decontextualized,* and even in the organizational structures where disciplines can be *isolated* and protected within their own departments. Despite the evidence that these characteristics are changing in some settings, educational decisions made many decades ago are now institutionalized in physical and bureaucratic structures and continue to exert tremendous influence over what is possible.

The energy required to modify our work, given the power of traditional frames of reference, has to be factored into the calculations of what will be possible for faculty and faculty groups when they consider changing their methods. Consequently, in our conceptualization of CEUT's mission and activities, we determined to remember that even as faculty and students may move into new relationships and contracts with respect to academic work, those changes need to occur in supportive contexts. Just as we think about the scaffolding that students need when they move into new territory with regard to concepts and skills, faculty require the same consideration. For the teaching center, the three key resources we can provide or advocate for are (a) continuing access to information and critical dialogue, (b) time to pursue new directions, and (c) access to supporting collaborative networks among peers.

With these ideas in mind, CEUT quickly established a significant track record in terms of providing an array of services in support of instructional faculty. The CEUT's yearly profile of activity includes the following:

- Workshops: Approximately 50 events covering a range of topics related to learning, teaching strategies, assessment, student characteristics, and the like
- Grants: Funding for course development, instructional improvement, and experimentation—an average of 40 projects each year
- Consultation: Support for individuals who request assistance
- Collaborations: Maintenance of ongoing collaborations with as many as 25 different units and entities on campus that have missions relating to support for teaching
- Resources: Maintenance of written and electronic materials on teaching that faculty can access
- Study groups: Support for small faculty groups to work on teaching over extended periods of time—1 to 4 years in some cases

Certainly these activities and resources are standard fare for many teaching centers or other entities that provide faculty development support. In our view, however, the type and quantity of support are not the only issues. We also concern ourselves with the nature and quality of our interactions with faculty. This focus has practical advantages in terms of participant satisfaction and also actively supports the messages we promote and endorse about learning environments needing to be invitational, supportive, and respectful of participant needs. In particular, we are concerned about establishing the trust that is necessary when promoting change that may carry levels of risk. We seek to convey the idea that the environment we create in working with faculty (as it is for students) is more than just a key part of the message—it actually coproduces the outcomes we plan for and anticipate.

Thus, in a gentle and sometimes indirect manner, the stage is being set in our faculty development work for models of teaching that are increasingly learning centered and less content driven. This work is invitational in nature, and participation is voluntary. In the past 8 years, a special cadre of faculty has emerged who have regular contact with CEUT and who generously participate in planning, supporting, and delivering some of the programs. These faculty members, who have increased in number to perhaps a fifth of the total number of faculty on campus, are essentially ambassadors for academic change; they talk and work with other faculty who in turn are influenced to varying degrees. This is not to say at all that beliefs and goals among this large array of faculty are uniform, but certainly the groundwork is set for serious consideration of frameworks such as the Learning Partnerships Model.

Initiatives That Localized and Focused the Need for Change

In 1997, we began one particular initiative that almost immediately opened a significant opportunity to disseminate and discuss the work that we have done with Baxter Magolda. The university initiative was designed to explore and develop the concept of learning communities. The Learning Communities Initiative was part of a larger strategic plan to invest in key areas of research and educational strength, most of which related to programs and initiatives in science, engineering, and technology. The decision to explore and develop the concept of learning communities provided a signal, welcomed by many, that a research university should concern itself with more than just the purely academic features of a college education. Already, the strategic plan for the university had included explicit references to "education of the whole person," but until we began this investigation into the meaning of learning communities, that phrase was not much in the forefront of the university dialogue.

Self-Assessment

The Learning Communities Initiative unfolded in stages. The first phase, begun in the fall of 1997, was essentially a self-assessment of where we stood as an institution with respect to the central concepts embodied in the learning communities movement, including an analysis of whether we were even building and supporting such communities. The responsibility for this analysis was placed with an appointed university committee, chaired by the director of the teaching center. Three years were initially allocated to the initiative, with the needs assessment due at the end of the first year.

The results of the self-assessment were mixed. On the one hand, we could find few specific curriculum models (e.g., linked courses, freshmen interest groups, or federated learning communities) that met the formal definition of a learning community and that students could negotiate in cohorts. We simply had not invested in such curriculum models, even though the movement in this direction was at least 10 years old by the time our work began. However, when we shifted our focus to an examination of the basic learning principles and values that underlie learning communities more generally (see, e.g., Boyer, 1995; Bruner, 1990, 1996; Lave and Wenger, 1991; Palmer, 1997), we began to see that the fundamental issue was really about the arrangements and conditions for *meaning making* as well as student participation in meaningful practices (as contrasted to implementation of strictly defined curriculum structures). Our spirits lifted significantly as we began to discover a number of programs, projects, and educational experiments throughout the university that seemed to be successfully organized around the key principles of interest.

One of the first examples we explored in this regard is the studio model for preparing architects. At our school, the early preparation of architects has long been designed around the explicit awareness that the curriculum should be oriented to the student and the mix of individual and collaborative work that involves issues of social, economic, and environmental importance. The studio itself is a place with distinct qualities, essentially serving multiple roles as a work site for students and faculty, a social home base for the emerging professional community, and a direct connection to the culture of architecture. The studio model is also applied in different configurations in theater, art, interior design, engineering, and other disciplines.

We began to make the case, then, that learning communities must be understood and enacted, at least in part, within the context of legitimate social practices. Jerome Bruner, one of the original architects of the cognitive revolution, which began in the 1950s, reminded us in his 1990 book *Acts of*

Meaning that our modern study and treatment of the learner does not always place the construction of meaning at the center. Rather, he claims, we have allowed the conventional goals of a "positivist science . . . with its ideals of reductionism, causal explanation, and prediction" (p. xiii) to dominate not only the production of knowledge but also the sharing and use of knowledge. Missing, he says, is the understanding that learning involves participation in culture, where "life depends upon shared meanings and shared concepts and depends as well upon shared modes of discourse for negotiating differences in meaning and interpretation" (p. 13). The question, then, of how to put meaning making back at the center of teaching and learning is one that needs to be kept on the table and in the center of our ongoing dialogue.

During the past several decades, the research on learning has matured and developed to the point where learners are no longer seen simply as individuals to be shaped and molded independently of others or the culture around them. Lave and Wenger's (1991) groundbreaking work on the "situated" nature of learning provides a rich framework for understanding the nuances of participation within communities of practice. As participants in social practices, learners are seen as whole persons who develop through knowing in context, by becoming agents of their own learning, and through the construction of identities within the community in question. Clearly, these understandings about learning are qualitatively different from the concepts that have guided instructional practice for most of the past century.

Two things happened as we began to apply the conceptual framework of a learning community, or a community of practice (Wenger, 1999), to our thinking about our own programs. First, as noted with the architecture studio example, we began to see some encouraging developments we had not noticed before. In a matter of weeks, we identified programs, individual courses, capstone projects, outreach and extension projects, and some experimental programs that held as their main organizing principles at least some of the ideals about learning expressed previously. However, most of these examples had one unfortunate thing in common in that they were not well known outside their immediate environment, department, or college. This gave us the sense that the institution as a whole was not functioning exceptionally well as a larger community of practice. We were not learning very well from each other—we were not developing common language with which to share the work we were doing.

Second, we began to see the large number of structural barriers to community that existed in our institution. We talked extensively about the physical barriers in classrooms and other settings that dramatically dampen the opportunity for shared work and discourse among students, faculty, and other stakeholders. We discussed difficulties inherent in the hierarchical organization itself, noting that college and departmental structures are frequently discussed nationally as barriers to good practice. We also looked with concern at the prevailing reward structures in a research institution, the bureaucratic means of accounting for productivity, and the overall organization of time and space. The way we frame our work has a powerful influence on what we interpret as important. Consequently, when we submitted our initial report following our first year of study, we placed the recommendation to address structural barriers to community first on our list.

Consideration of Student Development

Following a year of analysis and identification of institutional strengths and weaknesses, the Learning Communities Initiative entered a longer, second stage. This phase involved further identification of naturally occurring learning communities, dissemination of our findings internally via workshops and other events organized through CEUT, and the formal introduction of the developmental research of Marcia Baxter Magolda. Our first introduction to her research actually reveals one additional key outcome of our work with learning communities: the rapid development of closer ties with student affairs. Baxter Magolda's work, as well as related research on student development, was well known within the mainstream of professional thought and consideration in student affairs work but less so on the academic side of campus. As soon as we made this connection, however, we invited her to campus for an initial lecture and some discussions.

Two things happened at that point. First, it was immediately clear that our investigation into the role of learning communities was missing a key feature: developmental models of student learning. I think we saw the imperative to infuse our work with developmental considerations so readily because the Baxter Magolda presentation also included a general model or scheme for how to think about the pedagogical challenges inherent in the goal of pursuing development in addition to disciplinary knowledge. The model, while complex, focused on just three core assumptions about learning and three principles for supporting students' development as knowers. Further, the language of self-authorship may have captured metaphorically the ideal that many faculty seem to innately hold that students will come to take ownership for their own learning. For some, the ideas were totally new and surprising; for others, the model provided a way to think and talk about ideals they had long held but perhaps could not express systematically.

As we continued to promote the idea and ideals of learning communities, Marcia was invited to return to campus at important junctures to continue the discussion about her developmental research and especially to participate in dialogue about pedagogy and curriculum. Over the past 4 years, approximately 250 faculty members have participated in these lectures and discussions. With few exceptions, these individuals have not been followed in any systematic way, but the ongoing contact we have with many of the faculty through the teaching center provides a sort of "listening post" that allows us to detect instances in which the model may be at work. For example, we can see references to the concept of self-authorship in grant applications, workshops, learning community projects, and the discussions that occur in our faculty study groups. Many of these indicators that the language and ideas are alive and working are isolated instances that are not cultivated or supported in any systematic way by the teaching center or other university entity. Clearly, some of the seeds that have been sown have taken root, and the results are showing up across the landscape.

The Residential Leadership Community

One of the most successful and dramatic examples of the learning communities movement at Virginia Tech is a program designed to prepare students as citizen leaders. The Residential Leadership Community (RLC) is a collaborative program cosponsored by the Division of Student Affairs, the Center for Interdisciplinary Studies, and the University Honors Program and supported by other partners, including Residential and Dining Programs, University Unions and Student Activities, Alumni Relations, the Women's Center, Pamplin College of Business, Office of Multicultural Affairs, and CEUT.

The program welcomed its first cohort of students in 1998–1999, added a second-year component in 2000, and presently serves approximately 225 students each year. The program seeks to prepare individuals to participate responsibly as citizen leaders in an increasingly complex global context. Students who complete the 2-year program may then elect to continue their leadership development through one of several leadership options or minors available in colleges across the university.

The RLC is distinguished by its curriculum and pedagogy. To begin, the program is conceptualized and enacted within a carefully constructed residential learning community. Utilizing a praxis framework and service learning pedagogy, students in the first year are introduced to leadership concepts in course work offered within the residential community and in leadership praxis experiences situated within the campus environment. Praxis, a concept basic to Freire's (1970) work, consists of the elements of action and reflection arranged in a nonlinear relationship so that action and reflection, or theory and practice, build on each other. A praxis curriculum, as described by Grundy (1987), is informed by an emancipatory interest that not only entrusts the construction of knowledge to learners and their communities but also recognizes that "the curriculum itself develops through the dynamic interaction of action and reflection" (Grundy, 1987, p. 115).

The learning community, following the work of Kegan (1994) and Baxter Magolda (1999, 2001), is designed to provide a carefully constructed "holding environment" in which the interplay of challenge and support can be artfully negotiated as students develop across intellectual, ethical, and civic awareness dimensions. The first-year leadership courses carry core curriculum credit and approach leadership through both humanities and behavioral and social science frameworks. Following a treatment of leadership as a contextual phenomenon across cultures and historical time frames, students move in the spring semester into action projects utilizing behavioral and social science methodologies. These action projects are situated in the campus and local communities. They provide students with the opportunity and challenge of designing service and learning projects that often have real consequences for real people and organizations. Implemented through a leadership course titled "Exploring Citizen Leadership: Communities of Praxis," students in the spring of 2003, for example, could choose from among a variety of course sections, distinguished as follows by the action research undertaken within the community:

- A benchmarking project for the campus police department, involving research conducted in 25 police departments in the eastern United States
- Instructional support for English and journalism classes in a local high school
- Exploration of health delivery systems across the region surrounding Virginia Tech and participation in related volunteer and fund-raising activities
- Design of mentoring experiences, a speaker series, and career networking within the context of Alumni Relations at Virginia Tech
- Sponsorship of a daylong leadership conference for local high school students
- Organization of issues forums around concerns of the campus community and especially of first-year students

Twelve such sections offered in this particular semester varied with the instructors' expertise and the availability of opportunities within the local community.

As the program matured, a peer component was added that involved carefully selected second-year students (approximately 42 each year) serving as peer group facilitators or community service organizers for the first-year students. In this manner, the program systematically builds in opportunities for students to gain significant ownership of the RLC as they work in instructional teams with faculty from student affairs and academic departments. The strong orientation toward student leadership within the community, as well as student acceptance of responsibility for the community, ensures that the program maintains a fluid and dynamic quality. This is both a desirable feature and a challenge for the faculty involved.

Finally, to ensure that students recognize and experience the full extent and promise of citizen leadership, plans are under way to create a course that explores active leadership and service in a global context. This component includes potential study-abroad experiences that can be linked with nonprofit international educational organizations to provide students with service-learning experiences in cross-cultural contexts. In January 2001, the RLC piloted an international service-learning course in Kenya. This experience has further inspired the students and faculty to pursue more intensely the ideal of the RLC as developing citizen leaders for a global context.

The RLC is of particular interest as a "case" to be examined in this chapter because of its underlying theory of student development and its intent to bring conceptual clarity to its curricular organization. Rather than approach the curriculum from a strictly skills development point of view, the focus is to equip students with the tools to continually construct new paradigms for leadership that require continuing to examine the critical questions of what is ethical and effective leadership behavior and how such behavior changes and moves in a complex and interdependent world. The praxis approach to such development requires that the community itself learn through practice, reflection, and inquiry. The program director contends that through the goals and pedagogies established for the program, students and faculty will be engaged in exploring a "new ethical frontier" imposed by rapid globalization (Johnston, 2002).

With leadership and support from the Division of Student Affairs, the RLC has also benefited from a significant appraisal process. Participants were compared with matched samples based on grade-point average and were also examined in terms of their responses to a 46-item self-report survey designed after research on participation in communities of practice (see, e.g., Lave & Wenger, 1991; Wenger, 1998). These evaluation data demonstrated that students participating in the RLC (and sister communities not featured here) significantly exceed matched samples on academic achievement as measured by course grades. Students in the RLC cohort reported being actively engaged in the community and its work, confident of their learning gains across a variety of skill and knowledge domains, cognizant of gains in problem solving and the responsibilities of working in a community setting, and aware of changes in their identity as participants in a purposeful community. Anecdotal data based on experience with individual students provide even more compelling evidence that the educational process is deeply enhanced when students are provided with supported opportunities to "make their own way" when immersed in issues and problems of importance to their immediate community and context.

The success of the RLC in stimulating student development, even within the 2 years of its inception, is remarkable to all who know the program and interact with its "graduates." The gains and the successes do not seem to be the result of anyone "trying harder" or selecting better students, even though the program attracts its share of exceptional students. Rather, the results seem connected to one deceptively simple understanding: Learners gain intellectual power and identities that go with such power when the curriculum is structured to give power away. The Learning Partnerships Model clarifies this claim and gives it depth and coherence through its anchorage in an empirical framework that demonstrates the complex route that must be followed to achieve these outcomes. The RLC, following the Learning Partnerships Model and other related theory and evidence, clearly shows that it is possible to *design for* student growth through innovative courses and curricula. When we truly do place student growth at the center of our plans, students' own designs begin to emerge within the program as a result of their taking up the power given through the program.

The Importance of Contexts for Faculty Dialogue and Scholarship on Teaching

A significant challenge in supporting institutional consideration of alternative models of instructional practice is overcoming constraints that faculty face in accessing opportunities for rich dialogue around their teaching. The entrepreneurial culture common to the research university makes it possible, even likely, that the faculty will experience a teaching life that is solitary and unreflective because teaching itself does not become a readily accepted form of scholarship. The academic department, the "home base" of most faculty, represents a possible site for such reflection and collaboration but in reality may not provide the support needed to overcome the organizational tendencies to view teaching as a practice conducted by individuals who carry out their assignments mostly alone. Indeed, faculty members are evaluated on the basis of their individual productivity in terms of credit hours, their teaching scores, and their ability to cultivate their own personal space within the overall curriculum. Less appreciated is the idea that teaching is a complex social practice where meanings derive not so much from technical moves that individuals can learn and master but from the mutual engagement of participants who negotiate their work together.

The Faculty Study Group Program

Recognizing these institutional constraints, CEUT began in 1997 a program designed to bring faculty together, in cross-disciplinary groups, to study their own teaching. We called this arrangement the Faculty Study Group Program. (On other campuses, such arrangements might be called teaching circles.) As a pilot project, we initially wanted to explore the idea with two or three groups of five to six participants each; this invitation was extended to faculty and administrators campuswide. We were surprised when the response exceeded 50 individuals who participated in an initial information session, resulting in 42 participants across six faculty study groups (FSGs) that began meeting in the 1997 spring semester.

In the initial invitation to faculty, the general FSG goals proposed included studying and improving individual teaching practices, sharing instructional strategies related to student success, building a process of inquiry around one's own teaching, and creating strategies (such as teaching portfolios) to support reflection and to document one's work. We emphasized, however, that the groups were invited to determine their own specific agendas. We also implemented other supports and incentives for participants that included a $300 professional development stipend provided through CEUT's operating budget, meeting spaces, and staff support to encourage development of meeting protocols conducive to collaboration and the building of trust among participants. The groups met approximately twice monthly during the course of a 16-week semester.

This program has grown during the past 5 years into one of our primary contexts for supporting inquiry into teaching. During the 2002–2003 academic year, 26 groups actively engaged nearly 170 faculty members. We have continued to maintain the professional development stipend for participants, and two CEUT staff members devote significant amounts of their time supporting the program and working with individual groups.

As we have studied the program (see Wildman, Hable, Magliaro, & Preston, 2000), it is clear that there are some important considerations in the establishment and support of these small "communities of practice." Four understandings that flow from this work are important to consider:

1. It takes time for groups to mature as communities. Many of our current FSGs have been in place for 2 to 4 years. From year to year, the membership may change somewhat with the loss of a member and the addition of another, but the agendas of the groups develop slowly and tend to progress in a manner that suggests a longer life span than we had first anticipated.

2. The progression of group agendas tends to follow a pattern beginning with simple dialogue about teaching—sharing the good and the bad, the puzzling features and the discoveries, and finding out that self-disclosure can be a positive thing in a protective and trusting environment. What seems to be compelling about these conversations is the "good problem" that teaching presents. Teaching is complex, tending not to yield to fixed solutions, and the contexts in which individuals practice their craft, even in a single institution, are amazingly variable. Thus, the groups seem well satisfied to share their stories of teaching and the meanings they can derive from these stories for quite some time. Eventually, the agendas shifted to specific projects that extended beyond these initial conversations, perhaps growing from them.

3. The interdisciplinary nature of these groups supports disclosure of personal teaching issues and enriches the dialogue about teaching. Participants report a feeling of protection in these conversations that may not be possible within the departmental context, and they almost uniformly report appreciating the discovery that their particular challenges are shared in other precincts of the university.

4. The study groups, as small communities of practice, choose to consider new ideas about teaching in ways and on schedules that were natural to their needs and emerging agendas. In the early going, the groups may profitably spend many weeks or months engaged in the sharing of stories about their own practices. Rather than viewing this ongoing dialogue as wasteful of time, we tend to adopt the notion advanced by Bruner (1990) that storytelling is the premier vehicle for the social construction of meaning and that storytelling can in fact be a prime indicator of movement from peripheral participation in the community to more central roles.

As we attempt to build on these observations, it is increasingly clear that rich, supportive environments for reflection on teaching are possible to nurture even in institutional contexts that do not naturally require or support such behavior. These settings in turn become sites for new ideas to take root, such as promoting self-authorship through the Learning Partnerships Model. The important caveat, however, is that each little community will create its own story.

Women in Information Technology

One case from the faculty study group program is of particular interest in revealing the potential power of an organizing frame such as the Learning Partnerships Model. This case revolves around three faculty members who formed a study group that is now entering its third year together. At any given time, there were as many as five members of the group, but the core always revolved around the three participants featured here. One is a senior university administrator and professor in the human sciences domain, returning to the classroom and teaching undergraduates for the first time in 10 years. Another is an accomplished biology professor who has recently moved to a faculty position more aligned with programs in the humanities and to a different teaching culture. The third is a professor in the social sciences who was already familiar with the work around which this book is oriented. Two members of the group had previously been engaged with another study group that focused on feminist pedagogies, but when the opportunity came at the beginning of a new school year to form new group configurations, these three faculty decided to initiate a study group oriented specifically to Baxter Magolda's research. In part, the motivation was to initiate a process in which two of the members could chart their way into a new teaching life, particularly focused on constructivist teaching philosophies. A second motivation for these three faculty was a common interest in an emerging research project dealing with the barriers confronting young women in terms of moving into technology careers. It turns out that the constructive-developmental work and philosophy of Baxter Magolda was to play a key role in both domains of interest.

The group's objectives were achieved to a significant degree within 2 years. The biologist reported profound changes in teaching philosophy and strategies that were also noted in interviews with the other two colleagues. All three participants found the mutual support and coaching provided within the group to be helpful in thinking through the nuances and challenges of constructivist teaching. In terms of the group's research interests, a National Science Foundation grant proposal developed by the group yielded a $650,000 award, the success of which was attributed in part to the ability to situate the work within the Learning Partnerships Model. Currently, the group is implementing the research project (as a task separate from the study group) and continuing to meet to focus on teaching. The group plans to continue their work together for an additional year, with perhaps the addition of new members.

Beyond these highlights, however, the story of how the group managed to work together and achieve their successes suggests some complexities. From structured interviews with these participants, three findings seem especially salient in terms of understanding how faculty work together to study and change their practices. First, the participants affirmed the importance of differences in backgrounds, work histories, and philosophies. The effort and collaboration required to understand and negotiate participant differences not only deepened their working relationships over time but also added to their understanding of concepts, such as self-authorship, that are central to the work they were studying and attempting to apply. Through the grant writing process they entered into during their first year together, they were able to explore and test the concept of self-authorship in a research context before moving to the more personal contexts of their own teaching. In essence, the Baxter Magolda framework and associated research provided the common interest and the external reality that transcended what each individual brought to the discussion.

The second finding is simply that time is required to establish the trust and mutual understandings needed to delve into the nuances of one's teaching life. The most significant progress in rethinking teaching—revolving around issues such as sharing of authority, designing work for students, and changing classroom strategies—did not occur until the second year, and there was doubt expressed that the group could have come easily to those discussions and related resolutions without having the first year to lay the groundwork for the more intense work.

A third finding from the interviews concerns the importance of the structure and resources provided by CEUT and its staff. The agreement to set aside structured time, the commitment to follow through with scheduled meetings, a powerful theme of interest (self-authorship), and encouragement from a member of CEUT's staff to set meeting agendas and share meeting notes all were mentioned as important to the overall success of the group.

Our experiences with the study groups in general suggest that there is a natural flow to the collaborations that faculty experience when examining their teaching, considering changes in their practice, and negotiating meanings with colleagues. Frameworks such as the Learning Partnerships Model can have powerful effects on how educators think about and enact their professional work, but the route may well be more interesting and less linear than might be expected in a traditional faculty development model involving more direct intervention via workshops and seminars.

Enlarging the Scope of Application

We have examined faculty and institutional considerations of the Learning Partnerships Model to this point more as an avenue to a deeper understanding of how our students develop intellectually and what we can do as individual faculty to better inform our own work. But there is a larger and potentially more fruitful venue for the application of the constructive-developmental frameworks, namely, the larger curriculum our students must negotiate. What happens when the scope of analysis extends beyond individual courses or clusters of courses to the university core curriculum, a set of courses that constitutes one third of credit hours required for graduation?

This is exactly the question we have been asking during the past year as the university has opened a new set of discussions aimed at testing the efficacy of the existing general education program. The present core curriculum was established via a major university forum in the early 1990s, and that effort in turn was informed by a major report on the role of liberal education during the early 1980s. Between these major efforts to explicitly study general education, the system tended to move forward with only minor adjustments as determined by ongoing and routine faculty governance activity. It is safe to say that the curriculum we count on to provide the foundation for later study in the disciplines and majors is often left to function in a state of ambiguity with respect to purposes, clear methodology, and ownership. While these characteristics, to the extent that they are accurate, sound like severe indictments of the system, studies of general education more broadly indicate that these issues are widespread and particularly common (albeit troublesome) at large research universities (see Boyer Commission on Educating Undergraduates in the Research University, 1998; Penn State Symposium on General Education, 2002).

Our own recent (and ongoing) study of general education at Virginia Tech identified the predictable range of issues of concern, including funding and organizational concerns, ownership issues, questions about overall design, faculty participation, and integration of the core experiences with students' participation in their majors. What distinguished these discussions from previous deliberations, however, is the more explicit focus on issues of student learning and development. This focus is the point of contact with the Learning Partnerships Model.

Though it is too early in this most recent study of general education to identify a clear path to specific reforms, several recommendations are now on the table for consideration, and these are directly connected to our engagement over time with the Baxter Magolda research and related educational concepts from the cognitive and social constructivist movements. First, we have begun to talk explicitly about what it means to grow and learn and what it means to consider all aspects of our students' development. It takes only a short journey into these conversations to realize that one of the chief design flaws in the university curriculum, particularly at the lower levels, is *excessive fragmentation.* The "check-sheet" mentality to managing courses that are largely isolated from each other is readily acknowledged in current practice and when viewed strictly from a management perspective could likely be accepted as an undesirable but necessary way to continue to do business. Applying any contemporary research-based conception of intellectual development, however, reveals more clearly the deleterious effects of such curriculum design and management on learning and development.

A second insight now on the table for consideration is the necessity for increased student ownership of their learning. Already, changes in our concept of student advising have highlighted the desirability to stress *students' responsibility* to think through and plan their own paths. As Marcia has reminded us across some of these conversations, "The University can provide maps, guides, and resources, but it is really the students' journey." The question then becomes more one of how we can provide company and support for the journey. In this regard, our previous discussion of the RLC highlights the fact that we do have programs in place that provide clues for broader institutional reform. The challenge is to move these ideas from the smaller contexts of residential communities and honors programs to the larger cross section of students.

Assessment practices are also coming under scrutiny. Here again, the practice of looking at specific courses and particular outcome areas of the core curriculum (e.g., writing, quantitative analysis, or global awareness) independently of the whole serves to reinforce a conception of the curriculum as a simple additive process that individual faculty and departments can pursue entirely on their own.

As we continue this work, the power and importance of the particular frameworks we employ to guide our efforts come into sharper focus. On the small scale of a single faculty member developing or modifying a single course, the effects of errors in basic design may have only limited effects. But when we design for thousands of students and expect that the effects will play out over years and decades, the matter of design and design error becomes a more serious concern given the significant magnification of even modest changes in design. The fact that we are really talking about large differences in design philosophy, magnified many times, provides some sense of the potential scope and importance of these deliberations.

Frames and Their Implications

The Virginia Tech case briefly summarized here is certainly not one that brings a set of ready-made solutions to the question of how to implement the Learning Partnerships Model. What this story does convey is that through a rich set of experiments involving significant numbers of faculty members, a new set of narratives can emerge as we experiment with the powerful ideas contained within the Learning Partnerships Model.

As asserted in the beginning of this chapter, frames are important. They are important in one sense because they place constraints on what we do and think we can do. They certainly influence what we see and what we hear. Just as frames can limit our perspectives and our perceptions, they can also help us establish a compass in terms of future directions. I tend to view the Learning Partnerships Model in terms of how it can shape personal and institutional thinking and hope that its potential power can be more fully explored.

Frames such as the Learning Partnerships Model help us see old actors in new ways—and in new roles. In the discussion here about Virginia Tech's explorations with the Learning Partnerships Model, the key characters have been the students, the faculty, the other educators we generally find in student affairs units, and perhaps those carrying the title of administrator. What roles are given to these actors under our traditional models of educational delivery? Perhaps the word *delivery* too easily gives away the distinctions that are so potentially dramatic when the pedagogy and curriculum designs flowing from the Learning Partnerships Model are placed in close proximity with designs flowing from a metaphor of learning as primarily the acquisition of knowledge. The roles of faculty clearly shift in powerfully different ways, as do the roles of students and the roles of those who work in the student affairs domains. Our experience with the RLC demonstrates in a very local community how these roles shift, but what about the larger institution? Until we can really embrace these fundamental differences in roles and role definitions, our attempts at reform will likely remain hamstrung by the awkward gyrations that old actors have to perform to temporarily configure themselves in new ways for the particular experiment of the day.

Frames also help us see familiar structures in new ways. Classrooms, time frames, reward structures, and administrative policies are just a few of the constraints on everyday practice that we take for granted because they *fit with the frames we tacitly accept that organize and govern how we do business*. Again, when we desire to play with a new frame, such as the Learning Partnerships Model and its family of related constructs, we exert tremendous energy working around familiar structures that may no longer serve us well or even make any sense. At CEUT, we are routinely engaged in conversations with faculty who are valiantly attempting to overcome structural barriers. We allocate resources to aid faculty in the construction of detours around barriers. We hold endless meetings to discuss what to do, how to adapt, and how to cope. In our faculty study groups, individuals tell stories to ease their frustrations and sometimes to celebrate small victories. But what if we could use a promising frame, such as the Learning Partnerships Model, to really rethink the structures that constrain our work?

Frames help us see familiar goals in new and sometimes disturbing ways. I see it as no accident that faculty who eagerly approach the Learning Partnerships Model may also have close to their desks the works of Paulo Freire or bell hooks. How do we define the work that our students are asked to accomplish, and how do we conceive of the contexts and manner in which they are asked to perform? When we examine the work of our own RLC, one concept central (and familiar) to so many educational settings is conspicuously missing. That concept, an implicit goal of much of the educational enterprise, is *compliance*. This is a concept not much in evidence when we look at the world of education through the lens of the Learning Partnerships Model. The traditional expectation for student compliance, compared to a different goal oriented to empowerment and liberation, is only one of the by-products of our mainstream system that may be viewed differently through an alternative frame such as the Learning Partnerships Model.

We could continue with the analysis of how frames help us see and discover new tools, find new relationships, and discover new meanings. However, I want to leave this discussion with a relatively simple idea: The most powerful role of frames like the Learning Partnerships Model is not to immediately aid instrumental problem solving, as in how I might design a new exercise for a particular course, but in how to reexamine the fundamental workings of the system itself. With so much converging data showing the essential validity of the Learning Partnerships Model's basic propositions about human development, we have a powerful compass to implement systems, roles, and expectations that are better attuned to supporting student learning and development. The stakes of the status quo are too high to do otherwise.

References

Baxter Magolda, M. B. (1999). *Creating contexts for learning and self-authorship: Constructive-developmental pedagogy.* Nashville: Vanderbilt University Press.

Baxter Magolda, M. B. (2001). *Making their own way: Narratives for transforming higher education to promote self-development.* Sterling, VA: Stylus.

Boyer, E. L. (1995). *The basic school: A community for learning.* Princeton, New Jersey: Carnegie Foundation for the Advancement of Teaching.

Boyer Commission on Educating Undergraduates in the Research University. (1998). *Reinventing undergraduate education: A blueprint for America's research universities.* Stony Brook, NY: SUNY at Stony Brook for the Carnegie Foundation for the Advancement of Teaching.

Bruner, J. (1990). *Acts of meaning.* Cambridge, MA: Harvard University Press.

Bruner, J. (1996). *The culture of education.* Cambridge, MA: Harvard University Press.

Freire, P. (1970). *Pedagogy of the oppressed.* New York: Herder & Herder.

Grundy, S. (1987). *Curriculum: Product or praxis.* New York: Falmer.

Johnston, S. N. (2002, August). *Leadership education for global citizenship: Engaging leaning communities in a new ethical frontier.* Paper presented to the Wabash Center for Teaching and Learning in Theology and Religion, Crawfordsville, IN.

Kegan, R. (1994). *In over our heads: The mental demands of modern life.* Cambridge, MA: Harvard University Press.

Lave, J., & Wenger, E. (1991). *Situated learning: Legitimate peripheral participation.* New York: Cambridge University Press.

Mandler, J. M. (1984). *Stories, scripts, and scenes: Aspects of schema theory.* Hillsdale, NJ: Erlbaum.

Minsky, M. (1975). A framework for representing knowledge. In P. H. Winston (Ed.), *The psychology of computer vision* (pp. 211–277). New York: McGraw-Hill.

Palmer, P. J. (1997, November–December). Teaching and learning in community. *About Campus, 2*(5), 4–13.

Penn State Symposium on General Education. (2002). *Students in the balance.* Penn State University.

Schon, D. (1983). *The reflective practitioner.* New York: Basic Books.

Wenger, E. (1998). *Communities of practice: Learning, meaning, and identity.* Cambridge, England: Cambridge University Press.

Wildman, T. M., Hable, M., Magliaro, S. G., & Preston, M. (2000). Faculty study groups: Solving good problems through study, reflection, and collaboration. *Innovative Higher Education, 24*(4), 247–263.

10

ORGANIZING FOR LEARNING IN A DIVISION OF STUDENT AFFAIRS

Rebecca Mills and Karen L. Strong

When we make a commitment to practice transformative leadership,

> we also necessarily open ourselves to questioning some of our most cherished individual habits and long-standing institutional traditions. . . . Most importantly, once we recognize the constraints imposed by our current beliefs and habits and by the organizational structures that emanate from them, we can begin to open our minds and hearts to one of higher education's greatest paradoxes: inherent in many of our "limitations" and "constraints" are some of our greatest opportunities and potentials for transformative change. (p. 88)

This quote, from *Leadership Reconsidered* (Astin & Astin, 2000), challenged us as student affairs educators to fully explore existing constraints and transform organizationally to promote self-authorship both among today's university students and among student affairs educators. Indeed, fostering self-authorship among student affairs educators is key to promoting the development of students on their journey toward self-authorship. This chapter explores the reorganization of what was a highly independent, departmentally focused division of student affairs into what is an emerging, interdependent, student-focused learning organization. The resulting transformation was designed to promote self-authorship among staff by creating a work environment that encourages and rewards cognitive complexity, mature relationships, and effective citizenship (Baxter Magolda, 2001; see also chapter 1 of this volume). This chapter includes a description of the context and results of the reorganization as well as an explanation of the implications of the reorganization for student affairs educators and for students. The Learning Partnerships Model is inherent in both the reorganization process and the resulting learning organization.

Context: The Division of Student Life

For years, the student affairs division at the University of Nevada, Las Vegas (UNLV), functioned satisfactorily in a traditional organizational structure. Individual directors of 16 departments reported to either the vice president or assistant vice president. All directors set goals and objectives for their departments, and directors' successes were measured by their ability to move their departments forward. There was little expectation that directors would see themselves as divisional leaders; their roles were defined, more traditionally, as departmental leaders. Meetings among the directors focused minimally on divisional or institutional goals; rather, they consisted mainly of exchanges of information between and among the vice president, assistant vice president, and directors.

Internally, UNLV struggled to respond to sustained, dramatic growth. Since 1996, headcount enrollment increased by more than 6,000; in the same period, full-time equivalent enrollment increased by more than 30%. In 2000, the Division of Student Life served more than 2,500 additional students with virtually the same human resources and state support they had worked with since 1993. These circumstances stimulated divisional conversations about change to ensure that creative ideas could be explored and that resources were used most effectively and efficiently to maximize benefits to students. Externally, contemporary higher education faced the need to respond to increasing demands for accountability for undergraduate student learning, increasing enrollments with dwindling resources, and the changing nature of the student body (Wingspread Group on Higher Education, 1993).

As the institution changed and the impact of change became more profound, the division began to discuss ways to respond to student expectations, external demands, and diminishing resources. These conversations had been under way for a short time when the vice president of 15 years resigned, an interim vice president (Mills) was appointed, and the assistant vice president was promoted to associate vice president. The change in vice presidents served as the catalyst to begin an intentional process of exploration that included broad-based conversations about students' needs, learning opportunities, divisional leadership, and working relationships. We undertook an audit of internal resources, staffing patterns, and assessment results in order to explore possible organizational structures. We identified core functions in each department and sometimes needless duplication of services or efforts. Shortly after the preparation for a restructuring of the division began, the associate vice president left UNLV, and the director of campus housing (Strong) was appointed as the interim associate vice president. Throughout these changes, the divisional leaders continued to engage in a series of future-oriented conversations and reflective activities designed to help the group reach consensus about the desired characteristics, goals, and structure of the division.

Senior administrators were aware that they needed to provide guidance and support as directors worked together to create a new organization. Rather than senior officers "unveiling" a plan for others to implement, they asked directors to actively participate in designing a new plan for the division in order to mutually construct the division's future. Experiences were structured so that directors would think critically and broaden their perspectives from those of departmental leaders to divisional leaders. Over the course of several meetings, individual perspectives were shared publicly through collegial interactions. These interactions, along with written assignments, supervisory conversations, and problem-solving activities, served to validate directors' knowledge, situate learning in their experiences, and develop frameworks for future interactions (Baxter Magolda, 2001; see also chapter 2 of this volume). The topics for the first year of meetings and the directors' "homework" in preparation for those meetings are outlined in Table 10.1.

Table 10.1   Timeline of Year 1: Content of Directors' Meetings Including "Homework"

May 22, 2000	Interim vice president (Mills) appointment announced. At initial meeting with the directors, the vice president shared her expectations of directors in their role as leaders and scheduled individual appointments with directors and visits to departments.
May 24, 2000	The directors discussed the characteristics of their past meetings and what they wanted in future meetings. Vice president engaged group in a discussion on the name change (per president) from Student Services to Student Life.
	Homework: Continue, Stop, Start (ala Covey, 1989): Directors were asked to think about the nature of directors' meetings and what they would like to continue, to stop, and to start. *Note: This was the first time that directors were asked to complete a "homework" assignment and to think critically about how they were spending time with their colleagues.*

(Continued)

Table 10.1   Continued

June 7, 2000	Discussion of May 24 homework—vice president presented a summary of the homework. Directors were asked if they agreed with the new "nature" of director meetings and, if not, to offer other suggestions. By the end of the discussion, the group had come to an agreement. *Note: Discussion at this point was minimal, and agreement was lukewarm because of limited relationship between directors who did not all see the value of these meetings.*
	Homework: Name one entrepreneurial idea for the department or division to try.
July 26, 2000	Discussion of June 7 homework—the vice president presented a summary of the ideas and asked the group to engage in a discussion about these ideas—to talk about the merit and the obstacles of implementing such ideas. *Note: The discussion level continued to be minimal as directors were not used to engaging in these types of discussions.*
	Homework: The directors were asked to think about the existing divisional committees—Mission and Goals, Training and Development, and Assessment—and indicate if these committees should continue. They also were to indicate if they thought additional committees should be created and why.
August 9, 2000	The vice president's Search Committee was to be created by the president, and the directors were asked how they wanted to identify student life representatives for this committee.
September 13, 2000	The vice president initiated a discussion of institutional characteristics and goals and asked directors to talk about the role the division should play given this information. *Note: The vice president was attempting to engage the directors in a discussion that went beyond their departments and to look at the division as a whole.*

Table 10.1 Continued

September 27, 2000	The vice president presented a framework for planning conversations that would occur over a 4- to 6-month period. The focus was to position the division within the institution based on the assumptions that we wanted to create a cohesive unit and shared sense of identity in order to better serve UNLV students.

Questions to Guide Discussion

- What is really changing? Is it the nature of students? Our interactions with students?

- Given assumption of continuing focus on research, what does this mean for the division in terms of structure and organization?

- Who are we as a division; what should be our roles?

- How do we/can we implement needed changes?

Note: This provided a preliminary introduction to start the directors thinking differently about the work they do and the organization in which they work.

October 11, 2000	The vice president continued to prepare the directors' involvement in planning for a changing student population by presenting information on university students of the 21st century, UNLV's new students today, and the nature of relationships with students.

Homework: The directors were asked to assume that UNLV will become more selective and the Division of Student Life will become a more cohesive unit with new resources next year. Based on these assumptions, they were asked to respond to the following questions:

- What should these changes mean for the division in terms of goal achievement and role of division?

- What should it mean for the organizational structure for student life?

(Continued)

Table 10.1 Continued

	• Propose one specific organizational change at the divisional level and one organizational change at the departmental level.
	Note: The directors are now being asked to think from a departmental perspective, divisional perspective, and institutional perspective.
November 8, 2000	The division received some unexpected additional resources, and the directors were asked to help develop institutional priorities for the allocation of these resources. *Note: This is the first time the directors had to identify areas of need, justify requests, and negotiate with their colleagues in how the new resources would be allocated. Formerly, directors shared ideas with supervisors, and the vice president and associate vice president determined priorities. The new vice president expected directors to share in the decision making, understand rationale, and "own" the outcome even though all requests could not be met.*
	Homework: The directors were asked to read all the responses from October 11 homework. As they read, they were asked to consider similarities and differences with individual responses and detect patterns. As a result, directors were asked if they would make changes in their previous suggestions from October 11.
November 15, 2000	The directors were asked to present the ideas from their November 8 homework to their colleagues. This meeting was for sharing only—no questions or comments from other directors were allowed—in order to ensure that everyone was listening to understand what was being presented. *Note: This was the first time that directors publicly shared their ideas and perspectives. We reinforced the idea that all perspectives could be heard and considered.*
	Homework: The directors were asked to think about what the next step was in the process of reframing the Division of Student Life.

Table 10.1 Continued

December 6, 2000	As the directors continued to engage more deeply in the discussions about the role and structure of the student life division, some staff members began to express concerns about what that might mean for them as professionals within the organization. The vice president spent some time reassuring the directors that directors would retain their titles, that reorganization would not result in a loss of jobs, and that directors and others likely would be asked to work differently or assume different responsibilities.
	The vice president ascertained that the directors needed to spend some significant time away from the workplace in order to fully immerse themselves in the planning process, so a retreat date was set for the spring semester.
	Homework: All directors were asked to analyze their respective departments and list all functions using broad categories (i.e., advising, health care, budgets).
December 20, 2000	Semester Wrap-Up
January 10, 2001	Each department displayed its functions on the wall (each function was on an 8×11 paper). Directors spent some time analyzing the various functions and then were asked to rearrange them—clustering by similar and duplicative functions. Once this was completed, the directors started identifying themes, such as advising, counseling, programming, tutoring, budget administration, and so on.
	The vice president announced the resignation of the associate vice president and the interim associate vice president appointment (Strong).
January 24, 2001	The directors spent some time debriefing the January 10 exercise—sharing reactions and talking about how they made meaning of the activity. The vice president provided a synthesis of January 10 work (clustering functions around themes) as a handout.

(Continued)

Table 10.1 Continued

	Note: This continued the effort to assist directors in understanding all the functions within the division in order to break down perceptions that individual departments were totally unique.
	Homework: The directors were to use this handout from January 10 and write a response to the following: Does this synthesis make sense? Did we cover everything?
	Homework (for retreat): In preparation for the retreat, directors were asked to read *Who Moved My Cheese?* (Johnson, 1998).
February 15 and 16, 2001	During the retreat, the directors engaged in the following discussions and activities:

- Discussed departmental functions and identified divisional core purposes.

- Group presentations: Directors were assigned to a group and were given significant time to prepare a 20-minute presentation that responded to: How can we best use existing resources (personnel and facilities) to achieve core purposes? There were no other instructions, which was intentional.

- After the group presentations, the entire group of directors began a dialogue on reorganizing. Given these purposes and existing resources, how could we redefine the way we work so that we work collaboratively to achieve these purposes and minimize obstacles, maximize efficiency, create flexible and adaptable systems, take advantage of the talent we have, and take advantage of the facilities we have. As they engaged in this discussion, they were challenged to continue to work to understand the complexities and commonalities in our work and to organize around purposes so that new organizational structure makes sense to *students*.

Table 10.1   Continued

	Note: During this retreat, differing perspectives about the purpose of Student Life and its various departments became more apparent. Some staff members were becoming more concerned about the direction of Student Life and the possible impact on their positions. Other staff members assumed that a grand plan was already in existence and wanted to know what it was so they would not have to deal with the level of ambiguity that existed. Many did not believe that everyone would create the division's future together.
February 28, 2001	Retreat follow-up: Conversation continues—the directors were to have shared the content and outcomes of the divisional retreat with their respective staff members and come prepared to share their staff responses. *Note: This was done to get an overall sense of where the division was in terms of pending changes, to begin to ascertain how directors were sharing messages and perceptions with their staff members, and to determine if feelings of unease were being escalated unnecessarily.*
March 21, 2001	Reorganization conversation continues.
	Homework: Directors were to consider carefully existing resources and respond to the following:
	• If money were to become available for enhancements, what amount, if any, would you request for your department? Justify.
	• If new state positions were to be assigned to the division, what positions would you request for your department? Justify.
	• What do you believe are the three most pressing needs for positions *in the division*? (those that would have the greatest impact for service to students and accomplishing division goals.)

(Continued)

Table 10.1 Continued

March 28 and 29, 2001	Rebecca interviewed for vice president position. Discussions that were theoretical and planful in nature had concluded, and there was little remaining to be done until a decision about organizational structure could be made by the new vice president. Time for an ongoing national search created a "pause" in the process until a vice president was named.
April 22, 2001	Rebecca Mills selected as vice president.
April 25, 2001	As the newly appointed vice president, Rebecca led a discussion—Leadership: A Shared Perspective. During this discussion, directors were asked the following questions: • Where we are now; where we are headed? • What do you, as leaders in the division, want from your vice president? The vice president then shared how she wanted to function as vice president. Finally, the directors agreed to meet weekly to reach decisions about reorganization.
May 9, 2001	During this meeting, the directors outlined the process for finalizing reorganization plans and beginning implementation. Because of the delay with the search process, we needed to consider moving quickly in order to implement the changes in the fall. **Homework:** Given the current context for reorganization and the assumption that we will reorganize by fall 2001, please respond to the following questions: • What would be the advantages of accelerating the process of decision making and implementing the reorganization? • What would be your concerns about accelerating the process? • List issues that you believe would be essential to resolve before moving forward.

Table 10.1 Continued

	• List issues that you would prefer to have resolved before moving forward.

Note: The vice president continued to provide opportunities for directors to have input into the reorganization process as well as the opportunity to express concerns. Both were crucial—one to continue to emphasize that everyone would have input into the creation of a different structure and way of working and the other to continue to address and reinforce staff concerns as valid.

May 16, 2001 — "That Vision Thing"—The directors spent significant time discussing the May 9 homework. Summer plans were finalized in preparation for the fall 2001 reorganization process. The directors were asked to look forward 5 years and talk about the following:

• What do you want to be the characteristics of this Division of Student Life?

• Identify the essential characteristics of cluster leaders.

The vice president then presented possible organizational structure by clusters, which was formed from all the previous discussions, homework, and vice president's and associate vice president's thoughts.

Directors were asked to place their names along a reorganization readiness continuum labeled from "not at all ready to reorganize" to "past ready to reorganize" to provide a visual commitment to moving forward.

Homework: Based on the assumptions that CAEO, Public Safety, and Administration will remain as direct reports to the vice president and we will create Campus Life, Academic Success, and Health and Safety Services Clusters, where would you place your department's functions across those clusters? If you were designing the clusters, what would you change from the descriptions provided and why? If you were vice president, who would you appoint as cluster leaders

(Continued)

Table 10.1   Continued

	for Campus Life, Academic Success, and Health and Safety? Ideally, what would be your role in this newly reorganized division? What role would best use your talents and interests?
May 23, 2001	Response to cluster concept
	Role of directors following reorganization
	Staff involvement through reorganization
	Timeline for reorganization
June 6, 2001	Announced organizational framework and cluster leaders for reorganization. *Note: At this point, the group's "planning" became reality. Directors' reactions were mixed despite the commitments made during the previous discussions. Some wanted to articulate how other individuals and/or departments would change without realizing there was an assumption that all would change in order to redefine working relationships, achieve shared expectations, and allow new "ways of working."*

As the directors' group genuinely began to construct the plan to restructure, we envisioned a division that served students well, fostered learning among students and staff, promoted collaboration, fostered shared leadership, and eliminated needless duplication of resources and efforts. We understood that both the organizational structure and the ways that we worked with students and with one another needed to change. Essentially, we hoped to create what Senge (1990) called a learning organization by changing what Kegan and Lahey (2000) called "social arrangements" to support "sustained learning of a transformational sort" (p. 9).

Reorganization: Creating Contexts for Collaboration

Over time, we were able to articulate the characteristics of leadership and the structure necessary for the organization that we envisioned. As a result, we clustered entire departments or individuals with similar functions into the following major areas with broader missions: Academic Success, Administration (including technology), Campus Life, Center for Academic Enrichment and Outreach (TRIO and GEAR UP), Public Safety, and Student Wellness. Each cluster leader was a former director; these individuals and the executive director for student life facilities formed the vice president's council, the new leadership group for the division. Needs for additional staff meant that the cluster leaders retained administrative responsibility for their former departments; this helped refute initial perceptions that we might create a "top-heavy" administration, but it also created competing demands for time as cluster leaders undertook a variety of additional responsibilities.

The members of the vice president's council began immediately discussing ways to foster a collaborative environment that would empower individuals, engender trust, and capitalize on the diverse talents of group members. We hoped members of the division would come to see this learning organization as a place where they could not only learn about each other and themselves but also acquire the shared knowledge, interpersonal competencies, and technical skills required to function more effectively within the organization. Recognizing that differences in perspectives would be inevitable and at the same time desirable, divisional members spent a year sharing their insights, perspectives, and feelings about what a reorganization of the divisional structure could accomplish. It was crucial that all perspectives were shared and voices heard in order to create an atmosphere where problem solving and decision making were conducted with mutual respect and trust. This type of atmosphere could be created only if we were willing to embrace all perspectives, even those that did not agree with what we had envisioned. Staff members needed to know and trust that they could be honest—even when disagreeing—and still be heard without judgment. Engaging staff members in activities that intentionally provided opportunities for all perspectives to be shared moved us closer to creating a divisional approach to our work. In addition, staff members, through engagement in the process, learned that voicing a perspective did not necessarily mean that the decisions and changes they advocated would be implemented. We confronted often the need for consensus and compromise, and we endeavored to explain the rationale for decisions as they were made. With their colleagues, staff found common ground from which to interact and in turn began to develop a common language. This resulted in consistent experiences for staff as they established cluster identities and engaged in divisional conversations.

As a leadership group, we focused internally on trust building, information sharing, open communication, and data-driven decision making. Early in the group's formation, we reviewed processes and policies that had the greatest divisional impact. A careful review of such things as divisional budgets, resource allocations, performance evaluations, and merit procedures led to intense conversations so that we could achieve our goals: collaborative decision making, appropriate resource allocation, and effective organizational structure. In the process of articulating and clarifying assumptions (some of which were long held) about one another, the division, and/or departments, we reached a common perspective and coalesced as a team.

Not unlike the experiences of the divisional leadership group, as departments transformed into the more seamless cluster format, the complexity of staff interactions and functions increased. New and existing relationships had to be renegotiated as several positions were reframed and teams were redefined. Differing expectations and perspectives among cluster leaders and staff members often caused frustration as clusters were being formed. For example, cluster leaders initially approached the formation of clusters from a logistical perspective, realigning positions to better serve students and to enhance efficiency. This resulted in some high-performing staff being promoted to new positions with broader responsibilities. Other staff members assumed they also would be promoted. In some cases, individuals expected the formation of clusters to automatically result in title changes and promotions without broader responsibilities and without considering past performance issues. The number of different perspectives shared increased as programmatic initiatives, policies and procedures, and functional responsibilities were reviewed and often realigned as a result of these discussions. Staff members were encouraged to think outside their own areas of responsibility, to share their expertise, and to hear others as they worked together to create their cluster's future.

As a strategy to enhance collaboration and broad communication, we created cross-cluster planning groups comprised of staff inside and outside of respective clusters. These planning groups addressed new initiatives in areas of our work, such as leadership, facilities use, student learning, diversity, and student wellness. Table 10.2 summarizes major recommendations from the cross-cluster work. Staff members worked collaboratively to develop short- and long-term recommendations for approval and implementation. Recommendations were formed after the groups assessed work currently being done, discovered duplication of resources, identified resource needs, and created an implementation timetable. At the end of the first year, the planning groups presented their recommendations to their respective clusters and to the vice president; the resulting reports set forth well-conceived, creative, essential, and beneficial projects. Such opportunities for collaborative work reinforced many of the benefits of the organizational change that we envisioned. As the organization changed, implications for student affairs educators became increasingly apparent; we discuss these next.

Table 10.2 Divisional Planning Groups: Charges and Recommendations

Diversity Planning Group

Charges	• Assess current interventions/programs currently in place, such as outreach, educational, programmatic, and training
	• Determine the sense of identity for student populations and student organizations
	• Examine all levels of staff training and education
	• Assess cultural organizations and clubs. Obtain a sense of their purpose; who they serve/represent; their funding, activities, and functions; and how they communicate their business to the university
	• Compare recent assessments (CSEQ, Kuh Report, Cultural Audit) to identify themes/patterns regarding student populations
Recommendations	• Create a divisional diversity statement
	• Implement a series of interactive workshops so that all student educators would become culturally competent in working with a diverse university community
	• Create a divisional diversity committee

Student Professional Goal-Setting Team

Charges	• Broaden the impact of career services through collaborative efforts:
	○ Increase faculty involvement in career services
	○ Enhance career counseling in advising sessions
	• Address student career development issues particularly as related to:
	○ First-year students
	○ Exploring majors
Recommendations	• Coordinate pilot test of vendor software for Web recruiting

(Continued)

Table 10.2   Continued

- Support and expand the Career Services Library

- Assess needs of underrepresented populations in response to career explorations

- Form a universal schedule for career-focused programs

  ○ Enhance outreach through additional classroom presentations

- Create Academic and Career Exploration through Student Development Center

  ○ Focus on exploring majors (Student Development Center); using career counseling to support decisions about academic major

- Pilot small-scale portfolio program with student leaders to increase student learning and connect experiences to preparation for the world of work

Campus Life Facilities Use Planning Group

Charges
- Identify the campus/student life facilities and who they currently serve; review existing policies

- Examine reservation/scheduling processes and fee structure

- Determine what other facilities could be used and review the procedures for reservations

Recommendations
- Create and implement a centralized scheduling office within the Division of Student Life to serve student organizations, university departments, and nonuniversity clients

Student Leadership Planning Group

Charges
- Assess what is currently in place in terms of student leadership

- Examine the intended needs and learning outcomes

- What do our programs/interventions/training experiences have in common?

Table 10.2 Continued

	• What is unique about our programs/interventions/ training experiences?
	• Conduct a leadership assessment with students and compare results of "involved" students with student body
Recommendations	• Develop a Leadership Advisory Board to guide further recommendations, continue the evolutionary process of leadership development at UNLV, and disseminate funds to encourage leadership training efforts
	• Create and implement a campuswide emerging leaders retreat
	• Develop a service learning program
	• Develop and implement a leadership certification program

Student Wellness Outreach Team

Charges	• Provide innovative programs and professional training for students, staff, and faculty to result in demonstrable impact on students' academic success and wellness
Recommendations	• Form a divisional outreach programming committee to facilitate collaboration and communication among student life departments
	• Add funding and staff time to implement new programs (e.g., curriculum infusion and student wellness outreach Web site)
	• Undertake campuswide needs assessment project
	• Revise job expectations to accurately reflect the amount of time needed to achieve the goals of the committee

Student Activities and Traditions Planning Group

Charges	• Assess current initiatives and why they are in place. Look at student impact versus funds expended.

(Continued)

Table 10.2   Continued

	• Explore how events are communicated to students, the university, and the community
	• Determine what we are directly responsible for and what we support in terms of money and personnel
	• Identify student needs and develop a student activities curriculum that addresses these needs
	• Identify programming duplication within the division
Recommendations	• Create and implement the hub that will standardize and centralize all program planning and evaluations, create and maintain a calendar system, and provide a connecting point ensuring collaborative interactions between programmers, processes, and information within student life

Implications of the Reorganization for Staff Members

Quite consistently, we emphasized the message that the organization had to change and that the division's collective view of leadership needed to shift. As we were leading the division, we were simultaneously working to make sense of our new roles of interim vice president and interim associate vice president within the division. We needed to develop a "blended" leadership style to ensure that messages were consistent and expectations were congruent. The two of us also had to find a way to blend our styles: Rebecca's relationship focus and Karen's task focus. In addition, we had to support former directors who had been promoted to assistant vice presidents as they learned their new roles within the division and worked with staff to develop cluster identities.

Members of the vice president's council—who were simultaneously grappling with expanded, complex roles and the transition from peer to supervisor—worked quickly to learn about new areas under their supervision and about divisional data. Members of the council used the term *shared leadership* frequently and encouraged staff to share good ideas and to feel empowered to take action, make mistakes, challenge thinking, and express concerns. We talked about creating new relationships between and among staff and supervisors. We continually challenged hierarchical thinking, reinforced enhanced accountability, and encouraged diverse perspectives. Student life educators also were struggling to make sense of this new organization as we challenged them to consider themselves to be leaders regardless of their role in the division.

For example, at the early stages of the divisional changes, a staff member who had been at UNLV for 5 years expressed frustration at what he was hearing from the division and his supervisor. His understanding of collaboration was that he would no longer be able to do the work for which he was hired; in fact, he interpreted the goal of collaboration and learning about the work of others to mean *doing* the work of others. In addition, he questioned how decisions would get made and responsibilities aligned if we were going to create a flat organization; his questions reflected how he "heard" (i.e., how he interpreted) the idea of shared leadership. We continually created opportunities in which such issues could surface. We did this not only to create environments in which individuals felt free to share how they were making meaning of events around them but also to surface concerns and perceptions so that misperceptions could be addressed. Had these important issues—collaboration and shared leadership—not been articulated in a divisional meeting, we might not have anticipated the need to have divisional discussions and develop a shared language to explain the concept of shared leadership within a hierarchical structure.

At the same meeting, a first-year staff member expressed a completely different sentiment when he stated that the direction of the division was "very clear" and that "everyone just needed to use a different lens to understand and not be afraid of change." A midlevel staff member commented that she thought the work of reorganizing was "finished" because all the physical changes had been completed and reporting lines had changed. As divisional staff engaged in these discussions, it became apparent that there were many individually held interpretations and assumptions about the restructuring process and that these would create conflict if not mediated.

These differing interpretations of the change process—which were being shared at divisional staff meetings and in cluster discussions, supervision sessions, and informal conversations—led to a variety of staff reactions: fear, resistance, frustration, excitement, and impatience. The different perceptions resulted in friction among staff members who did not view the restructuring in the same light. In addition, terms such as *collaboration* and *shared leadership* were used with differing interpretations. This led to confusion as to what really was expected in terms of job performance. As a result, some staff members began to be perceived as intentionally resisting the change process.

The initial approach to the divisional restructuring was grounded in organizational development, and we read and talked a great deal about the literature on organizational change. As the process moved forward, members of the vice president's council sometimes found ourselves "labeling" staff members who were more vocal about their discomfort with the process as being resistant. Over time and in other settings, these individuals had demonstrated similar behaviors when faced with change; therefore, we attributed their concerns to be "typical" for those individuals. But as we got further into the reorganization process, it became more apparent that it was not just the more recalcitrant individuals who were having difficulties; staff at all levels were beginning to express varying degrees of concerns about the reorganization. These ranged from dealing with ambiguity to the increasing awareness of different and more rigorous expectations for performance.

As Fullan (2001) remarked in *Leading in a Culture of Change,*

> Internal commitment . . . cannot be activated from the top. It must be nurtured up close in the dailiness of organizational behavior, and for that to happen, there must be many leaders around us. Large organizations can never achieve perfect internal commitment, but with good leadership at all levels, they can generate a great deal of it, and this will feed on itself. . . . Strong institutions have many leaders at all levels. (pp. 133–134)

It quickly became apparent that it was not sufficient to tell the staff that their supervisors wanted them to "assume ownership" for the plans for a "new division." Building leadership capacity at all levels and broadly held commitment to shared leadership became an essential component of the reorganization.

We realized that as a division we had to make meaning of what we were experiencing as a result of the structural reorganization. Before we could move forward to implement the changes we envisioned, we needed to create structured opportunities for staff to come together across clusters to address issues of concern and areas of need. We realized that we needed to focus on individual staff responses before we could genuinely focus on students and their development. In spring 2002, we invited Marcia Baxter Magolda to campus to help us understand where staff members were on the journey toward self-authorship and how their meaning making might mediate how they would participate in the evolving reorganization. The three goals we outlined for Marcia and for divisional staff were to (a) engage in discussions to gain insight into how we construct meaning about ourselves and our relations with others, (b) explore how these contributions mediate our work lives, and (c) explore aspirations and apprehensions about the reorganization that would be useful to surface as it moves forward. Marcia served as an "outsider" to allow people to share their concerns. Her developmental lens allowed us to look differently at the staff reactions.

Marcia spent 3 days on campus in a series of meetings with the professional staff in the division to help us intentionally explore the personal transformations necessary to achieve the objectives of the reorganization. First as individuals and then in clusters, staff articulated their aspirations and anxieties as they engaged in their work to transform the organization. As the result of this intervention, staff members realized that the vice president's council members' understandings of and concerns about the change process were similar to those of other divisional staff. This realization served to unify the division as we moved to mutually construct the future.

We summarized the aspirations that seemed to be held widely by division staff; they included the need to enhance communication, understand and value what others do, collaborate frequently, share knowledge, improve outcomes for students, encourage professional development, and promote sharing expertise. Commonly held apprehensions included concerns about workload (e.g., does "working differently" mean "working harder"?), burnout, and failure. Some individuals questioned whether we were doing the right thing and what would happen if the reorganization did not work. We discussed the difficulty of finding time to allow us to create new ways of working and define new relationships simultaneously with accomplishing the "daily work" of the division. Staff expressed concern about the long-term impact of working in a dynamic environment. Initially, they especially wanted to know that good efforts planned previously would be maintained. Long-term, they worried about their ability to serve students and manage continual change.

At the end of those divisional discussions, members of the vice president's council recognized more fully the need to support what Marcia calls learning partnerships among staff and with students. We understood more fully what she meant when she said to the two of us at breakfast on her last day that "what we bring to work is the organization; we organize together and personally as individuals." We saw clearly that the staff in the division—with their strengths, weaknesses, distractions, and commitments—would determine the nature of the organization. We understood that theoretically; however, the discussions made the concept more concrete and obvious. Marcia further helped the vice president's council focus on the personal development of staff as she talked about the division as educators on a journey toward self-authorship.

She reminded us that meaning making mediates how individuals participate in the evolving organization. She also helped us interpret the behaviors we were seeing. As we shared our concerns about some individuals who we perceived to be resistant, she simply asked us whether we understood the complexity of how we were asking people to work. Somewhat embarrassed, we realized that we had not carefully considered the preparation necessary to think, interact, and participate in the organization we hoped to create. Marcia talked with us about issues of developmental readiness. What at first seemed like resistance was in reality an issue of readiness; this gave us a new lens through which to view and influence behaviors. As a result, we shared even more about expectations, crafted consistent messages, and acknowledged the developmental issues inherent in the creation of a learning organization.

We publicly acknowledged that this process was chaotic, confusing, and often frustrating. At the same time, we publicly validated the abilities, expertise, and contributions that every staff member brought to this process, and we attempted to acknowledge and communicate results of shared leadership and collaboration. One of the council members wrote in a memo to her cluster that

> part of working in a dynamic organization is that we can make changes as necessary because we are constantly monitoring the environment. And while there are days I wish I had a crystal ball to help guide us, I don't. And really that is for the better because while some of you may be tired of the ambiguity, the chaos, the constant discussions as we continue to create our environment, what you all have contributed is outstanding . . . after a year of hard work we are going to implement our first set of changes. And they may work or some may need tweaking—and it is chaotic, and it may raise more questions and challenges than we realized. But that is okay. As a team, we will answer those questions and find solutions to the challenges. I know that this can feel scary and overwhelming, but given what you have all demonstrated thus far, I have complete confidence we will continue to be very successful. We just need to acknowledge our discomfort, admit we are human and mistakes will be made, and that we will continue to learn.

When we focused on individuals and their readiness, we could support more intentionally their continued growth and development.

As the vice president's council members reviewed the feedback that was generated during Marcia's visit, one issue consistently surfaced: the need to create a common language. While the division had talked about fostering collaboration, practicing shared leadership, and expecting staff to work in a dynamic, learning organization, we had not engaged as a group to create or agree to divisional definitions. As a result, staff at all levels were invited to help create and facilitate a series of divisional conversations in which student life educators would create and agree to a common set of definitions that would guide the ways in which we would work and interact with others. This "construction of knowledge" was an intentional strategy for enhancing self-authorship among staff; as diverse perspectives and expectations were shared, suggestions were negotiated. Through dialogue, where all voices were heard and valued, a shared language was created. The dialogue led to what Kegan and Lahey (2000) called "the language of public agreement." Over time, we created a vision statement for the division: "The Division of Student Life is a dynamic environment characterized by shared leadership that fosters learning and human development." Conversations revealed the need to acknowledge the changing nature of our institution, the commitment to shared leadership, and the need to support both student and staff learning. This vision statement exemplifies the integration of learning from many individuals into what Allen and Cherrey (2000) called collective organizational intelligence.

As staff interactions began to mirror the educational assumptions of Baxter Magolda's (2001; see also chapter 2 of this volume) Learning Partnerships Model to promote self-authorship (that knowledge is complex and socially constructed, that self is central to knowledge construction, and that authority and expertise should be shared in construction of knowledge among peers), staff members at every level had the opportunity to learn about themselves as they examined current ways of doing things in light of the new organizational goals. As part of the restructuring of the division, an older, long-term, highly respected staff member was transitioning from his position as a director of a multiuse recreation facility into a divisional leadership position (Executive Director for Student Life Facilities) with broader responsibilities. For years, this staff member literally developed all the policies and procedures for his area, determined and assigned job responsibilities unilaterally, and rarely looked at what could be done differently. As he began his transition, an interim assistant director and his staff began to have conversations about changes that needed to occur with his pending absence from the facility. During these discussions, issues were raised about the need to redo the policies and procedures so they were more in line with the Facilities Use Planning Group recommendations. With the executive director as an active participant, they re-created policies and procedures, revamped programs, and realigned position responsibilities. By the end of the discussions, what the former director had created and implemented for several years had been completely revised.

As the staff worked their way through the complexities of developing new policies and procedures that better reflected the new organizational structure and as they negotiated job responsibilities, their confidence in their ability to solve problems and make decisions increased. Rather than telling them what they needed to do to ensure that all his job responsibilities were covered when he left, the former director supported the interim assistant director and posed questions that empowered the staff to reflect, analyze, and create a new way of working together. Staff began to understand and work with the complexity of issues inherent in the proposed changes rather than see themselves only as implementers of others' decisions. In this context, staff felt safe to re-create and redesign rather than afraid to surface ideas about new ways of doing things.

Through this renegotiation, staff members were not the only ones who were affected. The former director, who had worked so diligently to successfully manage an underresourced, highly used facility meeting the university and community demands for service, struggled to internalize the changes as they occurred. In his new position, he had to examine resource allocation, facility policies, long-standing procedures, and staffing expectations from a new lens. On the one hand, he realized that the staff members were not criticizing his past decisions; but because he was so deeply invested in the recreation facility, their suggestions often felt personal. Changes were being made in procedures he had developed over the years, and staff members were very vocal about their not wanting to put in the long hours that were a standard for the former director.

He realized that the changes were necessary to implement this new concept, so during the meetings the former director continually encouraged his staff to review and revamp to better fit the cluster concept. Simultaneously, he spent quite a bit of time reflecting on the conversations and his reactions, and he worked hard to put all those feelings into perspective. Over time, he grew to truly value the process of group discussion. Recently he shared,

> The entire process worked out well, and ultimately, upon reflection, the experience benefited the staff, students, university and me. I knew the concept of shared leadership would require patience, understanding, shared values and time in order to reach a new common ground. The new commitment of the division leadership facilitated this process. By actively and willingly participating in the process, I believe I grew as a leader and at the same time learned a little more about myself.

Baxter Magolda (1999) found that self-authored individuals are capable of mature relationships and negotiated expectations. In her research, she discovered that a strong internal sense of self supported participants as they engaged in authentic relationships and renegotiated old relationships. We wanted to structure the work of the division in such a way that student affairs educators forged more mature relationships with colleagues, manifested by increased mutual respect and productive collaboration that integrated multiple perspectives while accomplishing divisional goals.

Staff members were assured that they would have the opportunity to contribute their ideas, knowledge, and expertise within their own clusters and in other clusters. All planning groups were structured to allow members to look at their work both within individual clusters and within the division and to allow staff to work collaboratively sharing ideas, expertise, and perspectives. "Active engagement is one of the capacities necessary for influencing change on both an individual and organizational level" (Allen & Cherrey, 2000, p. 112).

Ongoing committees and short-term work groups selected issues that were articulated in the original planning process, researched them, and proposed ways to address them. For example, groups considered promoting diversity, supporting leadership development among students, streamlining programming efforts, implementing centralized scheduling, and consolidating learning enhancements for students. These action-oriented groups allowed individuals to come to the table—regardless of their developmental location on the journey toward self-authorship or divisional position—to help move the division forward.

Over the course of a year, the divisional planning groups met to assess current status, identify deficit areas, develop and administer needs assessments, and recommend implementation schedules. Planning groups shared updates on their progress at each cluster meeting, which allowed for the entire cluster to understand the recommendations, ask questions, and provide feedback. In addition, they posted meeting minutes to the divisional listserv and invited feedback from others in the division. As a result of these highly collaborative examples of working "differently," the division began the implementation of a cocurricular agenda based on student learning outcomes, a leadership transcript, a leadership minor in the academic curriculum, a divisional diversity committee, a standardized assessment program, and a centralized facilities schedule. These planning groups engaged the staff in what Allen and Cherrey (2000) called "purposeful influencing" (p. 112) and served as examples of the enactment of shared leadership. Table 10.3 summarizes divisional accomplishments during the second year, which was a year of transition that focused on creating cluster identities and fostering a divisional perspective among staff.

Because this way of working is complex and staff members continue to be at different developmental places, we still renegotiate norms and expectations in small and large ways. Early in this process, it was not unusual for staff members in different areas to criticize one another to their respective supervisors. As staff learned that they could not play their supervisors against one another, small but important changes occurred. Members of the vice president's council worked to minimize these less-than-helpful occurrences by confronting staff; they modeled confrontation that was appropriate,

Table 10.3 Reorganizing for Learning: Accomplishments Across the Division of Student Life

Year 1

Implemented staff-led summer series on change

Created a student life newsletter complete with editorial board

Proposed organizational structure based on essential functions

Articulated purposes of and goals for organizing change

Realigned positions, changed work expectations, and redefined supervisory responsibilities

Year 2

Standardized planning paperwork for demographic and evaluation information collected for all student wellness programs

Merged two departments that provided advising to exploring majors and to athletes

Created Student Life Technology Committee

Created shared position to bridge gap between premajor advising and career decision making that led to programmatic changes

Created a divisional Diversity Committee

Standardized evaluation and merit procedures

Created a Student Life Awards Committee that designed and implemented the First Student Life Awards Night

Established an account to fund training and development opportunities for professional and classified staff

Held divisional conversations to create shared definitions on terms in vision statement

Sponsored professional discussions on leadership with Laura Osteen

Provided divisionwide training on self-authorship with Marcia Baxter Magolda

Year 3

Standardized chart information for Student Health Center and Counseling and Psychological Services

Table 10.3 Continued

Created a divisionwide orientation for newly hired professional staff

Implemented a centralized scheduling process for campus life facilities

Created a divisionwide student recognition ceremony: Rebel Achievement Awards Night

Pooled resources in order to address staffing needs and purchase necessary equipment

Centralized tutoring services previously coordinated by three student life departments

Provided divisionwide training on diversity with Kathy Obear and Jamie Washington

Created and administered a climate survey of all student life employees

Created Student Life Assessment Web site that included assessment calendar, results, goals, and committee records

---

Note: While at first this list might seem unrelated to the organizational structure, we feel strongly that it demonstrates a different way of working for the division. These accomplishments could not have happened without collaboration, shared leadership, and blended resources; the efforts were not mandated by the vice president and/or vice president's council members. Rather, they represent staff-initiated and staff-implemented ideas.

solution oriented, and professional. In fact, it was not uncommon for a vice president's council member to pick up the phone in the presence of the complaining staff member to investigate and resolve the complaint or disagreement. We also developed new norms about even more complex issues (e.g., interpersonal communication and problem solving) and focused on the development of interpersonal as well as intrapersonal skills.

At the beginning of the second year, one staff team used discussion to establish group expectations of how they would interact with each other, support each other's programs and initiatives, and provide feedback. These expectations were addressed at each staff meeting, feedback was provided, and expectations were reinforced. At the end of their first year, team members were divided: half the staff, those relatively new to the division, had worked diligently to meet the expectations set by the group; the other half, individuals who had been with the division for 5 years or more, had not met expectations despite continual feedback from peers and supervisors. By year's end, the team reached a point where some staff refused to interact with or support the team members who were not responsive.

During the summer, the director scheduled an all-day retreat with the team in which staff members spent time reviewing goal accomplishment, relationship development, and new expectations for the new academic year. Prior to the retreat, the director spent significant time with each staff member about how they were making sense of what had happened over the year. Those staff members who were talking about disengaging from the team were asked to think about where this reaction was coming from and what it would accomplish. Other staff members who had not met the agreed-on expectations were asked to think about why they chose not to meet these expectations and come prepared to talk about their choices at the retreat. While awkward and often uncomfortable, the staff members of this team did engage in a rich conversation about what had transpired during the previous year. Through this discussion, they developed new expectations and a system for holding one another accountable. The retreat helped clarify their individual perspectives and learn how to negotiate with others. This is representative of the clash of expectations that can occur in any transformative change process, and it is illustrative of the impact of individual developmental issues on work groups. Examples like these helped the vice president's council understand what Marcia meant when she explained to staff that "the ways you have learned to work may conflict with the ways you have been asked to work" (personal communication, May 2002).

Even through times of conflict and seeming divisiveness—when staff members encountered challenges through multiple interpretations, ambiguity, and the need to negotiate what to believe with others—staff members began to learn what was important in terms of relationships, forging work relationships that moved beyond mere "friendship" to colleagueship. Some staff members began to think beyond how others perceived them and what they had accomplished. They focused less on their need for personal recognition from others and more on students, those who should benefit most from the professional accomplishments of student affairs educators. Other staff members became more aware that even choosing to be less participative did not lessen the accountability to contribute and support the team's decisions. More recently, we have seen fewer conflicts about the quality of work completed by others or the failure to finish assigned work. Instead, these educators' sense of satisfaction and self-worth now derives from their work with students rather than how people see them as members of a department or group.

In other cases, staff worked effectively to refine and improve their work in accordance with divisional goals. Those whom Baxter Magolda (2001) referred to as "authors of their own lives" are true to themselves in their relationships because they have internal foundations that are grounded in mutual relationships. As groups solidified and individuals engaged in shared problem solving, peer accountability surfaced. Interactions like these helped shape the new ways of working and provided examples of mature relationships as individuals negotiated expectations of one another, reflected on their values, and forged professional partnerships.

Implications of Organizational Changes for Students

We discovered very quickly that our original intent to focus primarily on improving services and programs for students of necessity took a backseat to the need to focus on the continued development of student life educators. The time that we spent "stepping back" and rethinking priorities and timelines was well invested. As staff created new norms, they grew progressively ready to shift their focus from their own apprehensions, conflicts, and needs to encourage the development of students as self-authored individuals. By the end of the second year, we noticed dramatic changes throughout the division in services and programs for students and in student–staff interactions. We next offer several examples of these changes.

Tutoring Services

Prior to the reorganization, the interim vice president asked three directors, all of whom offered tutoring services in their departments, to work together to consolidate tutoring through consistent training, pay scales, schedules, and expectations. Despite a number of meetings, the directors were unable or unwilling to comply with the request. Two years later (in 2003), without administrative fiat, tutoring was centralized, and one cluster was managing the administrative functions (hiring, paying, and scheduling) while another was providing the training and learning enhancements. Through complex negotiations, what had once seemed impossible was completed, and the original idea was extended to provide even better services for students.

Student Leadership Opportunities

Staff members in Student Involvement and Activities, individuals well grounded in developmental theory, quickly confronted the need to serve as role models for students who were engaged in student programming, event planning, and Greek life. They created a student group called the Rebel Pride Council comprised of chairs for all major campus events and set expectations among the group for mature interactions, shared accountability, and collaborative endeavors. Instead of accepting any student who volunteered to chair a major activity or "begging" a particularly talented student to assume a leadership role, UNLV students are now expected to apply for leadership roles. This represented a major change; formerly, it was not unusual for campus activities to "belong" to the staff member who directed students as "worker bees." Now the focus was on student development through leadership opportunities.

Through intentionally planned and coincidental experiences, student chairs learned to interact with one another, challenge one another, interact with institutional administrators and policymakers, and solve problems together to encourage participation, create traditions, and develop leadership. As a group, they began to define what they wanted their committees to develop and identify where committees could work together; these efforts often led to a complete revamping of an existing tradition. As these students mutually defined their experience, staff facilitated and guided their development. Students are beginning to take a more divisional perspective as evidenced by the creation of a new student achievement award process. Historically, individual departments developed celebratory activities for their respective students and student accomplishments were not shared divisionally. In addition, the earlier events were typically created by professional staff with little input from the students. A committee was formed to develop a divisional recognition event for all students. The committee spent 18 months developing a philosophy, the award categories, and selection criteria as well as addressing the logistics of implementing such an event. In the spring of 2003, the first Rebel Achievement Award Ceremony was a resounding success. Staff encouraged students to try new things, supported them if they failed, and celebrated together when they succeeded.

Community Service Projects

In addition, staff worked with students to design the Rebel Service Council for students who wanted to engage in service projects designed to improve the quality of life for individuals in the local community. Guided by student affairs educators, experiences such as Tunnel of Oppression, Meals on Wheels, and Habitat for Humanity were planned and facilitated by students, and participation grew dramatically throughout the year. These service opportunities were congruent with the new focus on promoting self-authorship among students. In each, involved students implemented the service or program after research, planning, and collaboration. Staff structured expectations for students to share perspectives and learn from one another. Students were encouraged to reflect on their interactions, learning, and responses. For example, as students traveled from campus to homeless shelters, staff encouraged students to share their reasons for participating, their concerns about upcoming interactions, and/or commonly held misperceptions about the homeless.

Conversations on return trips were significantly different as students shared what they learned and experienced through face-to-face interactions with individuals who were hungry, lonely, and homeless.

Facilities Renovation

Another example of student involvement that promotes self-authorship grew out of the need for new student life facilities. For a long time, the institution hoped to remodel the student union and recreation center. Members of the vice president's council and staff throughout the division decided that the time was right to request a fee in order to meet this goal; members of the president's cabinet concurred. As a result, the Rebel Renovation Committee was formed, and, as a group, members defined the role of the committee. Individuals came with vastly different expectations about and motivations for their work.

Staff led discussions about institutional expectations, and student committee members reached mutual understanding about the projects by researching student unions and recreation centers, reading about their missions, and engaging in numerous discussions with their peers. Varied perspectives were solidified by the end of the project as individual perspectives melded into commonly held aspirations and mutual understanding. A common purpose was evident as students planned and implemented tours of the existing facilities and prepared and presented an effective presentation for the elected regents charged with deciding whether to implement the new fee.

Student Programming

The Student Wellness cluster consolidated efforts in programming through shared planning, scheduling, marketing, and assessment. As a result, resources were maximized to serve the most students while more efficiently using staff resources. This effort in one cluster led to a divisional group—self-initiated—that met regularly to discuss the philosophy and theory behind student programming and to consider the evaluation of programming as they planned. Through these and other examples, we began to see the results of divisional conversations focused on student learning, collaboration, and shared leadership in the staff interactions with students.

Summary

Through these efforts, we learned that the organizational structure of a division of student affairs may support or hinder practices that promote self-authorship among students. In order to support learning experiences that foster self-authorship among students, student affairs educators first may need to create organizations that promote self-authorship among staff. Inherent in the reorganization of the Division of Student Life at UNLV were the assumptions and principles of the Learning Partnerships Model for promoting learning partnerships.

Using the educational assumptions of the Learning Partnerships Model to guide our reorganization led to self-authorship. Baxter Magolda (2001) wrote, "Being supported to develop self-authorship through contexts characterized by these three assumptions yielded the *internal foundations*" (p. 190) characteristic of individuals who have shifted from external to internal self-definition. Through the experiences described here, we have come to believe that the Learning Partnerships Model is appropriate for promoting the development of self-authorship among staff as well as students.

Throughout the past 2 years, we intentionally structured learning experiences for staff that validated them as knowers (e.g., by reinforcing their expertise), situated learning in their experience (e.g., by acknowledging current learning and enhancing new learning), and defined learning as mutually constructing meaning (e.g., by negotiating the complexity of divisional reorganization). As divisional leaders, we tried to provide what Baxter Magolda (2001) called "good company" for their journey toward self-authorship by guiding and supporting their efforts toward new meaning making.

As we began the 2001 academic year in a structurally reorganized division, the vice president sent a "back to school" memorandum to all staff in the division that continues to guide our expectations of ourselves and of others. She challenged staff to consider the following from *Leadership Reconsidered* (Astin & Astin, 2000) and asserted that we each have a responsibility to do the following:

- Create a supportive environment where people can grow, thrive, and live in peace with one another
- Create a community of caring and shared responsibility, where every person matters and each person's welfare and dignity is respected and supported
- Collaborate with one another in order to empower individuals, engender trust, and capitalize on the diverse talents among our members
- Share our differences of opinion civilly in an atmosphere of mutual respect
- Create an environment in which we all have the opportunity to learn from and about each other
- Perform our work with competence and integrity demonstrating a commitment to the students whom we serve and the colleagues with whom we work

We have experienced a number of successes in our quest to enact our vision statement that says that we will create a "dynamic environment characterized by shared leadership that fosters learning and human development." We believe we have created an organizational structure that supports staff members who are on the journey toward self-authorship. We have experienced enhanced peer accountability and effective peer mentoring. The organizational structure has allowed new leadership roles and expanded opportunities for leadership through the assumption that leadership is not exclusively positional.

We have worked to ensure that student life educators have the resources they need to make decisions and the practice they need to become better decision makers. These resources, available to both professional and classified staff, include meaningful training, professional travel, focused supervision, and sufficient time. The division has focused efforts to articulate what it means to be a professional in a learning organization. We have structured conversations to foster among individuals the development of a clear professional identity based on goals for enhanced collaboration, shared leadership, and commonly held values. As an organization, we try to push individuals and groups to clarify what they think and believe. We ask such important questions as, How did you come to that decision? in order to encourage individuals to think critically, examine their decisions, and develop analytical skills.

Working in this way is not without its challenges. Chief among them is the need to provide adequate time for conversation, learning, and reflecting. Such work requires time for professional development, intense self-examination, and group negotiations. In addition, clusters move at different paces (much as individuals do); therefore, maintaining consistency becomes challenging as the varied pace yields different results.

We continue to struggle to maintain the divisional focus; as clusters establish mission and goals, they also form cluster identities. We continue to work to ensure that the clusters do not merely become "superdepartments" working separately from one another. Creating consistent experiences across the division requires that divisional staff come together frequently to make meaning as a large group; therefore, we have created what we call "divisional conversations" around a variety of topics, such as diversity, shared leadership, collaboration, and professional expectations. Such opportunities require careful planning, skillful facilitation, and uninterrupted hours. It is important that expertise is shared at the divisional level and that staff challenge one another and learn from one another.

Not surprisingly, we have begun to discover that we have staff who are not interested in or are not capable of working in this new way. We are challenged to handle these conflicts in ways that are consistent with our commitment to a developmental lens while not allowing individual staff members to derail the collective progress. Similarly, staff with varying functions—whether they are programmers, service providers, or clerical workers—are continually challenged to expand their perspectives and find connections within their work and across the division.

Ultimately, we want student affairs educators to partner with colleagues in academic affairs to ensure that the curriculum and cocurriculum appropriately support students' development. This means that student affairs educators need to understand both how to foster self-authorship among students and how to enact the principles of self-authorship in their own professional lives. The Learning Partnerships Model and the understanding of what is essentially a very human journey provide a foundation from which organizations may humanize bureaucracy, deconstruct mechanical ways of working, and, ultimately, serve students more effectively. Perhaps our most important lesson has been the realization that we are on an extended journey, one that requires continued commitment, self-reflection, and learning.

References

Allen, K. E., & Cherrey, C. (2000). *Systemic leadership: Enriching the meaning of our work*. Lanham, MD: University Press of America.

Astin, A. W., & Astin, H. S. (eds.). (2000). *Leadership reconsidered: Engaging higher education in social change*. Battle Creek, MI: W. K. Kellogg Foundation.

Baxter Magolda, M. B. (1999). *Creating contexts for learning and self-authorship: Constructive-developmental pedagogy*. Nashville: Vanderbilt University Press.

Baxter Magolda, M. B. (2001). *Making their own way: Narratives for transforming higher education to promote self-development*. Sterling, VA: Stylus.

Covey, S. R. (1989). *The 7 habits of highly effective people: Powerful lessons in personal change*. New York: Simon & Schuster.

Fullan, M. (2001). *Leading in a culture of change*. San Francisco: Jossey-Bass.

Johnson, S. (1998). *Who moved my cheese? An amazing way to deal with change in your work and in your life*. New York: Putnam.

Kegan, R., & Lahey, L. (2000). *How we talk can change the way we work: Seven languages for transformation*. San Francisco: Jossey-Bass.

Senge, P. M. (1990). *The fifth discipline: The art and practice of the learning organization*. New York: Doubleday.

Wingspread Group on Higher Education. (1993). *An American imperative: Higher expectations for higher education*. Racine, WI: Johnson Foundation.

II

CREATING LEARNING PARTNERSHIPS IN HIGHER EDUCATION

MODELING THE SHAPE, SHAPING THE MODEL

Patricia M. King and Marcia B. Baxter Magolda

Acclaimed American poet Nikki Giovanni (2002) wrote a memorable short poem in which she reflects on her own teaching and concludes that "the teacher is also learning" (p. 109). This insight emerges as a recurring theme in the stories of the educators who describe their experiences in this volume.

However, *what* the teachers learned as they used the Learning Partnerships Model to guide their work seemed to surprise even this experienced group of educators. These surprises set the context for this concluding chapter, acknowledging that educators both shape and are shaped by the conceptual frameworks they use to enact their practice. Indeed, educators as well as students construct meaning of their experiences; and just as the ways students interpret events shape their reactions to these events, so too do the ways educators interpret pedagogical models shape whether and how they choose to use them in their own practice.

At the heart of the Learning Partnerships Model is the assumption that a major goal of learning is self-authorship. The language of "self-authorship" may be unfamiliar to many, but like other lofty developmental aims (e.g., self-actualization and promoting intentional learning), it has a useful place in a lexicon of educational goals. In the preface to this volume, Baxter Magolda defined self-authorship as follows:

> Self-authorship is the capacity to internally define a coherent belief system and identity that coordinates engagement in mutual relations with the larger world. This internal foundation yields the capacity to actively listen to multiple

perspectives, critically interpret those perspectives in light of relevant evidence and the internal foundation, and make judgments accordingly.

In other words, self-authorship is about developing multifaceted capacities that enable learners to engage constructively and effectively in a learning process and to make decisions and take actions that reflect these capacities. Such learning could focus on deepening one's understanding of subject-matter content in college classrooms, finding a comfortable occupational niche in which to draw on one's interests and apply what one understands and can do, being involved as a member of one's community, or negotiating social relationships with peers and loved ones. It is a broad and ambitious educational goal—as demanding as the problems we as a nation face in the 21st century. If attaining this kind of internal foundation will help today's graduates address these problems, then this will be well worth our energy and effort.

Initial efforts bode well for achieving this ambitious goal. The collective chapters in this book provide encouraging evidence that educational practice can achieve particular learning goals and promote the self-authorship so crucial for 21st-century life. Haynes's interdisciplinary students were able to combine disciplinary knowledge to respond to a topic, present a rationale for taking an interdisciplinary approach, provide a new holistic understanding of the topic, engage with other thinkers, and have a clear understanding of themselves as scholars and thinkers. Hornak and Ortiz's students' experience with the Multicultural Education Framework increased their ability to change the way they thought about culture and society and to reconsider the ways in which they viewed their experiences and the world. Egart and Healy's Urban Leadership Internship Program students learned to critically analyze previously held views and decide for themselves what they valued and believed, yielding a transformation from being other-directed to self-directed citizens who are engaged in their communities. Yonkers-Talz' Casa de la Solidaridad experience enabled participants to refine their beliefs, identities, and relations with diverse others to arrive at a richer understanding of that which gives life deep meaning; doing so enabled them to envision their participation in creating a more peaceful and just world. Piper and Buckley's participants in the Community Standards Model learned to identify what they believed, value their own voice, and express it constructively with their peers, resulting in their taking more adult responsibility for their community. Rogers et al.'s graduate students came to self-author their belief systems, identities, and professional and personal relationships, enabling them to internally craft their professional futures.

Wildman's story of faculty development conveys that a rich set of Learning Partnerships Model experiments involving significant numbers of faculty members allowed a new set of narratives to emerge about learning in multiple contexts. Mills and Strong's organizational structure supported staff members on the journey toward self-authorship, yielding enhanced peer accountability, effective peer mentoring, expanded participation in leadership, and translation of Learning Partnerships Model characteristics to their work with students. Together with Baxter Magolda's longitudinal and course observation data, these outcomes illustrate that multiple educational contexts can be intentionally organized to effectively promote self-authorship. Students in these multiple versions of learning partnerships made substantial progress in building a foundation for self-authorship. Through these experiences, they made remarkable progress toward achieving what by most accounts is a difficult part of achieving maturity: They learned to internally define their belief systems and identities in ways that helped them organize and make decisions about how they would engage in mutual relations with others in the larger world. Similarly, faculty and student affairs educators using the Learning Partnerships Model refined and transformed their professional belief systems and identities to determine and coordinate the nature of their engagement in mutual relations with learners. Thus, placing self-authorship as the central goal of higher education can be achieved and is a goal that warrants our energy and effort.

Another central assumption of the Learning Partnerships Model is that learning is a partnership between learners and educators. As Haynes noted in her chapter, "I discovered that the problem did not really lie with the students themselves." This discovery may seem self-evident, but is an eye-opening admission for educators accustomed to either taking full responsibility for the conduct of an educational endeavor or assigning responsibility for disappointing performance solely to the students. There are many types of partnerships, of course, as seen through the examples offered in the prior chapters. As Dewey (1933) noted, "We never educate directly, but indirectly by means of the environment. Whether we permit chance environments to do the work, or whether we design environments for the purpose makes a great difference" (p. 22). Similarly, how these partnerships are constructed can make a great difference in whether students develop the capacity for self-authorship in a given educational environment. Creating partnerships through which learners engage in transformation from dependence on authority to self-authorship requires a corresponding transformation in educators. Wildman's discussion of faculty development and Mills and Strong's discussion of organizing a student affairs division address these transformations directly. A number of the chapter authors share their own transformations as they engaged in learning partnerships.

In light of the possibilities learning partnerships hold for both learners and educators, this chapter is addressed primarily to exploring how you, the reader, might apply the Learning Partnerships Model to your work. We first comment on some of the lessons shared by the authors of the preceding chapters of this book in light of their experiences using the Learning Partnerships Model, especially observations that illustrate issues that those implementing the framework might need to address. Next, we offer a framework for you to consider as you decide whether and how to use the Learning Partnerships Model in your own practice ("modeling the shape"), emphasizing that the model is not a static formula to be applied but an approach that can and should be adapted to various contexts ("shaping the model").

Underlying Questions Revealed by Early Applications of the Learning Partnerships Model

As noted previously, conceptual models such as the Learning Partnerships Model help educators shape their practice, and in turn these experiences shape them as educators. For example, the educators who described their experiences using the Learning Partnerships Model reported how they designed their practice to reflect the principles and assumptions of the Learning Partnerships Model; they also reported having reexamined their assumptions about the nature of teaching or supervising, about the kinds of relationships they were trying to enact with their students and colleagues, and even about themselves in these and other roles. Although none mentioned it directly, it is noteworthy that their comments reflected the three domains of development that underlie the Learning Partnerships Model; in other words, applying the Learning Partnerships Model provided the occasion for these educators to reexamine their assumptions about their knowledge of teaching and administration (the cognitive domain), about themselves as educators (the intrapersonal domain), and about the nature and quality of their interactions with others (the interpersonal domain). Several lessons shared by these authors can be used to alert others to some of the questions and issues they, too, might feel compelled to acknowledge and address. For example, reexamining assumptions about knowledge of educational practice includes a willingness to rethink educational goals. Related questions include the following:

1. Do I embrace promoting maturity as an overarching purpose toward which my own educational efforts should be directed? Is this goal consistent with or different from the current goals I hold that shape my practice?

2. To what degree am I willing to change my teaching or administrative practices to intentionally work toward self-authorship goals?

Rethinking educational goals, particularly considering self-authorship as a central goal achieved through mutual partnerships with learners, necessitates rethinking one's role as an authority. Related questions include the following:

1. What reservations do I have about forfeiting the power of authority that comes with many traditional educational practices in order to foster the self-authorship of those I teach and those with whom I work? Are there subtle ways I might try to retain this power?

2. Am I willing to ask of myself what I'm asking of my students and colleagues? For example, do I engage in deep reflection about my practices? Am I intentional about my interactions with others? How well do I author and communicate my own perspectives?

3. To what degree am I willing to scrutinize my own practices in terms of the principles and assumptions of the Learning Partnerships Model?

Finally, new conceptualizations of one's role as an educator and learner require reflection on relationships in the learning context. Key questions to consider are the following:

1. Do I currently interact with students and colleagues in ways that draw on, strengthen, and enact *my own* internal foundation?

2. Do I currently interact with students and colleagues in ways that draw on, strengthen, and support *their* internal foundations?

These questions might be asked of anyone implementing a new strategy for approaching their work. It is no coincidence that they are reminiscent of the kinds of reflective questions that the authors of these chapters encouraged their students and staff to ask as they experienced new opportunities and challenges.

Designing Educational Practice Using the Learning Partnerships Model

How can an educator interested in implementing the Learning Partnerships Model in his or her practice get started doing so? We (Baxter Magolda & King, 1998) designed a two-phase process—assessment and then design—for educators to use for this purpose. Assessment here is defined broadly, referring not only to students' entering characteristics but also to pertinent characteristics of the educator and the learning environment. Although it may be tempting to launch right into the design phase (e.g., "how could I implement these practices in my own course or program?"), we recommend a careful assessment phase as a beginning point; starting here honors Kegan's (1994) challenge to firmly ground developmental bridges on both sides. That is, the design should be directly linked to learner characteristics as well as to relevant aspects of the context. Engaging first in the assessment phase also conveys the idea that educators should be not only intentional but also reflective about their practice.

Each phase consists of a series of steps, described in the following sections. Table 11.1 provides an overview of the steps in the process. Because this is a reflective process, we begin each step with a basic explanation accompanied by a notepad that can be used to reflect on and respond to more specific questions about each step. A completed notepad, extrapolated from Carolyn Haynes's description of the interdisciplinary writing curriculum (chapter 3 of this volume), provides an example of the entire process.

Phase 1: Assessing Learning Goals and Learners' Capacities for Self-Authorship

In this phase, educators gather (or in some cases create) background information that will help them design or redesign educational programs. This phase includes defining learning goals for a selected educational context and identifying ways of making meaning that are required to most effectively meet

Table 11.1 Implementing the Learning Partnerships Model: An Overview

---

Phase 1: Assessing learning goals and learners' capacities for self-authorship

    Step 1: Select the context

    Step 2: Identify the learning goals for this context

    Step 3: Examine the learning goals from a self-authorship perspective

    Step 4: Consider the self-authorship characteristics of learners in this context

    Step 5: Identify consistencies and discrepancies between learning goals and learner capacities

Phase 2: Designing the "evolutionary bridge"

    Step 6: Outline the developmental "curriculum"

    Step 7: Address the three assumptions

    Step 8: Address the three principles

    Step 9: Review the consistencies and discrepancies

    Step 10: Outline plan to evaluate effectiveness

---

those learning goals and the degree to which students have already achieved the capacities for self-authorship to achieve these goals. Going through this process also allows the educator to examine the degree of alignment among three key elements of the teaching/learning process: learning goals (what successful learners should understand and be able to do as a result of this experience), what self-authorship capacities these goals require, and current learner capacities; these components are all necessary parts of the foundation on which to design educational practices to foster self-authorship.

Step 1: Select the Context

The first step in considering using the Learning Partnerships Model in your educational practice is to identify a context you perceive as appropriate to enhance self-authorship (see Table 11.2). A context selected for this purpose might be either one that has been identified as problematic, as was the case for the chapters in this book written by Haynes (the interdisciplinary writing curriculum) and by Piper and Buckley (increased damage, vandalism, and loss of community in residence halls), or one that is acceptably successful but not living up to its potential, as was the case for the Casa de la Solidaridad study-abroad program described by Yonkers-Talz or Rogers et al.'s master's program. Alternatively, you might consider whether special opportunities exist through which the learning goals might be achieved in a new way (e.g., development of new programs or curricula, availability of staff or financial resources, or change in administrative priorities) as a means of selecting a context suitable for this purpose. Frustrations with their experience of senior theses led Carolyn Haynes and her colleagues to initially identify the senior thesis as the context for promoting self-authorship. On further reflection, they decided to tackle the 4-year curriculum leading up to the senior thesis (see Table 11.3).

Step 2: Identify the Learning Goals for this Particular Context

There are many possible learning goals for educational experiences. However, placing them within the larger framework of self-authorship as an organizing goal creates a new lens for considering their larger purposes. For example, in contexts such as the one Piper and Buckley described, having administratively well-run systems is a common goal for many housing divisions on campuses across the nation. Unfortunately, this is sometimes interpreted primarily as keeping the common areas clean and keeping repair costs low. Placing these purposes within a self-authorship framework, however, can dramatically change how these purposes are implemented—and by whom and why this is important—as these authors explained. Notepad B (see Table 11.4) contains guiding questions to identify the learning goals for the context you chose in

Table 11.2   Notepad A

Step 1: Select the context. What would be an appropriate setting for you to adapt your interactions with students and/or colleagues to enhance their self-authorship using the Learning Partnerships Model?

Table 11.3   Notepad A—Example: Developing a Writing Curriculum (Haynes Chapter)

Step 1: Select the context. What would be an appropriate setting for you to adapt your interactions with students and/or colleagues to enhance their self-authorship using the Learning Partnerships Model?
We chose the senior thesis as a setting to enhance students' self-authorship because of our frustrations with working with students in this process. This eventually led to a focus on the 4-year writing curriculum.

Table 11.4   Notepad B

Step 2: Identify the learning goals for this context
(a) What are the current intended learning outcomes in this context?
(b) How would you adapt these learning goals to reflect self-authorship as an overarching goal?
(c) As a result of this learning experience, what would you like participants to better understand and address with more proficiency?

Step 1. Table 11.5 contains the learning goals Haynes and her colleagues identified as essential to successful senior thesis writing. The complexity of these goals already incorporated self-authorship.

Step 3: Examine the Learning Goals from a Self-Authorship Perspective

Step 3 involves interpreting the developmental demands the learning goals make on students. The central task is to identify the cognitive, intrapersonal, and interpersonal self-authorship capacities the learning goals require of learners. Notepad C (see Table 11.6) contains guiding questions for this task. To identify cognitive capacities, consider what ways of understanding concepts, analyzing and synthesizing information, contrasting multiple perspectives, and

Table 11.5 Notepad B—Example: Developing a Writing Curriculum (Haynes Chapter)

Step 2: Identify the learning goals for this context
(a) What are the current intended learning outcomes in this context?
(b) How would you adapt these learning goals to reflect self-authorship as an overarching goal?
(c) As a result of this learning experience, what would you like participants to better understand and address with more proficiency?

1. Answer a question, solve a problem, or address a topic by integrating disciplinary perspectives into a more comprehensive perspective.

2. Understand critically the differing aims, assumptions, and tasks of two or more disciplines while simultaneously possessing considerable proficiency in diverse forms of academic writing.

3. Demonstrate a range of critical thinking skills fundamental to good writing and interdisciplinary inquiry: comprehension, application, analysis, synthesis, and evaluation.

4. Operate in and understand critically the limitations and strengths of at least two disciplinary fields; additionally, attempt to take the additional steps of synthesis and application—that is, creatively explore ways in which insights from those fields can be combined or synthesized productively to respond to a real-life issue or problem.

so on these learning goals require. Does achievement of these goals require the use of assumptions associated with contextual knowing (Baxter Magolda, 1992) or reflective thinking (King & Kitchener, 1994; see also chapter 2 of this volume)? Could they be achieved through the use of assumptions associated with absolute knowing or prereflective thinking? Intrapersonal capacities include the ways of seeing oneself as a learner (i.e., student, staff member, leader, and so on) with a perspective to contribute that are required to achieve these goals. Are the goals achievable if learners define themselves predomi-

Table 11.6   Notepad C

Step 3: Examine the learning goals from a self-authorship perspective. What self-authorship capacities do the learning goals require of learners?
Cognitive capacities: What ways of constructing knowledge and making meaning about the concept at hand are required to achieve these learning goals?
Intrapersonal capacities: What ways of seeing and understanding oneself are required?
Interpersonal capacities: What ways of understanding oneself in relation to others are required?

nantly via external relationships? Finally, interpersonal capacities can be identified through determining ways of interacting with others (e.g., respectfully and nondefensively reacting to others' points of view) that the learning goals require. Haynes's interpretations of the developmental capacities required to meet the interdisciplinary writing goals serve as an example in Table 11.7.

Table 11.7 Notepad C—Example: Developing a Writing Curriculum (Haynes Chapter)

Step 3: Examine the learning goals from a self-authorship perspective. What self-authorship capacities do the learning goals require of learners?
Cognitive capacities: What ways of constructing knowledge and making meaning about the concept at hand are required to achieve these learning goals?   The ability to weigh evidence in context, understand that knowledge is not absolute—in other words, be contextual thinkers.
Intrapersonal capacities: What ways of seeing and understanding oneself are required?   For writers to identify their own position on a topic, they must have the ability to monitor their own and others' emotions and to discriminate among them.
Interpersonal capacities: What ways of understanding oneself in relation to others are required?   Thesis writers must learn to ask for and provide feedback in tactful but honest ways, assess the value of feedback given, and implement the useful feedback offered.   They must be able to differentiate their sense of meaning and the self apart from, but in relation to, other people and sources.

Table 11.8   Notepad D

Step 4: Consider the self-authorship characteristics of learners in this context. What underlying assumptions about knowledge, self, and relationships do they hold?
Cognitive capacities: What ways of constructing knowledge do these individuals commonly use?
Intrapersonal capacities: What ways of seeing oneself are exhibited by these learners?
Interpersonal capacities: What ways of one seeing oneself in relation to others do these learners exhibit?

Step 4: Consider the Self-Authorship Characteristics of Learners in This Context

To what extent do learners currently possess the self-authorship capacities required to achieve these learning goals? Identifying the underlying assumptions about knowledge, self, and relationships that learners currently hold is necessary to answer this question. Assessing learners' current capacities is the central task of Step 4. Notepad D (see Table 11.8) outlines the central questions for this step.

To identify learners' cognitive capacities, consider how they function in classroom interactions, how they interact with authorities regarding learning and decision making, how they make career decisions, how they interact with parents in decision making, and how they decide what to believe. As you reflect on these observations, interpret what kinds of epistemological assumptions appear to be guiding these approaches (e.g., absolute or prereflective thinking; transitional, independent, or quasi-reflective thinking; or contextual or reflective thinking). To identify intrapersonal capacities, consider whether learners exhibit an external or internal self-definition or something in between these two. Consider how students define themselves, what makes up their identity, to what extent their identity is solid or fluid, and to what extent they understand their gender, class, racial, and sexual orientation identity and how this affects their interactions with others. To identify interpersonal capacities, consider the extent to which students bend to peer pressure, why they choose to join groups (e.g., for affirmation or to further their own goals), their degree of sensitivity to others' needs, how clearly they identify their own needs, and the extent to which they seek out relationships with diverse others. To what extent do they take responsibility for personally defining and constructing the nature of their relationships with others? Table 11.9 shows Haynes's analysis of learners' meaning making in response to questions posed in Notepad D.

Step 5: Consider the Consistencies and Discrepancies Between Learning Goals and Learner Capacities

Notepad E (see Table 11.10) contains the guiding questions to determine the distance between learners' current capacity and the capacity required by the learning goals. Determining the gap between current and required capacity sets the stage for defining the developmental goals that necessarily accompany the learning goals. Considering how to organize both developmental and learning goals over time enables conceptualizing educational practice as a progressive curriculum that welcomes students in their current capacity while inviting them to stretch beyond that capacity. Table 11.11 shows Haynes's reflections for Notepad E.

The steps in this assessment phase are proposed as a framework for helping educators think through the myriad issues that arise in planning to use the Learning Partnerships Model in practice. Thinking through these issues is intended to provide a foundation of clarified assumptions and analysis of relevant background information for educators to use in making specific decisions in the next phase of this process: designing educational practices to promote self-authorship.

Table 11.9 Notepad D—Example: Developing a Writing Curriculum (Haynes Chapter)

Step 4: Consider the self-authorship characteristics of learners in this context. What underlying assumptions about knowledge, self, and relationships do they hold?

Cognitive capacities: What ways of constructing knowledge do these individuals commonly use?
Our first-year students tend to be absolute thinkers, believing that correct answers exist in all areas and are known by authority figures. Having already confronted in their first year an array of complex problems as well as a host of different disciplinary frameworks with which to view the world, sophomores begin to move to transitional knowing, increasingly coming to the idea that absolute knowledge exists in some areas while uncertainty exists in others. Most juniors are either transitional or independent knowers (seeing knowledge as open to many interpretations and viewing themselves as equal sources of knowledge).

Intrapersonal capacities: What ways of seeing oneself are exhibited by these learners?
Some combat an extreme fear of writing; others had never conceived of themselves as original thinkers or scholars.
They lack the conviction to pursue their own questions and ideas; they struggle to see themselves as knowers.

Interpersonal capacities: What ways of one seeing oneself in relation to others do these learners exhibit?
Students see feedback and assistance as a sign of weakness or as a form of critique that should be shunned.

Table 11.10 Notepad E

Step 5: Identify the consistencies and discrepancies between learning goals and learner capacities
(a) In what ways are the learning goals and self-authorship capacities of the learners in alignment?
(b) Where do you see discrepancies between these?
(c) What developmental goals would help bridge the distance between required capacity and intended learning outcomes?
(d) How could these developmental goals be organized over time to reflect learner capacities and the span of time for interactions within this context?

Phase 2: Designing the "Evolutionary Bridge"

Building a developmental bridge (Kegan's "holding environment") is necessary when learning goals require ways of making meaning that are beyond the learner's current capacity. This bridge is created by a well-designed "curriculum" that offers a series of experiences that are close enough to the learner's current experience to be meaningful yet involve increasingly complex goals as the learner moves through the curriculum. We use the term *curriculum* to convey the intentional organization of both classroom and out-of-classroom educational practice. The purpose of the bridge is to help students

Table 11.11   Notepad E—Example: Developing a Writing Curriculum
(Haynes Chapter)

Step 5: Identify the consistencies and discrepancies between learning goals and learner capacities
(a) In what ways are the learning goals and self-authorship capacities of the learners in alignment? They are not in alignment. The learning goals demand capacities that are beyond those students currently hold.
(b) Where do you see discrepancies between these? Students rely on external authority for knowledge, identity, and relationships. The learning goals require reliance on internal authority for constructing knowledge, identity, and relationships.
(c) What developmental goals would help bridge the distance between required capacity and intended learning outcomes? Move students out of external ways of knowing to internal ones, help them craft internal identities from which to speak, and help them engage with others' thinking in ways that do not depend on others' approval.
(d) How could these developmental goals be organized over time to reflect learner capacities and the span of time for interactions within this context? The writing curriculum of the School of Interdisciplinary Studies helps students progress steadily through three developmentally appropriate phases of increasing self-authorship, from engagement with expressive modes, to an increasingly critical awareness of and proficiency in disciplinary forms, to interdisciplinary scholarship. We determined that a 4-year curriculum was best suited for this purpose.

make the journey toward achieving the desired learning outcomes through developing more mature meaning-making capacities.

This phase is organized to help educators design learning partnerships in their selected contexts that craft the best balance of guidance and empowerment to promote students' maturity and achievement of self-authorship. Based on the results of the assessment phase, educators enter this process aware of the gaps that need to be bridged; the purpose of the design phase is to begin to sketch a picture of that bridge. As educators construct supportive learning environments, they help learners develop their capacities and stretch their perceived capabilities to meet learning goals. As Kegan (1994) wrote,

> Such supports constitute a holding environment that provides both welcoming acknowledgement to exactly who the person is right now as he or she is, and fosters the person's psychological evolution. As such, a holding environment is a tricky transitional culture, an evolutionary bridge, a context for crossing over. (p. 43)

The central task in designing practice is to build the evolutionary bridge from learners' current capacities to the ones required to achieve the learning goals.

Step 6: Outline the Developmental "Curriculum"

Given the distance between current and desired ways of making meaning, consider ways of bridging these gaps. Start by breaking down the developmental goals identified in Step 5 of the assessment phase into a sequence of steps. You can then use these steps as the basis for sketching out a plan (a "curriculum") that organizes these steps into a series of activities and accomplishments that culminate in the achievement of the learning goals. Notepad F (see Table 11.12) outlines this process. At the heart of Step 6 is figuring out what intermediate goals are appropriate and reasonable to accomplish in what time frame. Haynes's outline of her developmental curriculum appears in Table 11.13.

Step 7: Addressing the Three Assumptions

Three assumptions about learning serve as the foundation for Learning Partnerships Model practices: (a) knowledge is complex and socially constructed, (b) self is central to knowledge construction, and (c) expertise and authority are mutually shared among peers in knowledge construction. Each of these has been discussed in prior chapters; this step suggests that you think about your own area of practice in these terms. Guiding questions appear in

Table 11.12   Notepad F

Step 6: Outlining the developmental "curriculum"
(a) How can the learning and developmental goals be translated into steps over time?
(b) What form would the learning and developmental goals take in the first period of time (e.g., beginning of the term or first year of study), depending on the length of your involvement with these learners?
(c) Which of these steps are already in place, and which would need to be developed or enhanced?

Notepad G (see Table 11.14). For example, in determining the degree to which students mutually construct meaning with their peers and/or with you, how do you reconcile the tensions that sometimes arise among such roles as being a guide, an expert, and an authority figure? How do you offer your expertise without retreating into the role of expert whose role it is to disseminate information—or truths? In what ways do you portray knowledge as complex and socially constructed? To what extent do you invite learners to bring their experience to the learning enterprise? Rogers et al. spoke eloquently to the need to reexamine their own assumptions, even after thinking they had already done so. Do their experiences resonate with yours? That is, do you think rethinking or refining your definition of your role as educator could improve your practices? How might changes in your role definition

Table 11.13 Notepad F—Example: Developing a Writing Curriculum (Haynes Chapter)

Step 6: Outlining the developmental "curriculum"
(a) How can the learning and developmental goals be translated into steps over time? Year 1: Faculty validate students' experiences and knowledge and encourage them to identify their voice and position on various topics. Year 2: Faculty seek to reinforce and deepen this new development [to transitional knowing] by helping students to compare and contrast disciplinary frameworks, critically analyze the limitations and benefits of various ways of viewing the world, and begin to use various disciplines to think about their own questions. Year 3: Students should engage more systematically in interdisciplinary inquiry, using integrative theories and synthesized research methods. Year 4: The senior thesis requires navigating through uncharted waters and generating new ways of combining or making sense of disparate pieces of information on their own.
(b) What form would the learning and developmental goals take in the first period of time (e.g., beginning of the term or first year of study), depending on the length of your involvement with these learners? See above.
(c) Which of these steps are already in place, and which would need to be developed or enhanced? Initially, only the senior year steps were in place. For the 4-year curriculum that emerged from Haynes and her colleagues' analysis, see Table 3.1.

Table 11.14   Notepad G

Step 7: Addressing the three assumptions
Assumption A: Knowledge is complex and socially constructed.
Assumption B: Self is central to knowledge construction.
Assumption C: Expertise and authority are mutually shared among peers in knowledge construction.
(a) In what ways are these assumptions currently evident in your selected area of practice?
(b) How could you more effectively convey these assumptions to learners in your selected context?

influence the ways you construct your work and interact with students? Haynes's reflections on use of the three assumptions in the writing curriculum appear in Table 11.15.

Step 8: Addressing the Three Principles

Baxter Magolda identified three pedagogical principles that are central to connecting the three assumptions to learners' current ways of making meaning and thus provide three specific steps that educators can examine for application to their own areas of practice: (a) validate students' ability to know, (b) situate learning in learners' experience, and (c) mutually construct meaning with learners. The authors of the prior chapters found many creative ways to apply these principles, ways that were particularly appropriate for their contexts and purposes. Guiding questions for this task appear in Notepad H (see Table 11.16). For example, how could you strengthen opportunities for students to reflect on and expand their initial views on an experience (thereby validating them as

Table 11.15   Notepad G—Example: Developing a Writing Curriculum (Haynes Chapter)

Step 7: Addressing the three assumptions

Assumption A: Knowledge is complex and socially constructed.

Assumption B: Self is central to knowledge construction.

Assumption C: Expertise and authority are mutually shared among peers in knowledge construction.

(a) In what ways are these assumptions currently evident in your selected area of practice?

We encourage students to view writing as a process, a means of constructing and reconstructing meaning rather than recording one's ready-made thoughts.

Students are asked to compare and contrast disciplinary frameworks, critically analyzing the limitations and benefits of various ways of viewing the world; this prompts students to see themselves as knowledge producers and potential agents for change in these disciplines.

Faculty disrupt the notion that knowledge is universal. Although freedom of thought and expression is encouraged, faculty also continually challenge students to ground their ideas and pursue their inquiries in the academic context and to pursue their ideas by combining insights from multiple disciplinary lenses.

Students must decide what form their thesis will take.

(b) How could you more effectively convey these assumptions to learners in your selected context?

Offer ungraded and creative or nontraditional assignments, speak candidly about faculty's own writing process, and encourage tactful but frank discussions of one another's writing.

Course assignments spur students to take a clear stand on interdisciplinary topics.

Encourage learners to identify their own viewpoints and worldview by trying out extended, semester-long projects with some real-world significance and using interdisciplinary theory and research methods.

Table 11.15   Continued

Support students in gaining self-confidence and defining their own set of values that will influence their study.
Assignments that call for collaboration in which students must learn to distinguish their own viewpoints from others, learn empathy, and co-create meaning within a group context.
Urge students to engage seriously with the ideas of others and emphasize that writing and scholarship must be done within a community.

Table 11.16   Notepad H

Step 8: Addressing the three principles. Three pedagogical principles are central to connecting the three assumptions to learners' current ways of making meaning:
Principle A: Validate students' ability to know.
Principle B: Situate learning in learners' experience.
Principle C: Mutually construct meaning with learners.
(a) In what ways are these principles currently evident in your area of practice?
(b) How could you more effectively convey these principles to learners in your selected context?

knowers)? How could you encourage them to apply what they learn in this experience to other aspects of their lives (thereby situating learning in their experience)? How could students work together to develop the habit of drawing from multiple perspectives in coming to new ways of understanding the topics at hand (thereby mutually constructing meaning)?

Several authors illustrated the power of situating learning in learners' experiences as they noted that firsthand experience was a powerful source of insight. For example, recall that Mills and Strong (chapter 10 of this volume) described the changes in the way the staff in their division built on their experiences, taking a different kind of responsibility for how the division did business by applying these lessons in new contexts (e.g., in their interaction with students). What kinds of direct experiences or experiential learning are built in to your programs? What kinds of opportunities exist to apply lessons learned in new contexts? Table 11.17 reveals Haynes's analysis of addressing the three principles.

Step 9: Review Consistencies and Discrepancies

Now that you have conceptualized learning partnerships that bridge learners' current capacities with those that your learning goals demand, it is helpful to review the consistencies and discrepancies between the learning goals and the self-authorship capacities you noted in Step 5 of the assessment phase. Notepad I (see Table 11.18) contains the guiding questions for this task. Haynes's response to this notepad appears in Table 11.19.

In examining these elements of your selected learning environment, you might consider whether there are distinctive challenges to learning the content of this experience that contribute to these gaps. For example, Hornak and Ortiz discussed the challenge of helping students overcome their own personal defensiveness regarding issues of race to success in their multicultural education course.

Step 10: Outline Plan to Evaluate Effectiveness

In each of the examples described in this book, those implementing the programs had to figure out (mutually construct) what kinds of indicators could appropriately be used as measures of success. Meaning making as a goal may seem amorphous; however, it gets played out in many observable ways, from the kinds of questions students ask and the quality of projects they submit to the quality of their interactions with peers in cocurricular settings. In each case, the question of what constitutes appropriate evidence will vary by context and purpose and is a question worth raising among believers and skeptics alike. Notepad J (see Table 11.20) offers guiding questions for planning context-specific ways to evaluate the effectiveness of your newly designed

Table 11.17 Notepad H—Example: Developing a Writing Curriculum (Haynes Chapter)

Step 8: Addressing the three principles. Three pedagogical principles are central to connecting the three assumptions to learners' current ways of making meaning: Principle A: Validate students' ability to know. Principle B: Situate learning in learners' experience. Principle C: Mutually construct meaning with learners.
(a) In what ways are these principles currently evident in your area of practice? The opportunity to critique disciplinary frameworks helps students begin to hone analytical and critical thinking skills. Seniors confer weekly with a faculty adviser and meet as a group to share ideas, generate strategies for improving the writing process, and provide feedback on work in progress. Faculty help students identify their own analyses of disciplinary assumptions, codes, and conventions. Students conduct an original interdisciplinary thesis. Students engage in collaborative projects; peer reviews, individual conferences with students, and written comments on drafts all support writing as a process of constructing knowledge.
(b) How could you more effectively convey these principles to learners in your selected context? Create opportunities to experiment in new ways and to talk openly and honestly about writing obstacles and fears, without fear of judgment or penalty. Encourage students to complete more ambitious interdisciplinary projects. Select course topics and readings that are relevant to first-year students' lives, assign them writing that connects to their own experiences, help them analyze and take a stand on various readings, and provide them comfortable opportunities to share ideas. Assign students to create or take part in academic journals, annotated bibliographies, or electronic exchanges to cultivate the habit of dialoguing with other scholars.

Table 11.18   Notepad I

Step 9: Reviewing consistencies and discrepancies. Review the consistencies and discrepancies between the learning goals and the self-authorship capacities you noted in Step 5 of the assessment phase.
(a) Does the new plan appear to jeopardize the aspects that were in alignment (the consistencies)?
(b) Which discrepancies does this plan address?
(c) Which discrepancies remain to be addressed?

learning partnerships. Plans that Haynes and her colleagues used to evaluate their curriculum appear in Table 11.21.

Although there is a certain logic to these steps, in practice it is important to recognize that in the "real life" of program design and implementation, they may get addressed in many different ways and certainly not always follow the numbered steps here. Again, the purpose of offering this series of steps is not to provide a formula but to suggest the kinds of questions that would be profitable to address in practice designed to foster self-authorship.

Conclusion: Reshaping the Model

In this chapter, we have encouraged readers to explore the question, What does it mean to embrace maturity as an educational goal? We have encouraged you to do so from several perspectives, including the implications of your own definition of what it means to be an educator. Endorsing self-authorship

Table 11.19   Notepad I—Example: Developing a Writing Curriculum
(Haynes Chapter)

Step 9: Reviewing consistencies and discrepancies. Review the consistencies and discrepancies between the learning goals and the self-authorship capacities you noted in Step 5 of the assessment phase.

(a) Does the new plan appear to jeopardize the aspects that were in alignment (the consistencies)? No, because few things in the previous curriculum appeared to be in alignment. With the students' abilities and learning goals in mind, the Learning Partnerships Model curriculum more appropriately challenges students interpersonally, intrapersonally, and intellectually.

(b) Which discrepancies does this plan address? By establishing a purposeful sequencing of writing experiences, faculty created a curriculum based on Learning Partnerships Model principles that allows students to gradually progress from engagement with expressive modes to an increasingly critical awareness of and proficiency in disciplinary forms to the development of interdisciplinary scholarly inquiry. Such a progression helps students come to validate their own instincts and ideas (rather than relying too heavily on authorities), to understand that knowledge is never absolute but always under construction, and to see that understanding is dependent on context.

(c) Which discrepancies remain to be addressed? Sometimes, the specific needs of individual students do not fit the orderly progression outlined by the curriculum. For example, a few of the faculty members taught a course on the same topic to different levels of students (e.g., first-years vs. juniors); however, the writing assignments listed on both syllabi appeared to be the same. This suggests that not all faculty members are attuning their teaching to students' developmental needs. It is imperative that a writing curriculum such as this one not be followed too rigidly or monitored too closely. Faculty should meet, discuss, and revise it regularly in order to better serve their students' needs. Such flexibility models the Learning Partnerships Model, both in faculty sharing authority and expertise and in staying with students in mutual construction.

Table 11.20   Notepad J

Step 10: Outline plan to evaluate effectiveness
(a) What would you suggest be used as evidence in determining how successful this design was in promoting self-authorship capacities among its participants?
(b) How might this evidence be gathered?

as a central goal of higher education is itself a value stance. Like other aspects of teaching, promoting students' development (i.e., their maturity) is not value neutral; but unlike other aspects of teaching, this value permeates the goals, design of experiences, and quality of interactions with students. Respect for students (who they are, their lived experience, and what this learning experience is designed to enable them to do) is a first-order value of the pedagogy of the Learning Partnerships Model.

We have also encouraged readers to examine and address a series of questions in assessing and designing practices for this purpose. Many of these questions may not be answered quickly or easily. However, in the spirit of reflective practice, the investment will be worth the effort. These questions are written in a way that will assist you to use the Learning Partnerships Model in a variety of contexts (similar to the variety of contexts described in this book). However, the specific design of these educational practices will require creativity and inspiration on the part of you and your colleagues. In some cases, the changes you attempt in implementing this model may require a radical departure from more familiar ways of thinking about learning and learning environments. At the institutional level, it may

Table 11.21   Notepad J—Example: Developing a Writing Curriculum (Haynes Chapter)

Step 10: Outline plan to evaluate effectiveness
(a) What would you suggest be used as evidence in determining how successful this design was in promoting self-authorship capacities among its participants? For this context, the effectiveness of the plan can be judged by students' ability to integrate in a self-conscious manner two or more disciplines to respond to an interdisciplinary topic or problem. They would demonstrate this ability in the senior interdisciplinary thesis that integrates disciplinary insights and uses theory and/or methodology. Effectively completing such a project would require an ample number of self-authorship capacities that would benefit students in other aspects of their lives.
(b) How might this evidence be gathered? The rubric we developed for scoring the senior thesis is one means through which to evaluate the effectiveness of the curriculum. Faculty interviews also gathered perceptions of student progress.

be helpful to collaborate with those who specialize in organizational change for this to have broader impact.

Terry Wildman (chapter 9) made an astute observation about the uses of the Learning Partnerships Model that merits repeating here: "We expect the model itself will be shaped by the uses to which it is put and the contexts in which it is applied." This observation inspired the subtitle of this conclusion, "reshaping the model." We invite you to share the ways you use the model, including ways you have shaped it for your purposes and contexts and your suggestions for reshaping it.

Several authors (e.g., Rogers et al., Wildman, Egart & Healy, Yonkers-Talz) shared their own stories of engagement with this process; these stories illustrate the importance of reflecting on one's own prior experience and current situation as they affect how educators enter the process of attempting to redesign their own practices. We encourage you to reflect on the story that led to your current interest in educational practices and to philosophies and strategies that are directed toward substantive goals such as self-authorship.

We also encourage you to review the ways educational practices were designed and redesigned in the programs described in this book. What practices might be applicable to your own work? Did any of these authors experience challenges that you have faced? How have your ways of responding been similar and different?

We encourage you to creatively adapt the insights shared by these authors as well as the insights you gleaned from considering the questions posed here to your selected educational context. The process offered here is an organizing tool that is designed to serve as a resource in applying the Learning Partnerships Model. As noted previously, it is obviously not a formula; instead, it is designed to be adapted as appropriate for the purpose. At the same time, we believe these are important questions for educators to consider. By making the framework adaptable, we have tried to situate learning in the readers' contexts, recognizing the complexity of multiple learning contexts. In so doing, we have tried to validate readers of this book as knowers, those who know a great deal about their own context and what kinds of adaptations are possible and appropriate. We have tried to recognize that who you are as an educator affects how you see educational practice and to engage you via this chapter in particular in the mutual construction of meaning about your own practices. We offer this process of assessment and design to model the basic features of the Learning Partnerships Model and offer you a way to entertain it for your own learning contexts. We wish you well as you embark on your journey. And who knows? Maybe you will be inspired to describe your own program in this book's sequel.

References

Baxter Magolda, M. B. (1992). *Knowing and reasoning in college: Gender-related patterns in students' intellectual development.* San Francisco: Jossey-Bass.

Baxter Magolda, M. B., & King, P. M. (1998, October). *Enhancing student learning: It takes a whole campus.* Riker Student Affairs Lecture Series, University of Florida, Gainesville.

Dewey, J. (1933). *How we think.* New York: D. C. Heath.

Giovanni, N. (2002). *Quilting the black-eyed pea: Poems and not quite poems.* New York: William Morrow.

Kegan, R. (1994). *In over our heads: The mental demands of modern life.* Cambridge, MA: Harvard University Press.

King, P. M., & Kitchener, K. S. (1994). *Developing reflective judgment: Understanding and promoting intellectual growth and critical thinking in adolescents and adults.* San Francisco: Jossey-Bass.

INDEX